Story & Art by Shouko Akira

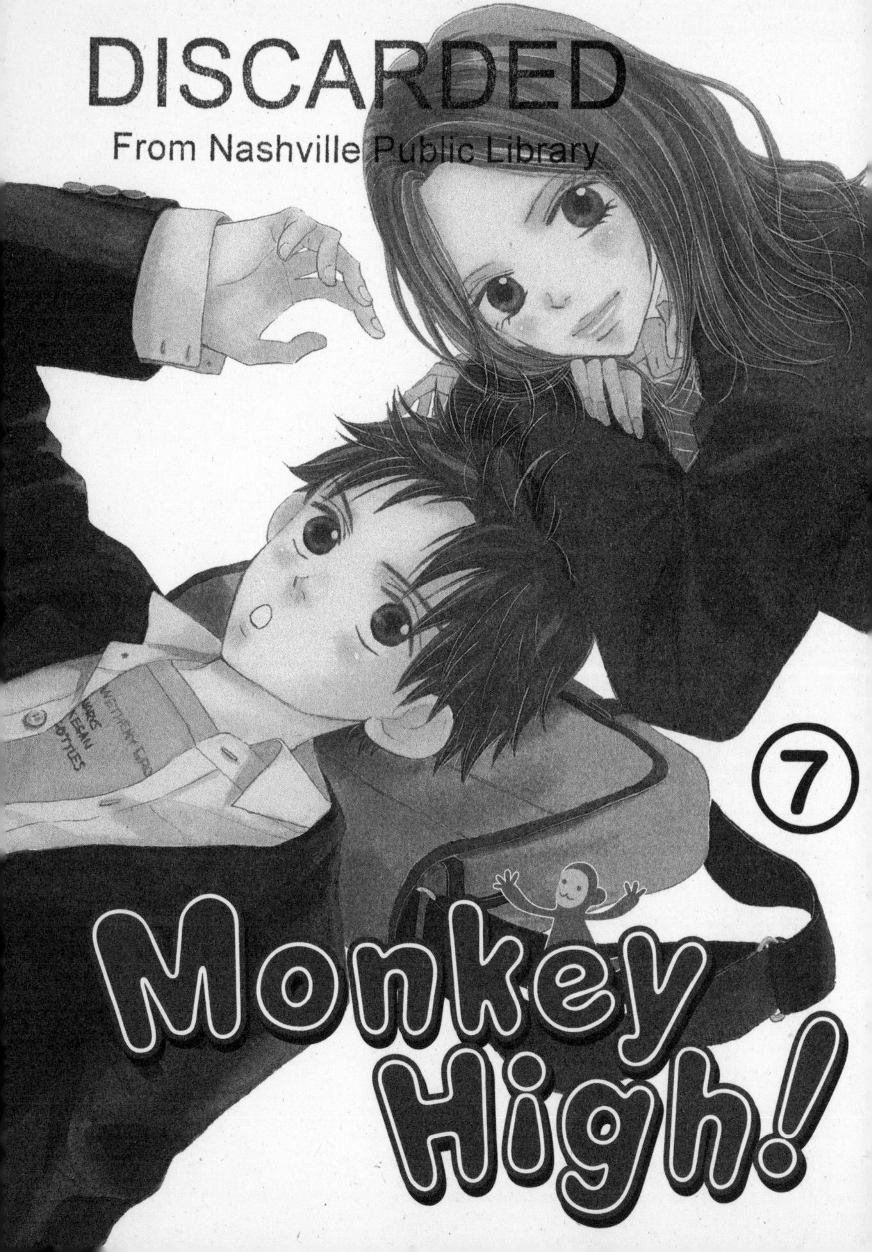
7
Monkey High!

Monkey High!

7

CONTENTS

Story Thus Far

Masaru Yamashita
(Nickname: Macharu)

It's been over a year since Haruna started going out with the monkey-like Macharu at the school she transferred into. Being in different classes as third-year students has created both increasing distance and new problems for the couple. The two can't seem to get past a kiss, but things may soon change...

Haruna Aizawa

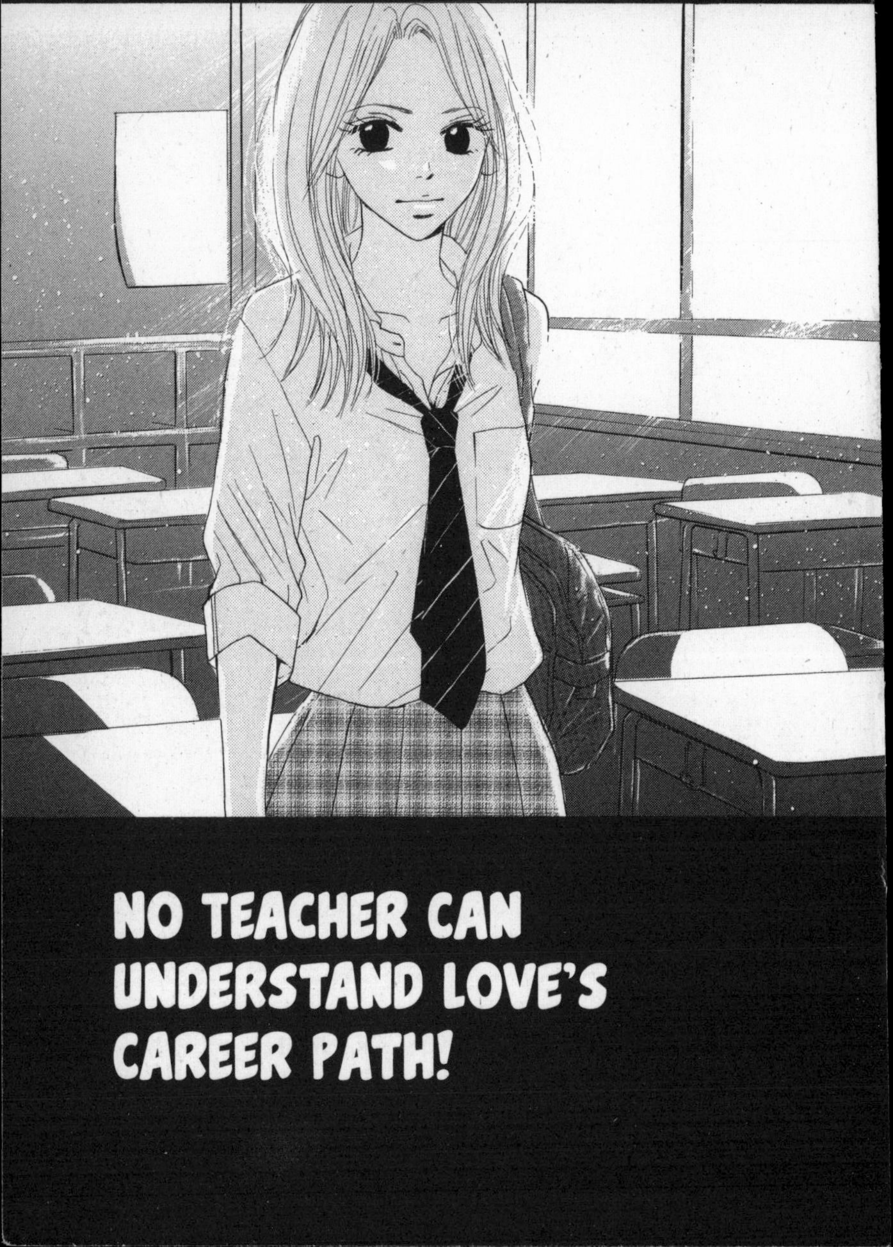

NO TEACHER CAN
UNDERSTAND LOVE'S
CAREER PATH!

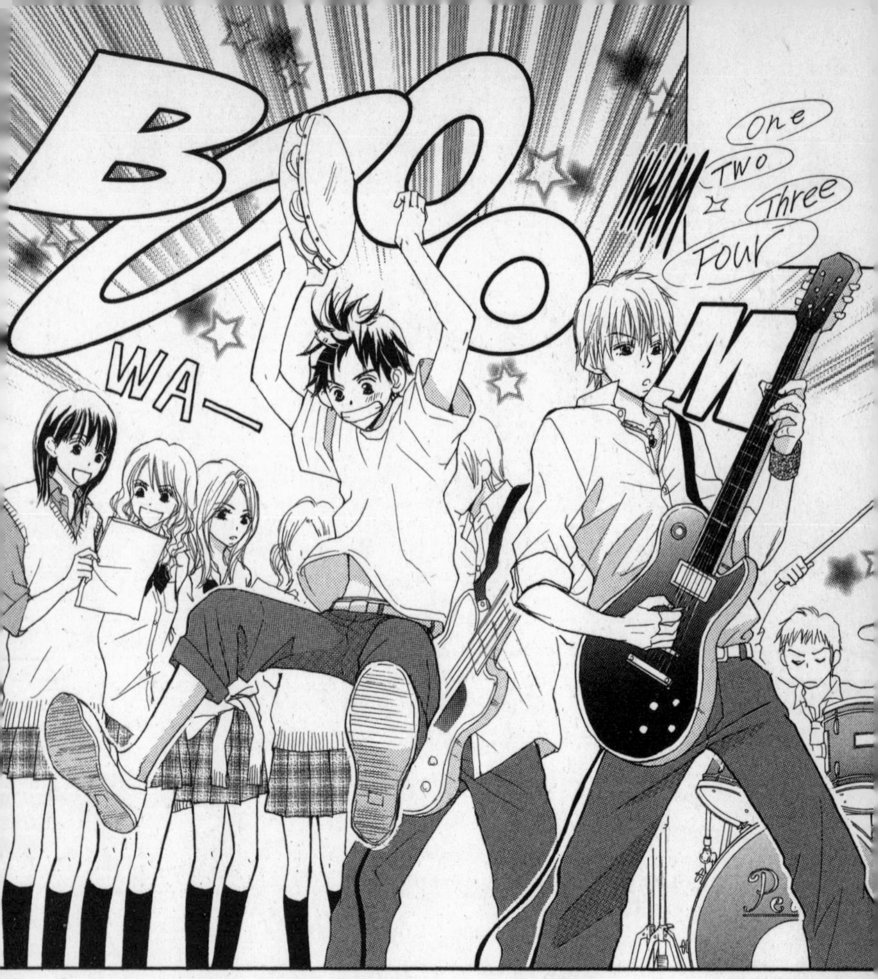
BOOOM
WA—
One
Two
Three
Four

Monkey High!

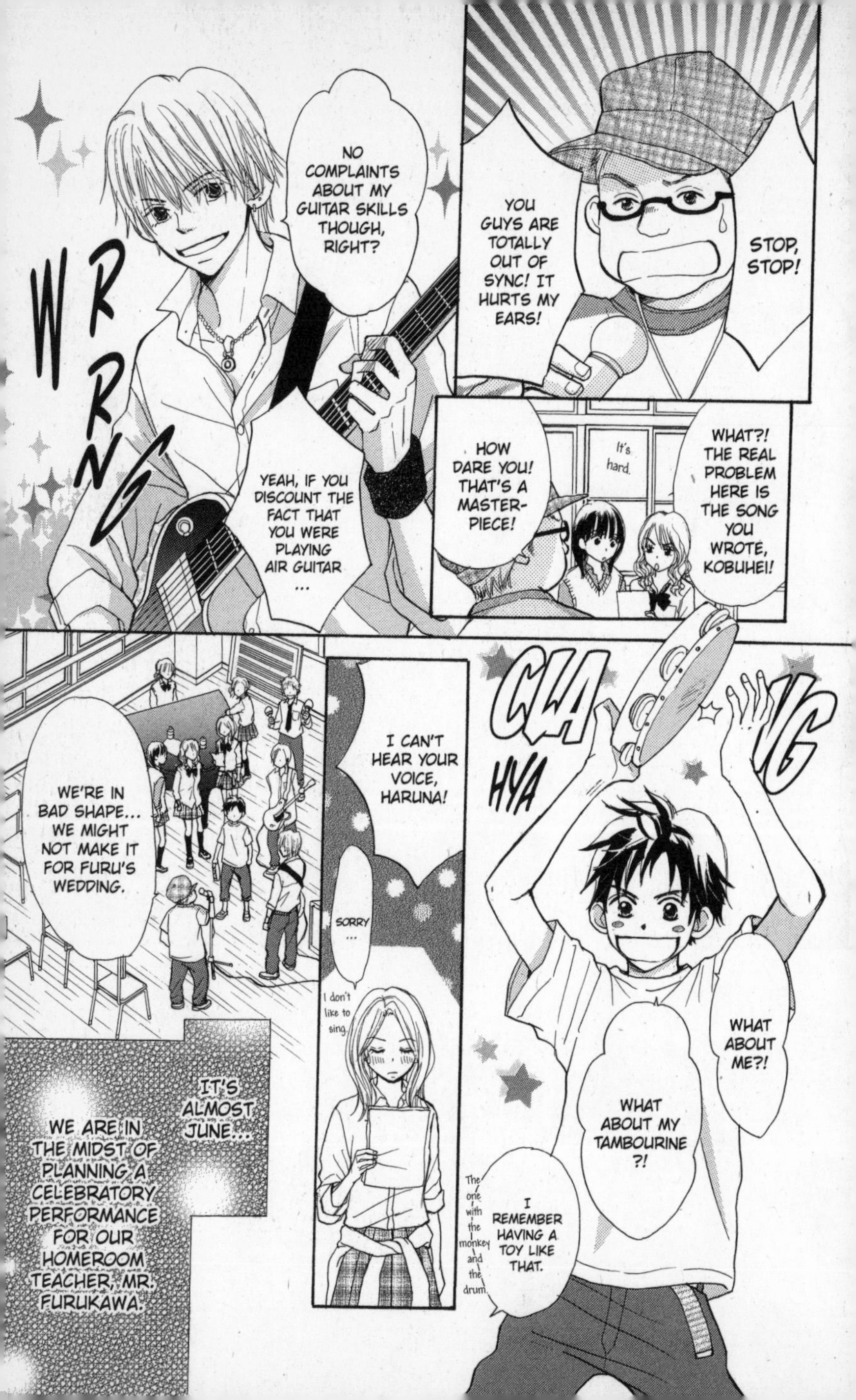

STOP, STOP!
YOU GUYS ARE TOTALLY OUT OF SYNC! IT HURTS MY EARS!
WHAT?! THE REAL PROBLEM HERE IS THE SONG YOU WROTE, KOBUHEI!
It's hard.
HOW DARE YOU! THAT'S A MASTER-PIECE!
NO COMPLAINTS ABOUT MY GUITAR SKILLS THOUGH, RIGHT?
WRRNG
YEAH, IF YOU DISCOUNT THE FACT THAT YOU WERE PLAYING AIR GUITAR...
CLA NG
HYA
WHAT ABOUT ME?!
WHAT ABOUT MY TAMBOURINE?!
I REMEMBER HAVING A TOY LIKE THAT.
The one with the monkey and the drum.
I CAN'T HEAR YOUR VOICE, HARUNA!
SORRY...
I don't like to sing.
WE'RE IN BAD SHAPE... WE MIGHT NOT MAKE IT FOR FURU'S WEDDING.
IT'S ALMOST JUNE...
WE ARE IN THE MIDST OF PLANNING A CELEBRATORY PERFORMANCE FOR OUR HOMEROOM TEACHER, MR. FURUKAWA.

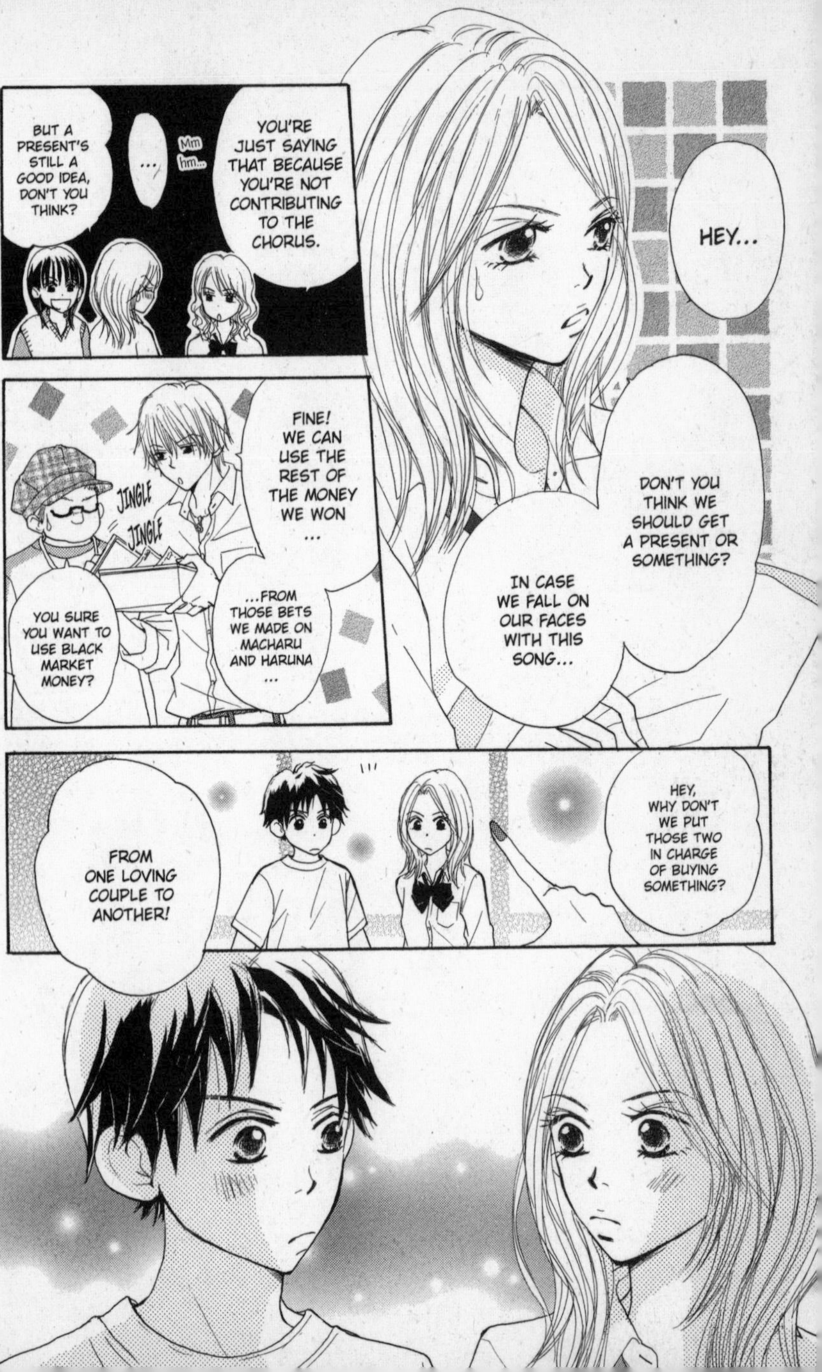
HEY...
DON'T YOU THINK WE SHOULD GET A PRESENT OR SOMETHING?
IN CASE WE FALL ON OUR FACES WITH THIS SONG...
YOU'RE JUST SAYING THAT BECAUSE YOU'RE NOT CONTRIBUTING TO THE CHORUS.
Mm hm...
...
BUT A PRESENT'S STILL A GOOD IDEA, DON'T YOU THINK?
FINE! WE CAN USE THE REST OF THE MONEY WE WON ...
...FROM THOSE BETS WE MADE ON MACHARU AND HARUNA ...
JINGLE
JINGLE
YOU SURE YOU WANT TO USE BLACK MARKET MONEY?
HEY, WHY DON'T WE PUT THOSE TWO IN CHARGE OF BUYING SOMETHING?
FROM ONE LOVING COUPLE TO ANOTHER!

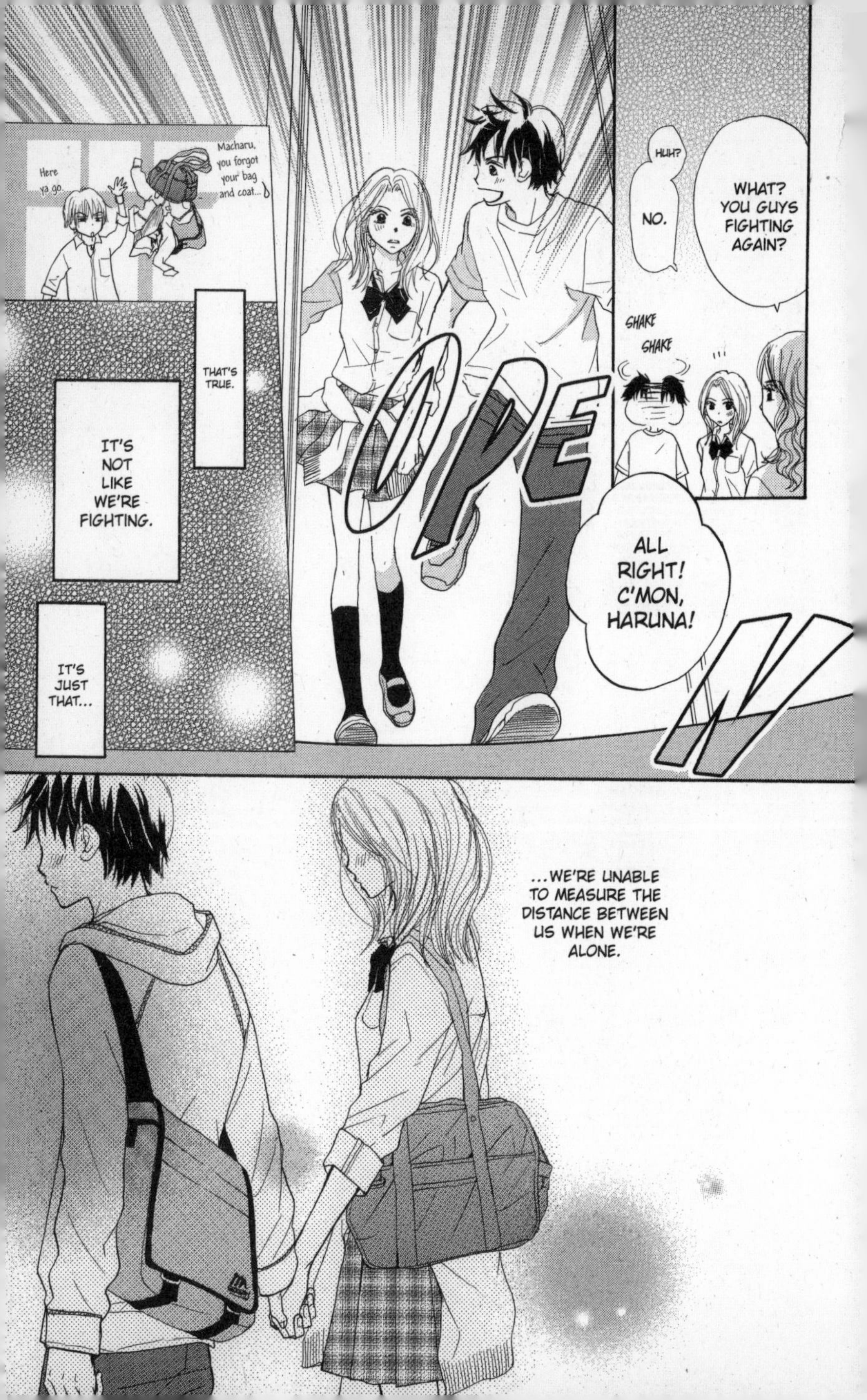
WHAT? YOU GUYS FIGHTING AGAIN?
HUH?
NO.
SHAKE SHAKE
OPEN
ALL RIGHT! C'MON, HARUNA!
Macharu, you forgot your bag and coat...
Here ya go...
THAT'S TRUE.
IT'S NOT LIKE WE'RE FIGHTING.
IT'S JUST THAT...
...WE'RE UNABLE TO MEASURE THE DISTANCE BETWEEN US WHEN WE'RE ALONE.

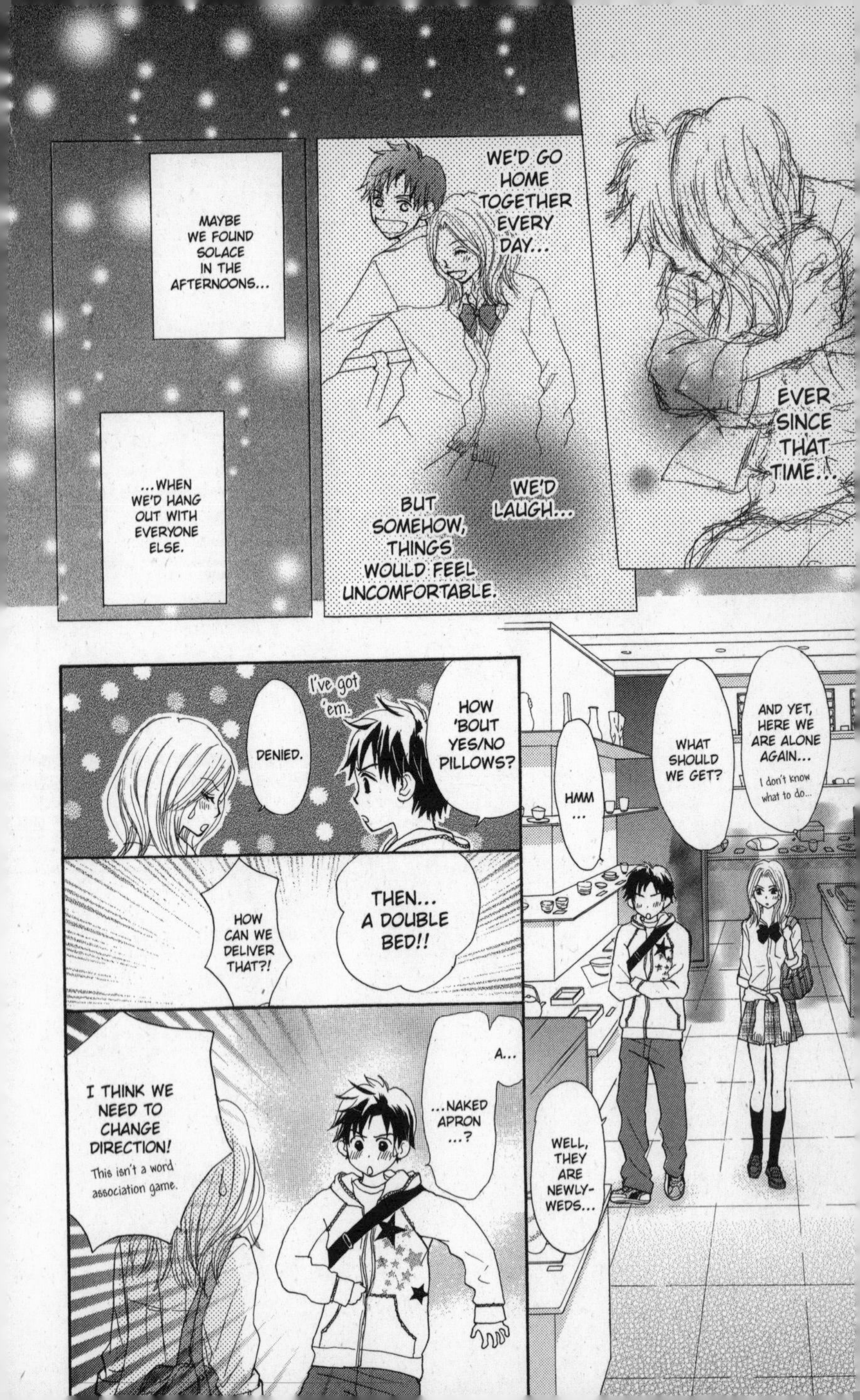
EVER SINCE THAT TIME...
WE'D GO HOME TOGETHER EVERY DAY...
WE'D LAUGH...
BUT SOMEHOW, THINGS WOULD FEEL UNCOMFORTABLE.
MAYBE WE FOUND SOLACE IN THE AFTERNOONS...
...WHEN WE'D HANG OUT WITH EVERYONE ELSE.
AND YET, HERE WE ARE ALONE AGAIN...
I don't know what to do...
WHAT SHOULD WE GET?
HMM ...
WELL, THEY ARE NEWLY-WEDS...
HOW 'BOUT YES/NO PILLOWS?
I've got 'em.
DENIED.
THEN... A DOUBLE BED!!
HOW CAN WE DELIVER THAT?!
A...
...NAKED APRON ...?
I THINK WE NEED TO CHANGE DIRECTION!
This isn't a word association game.

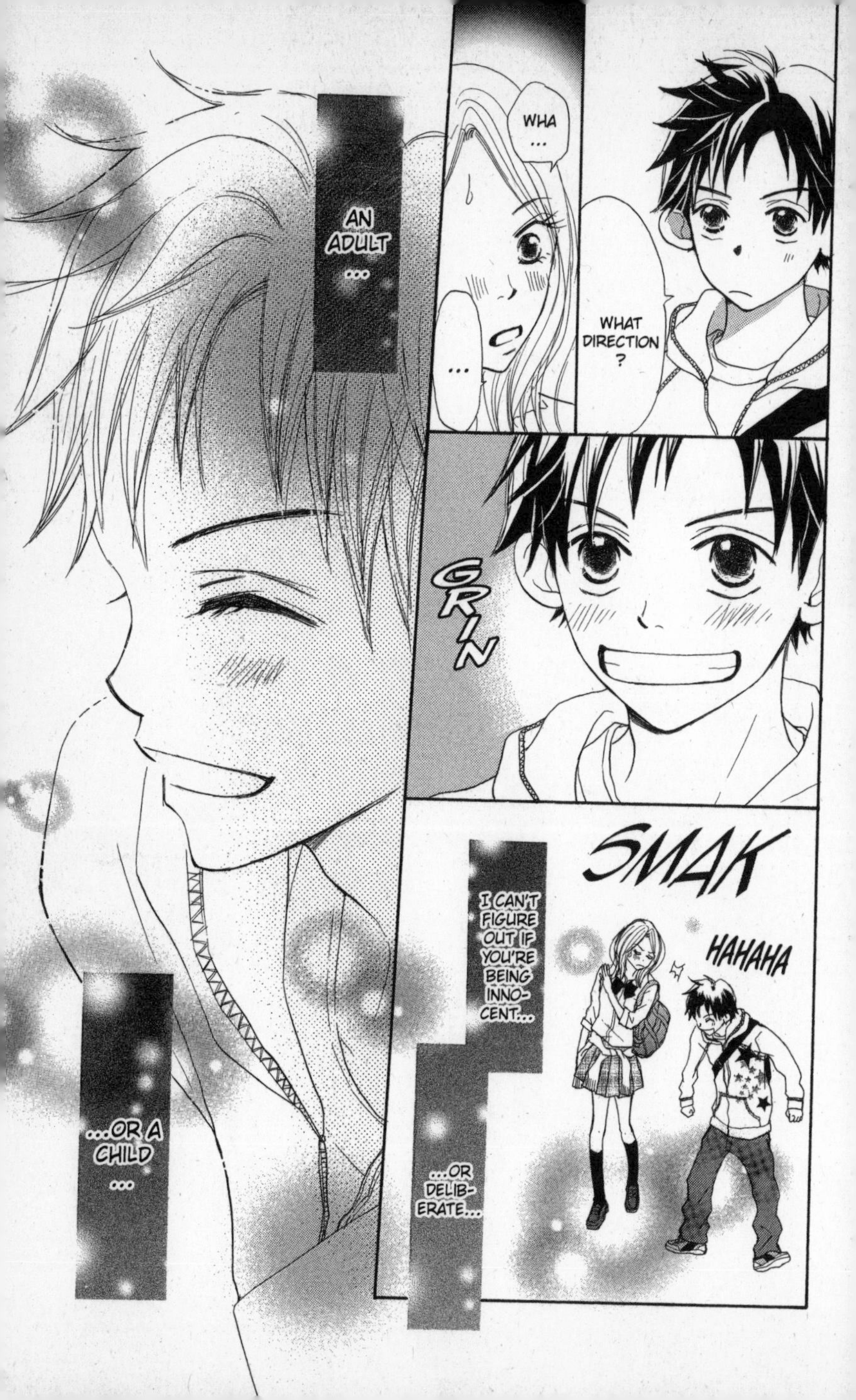
WHAT DIRECTION ?
WHA ...
...
GRIN
SMAK
HAHAHA
I CAN'T FIGURE OUT IF YOU'RE BEING INNO-CENT...
...OR DELIB-ERATE...
AN ADULT ...
...OR A CHILD ...

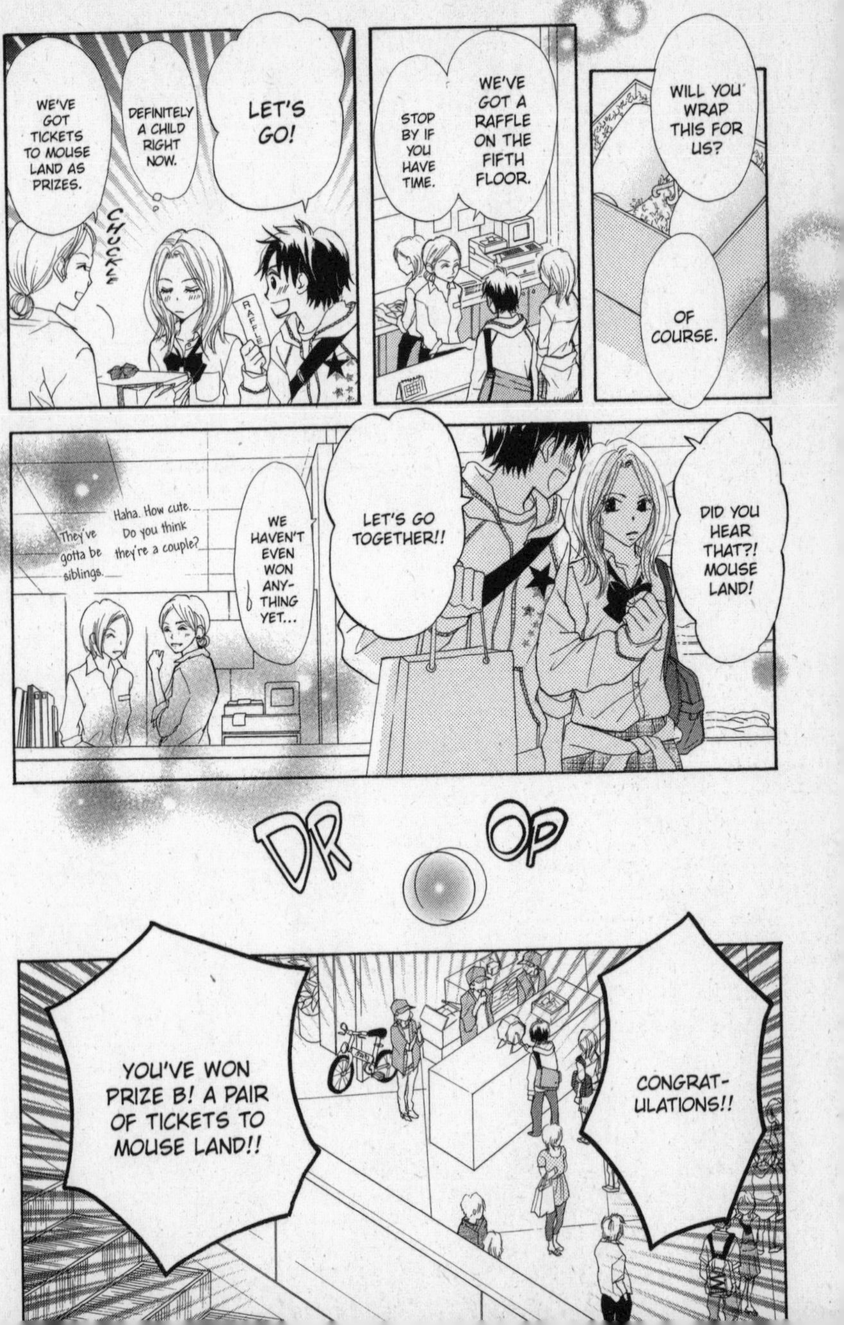
WILL YOU WRAP THIS FOR US?
OF COURSE.
WE'VE GOT A RAFFLE ON THE FIFTH FLOOR.
STOP BY IF YOU HAVE TIME.
LET'S GO!
RAFFLE
DEFINITELY A CHILD RIGHT NOW.
WE'VE GOT TICKETS TO MOUSE LAND AS PRIZES.
CHUCKLE
DID YOU HEAR THAT?! MOUSE LAND!
LET'S GO TOGETHER!!
WE HAVEN'T EVEN WON ANYTHING YET...
Haha. How cute. Do you think they're a couple?
They've gotta be siblings.
DROP
CONGRATULATIONS!!
YOU'VE WON PRIZE B! A PAIR OF TICKETS TO MOUSE LAND!!

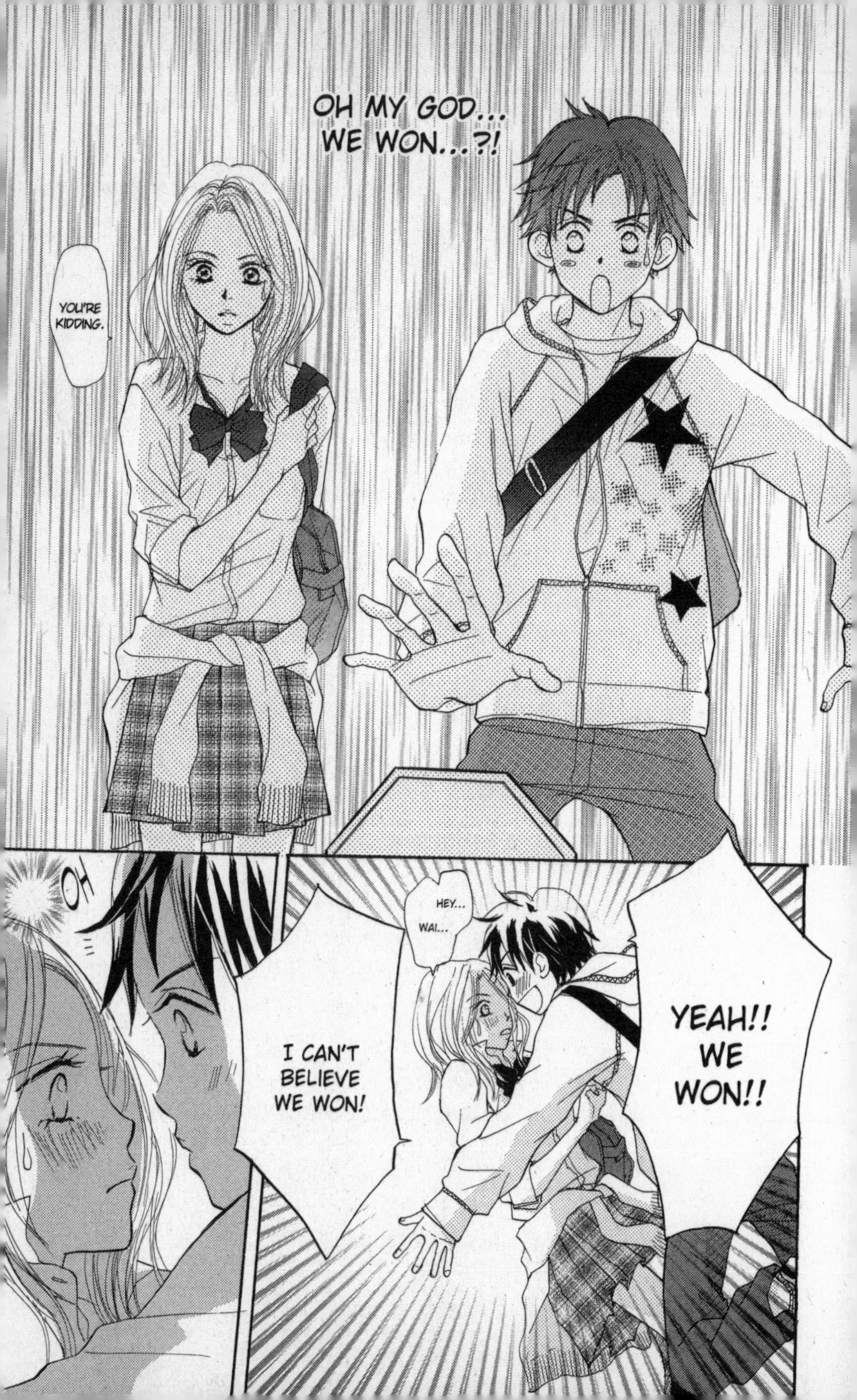
OH MY GOD... WE WON...?!
YOU'RE KIDDING.
YEAH!! WE WON!!
HEY... WAI...
I CAN'T BELIEVE WE WON!
OH

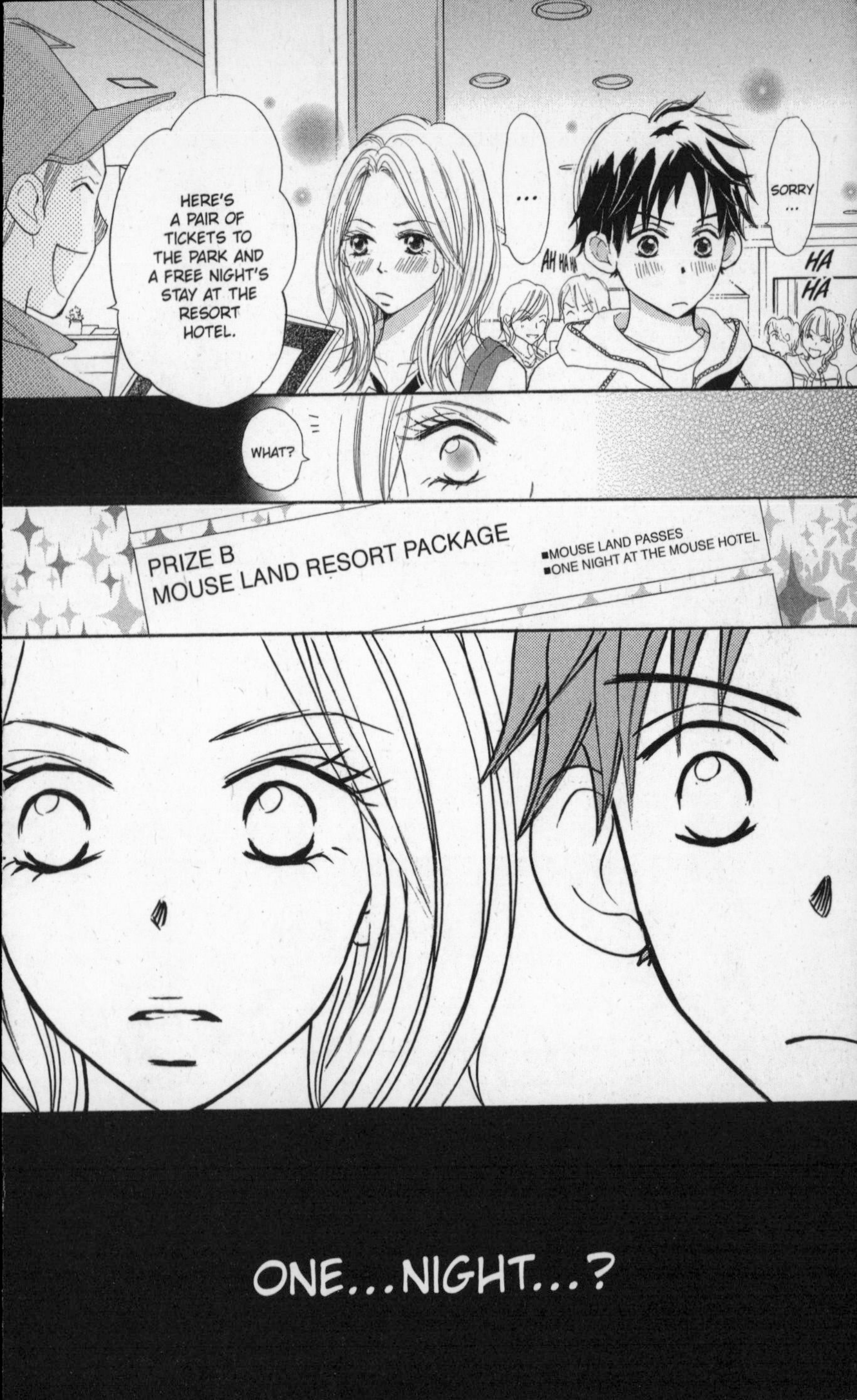
SORRY ...
HA HA
...
AH HA HA
HERE'S A PAIR OF TICKETS TO THE PARK AND A FREE NIGHT'S STAY AT THE RESORT HOTEL.
WHAT?
PRIZE B
MOUSE LAND RESORT PACKAGE
■MOUSE LAND PASSES
■ONE NIGHT AT THE MOUSE HOTEL
ONE...NIGHT...?

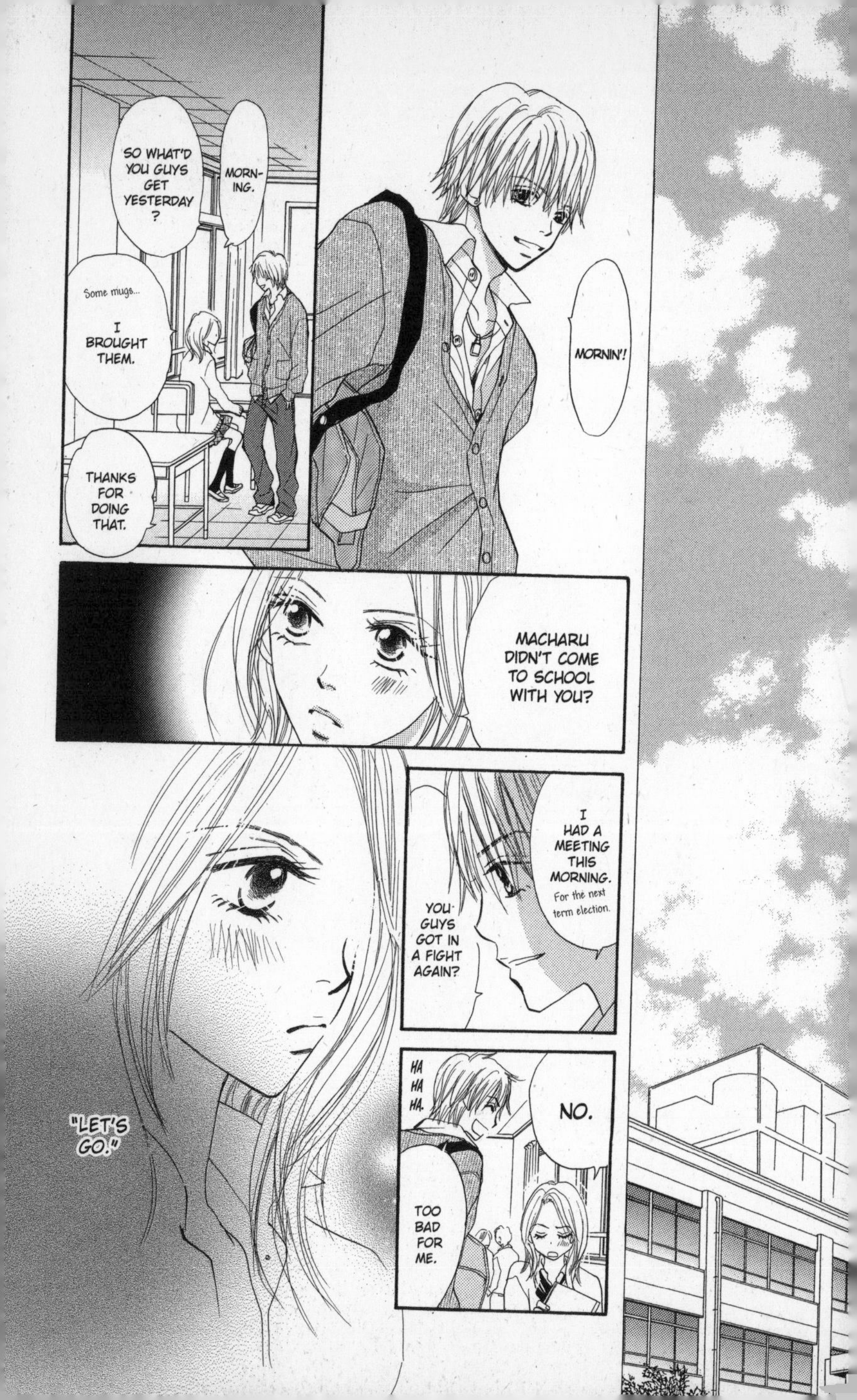
MORNIN'!
MORN-ING.
SO WHAT'D YOU GUYS GET YESTERDAY?
Some mugs...
I BROUGHT THEM.
THANKS FOR DOING THAT.
MACHARU DIDN'T COME TO SCHOOL WITH YOU?
I HAD A MEETING THIS MORNING.
For the next term election.
YOU GUYS GOT IN A FIGHT AGAIN?
NO.
HA HA HA.
TOO BAD FOR ME.
"LET'S GO."

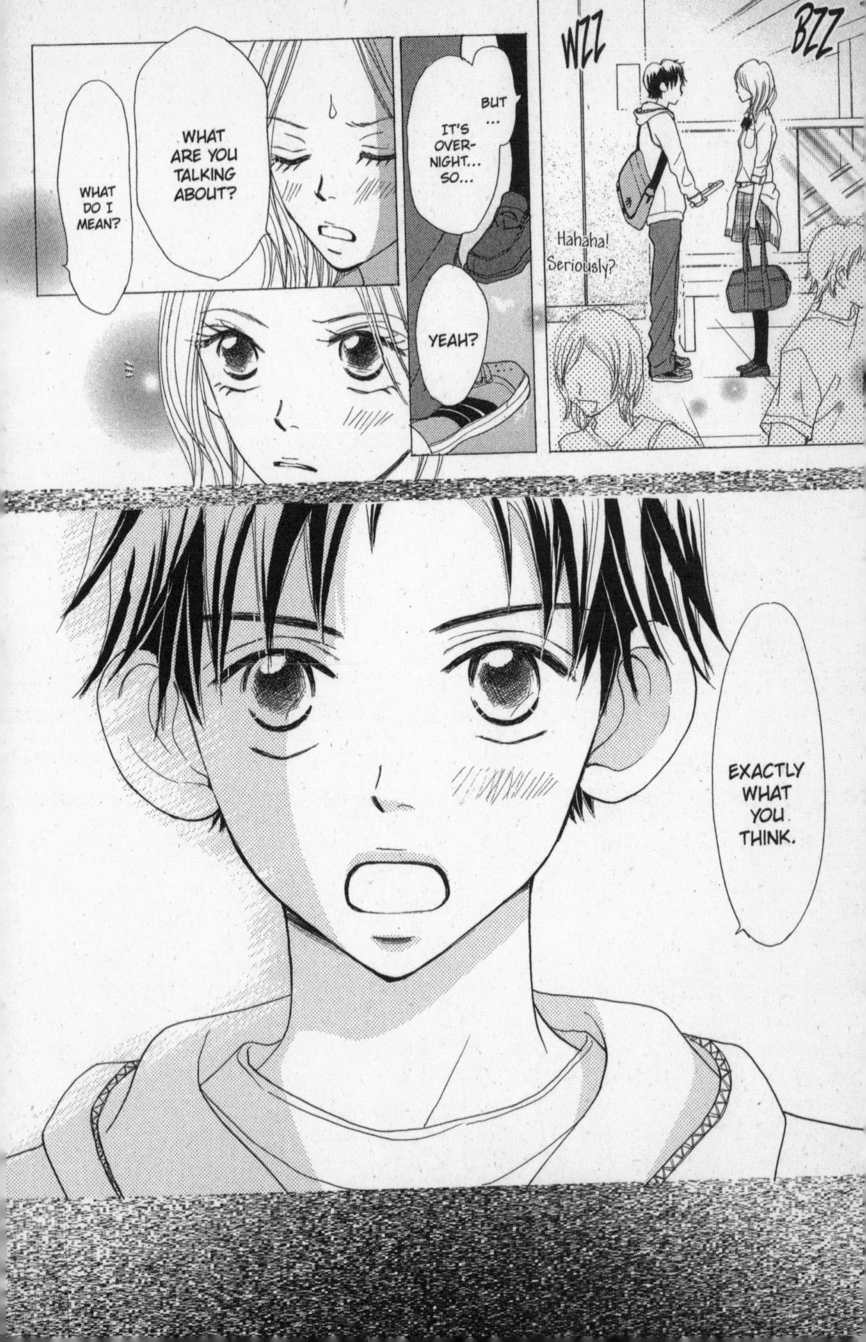
WZZ
BZZ
Hahaha! Seriously?
BUT ...
IT'S OVER-NIGHT... SO...
YEAH?
WHAT ARE YOU TALKING ABOUT?
WHAT DO I MEAN?
EXACTLY WHAT YOU THINK.

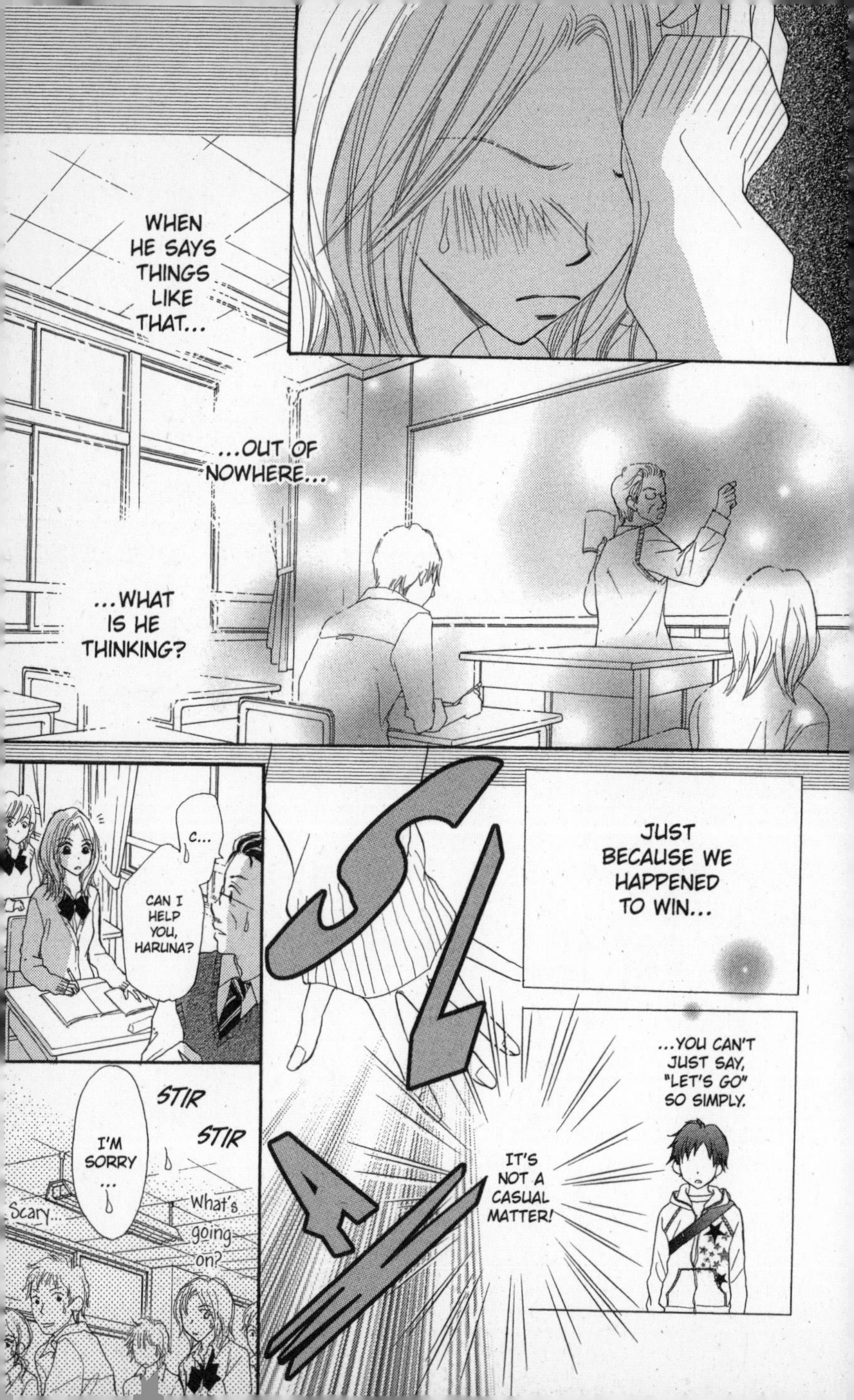
WHEN HE SAYS THINGS LIKE THAT...
...OUT OF NOWHERE...
...WHAT IS HE THINKING?
JUST BECAUSE WE HAPPENED TO WIN...
...YOU CAN'T JUST SAY, "LET'S GO" SO SIMPLY.
IT'S NOT A CASUAL MATTER!
C...
CAN I HELP YOU, HARUNA?
STIR
STIR
I'M SORRY...
What's going on?
Scary...

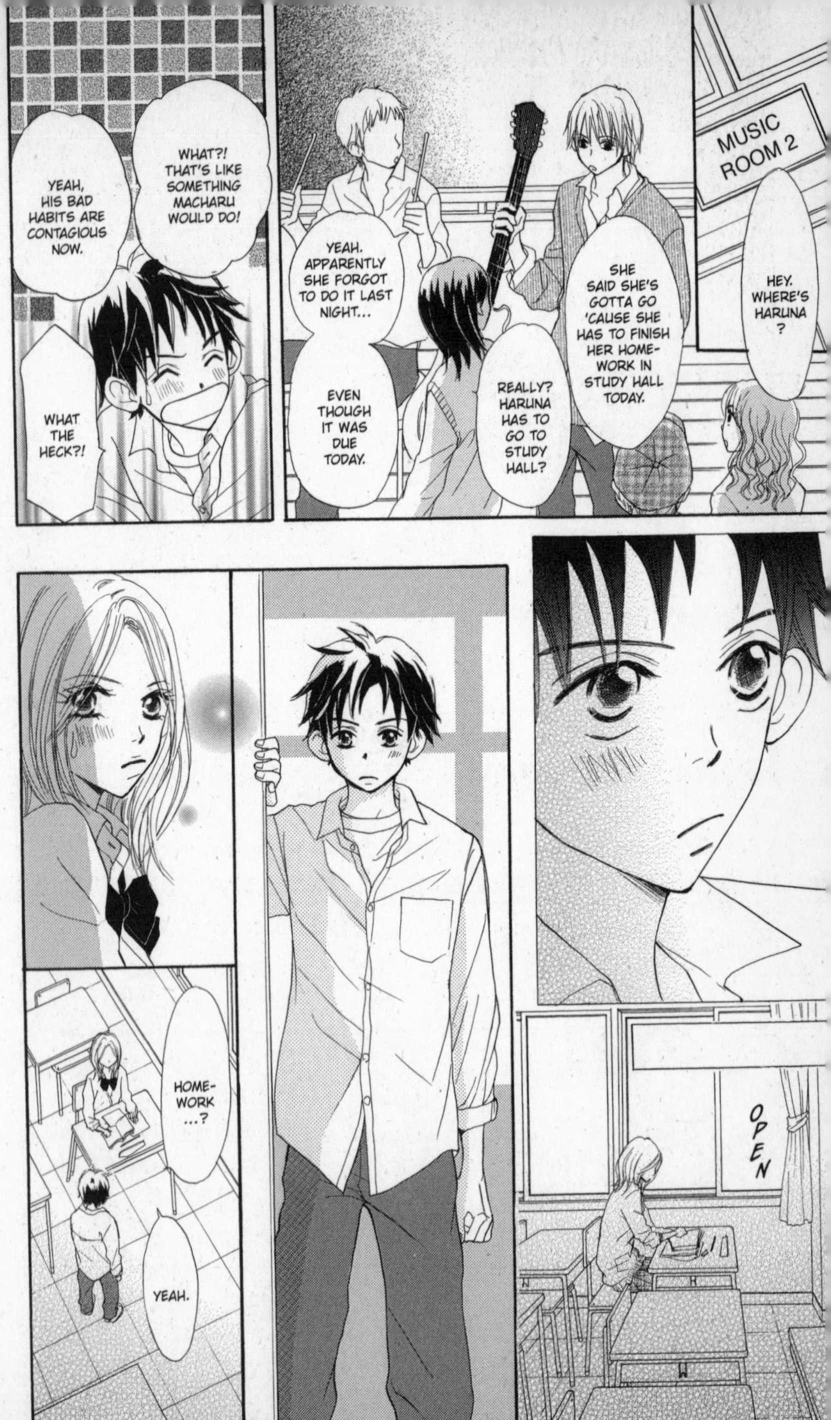
MUSIC ROOM 2
HEY. WHERE'S HARUNA?
SHE SAID SHE'S GOTTA GO 'CAUSE SHE HAS TO FINISH HER HOME-WORK IN STUDY HALL TODAY.
REALLY? HARUNA HAS TO GO TO STUDY HALL?
YEAH. APPARENTLY SHE FORGOT TO DO IT LAST NIGHT...
EVEN THOUGH IT WAS DUE TODAY.
WHAT?! THAT'S LIKE SOMETHING MACHARU WOULD DO!
YEAH, HIS BAD HABITS ARE CONTAGIOUS NOW.
WHAT THE HECK?!
OPEN
HOME-WORK...?
YEAH.

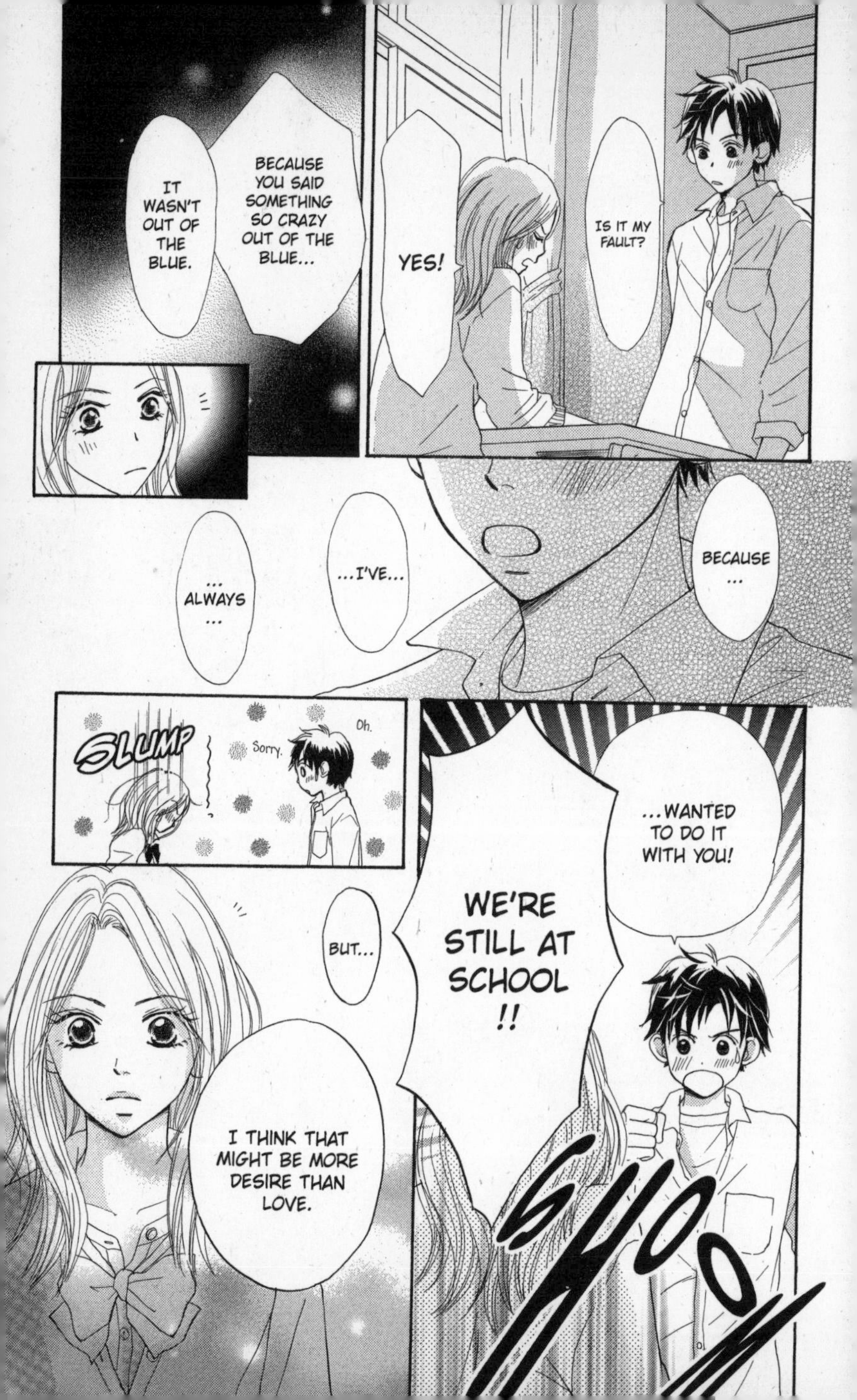
IS IT MY FAULT?
YES!
BECAUSE YOU SAID SOMETHING SO CRAZY OUT OF THE BLUE...
IT WASN'T OUT OF THE BLUE.
BECAUSE ...
...I'VE...
... ALWAYS ...
...WANTED TO DO IT WITH YOU!
WE'RE STILL AT SCHOOL !!
SHOOM
Oh.
Sorry.
SLUMP
BUT...
I THINK THAT MIGHT BE MORE DESIRE THAN LOVE.

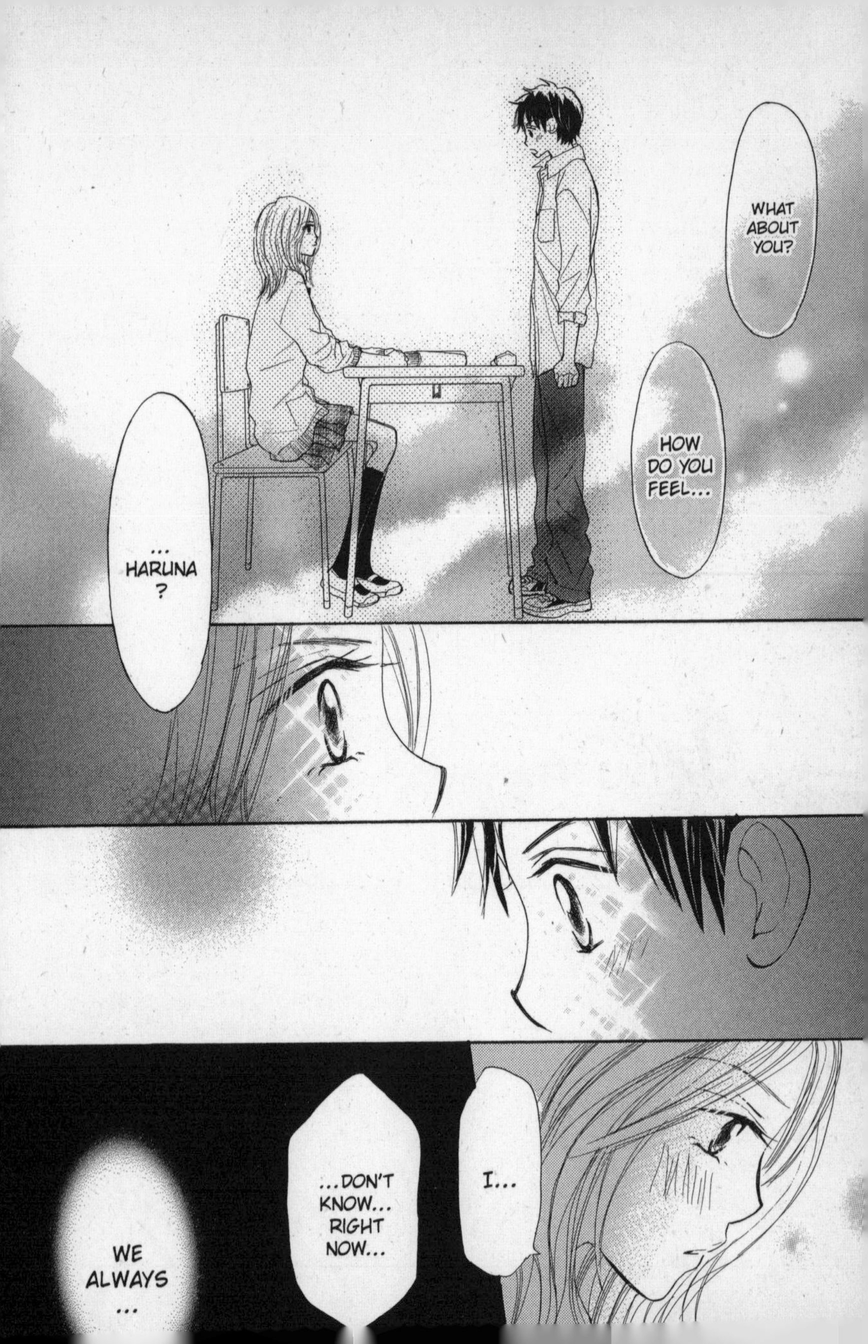
WHAT ABOUT YOU?
HOW DO YOU FEEL...
...HARUNA?
I...
...DON'T KNOW... RIGHT NOW...
WE ALWAYS ...

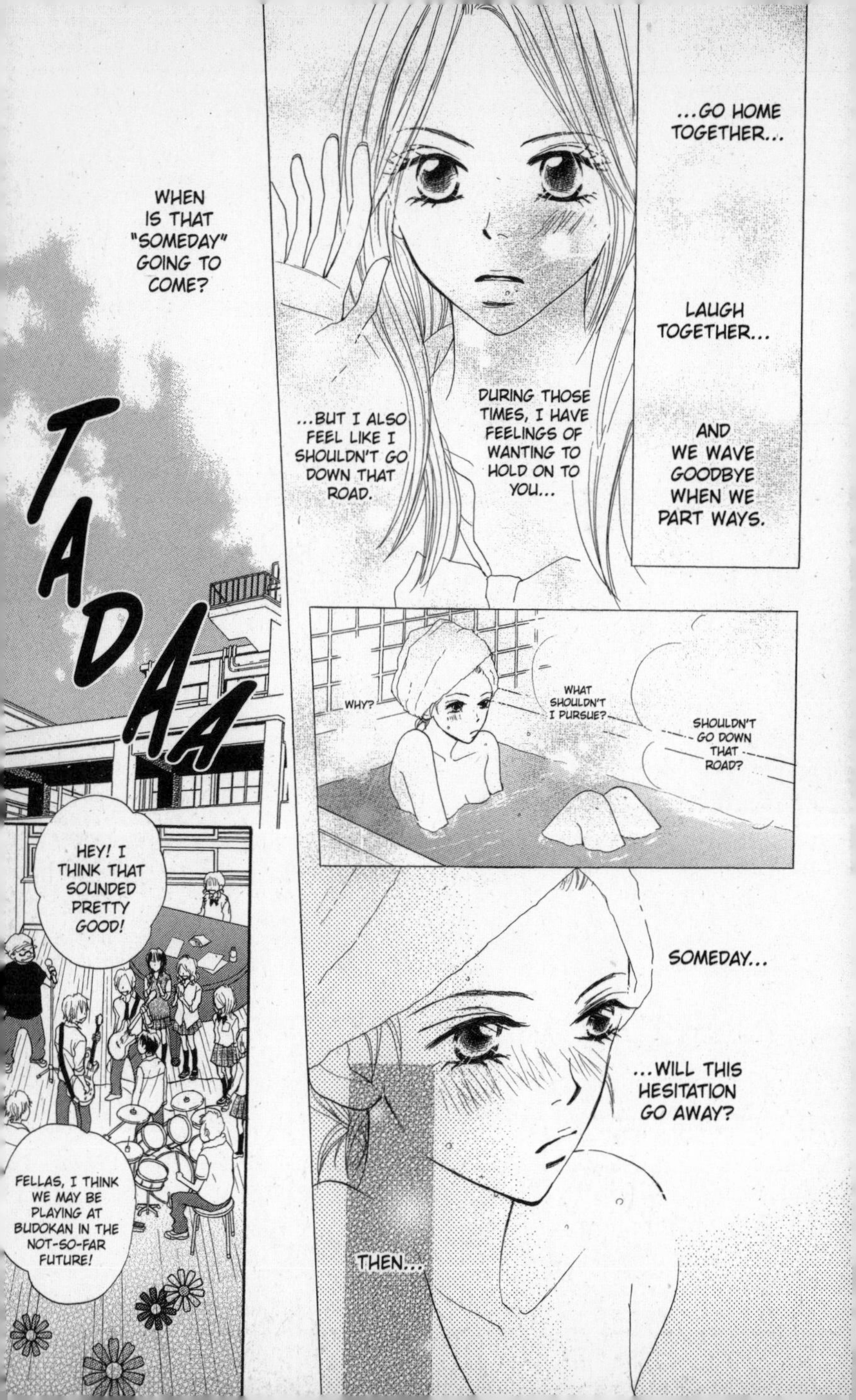
...GO HOME TOGETHER...
LAUGH TOGETHER...
AND WE WAVE GOODBYE WHEN WE PART WAYS.
DURING THOSE TIMES, I HAVE FEELINGS OF WANTING TO HOLD ON TO YOU...
...BUT I ALSO FEEL LIKE I SHOULDN'T GO DOWN THAT ROAD.
SHOULDN'T GO DOWN THAT ROAD?
WHAT SHOULDN'T I PURSUE?
WHY?
SOMEDAY...
...WILL THIS HESITATION GO AWAY?
THEN...
WHEN IS THAT "SOMEDAY" GOING TO COME?
TADAA
HEY! I THINK THAT SOUNDED PRETTY GOOD!
FELLAS, I THINK WE MAY BE PLAYING AT BUDOKAN IN THE NOT-SO-FAR FUTURE!

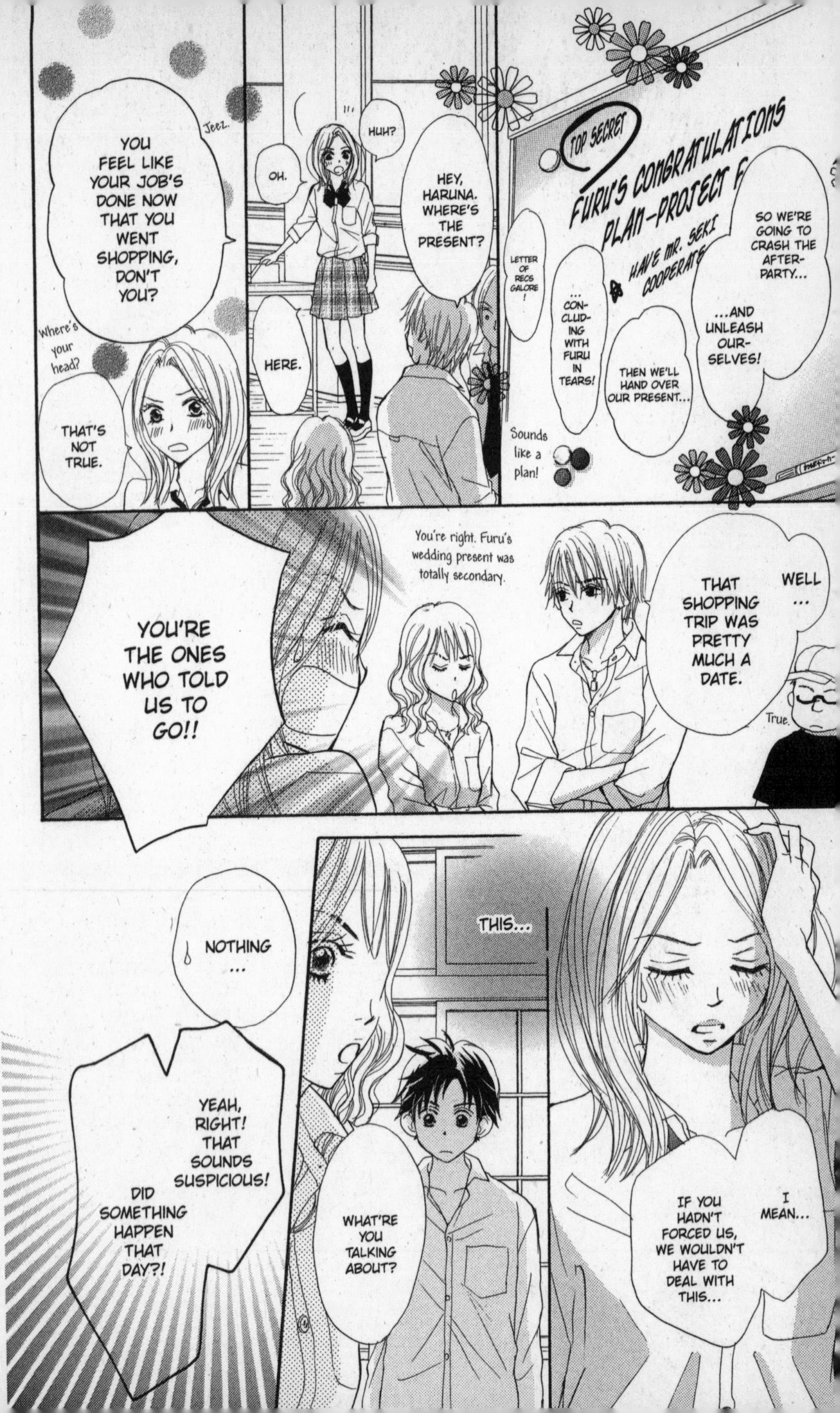
TOP SECRET
FURU'S CONGRATULATIONS PLAN-PROJECT F
HAVE MR. SEKI COOPERATE
SO WE'RE GOING TO CRASH THE AFTER-PARTY...
...AND UNLEASH OURSELVES!
THEN WE'LL HAND OVER OUR PRESENT...
...CONCLUDING WITH FURU IN TEARS!
LETTER OF RECS GALORE!
Sounds like a plan!
HEY, HARUNA. WHERE'S THE PRESENT?
HUH?
OH.
HERE.
Jeez.
YOU FEEL LIKE YOUR JOB'S DONE NOW THAT YOU WENT SHOPPING, DON'T YOU?
Where's your head?
THAT'S NOT TRUE.
WELL...
THAT SHOPPING TRIP WAS PRETTY MUCH A DATE.
True.
You're right. Furu's wedding present was totally secondary.
YOU'RE THE ONES WHO TOLD US TO GO!!
I MEAN...
IF YOU HADN'T FORCED US, WE WOULDN'T HAVE TO DEAL WITH THIS...
THIS...
WHAT'RE YOU TALKING ABOUT?
NOTHING...
YEAH, RIGHT! THAT SOUNDS SUSPICIOUS!
DID SOMETHING HAPPEN THAT DAY?!

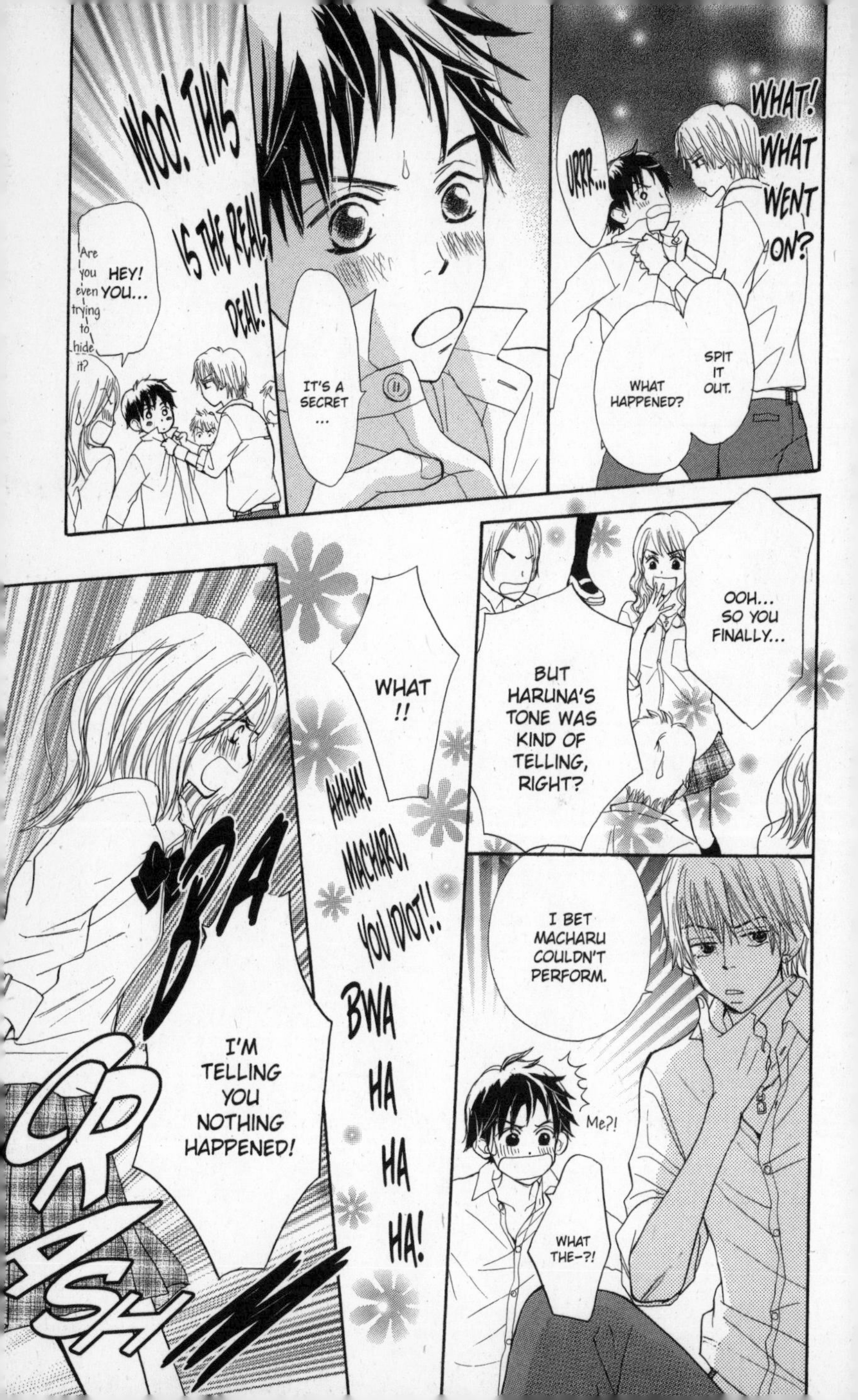
WHAT! WHAT WENT ON?
URRR...
SPIT IT OUT.
WHAT HAPPENED?
IT'S A SECRET ...
WOO! THIS IS THE REAL DEAL!
HEY! YOU...
Are you even trying to hide it?
OOH... SO YOU FINALLY...
BUT HARUNA'S TONE WAS KIND OF TELLING, RIGHT?
I BET MACHARU COULDN'T PERFORM.
Me?!
WHAT THE-?!
WHAT !!
AHAHA! MACHARU, YOU IDIOT!!
BWA HA HA HA HA!
I'M TELLING YOU NOTHING HAPPENED!
BA
CRASH

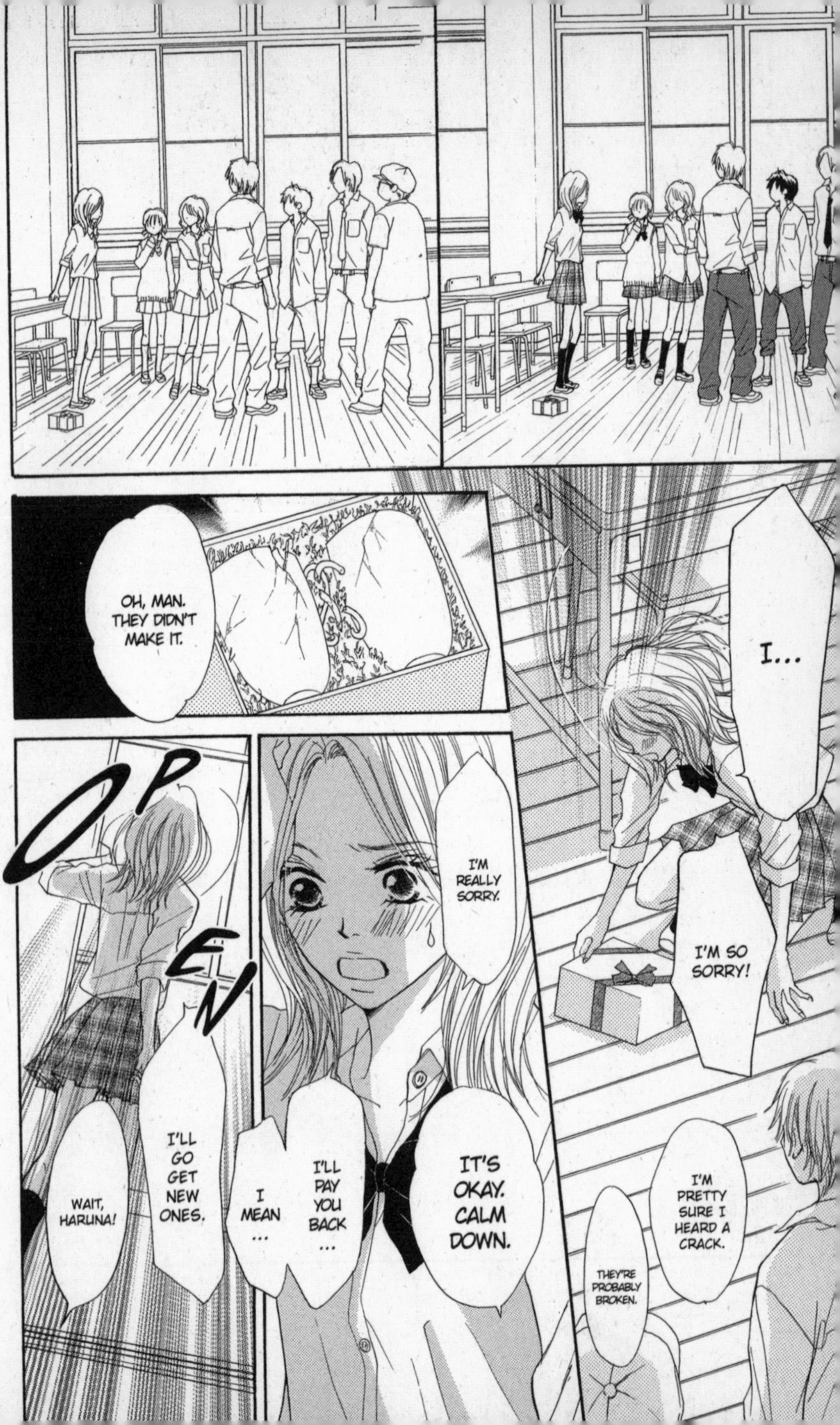
I...
I'M SO SORRY!
I'M PRETTY SURE I HEARD A CRACK.
THEY'RE PROBABLY BROKEN.
OH, MAN. THEY DIDN'T MAKE IT.
I'M REALLY SORRY.
IT'S OKAY. CALM DOWN.
I'LL PAY YOU BACK...
I MEAN...
OPEN
I'LL GO GET NEW ONES.
WAIT, HARUNA!

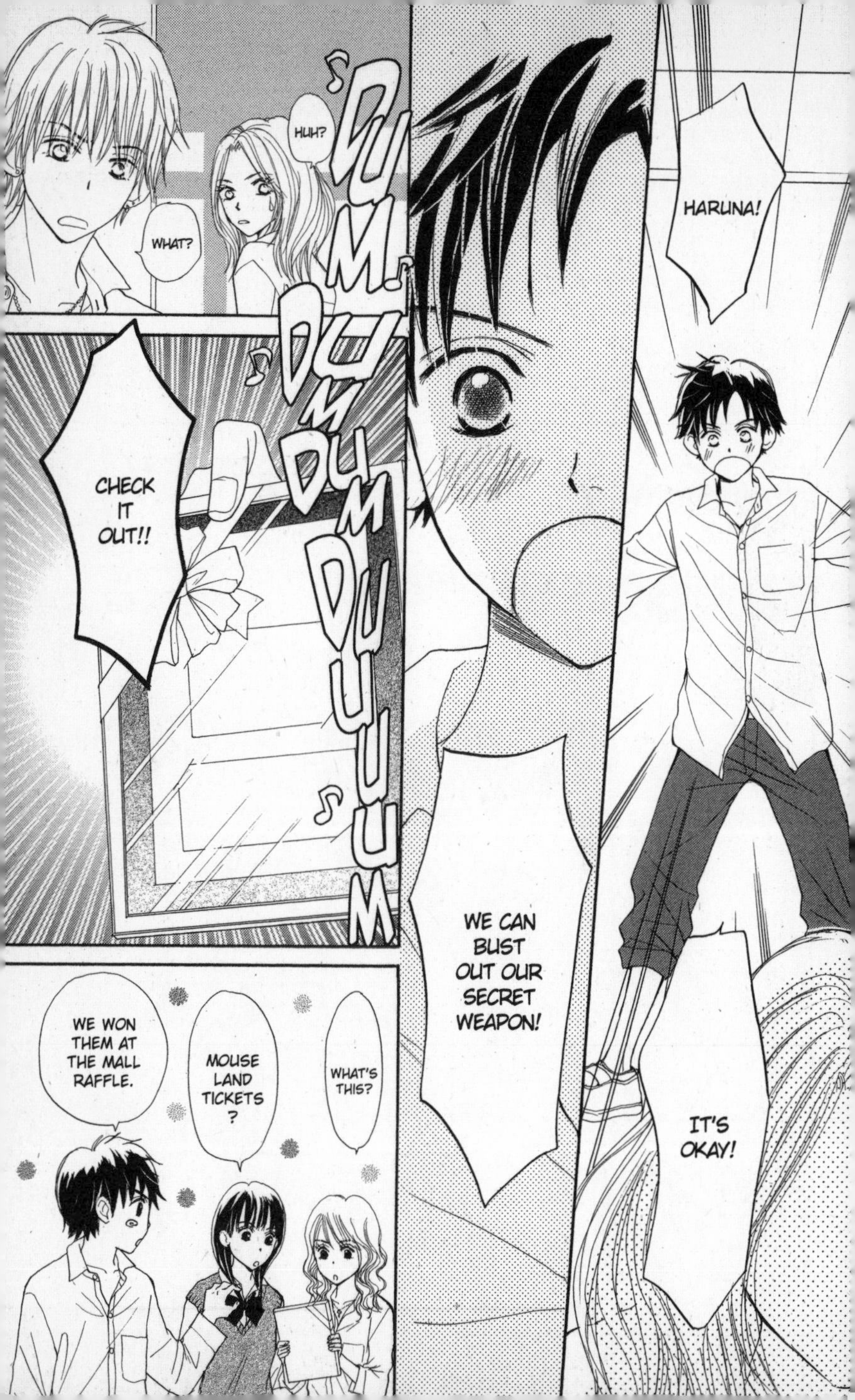

HARUNA!
IT'S OKAY!
WE CAN BUST OUT OUR SECRET WEAPON!
HUH?
WHAT?
DUM. DUM DUM DUM DUUUUM.
CHECK IT OUT!!
WHAT'S THIS?
MOUSE LAND TICKETS?
WE WON THEM AT THE MALL RAFFLE.

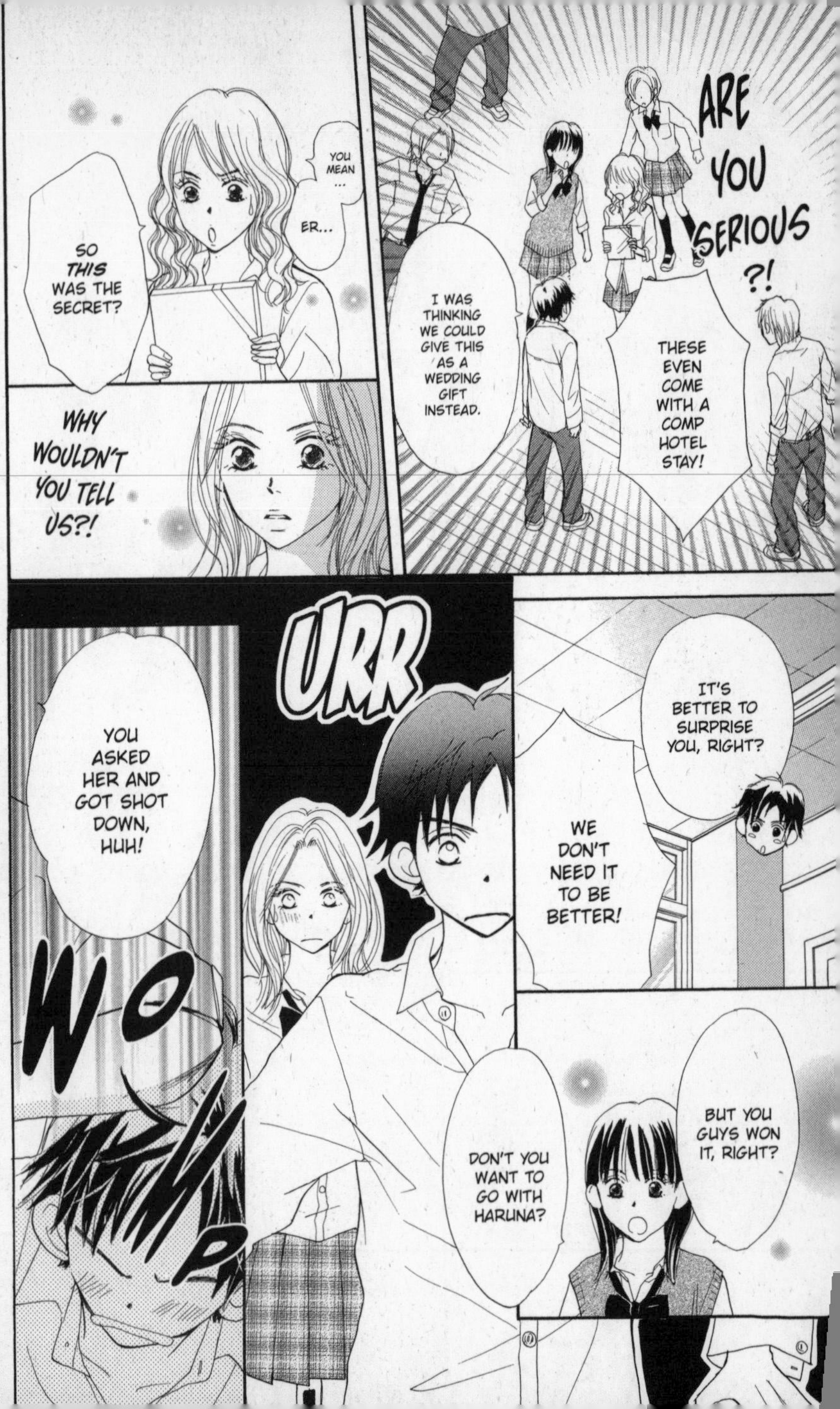

ARE YOU SERIOUS?!
THESE EVEN COME WITH A COMP HOTEL STAY!
I WAS THINKING WE COULD GIVE THIS AS A WEDDING GIFT INSTEAD.
YOU MEAN...
ER...
SO THIS WAS THE SECRET?
WHY WOULDN'T YOU TELL US?!
IT'S BETTER TO SURPRISE YOU, RIGHT?
WE DON'T NEED IT TO BE BETTER!
BUT YOU GUYS WON IT, RIGHT?
DON'T YOU WANT TO GO WITH HARUNA?
URR
YOU ASKED HER AND GOT SHOT DOWN, HUH!
WOMP

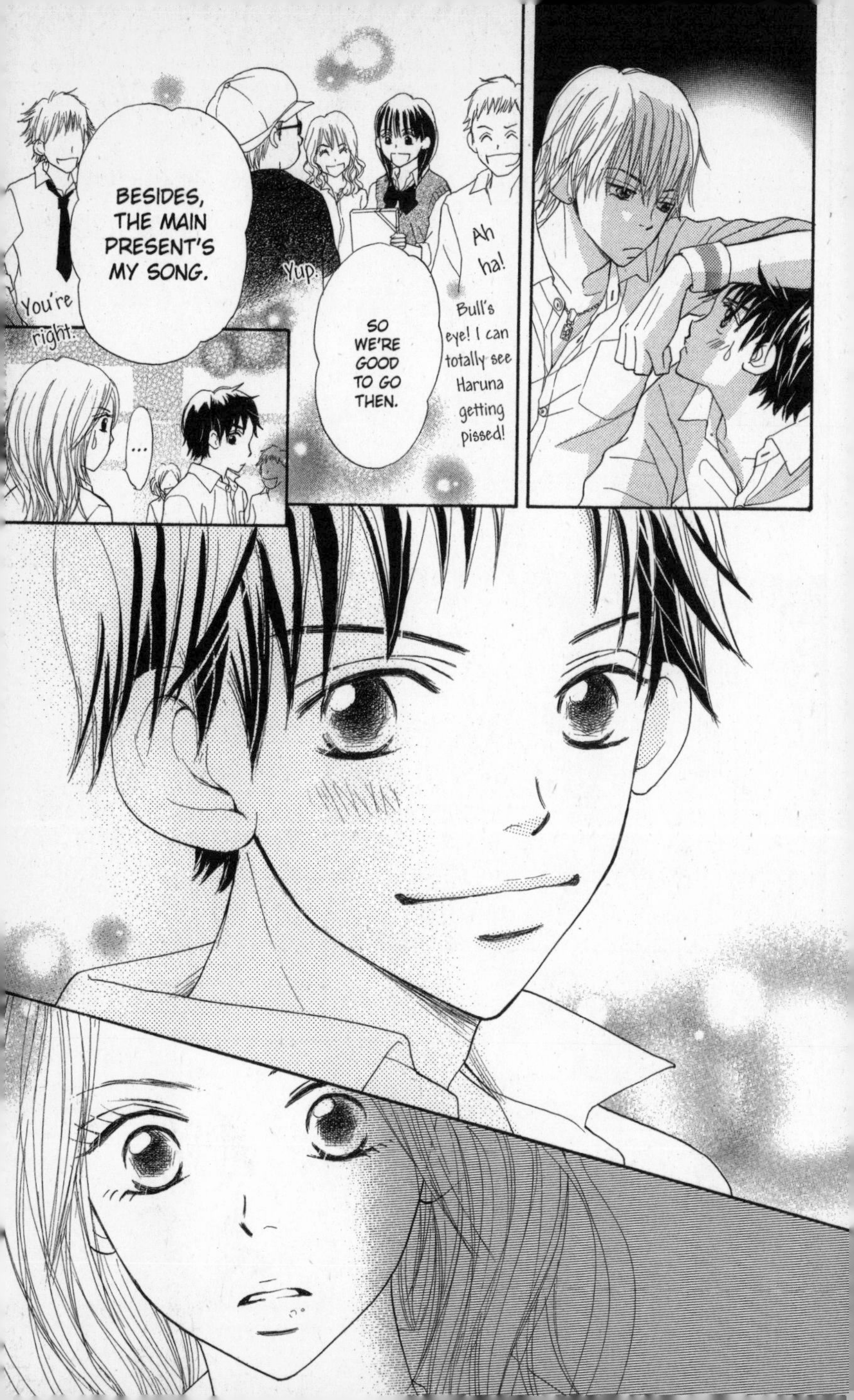
Ah ha!
Bull's eye! I can totally see Haruna getting pissed!
SO WE'RE GOOD TO GO THEN.
Yup.
BESIDES, THE MAIN PRESENT'S MY SONG.
You're right.
...

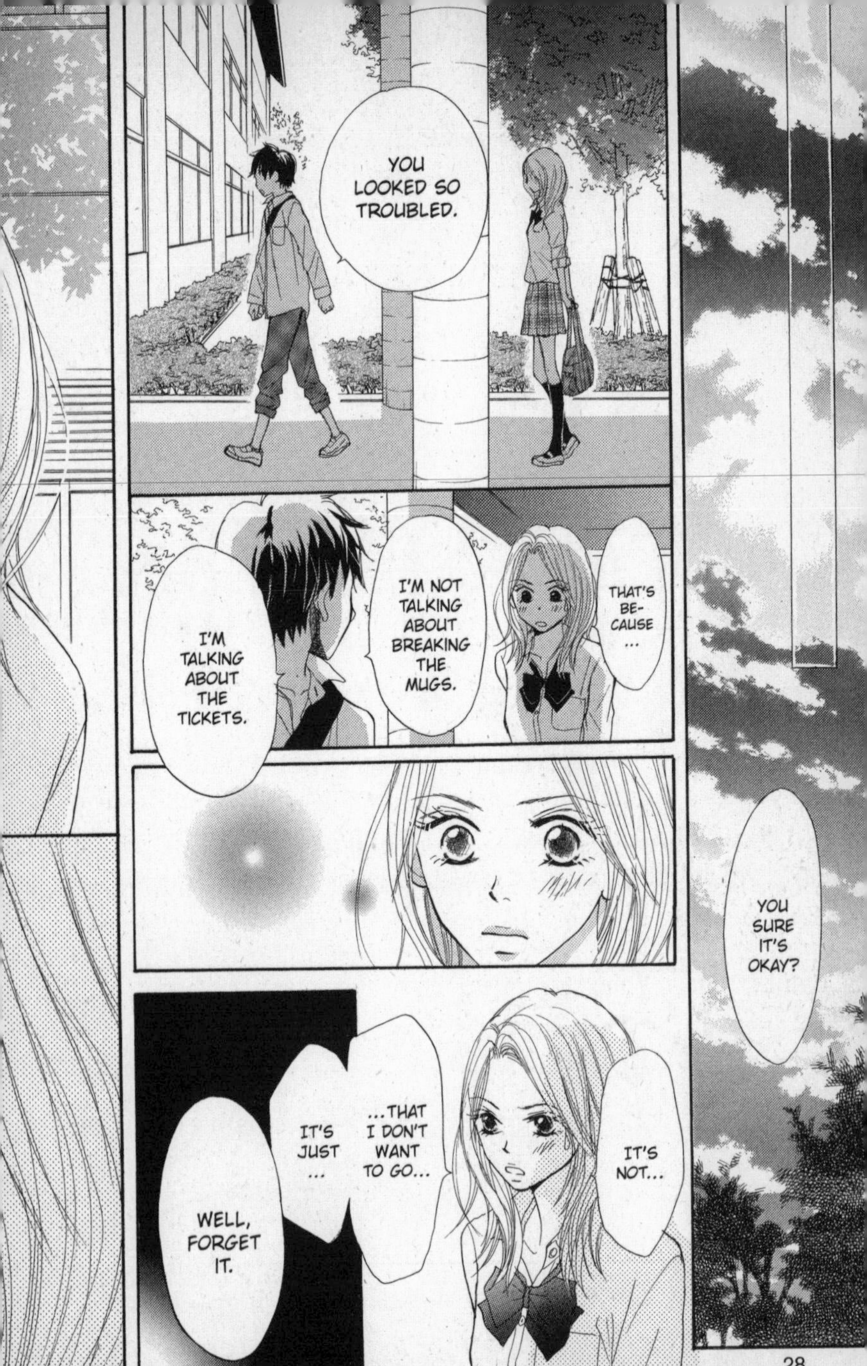
YOU SURE IT'S OKAY?
YOU LOOKED SO TROUBLED.
THAT'S BE-CAUSE...
I'M NOT TALKING ABOUT BREAKING THE MUGS.
I'M TALKING ABOUT THE TICKETS.
IT'S NOT...
...THAT I DON'T WANT TO GO...
IT'S JUST...
WELL, FORGET IT.

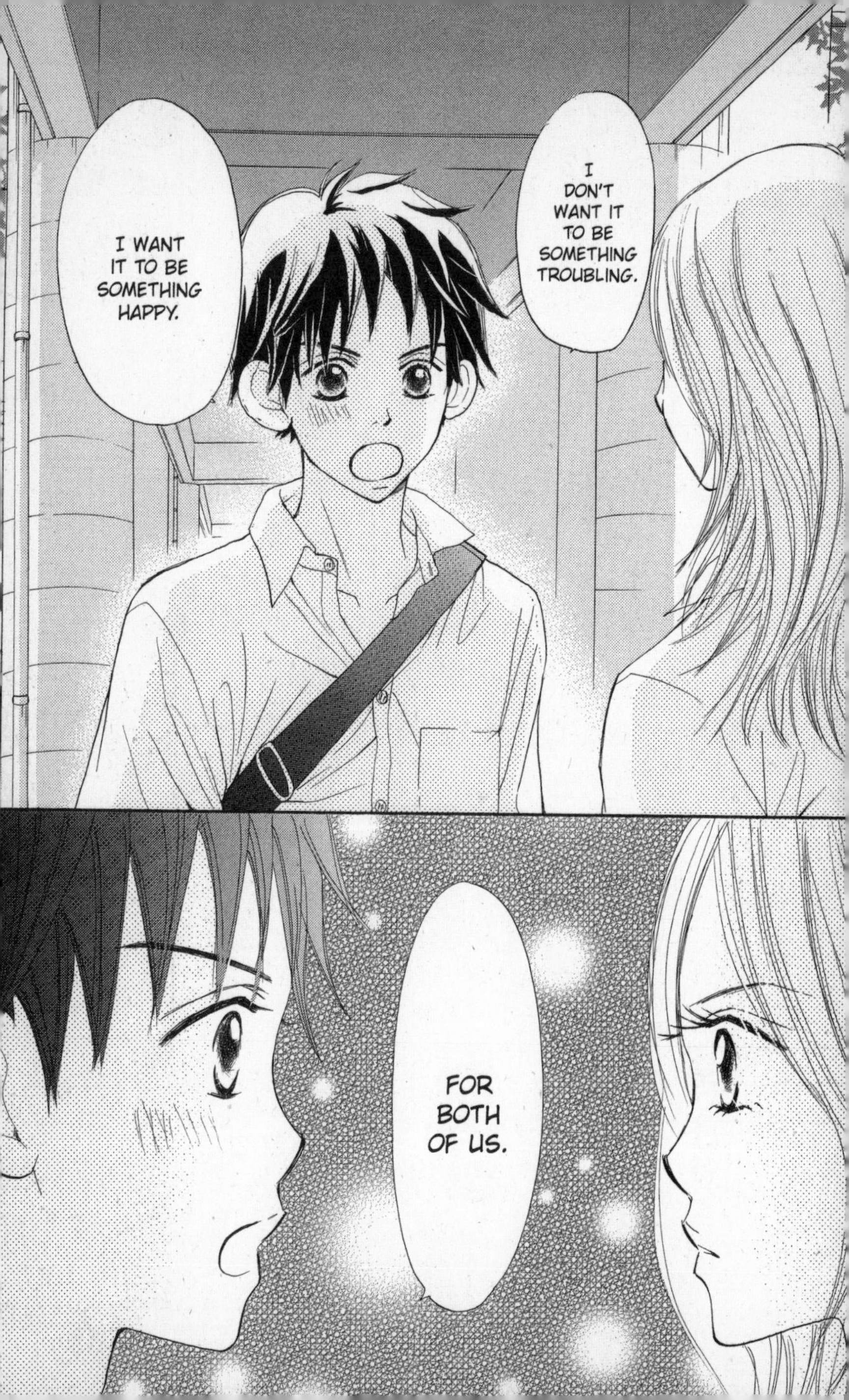
I DON'T WANT IT TO BE SOMETHING TROUBLING.
I WANT IT TO BE SOMETHING HAPPY.
FOR BOTH OF US.

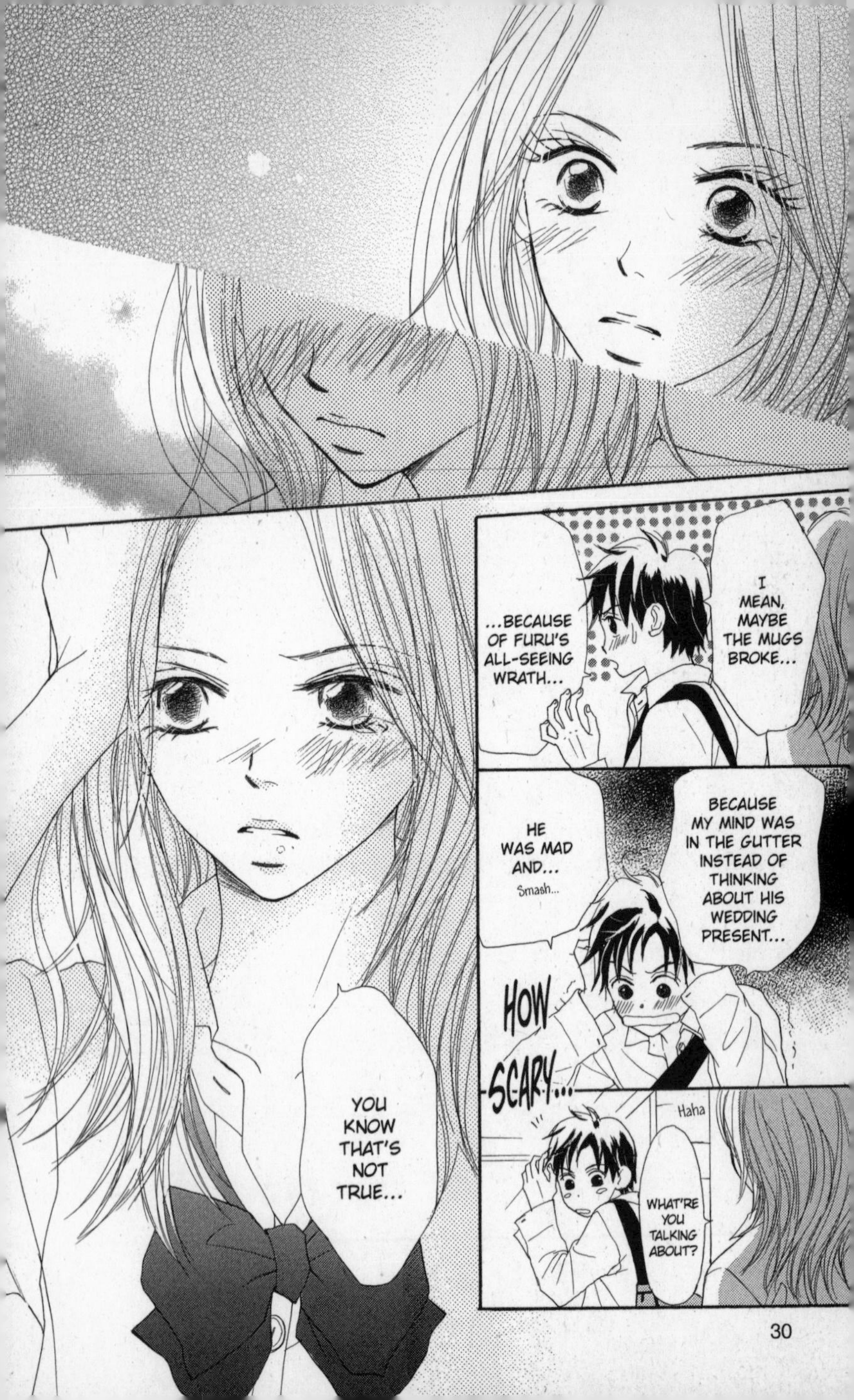
I MEAN, MAYBE THE MUGS BROKE...
...BECAUSE OF FURU'S ALL-SEEING WRATH...
BECAUSE MY MIND WAS IN THE GUTTER INSTEAD OF THINKING ABOUT HIS WEDDING PRESENT...
HE WAS MAD AND...
Smash...
HOW SCARY...
Haha
WHAT'RE YOU TALKING ABOUT?
YOU KNOW THAT'S NOT TRUE...

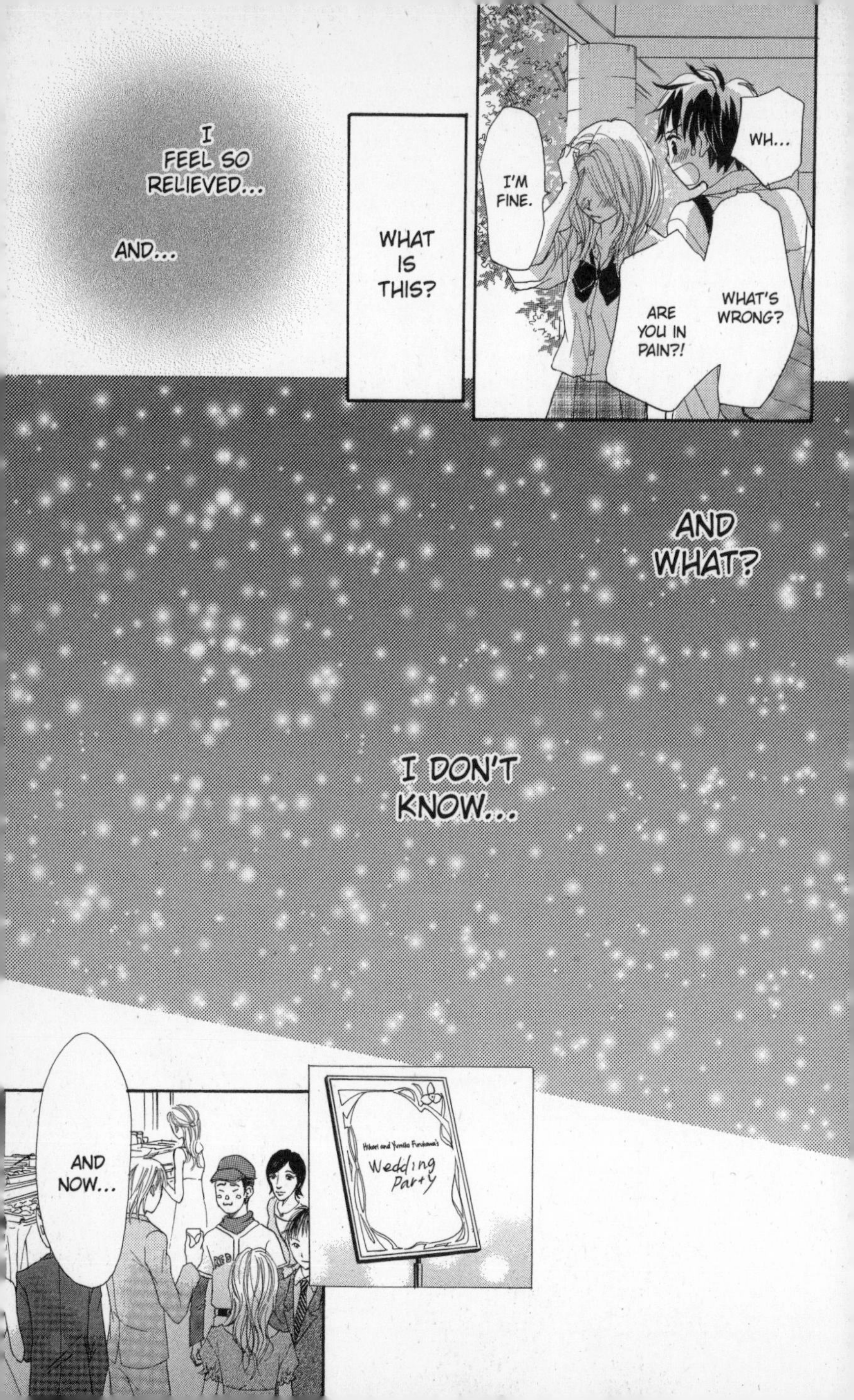
WH...
WHAT'S WRONG?
ARE YOU IN PAIN?!
I'M FINE.
WHAT IS THIS?
I FEEL SO RELIEVED...
AND...
AND WHAT?
I DON'T KNOW...
Hikari and Yumiko Furukawa's
Wedding Party
AND NOW...

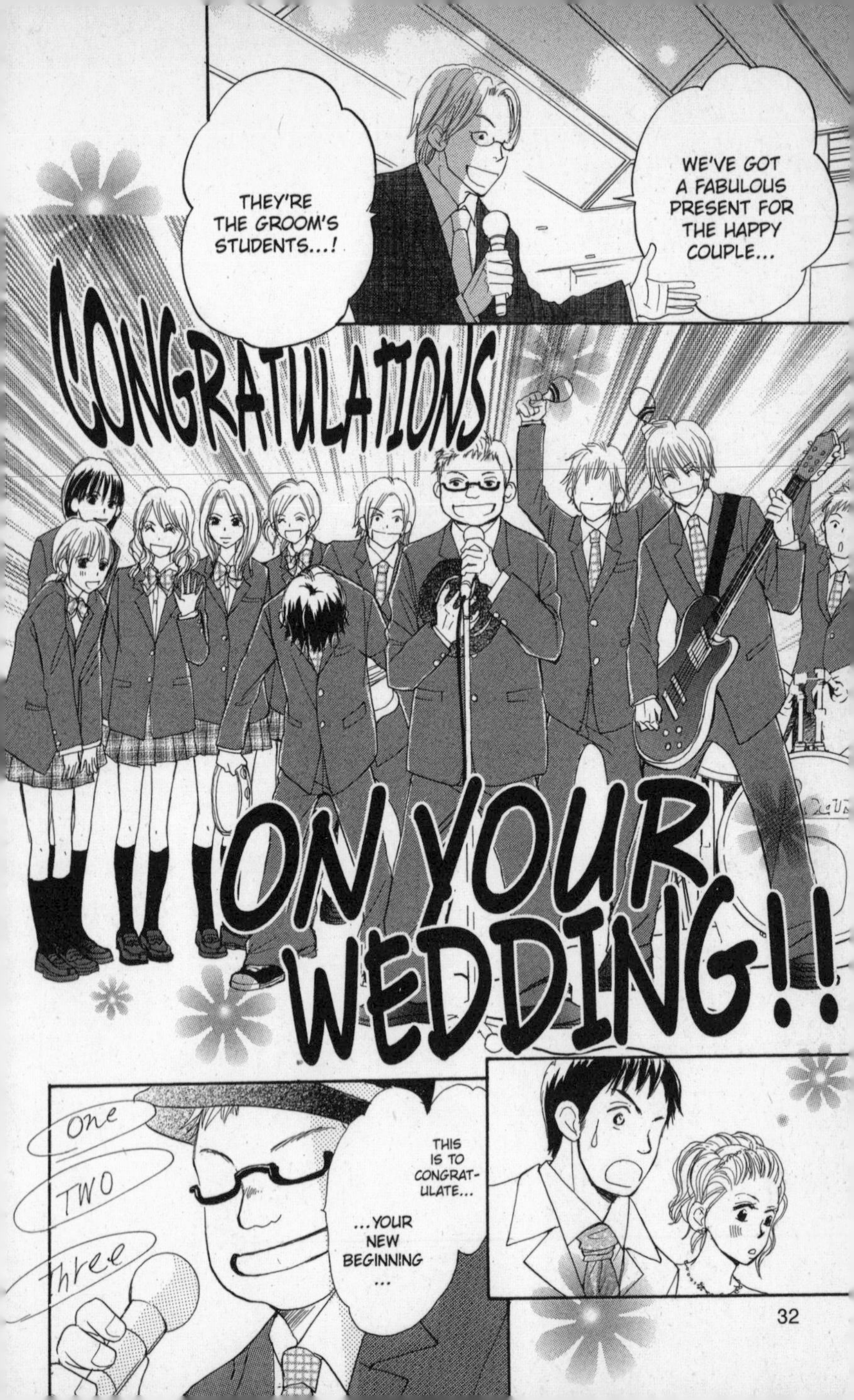
WE'VE GOT A FABULOUS PRESENT FOR THE HAPPY COUPLE...
THEY'RE THE GROOM'S STUDENTS...!
CONGRATULATIONS
ON YOUR WEDDING!!
One
TWO
Three
THIS IS TO CONGRATULATE...
...YOUR NEW BEGINNING ...

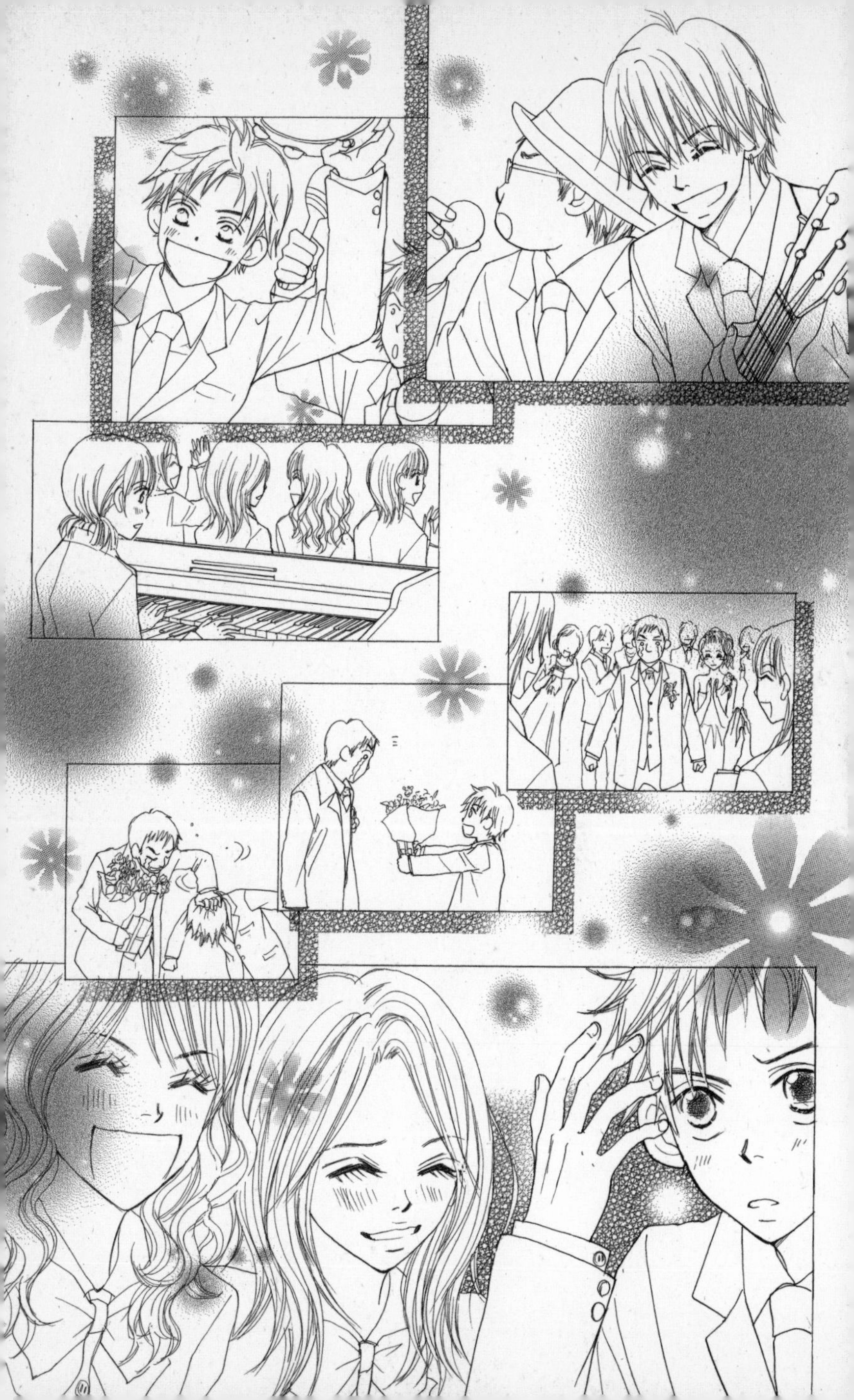

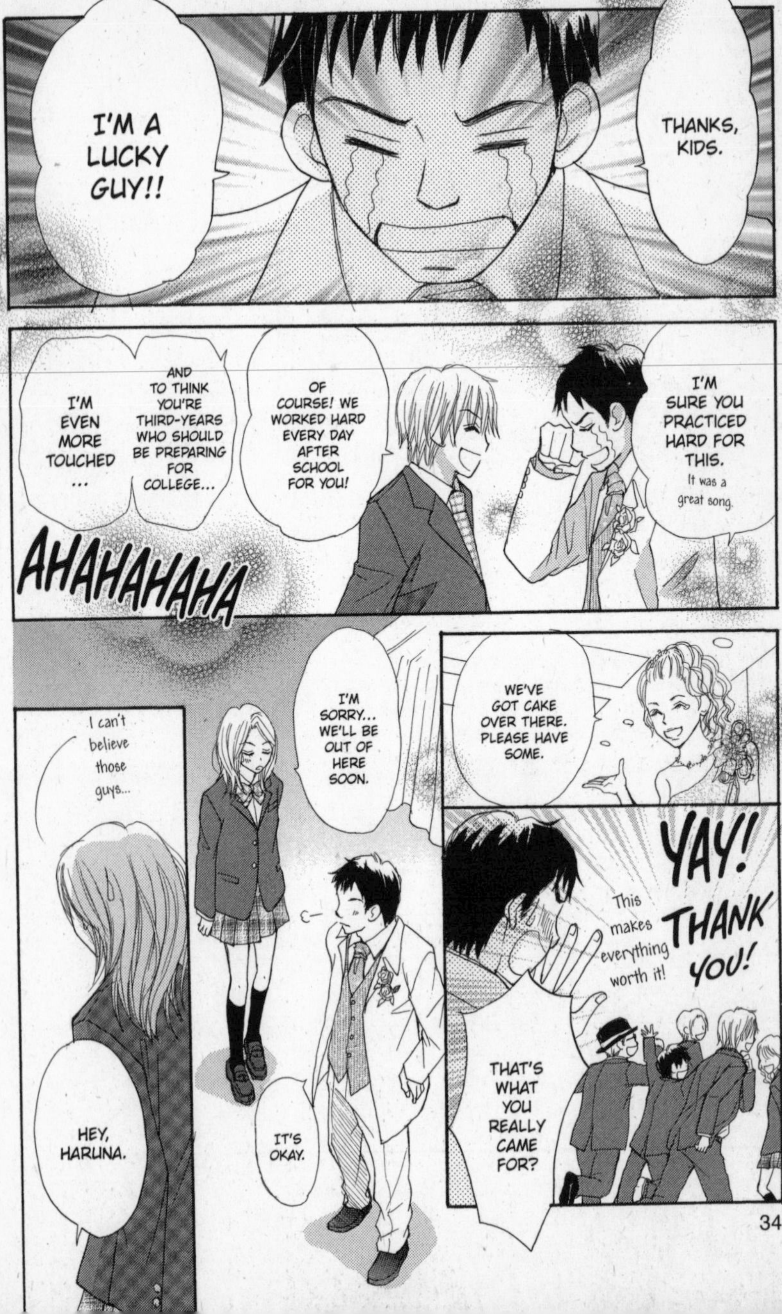
THANKS, KIDS.
I'M A LUCKY GUY!!
I'M SURE YOU PRACTICED HARD FOR THIS.
It was a great song.
OF COURSE! WE WORKED HARD EVERY DAY AFTER SCHOOL FOR YOU!
AND TO THINK YOU'RE THIRD-YEARS WHO SHOULD BE PREPARING FOR COLLEGE...
I'M EVEN MORE TOUCHED...
AHAHAHAHA
WE'VE GOT CAKE OVER THERE. PLEASE HAVE SOME.
YAY!
THANK YOU!
This makes everything worth it!
THAT'S WHAT YOU REALLY CAME FOR?
I'M SORRY... WE'LL BE OUT OF HERE SOON.
IT'S OKAY.
I can't believe those guys...
HEY, HARUNA.

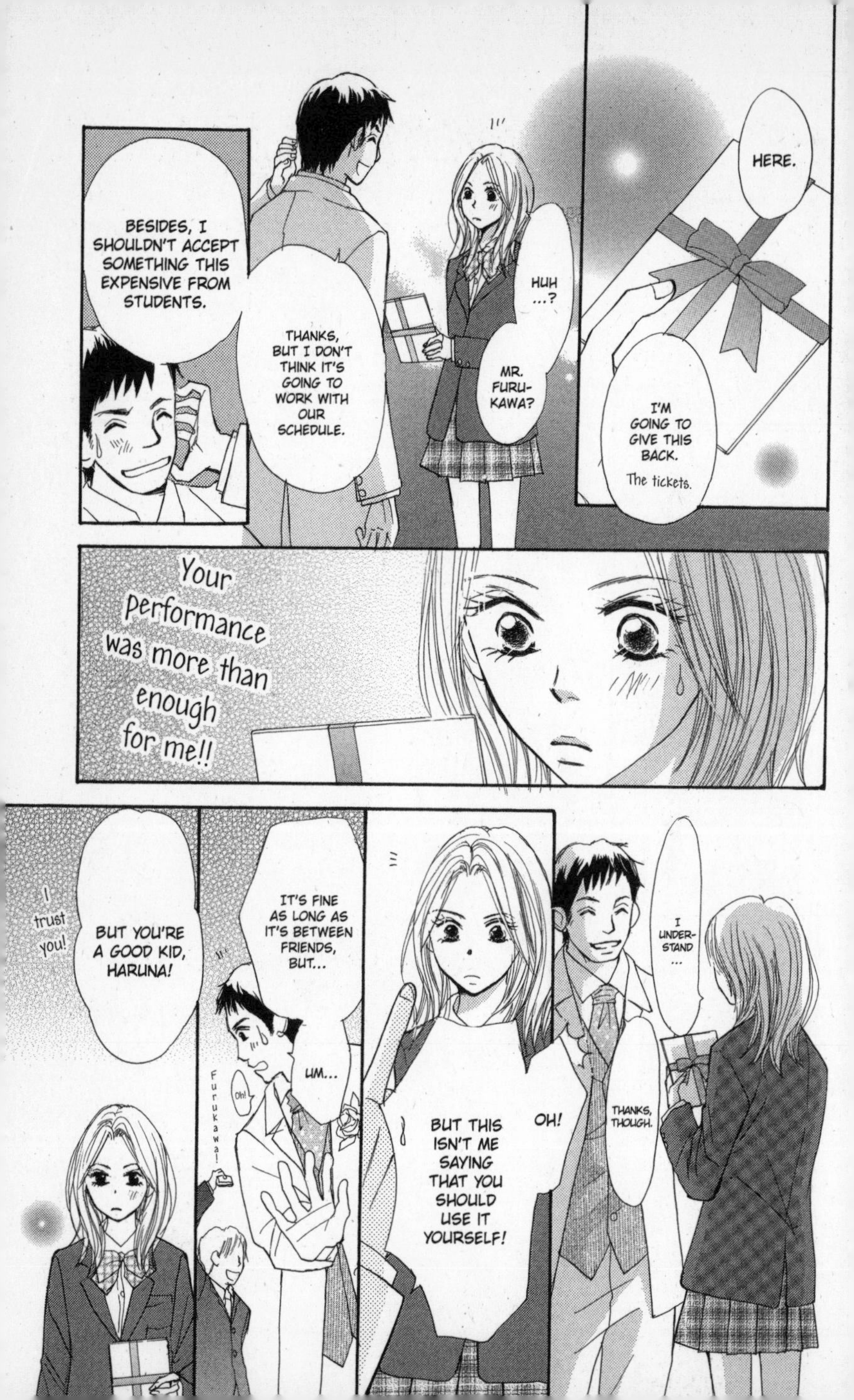
HERE.
I'M GOING TO GIVE THIS BACK.
The tickets.
HUH ...?
MR. FURUKAWA?
THANKS, BUT I DON'T THINK IT'S GOING TO WORK WITH OUR SCHEDULE.
BESIDES, I SHOULDN'T ACCEPT SOMETHING THIS EXPENSIVE FROM STUDENTS.
Your performance was more than enough for me!!
I UNDERSTAND ...
THANKS, THOUGH.
OH!
BUT THIS ISN'T ME SAYING THAT YOU SHOULD USE IT YOURSELF!
IT'S FINE AS LONG AS IT'S BETWEEN FRIENDS, BUT...
UM...
Furukawa!
Oh!
BUT YOU'RE A GOOD KID, HARUNA!
I trust you!

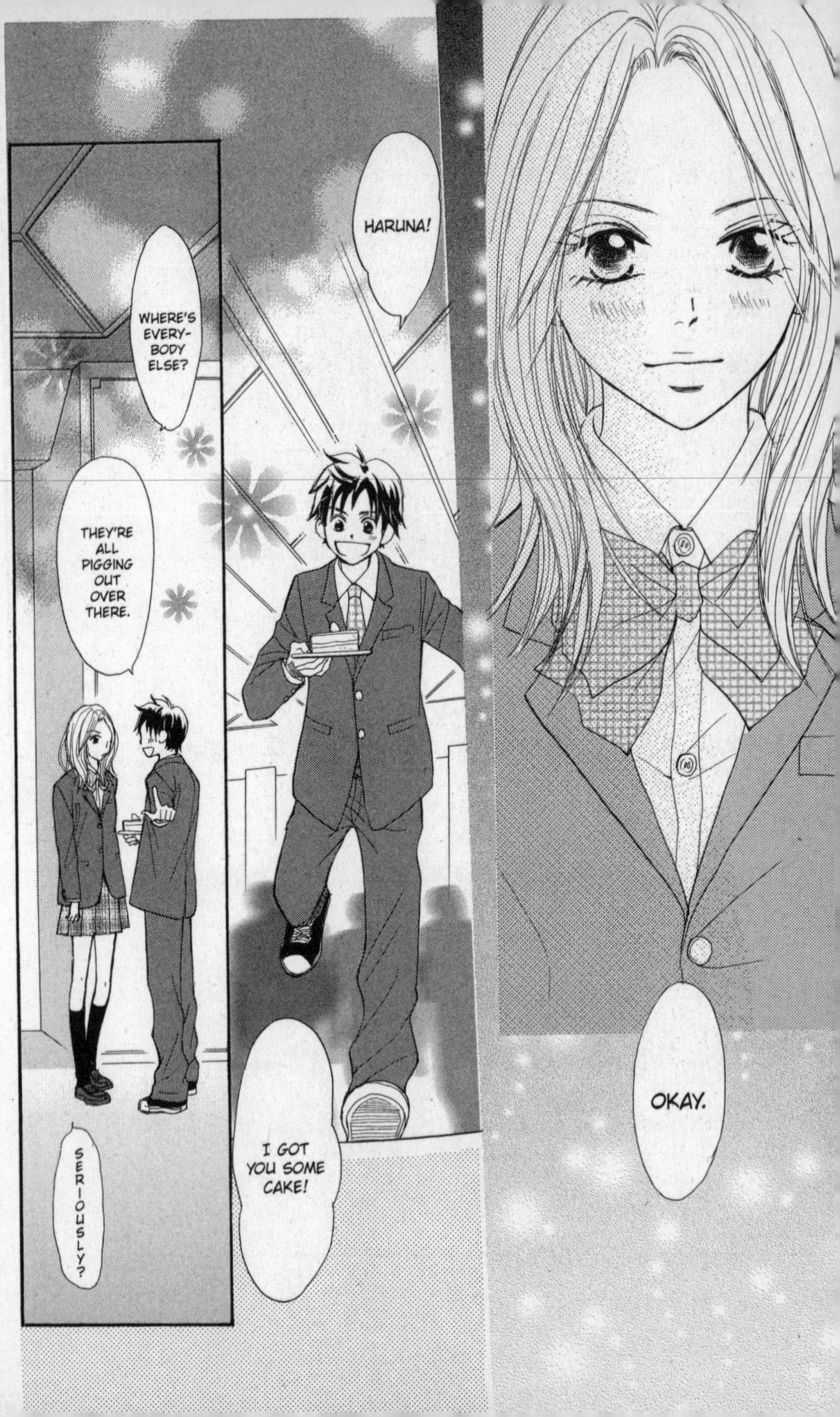
OKAY.
HARUNA!
I GOT YOU SOME CAKE!
WHERE'S EVERY-BODY ELSE?
THEY'RE ALL PIGGING OUT OVER THERE.
SERIOUSLY?

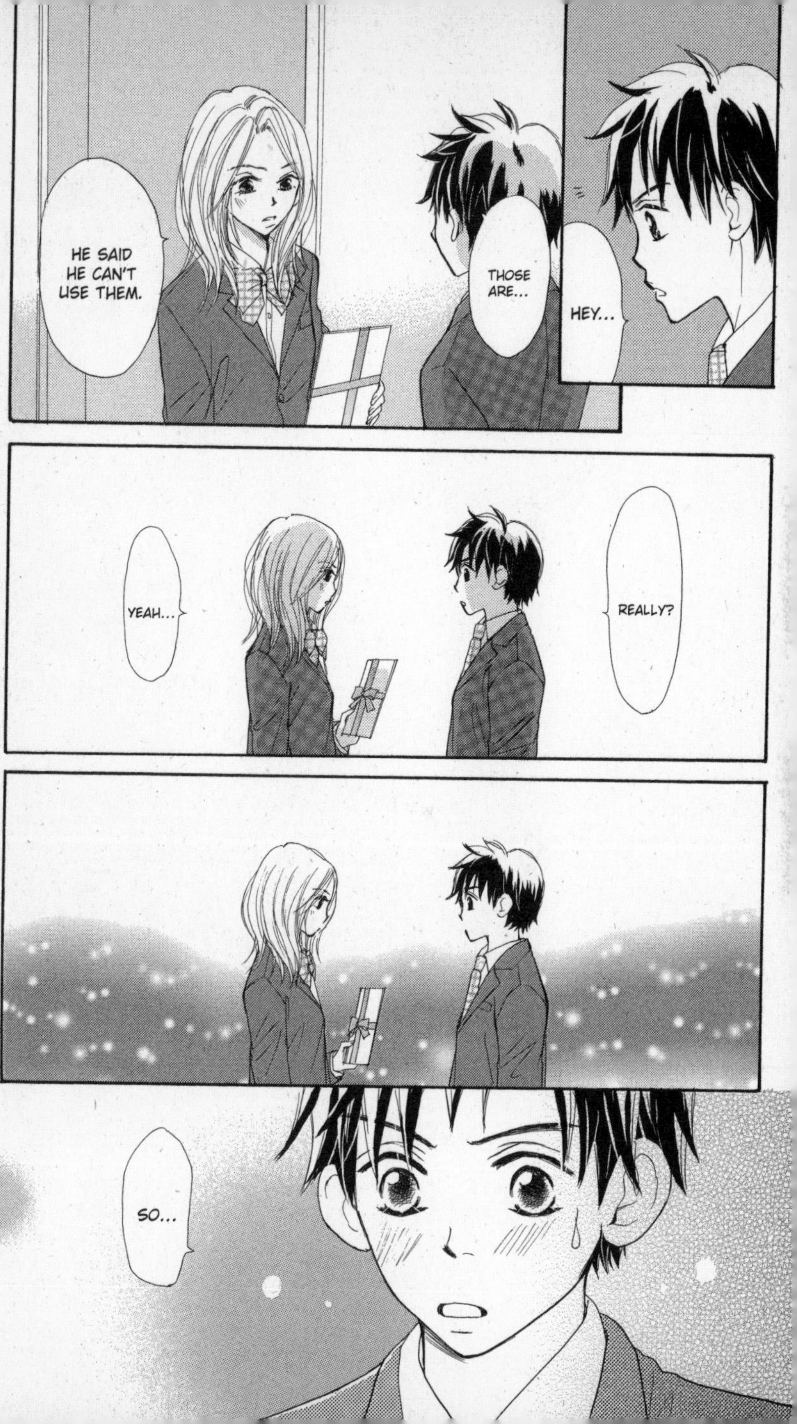
HEY...
THOSE ARE...
HE SAID HE CAN'T USE THEM.
REALLY?
YEAH...
SO...

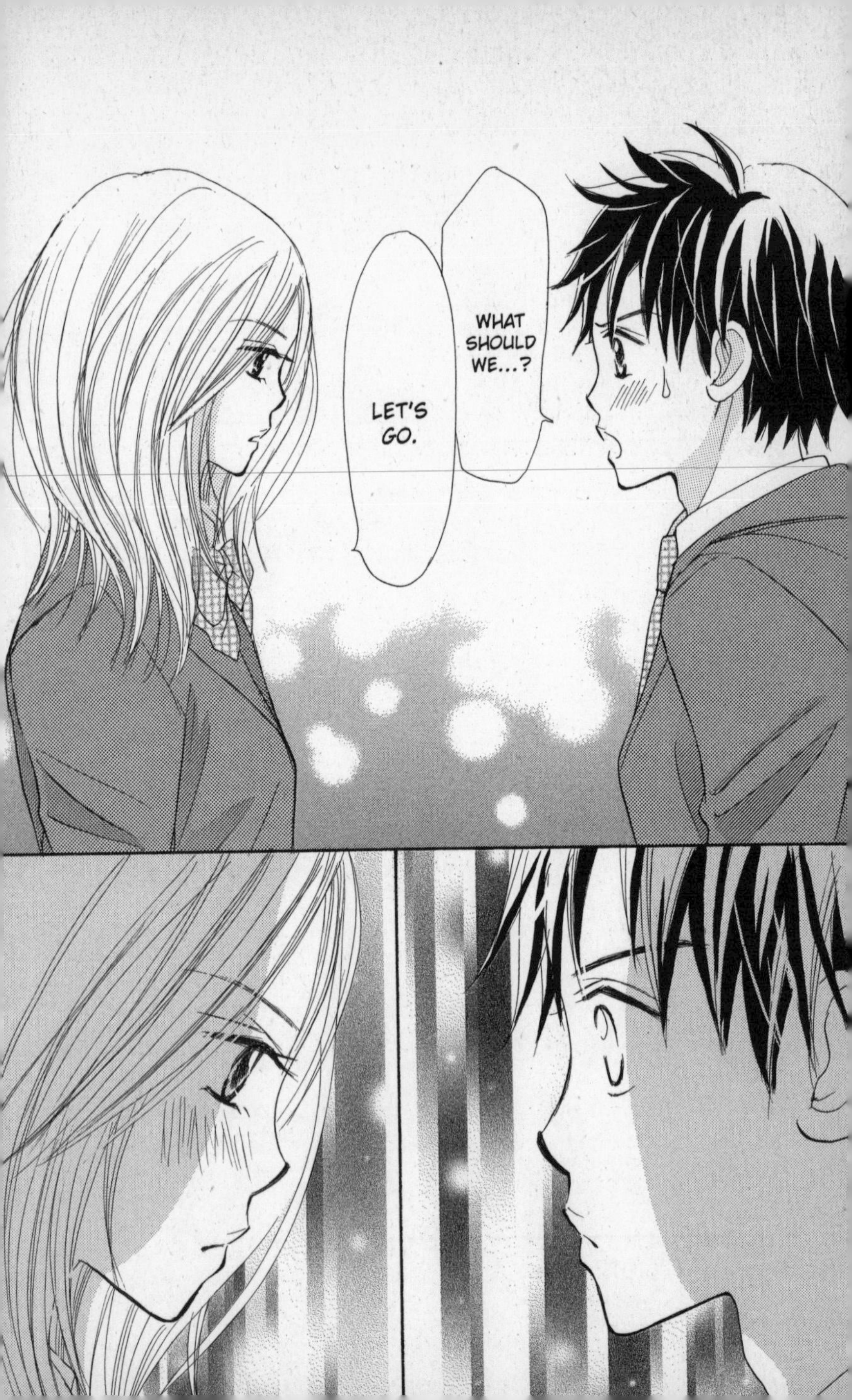
WHAT SHOULD WE...?
LET'S GO.

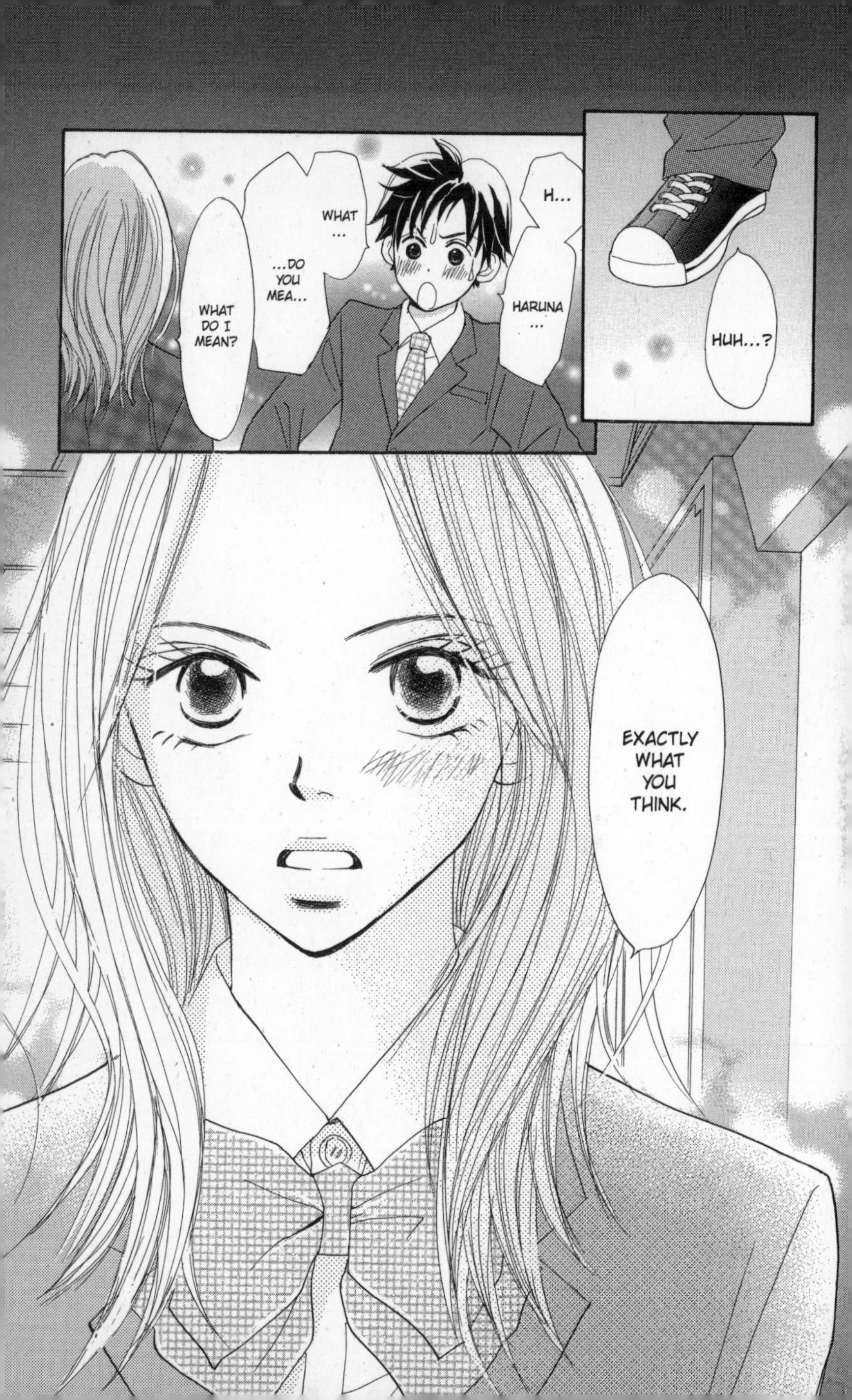
HUH...?
H...
HARUNA ...
WHAT ...
...DO YOU MEA...
WHAT DO I MEAN?
EXACTLY WHAT YOU THINK.

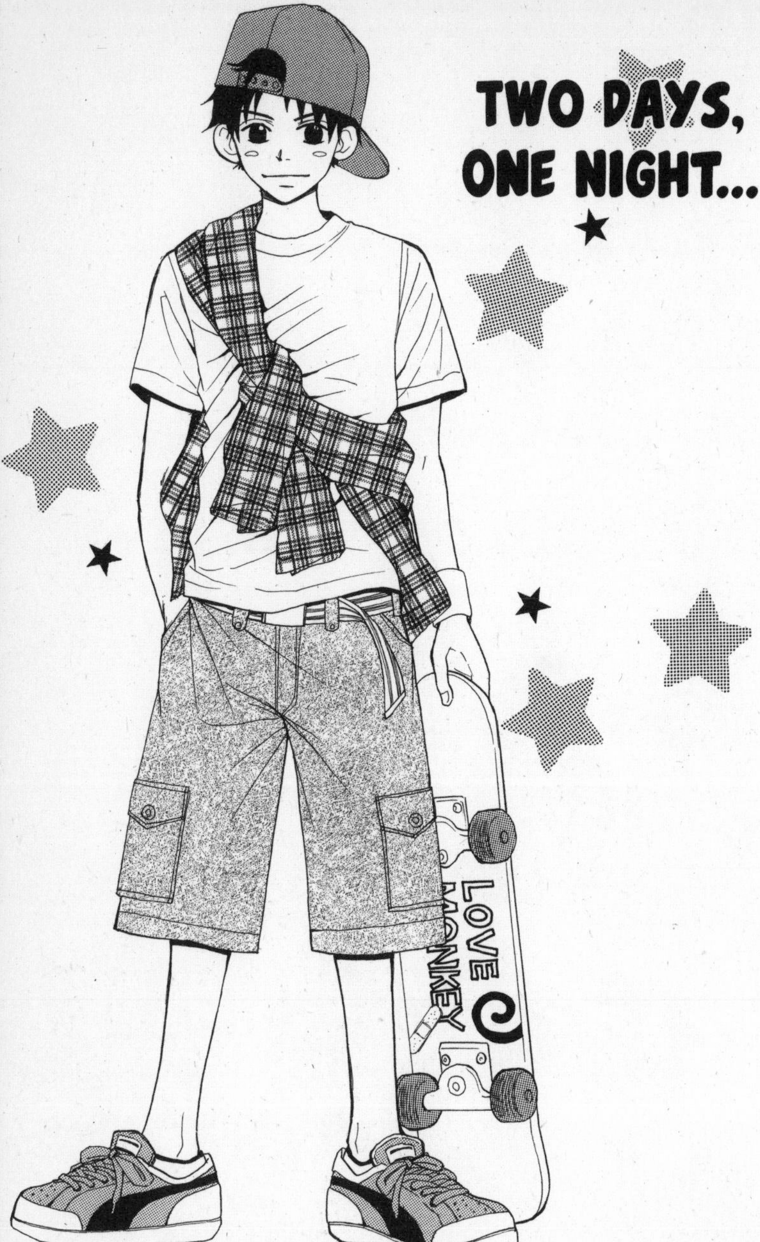
TWO DAYS, ONE NIGHT...
LOVE MONKEY

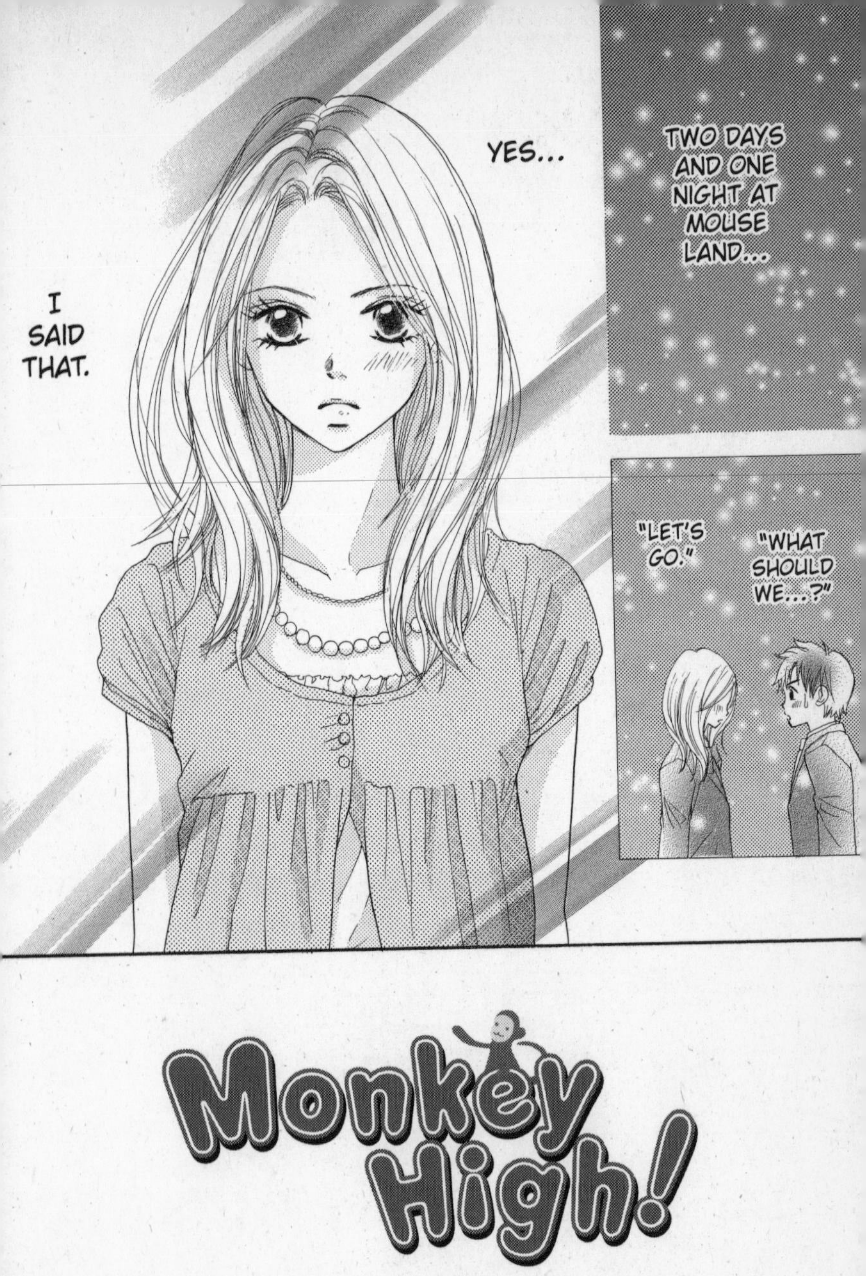
TWO DAYS AND ONE NIGHT AT MOUSE LAND...
"WHAT SHOULD WE...?"
"LET'S GO."
YES...
I SAID THAT.

Monkey High!

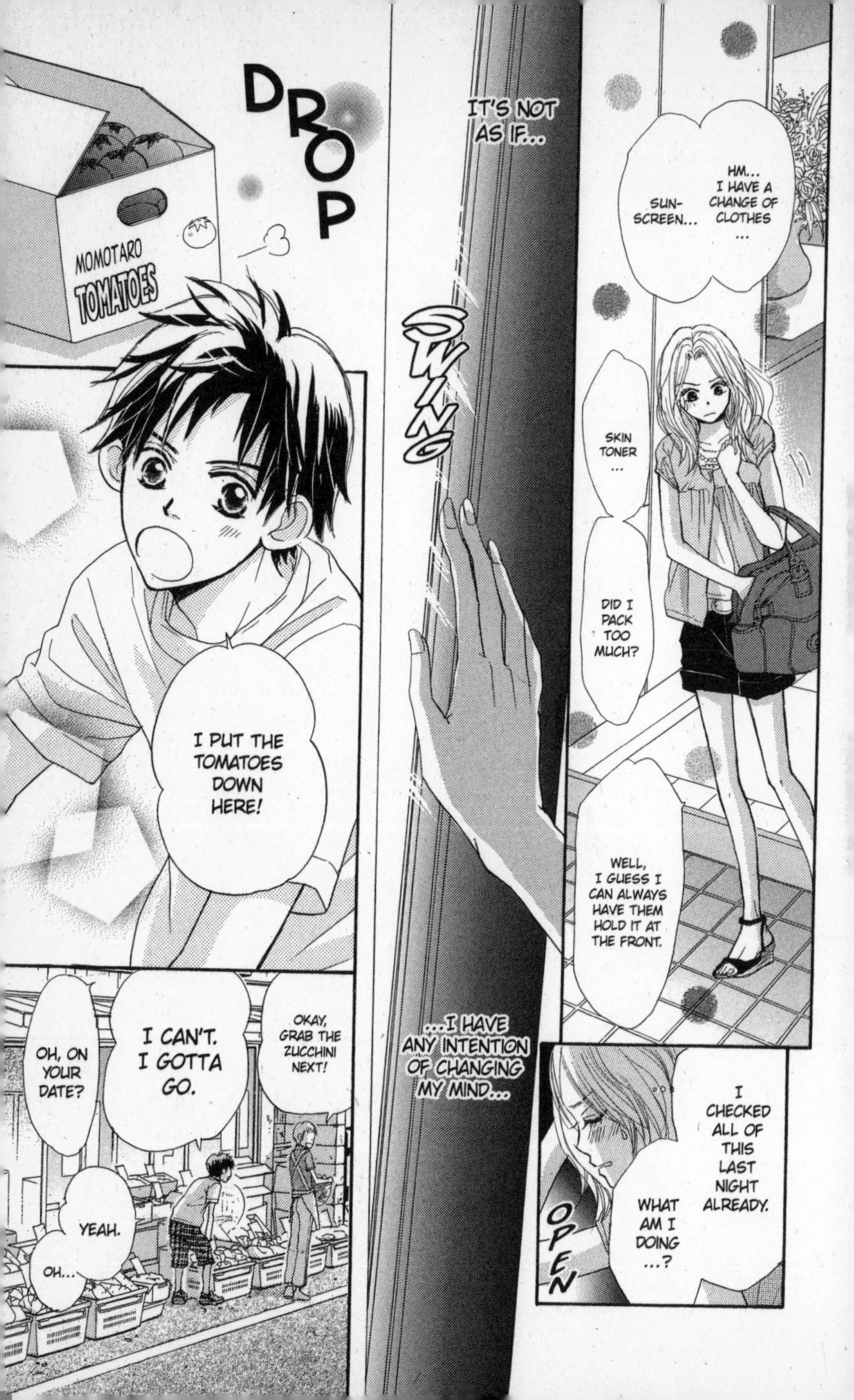
HM... I HAVE A CHANGE OF CLOTHES ...
SUN-SCREEN...
SKIN TONER ...
DID I PACK TOO MUCH?
WELL, I GUESS I CAN ALWAYS HAVE THEM HOLD IT AT THE FRONT.
I CHECKED ALL OF THIS LAST NIGHT ALREADY.
WHAT AM I DOING ...?
OPEN
IT'S NOT AS IF...
SWING
...I HAVE ANY INTENTION OF CHANGING MY MIND...
DROP
MOMOTARO TOMATOES
I PUT THE TOMATOES DOWN HERE!
OKAY, GRAB THE ZUCCHINI NEXT!
I CAN'T. I GOTTA GO.
OH, ON YOUR DATE?
YEAH.
OH...

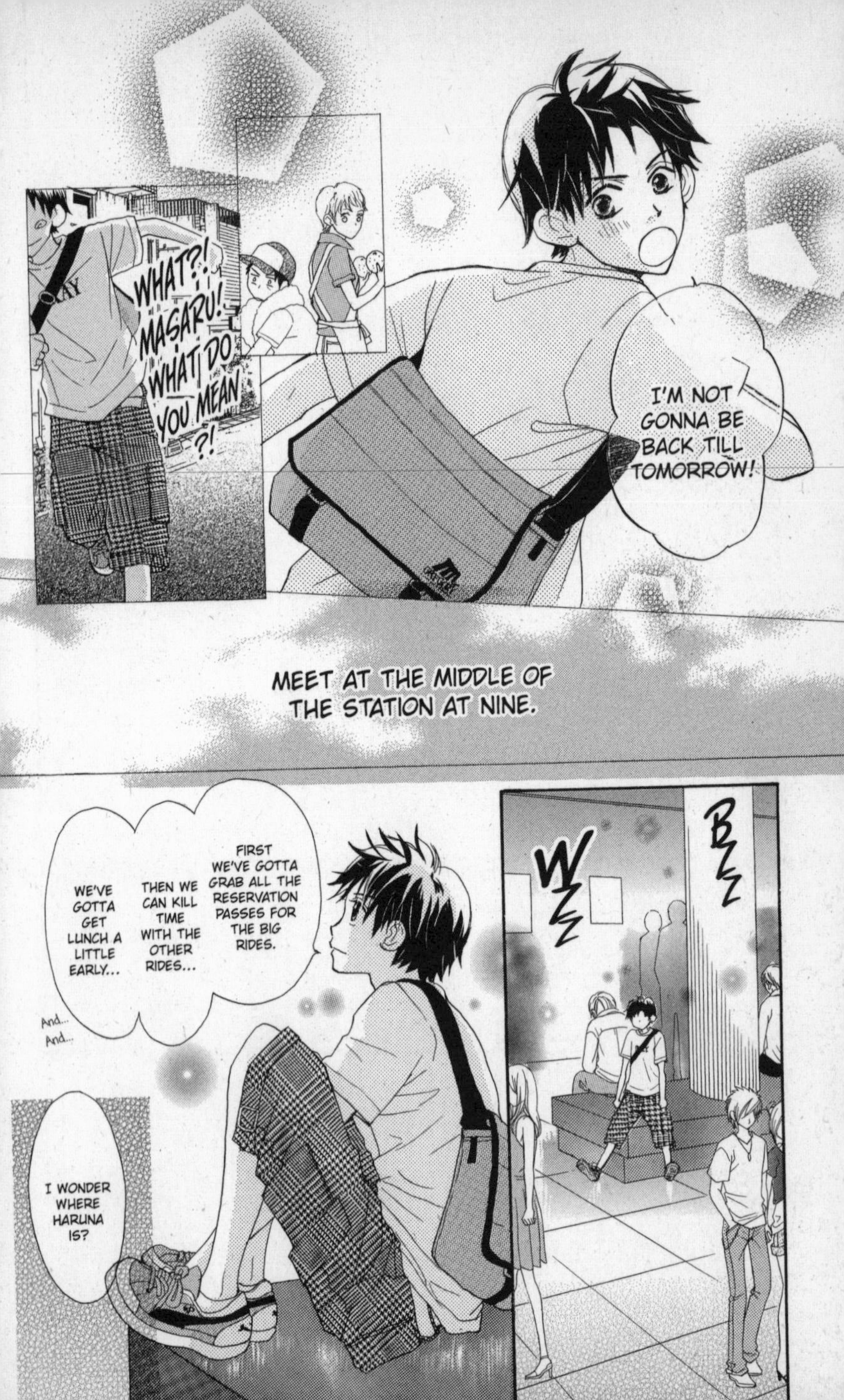
I'M NOT GONNA BE BACK TILL TOMORROW!
WHAT?! MASARU! WHAT DO YOU MEAN ?!
MEET AT THE MIDDLE OF THE STATION AT NINE.
BZZ
WZZ
FIRST WE'VE GOTTA GRAB ALL THE RESERVATION PASSES FOR THE BIG RIDES.
THEN WE CAN KILL TIME WITH THE OTHER RIDES...
WE'VE GOTTA GET LUNCH A LITTLE EARLY...
And... And...
I WONDER WHERE HARUNA IS?

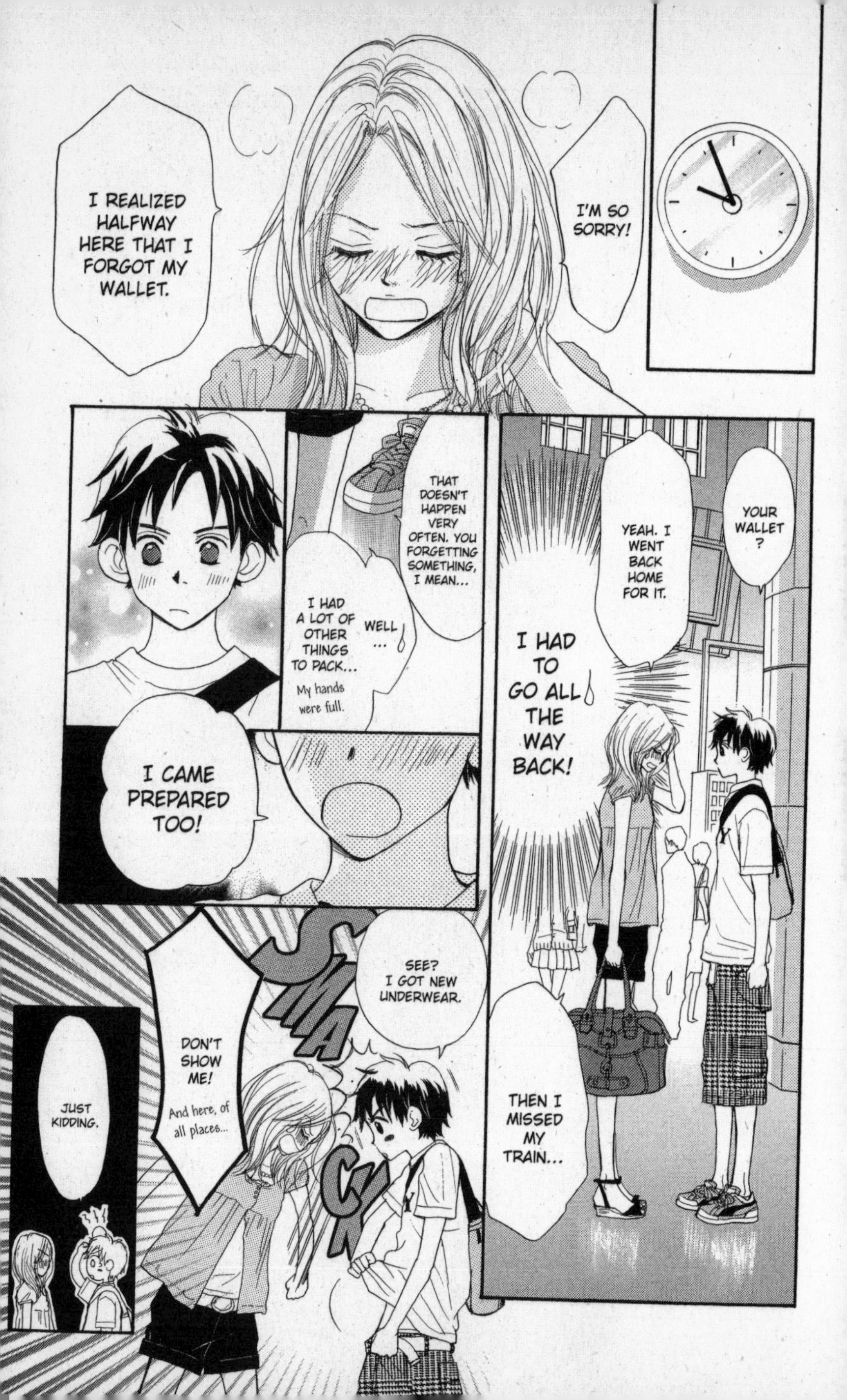

I'M SO SORRY!
I REALIZED HALFWAY HERE THAT I FORGOT MY WALLET.
YOUR WALLET?
YEAH. I WENT BACK HOME FOR IT.
I HAD TO GO ALL THE WAY BACK!
THEN I MISSED MY TRAIN...
THAT DOESN'T HAPPEN VERY OFTEN. YOU FORGETTING SOMETHING, I MEAN...
WELL...
I HAD A LOT OF OTHER THINGS TO PACK...
My hands were full.
I CAME PREPARED TOO!
SEE? I GOT NEW UNDERWEAR.
SMACK
DON'T SHOW ME!
And here, of all places...
JUST KIDDING.

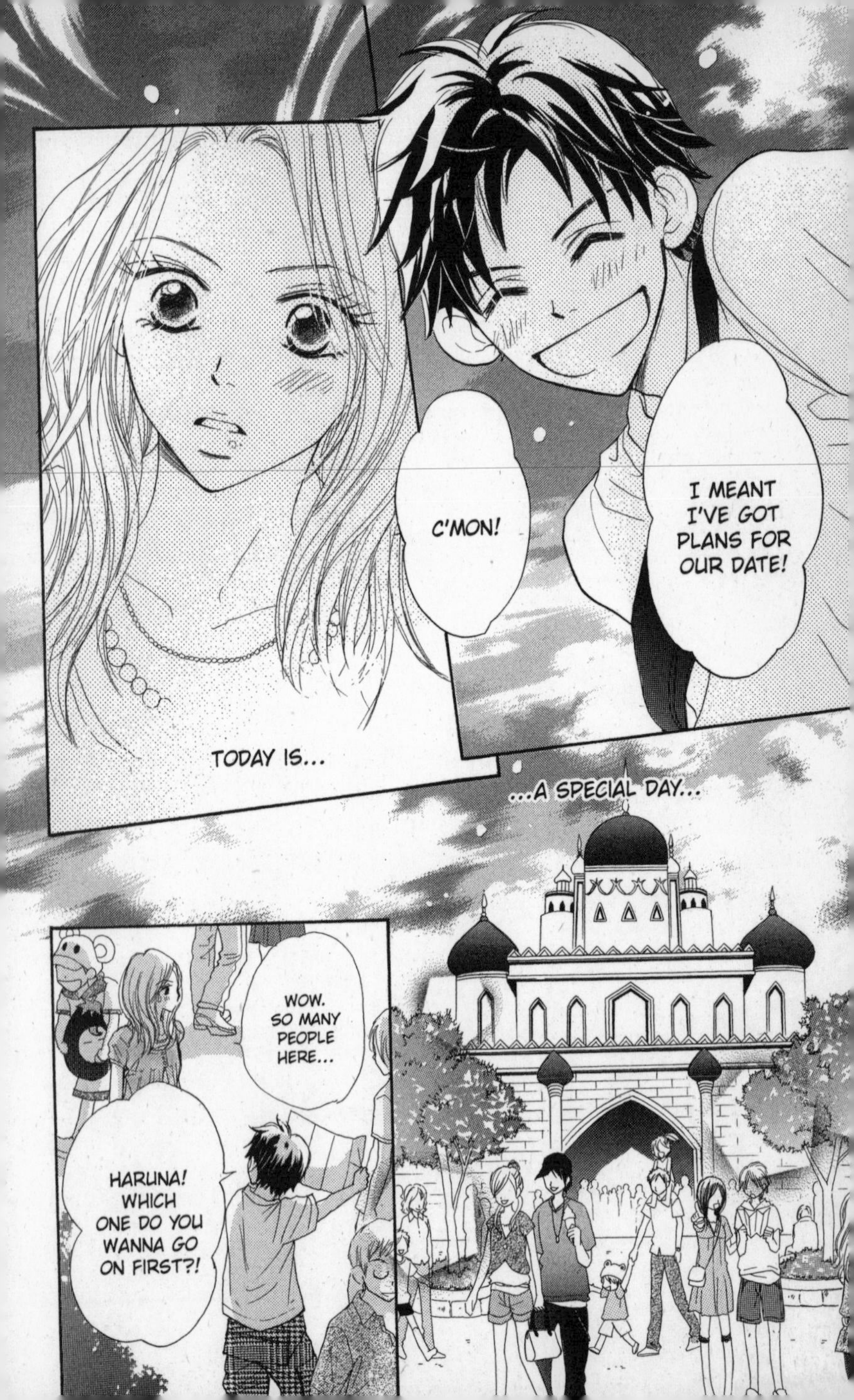
I MEANT I'VE GOT PLANS FOR OUR DATE!
C'MON!
TODAY IS...
...A SPECIAL DAY...
WOW. SO MANY PEOPLE HERE...
HARUNA! WHICH ONE DO YOU WANNA GO ON FIRST?!

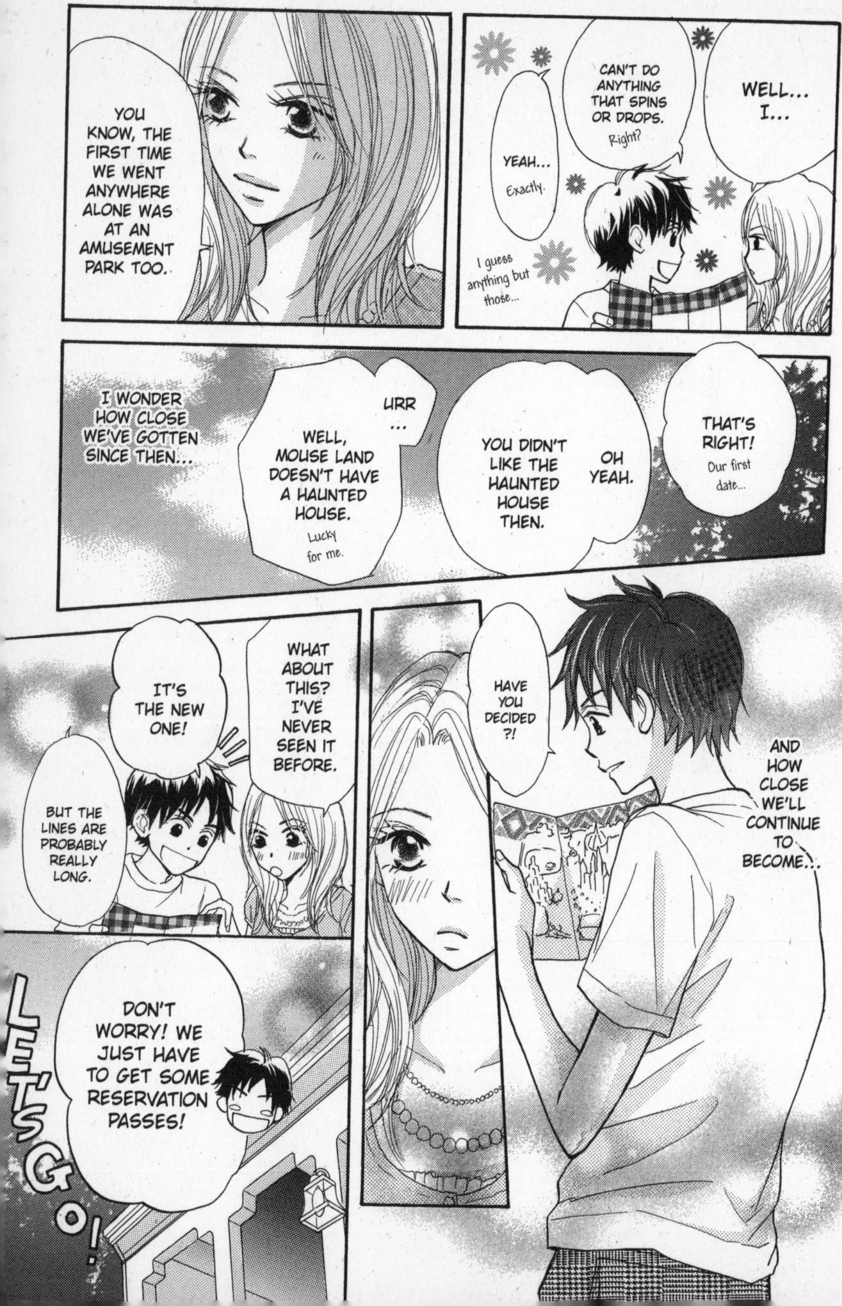
WELL... I...
CAN'T DO ANYTHING THAT SPINS OR DROPS. Right?
YEAH... Exactly.
I guess anything but those...
YOU KNOW, THE FIRST TIME WE WENT ANYWHERE ALONE WAS AT AN AMUSEMENT PARK TOO.
THAT'S RIGHT! Our first date...
OH YEAH.
YOU DIDN'T LIKE THE HAUNTED HOUSE THEN.
URR ...
WELL, MOUSE LAND DOESN'T HAVE A HAUNTED HOUSE. Lucky for me.
I WONDER HOW CLOSE WE'VE GOTTEN SINCE THEN...
HAVE YOU DECIDED ?!
AND HOW CLOSE WE'LL CONTINUE TO BECOME...
WHAT ABOUT THIS? I'VE NEVER SEEN IT BEFORE.
IT'S THE NEW ONE!
BUT THE LINES ARE PROBABLY REALLY LONG.
DON'T WORRY! WE JUST HAVE TO GET SOME RESERVATION PASSES!
LET'S GO!

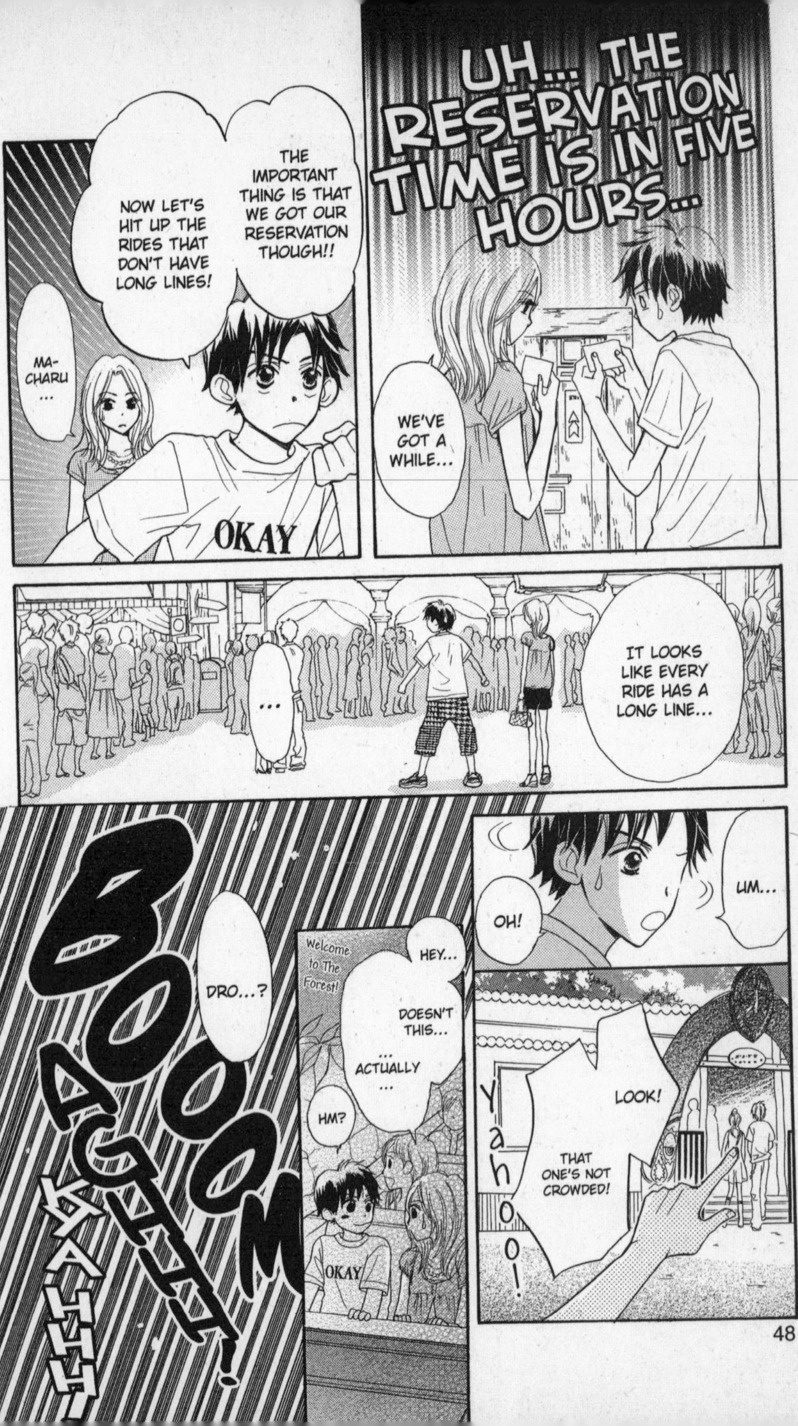
UH... THE RESERVATION TIME IS IN FIVE HOURS...
WE'VE GOT A WHILE...
THE IMPORTANT THING IS THAT WE GOT OUR RESERVATION THOUGH!!
NOW LET'S HIT UP THE RIDES THAT DON'T HAVE LONG LINES!
MA-CHARU ...
OKAY
IT LOOKS LIKE EVERY RIDE HAS A LONG LINE...
...
UM...
OH!
LOOK!
Yahoo!
THAT ONE'S NOT CROWDED!
Welcome to The Forest!
HEY...
DOESN'T THIS... ... ACTUALLY ...
HM?
OKAY
DRO...?
BOOOOM
AGHHH!
KYAHHHH

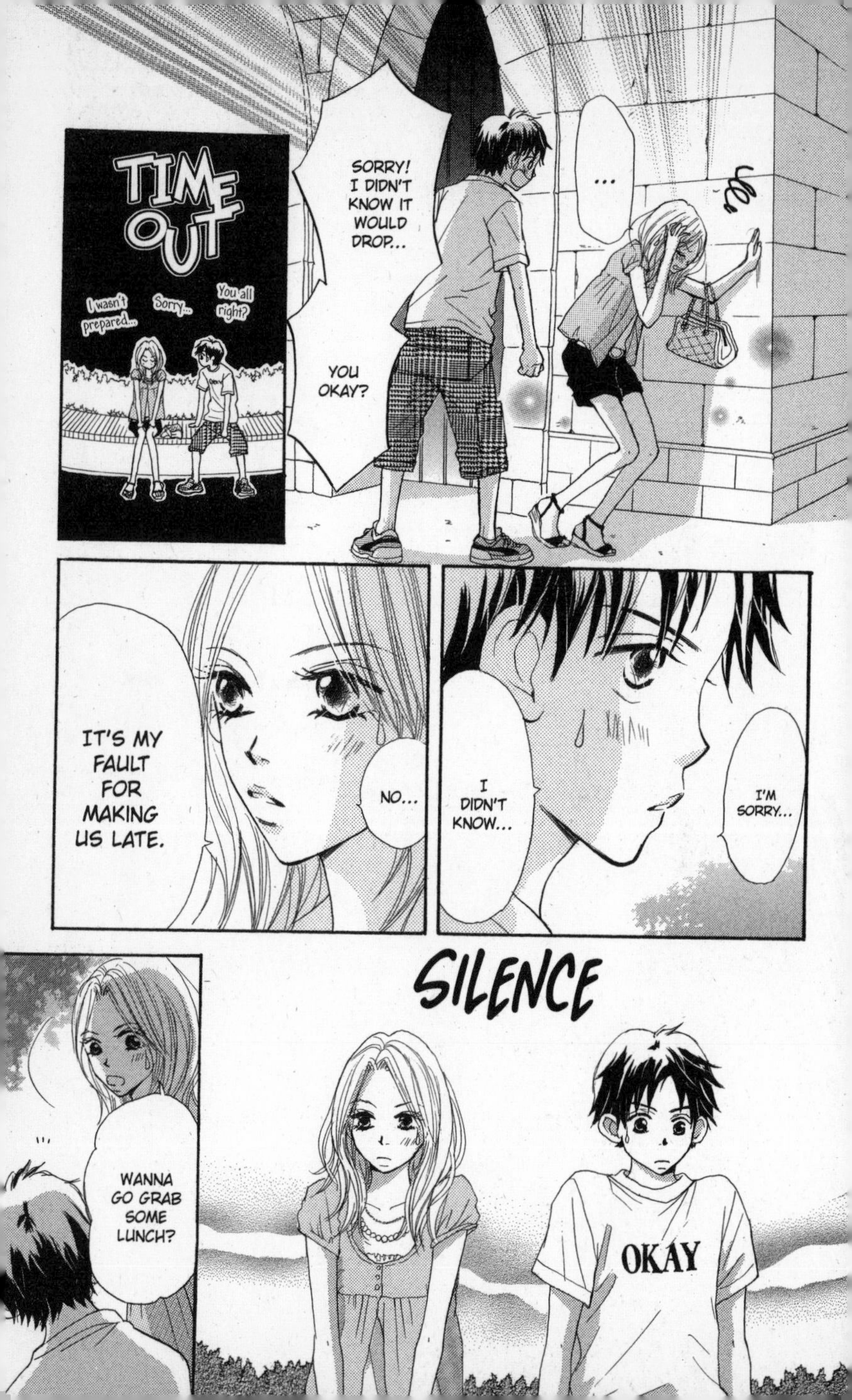
...
SORRY! I DIDN'T KNOW IT WOULD DROP...
YOU OKAY?
TIME OUT
You all right?
Sorry...
I wasn't prepared...
I'M SORRY...
I DIDN'T KNOW...
NO...
IT'S MY FAULT FOR MAKING US LATE.
SILENCE
OKAY
WANNA GO GRAB SOME LUNCH?

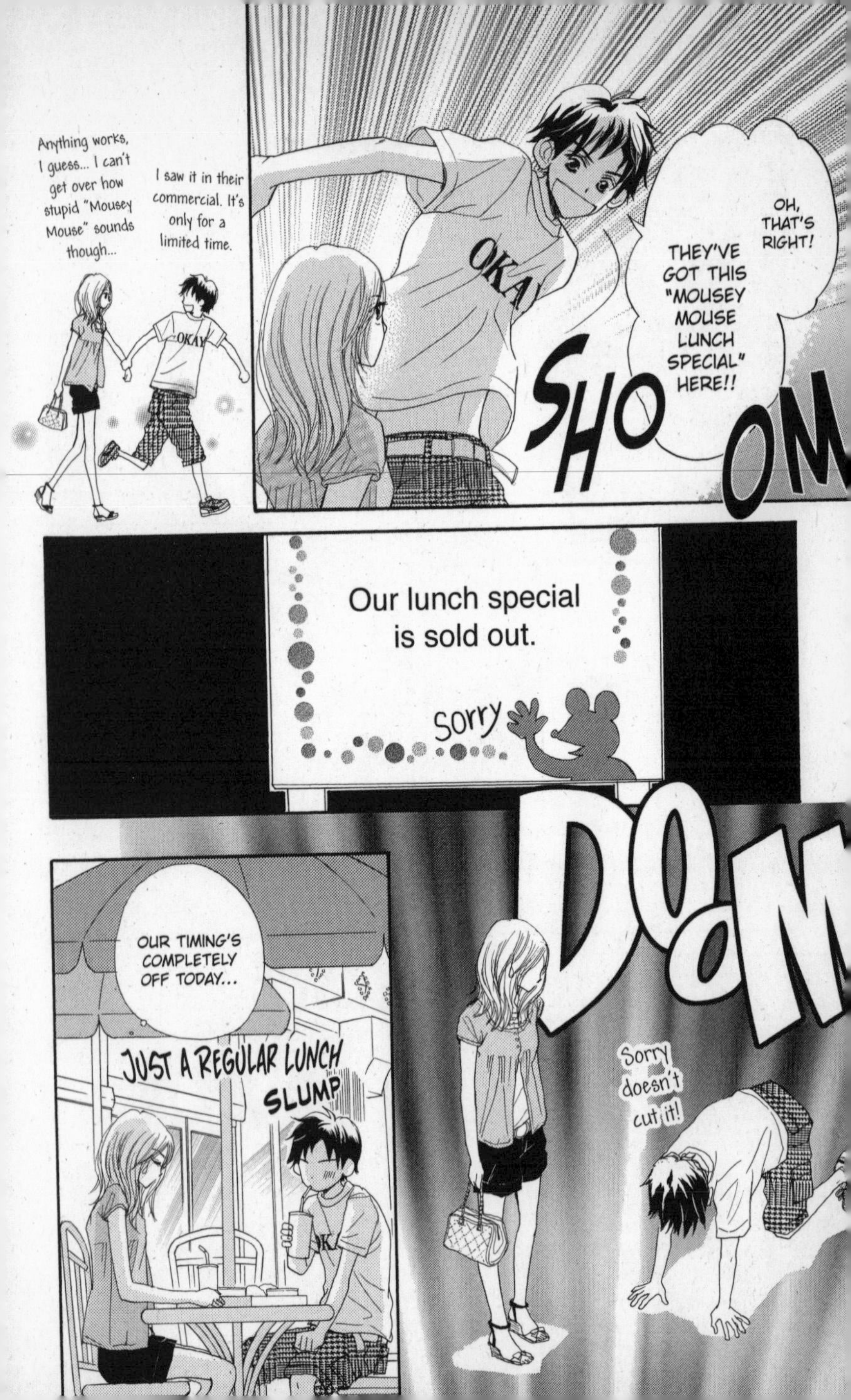
OH, THAT'S RIGHT!
THEY'VE GOT THIS "MOUSEY MOUSE LUNCH SPECIAL" HERE!!
SHO OM
I saw it in their commercial. It's only for a limited time.
Anything works, I guess... I can't get over how stupid "Mousey Mouse" sounds though...
Our lunch special is sold out.
Sorry
DOOM
Sorry doesn't cut it!
OUR TIMING'S COMPLETELY OFF TODAY...
JUST A REGULAR LUNCH
SLUMP

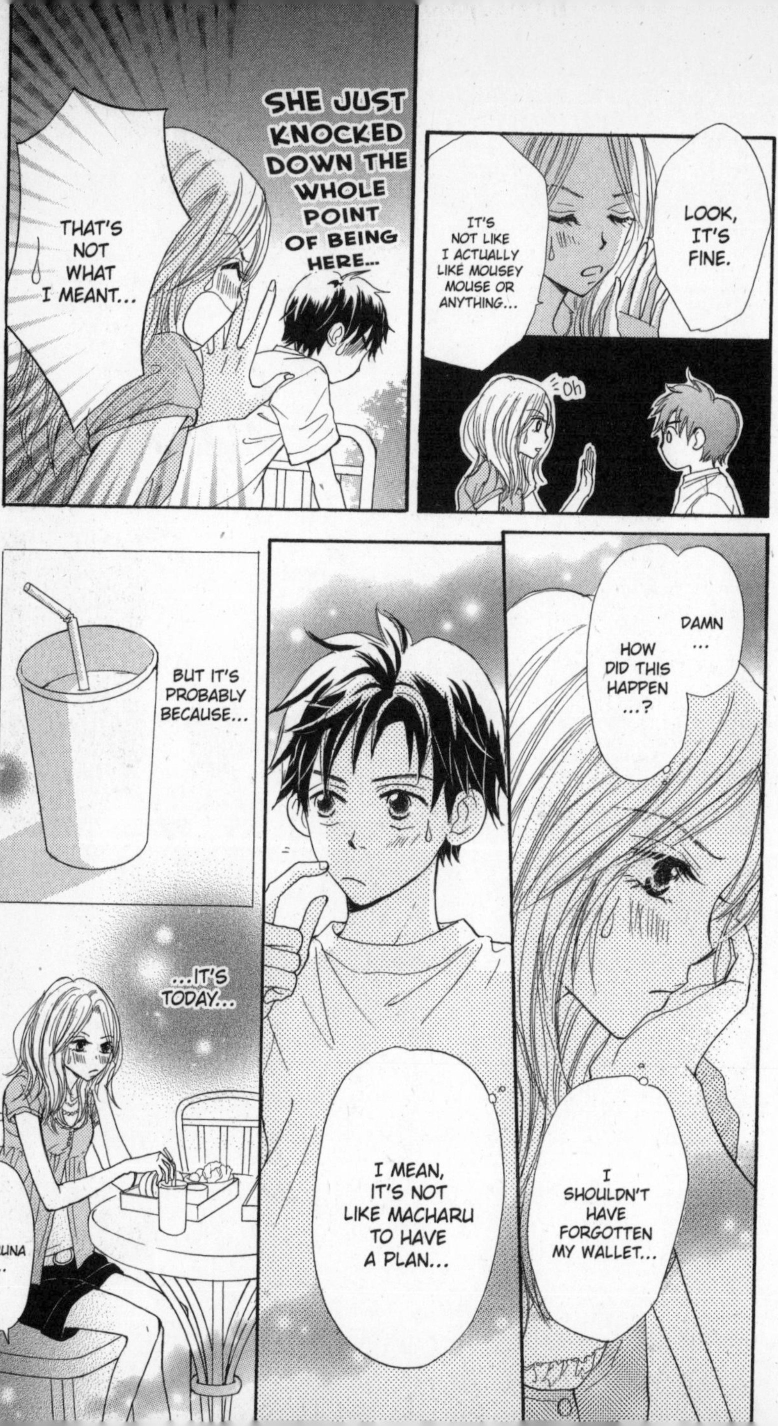
LOOK, IT'S FINE.
IT'S NOT LIKE I ACTUALLY LIKE MOUSEY MOUSE OR ANYTHING...
Oh
SHE JUST KNOCKED DOWN THE WHOLE POINT OF BEING HERE...
THAT'S NOT WHAT I MEANT...
DAMN...
HOW DID THIS HAPPEN...?
I SHOULDN'T HAVE FORGOTTEN MY WALLET...
I MEAN, IT'S NOT LIKE MACHARU TO HAVE A PLAN...
BUT IT'S PROBABLY BECAUSE...
...IT'S TODAY...
HARUNA...

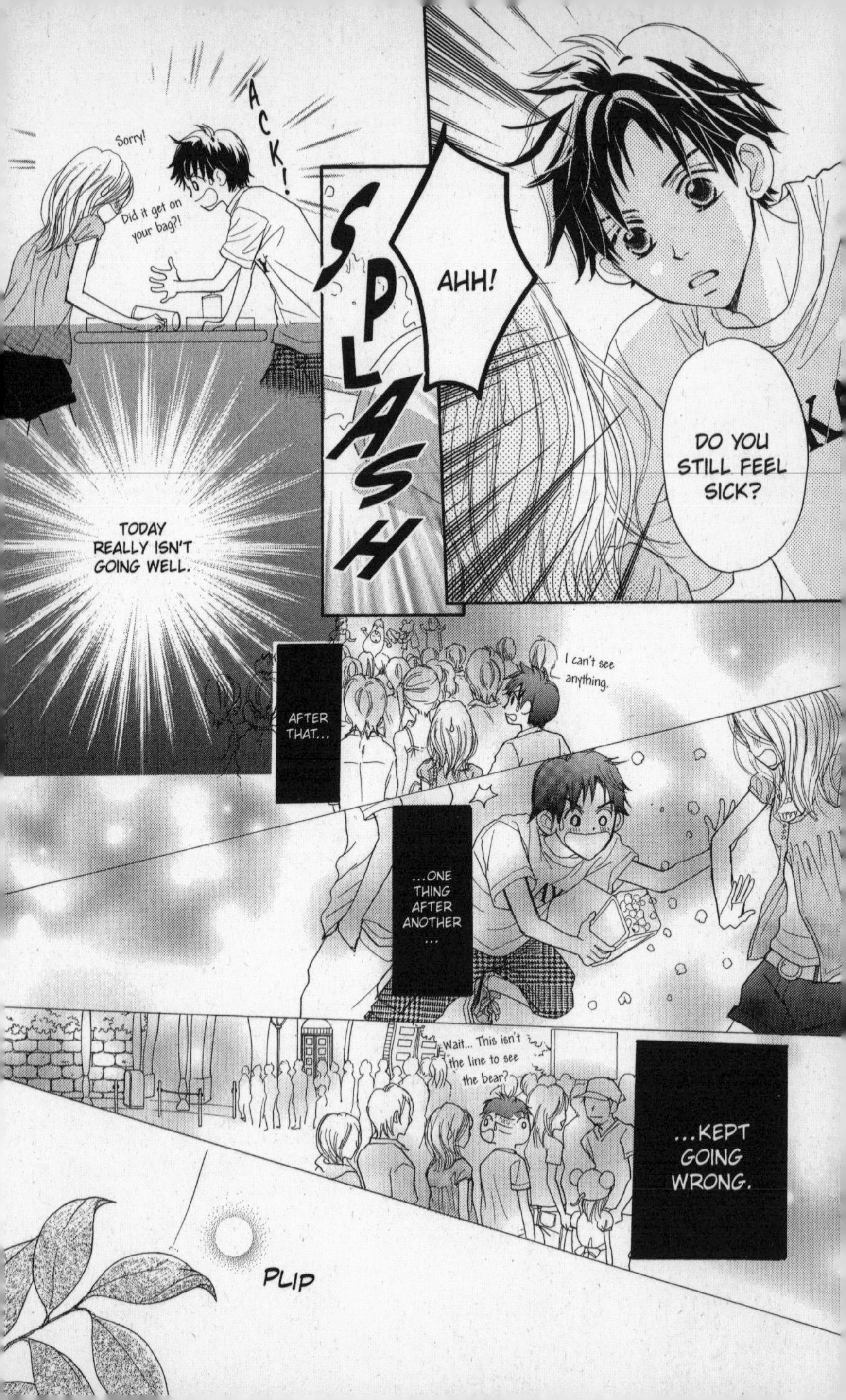
DO YOU STILL FEEL SICK?
AHH!
SPLASH
ACK!
Sorry!
Did it get on your bag?!
TODAY REALLY ISN'T GOING WELL.
I can't see anything.
AFTER THAT...
...ONE THING AFTER ANOTHER...
Wait... This isn't the line to see the bear?
...KEPT GOING WRONG.
PLIP

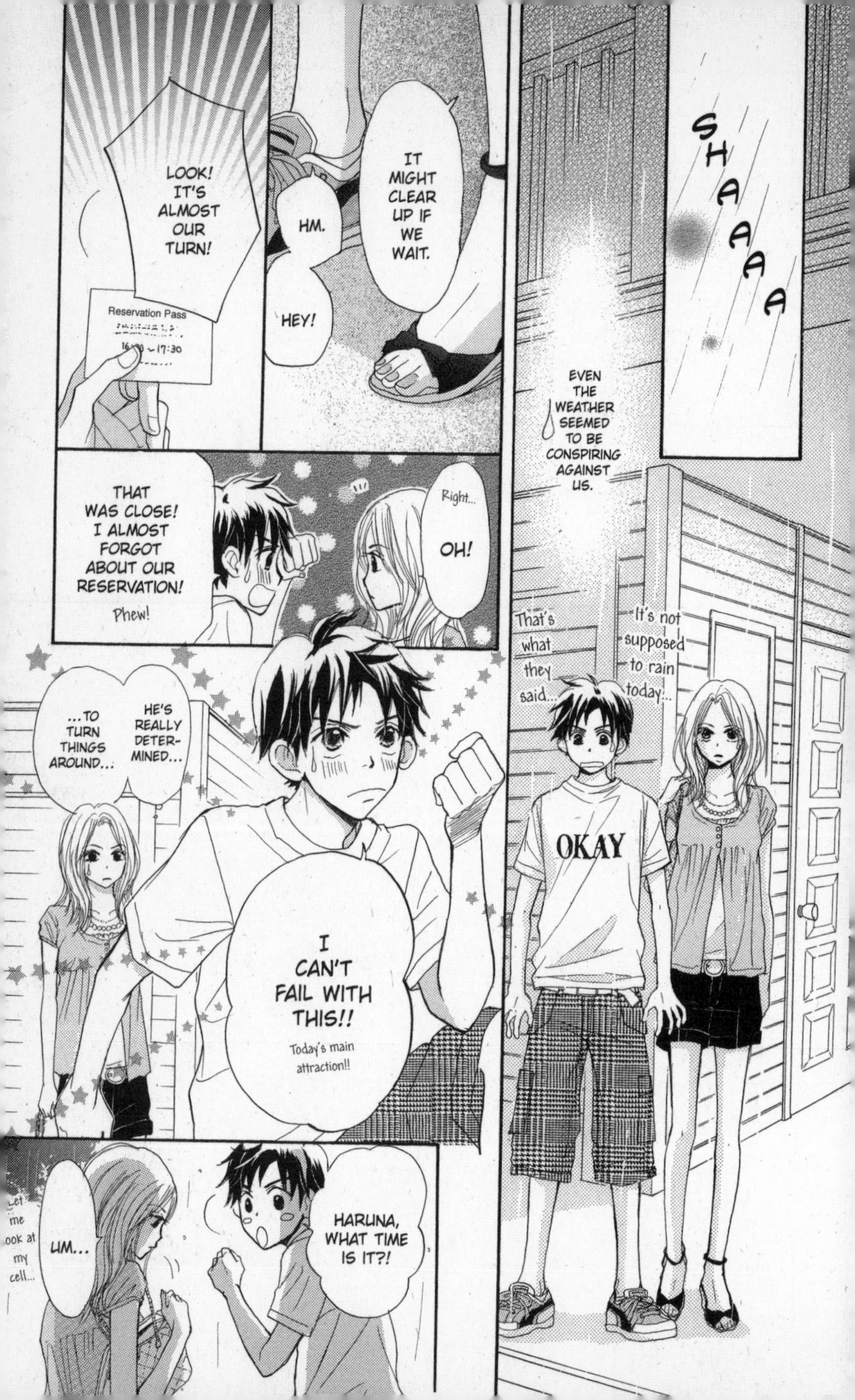
SHAAAA
EVEN THE WEATHER SEEMED TO BE CONSPIRING AGAINST US.
It's not supposed to rain today...
That's what they said...
IT MIGHT CLEAR UP IF WE WAIT.
HM.
HEY!
LOOK! IT'S ALMOST OUR TURN!
Reservation Pass
16:30 ~ 17:30
Right...
OH!
THAT WAS CLOSE! I ALMOST FORGOT ABOUT OUR RESERVATION!
Phew!
HE'S REALLY DETERMINED...
...TO TURN THINGS AROUND...
OKAY
I CAN'T FAIL WITH THIS!!
Today's main attraction!!
HARUNA, WHAT TIME IS IT?!
UM...
Let me look at my cell...

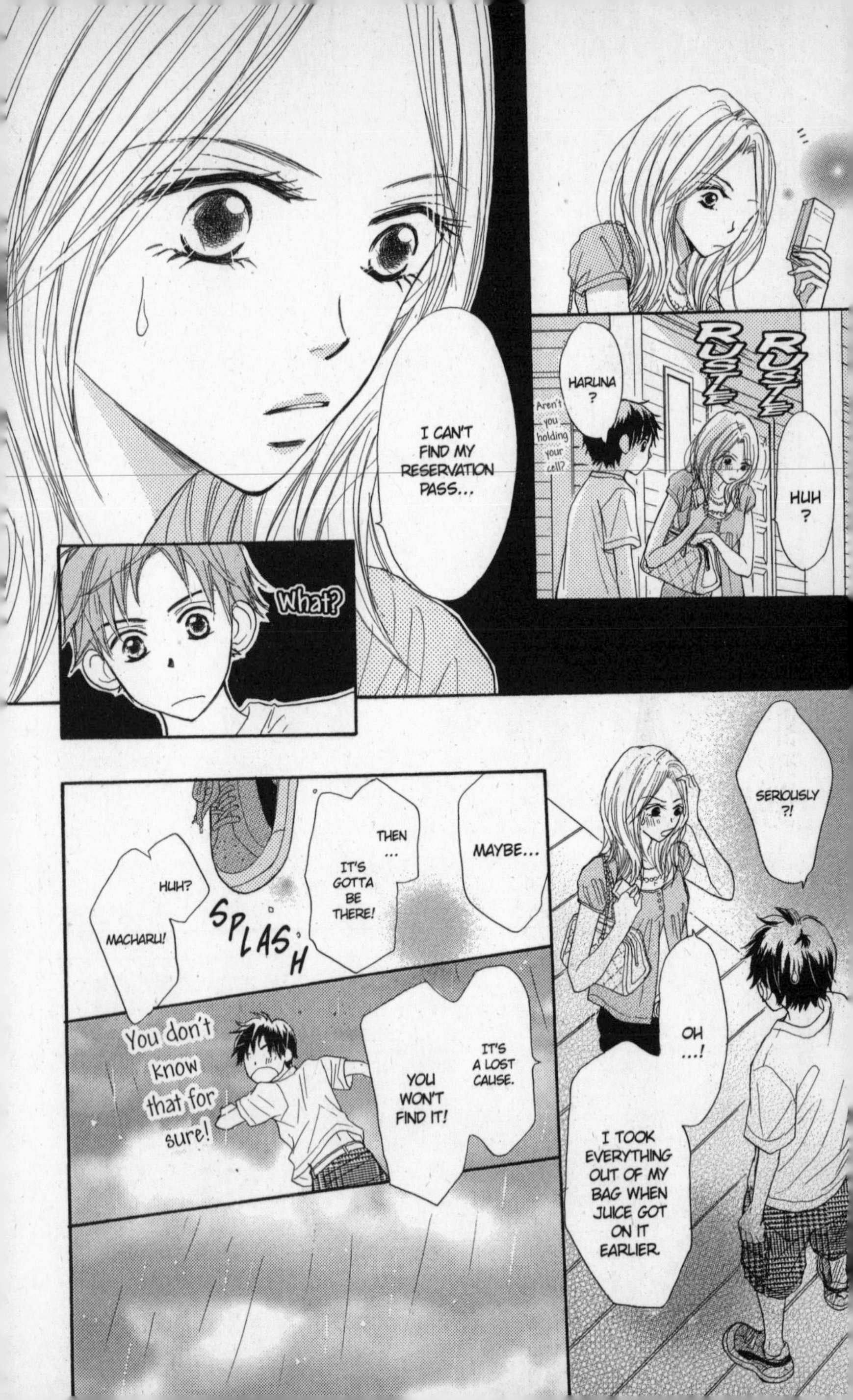
RUSTLE RUSTLE
HUH ?
HARUNA ?
Aren't you holding your cell?
I CAN'T FIND MY RESERVATION PASS...
What?
SERIOUSLY ?!
OH ...!
I TOOK EVERYTHING OUT OF MY BAG WHEN JUICE GOT ON IT EARLIER.
MAYBE...
THEN ... IT'S GOTTA BE THERE!
SPLASH
HUH?
MACHARU!
IT'S A LOST CAUSE.
YOU WON'T FIND IT!
You don't know that for sure!

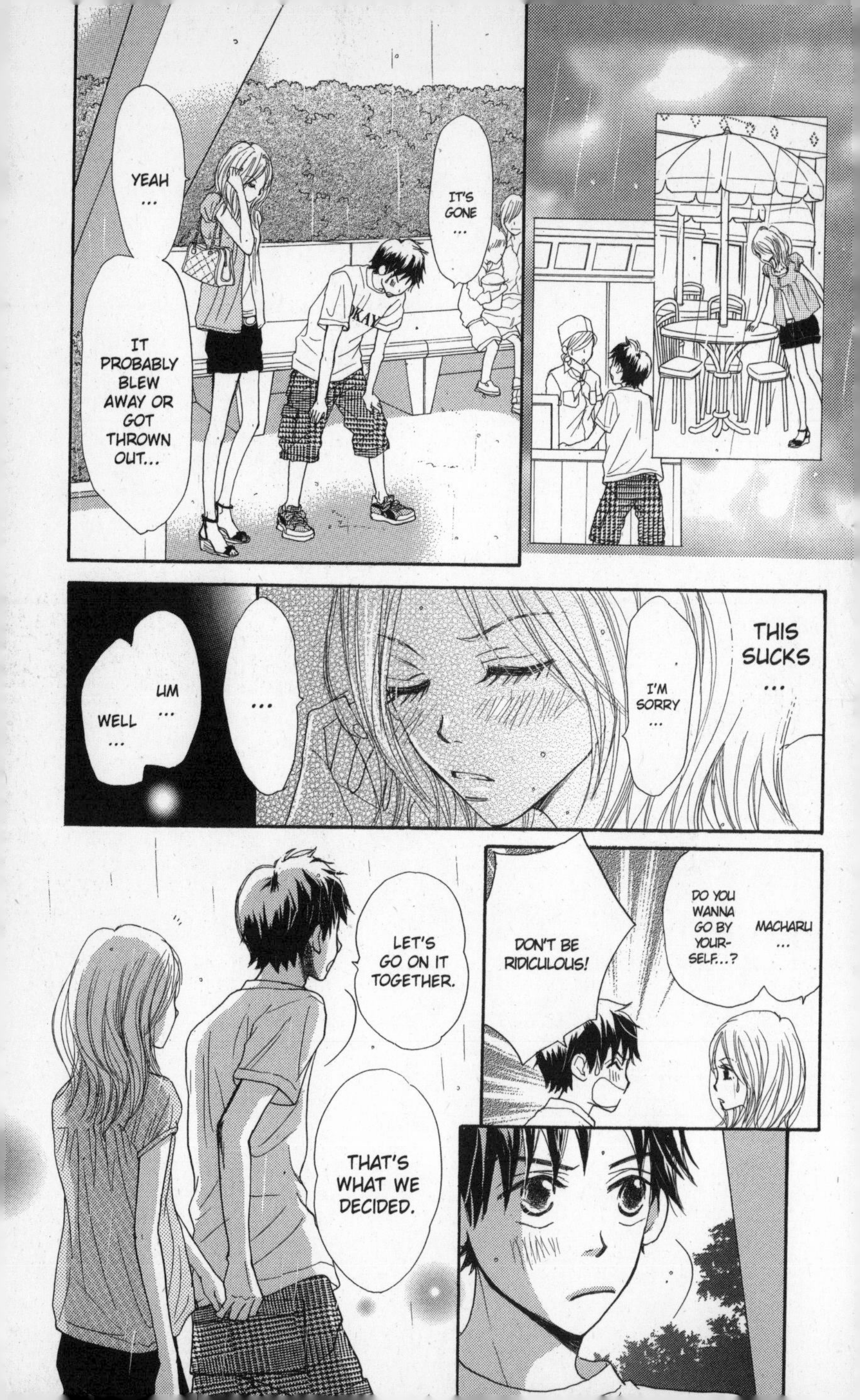
IT'S GONE ...
YEAH ...
IT PROBABLY BLEW AWAY OR GOT THROWN OUT...
THIS SUCKS ...
I'M SORRY ...
...
UM ...
WELL ...
MACHARU ...
DO YOU WANNA GO BY YOUR-SELF...?
DON'T BE RIDICULOUS!
LET'S GO ON IT TOGETHER.
THAT'S WHAT WE DECIDED.

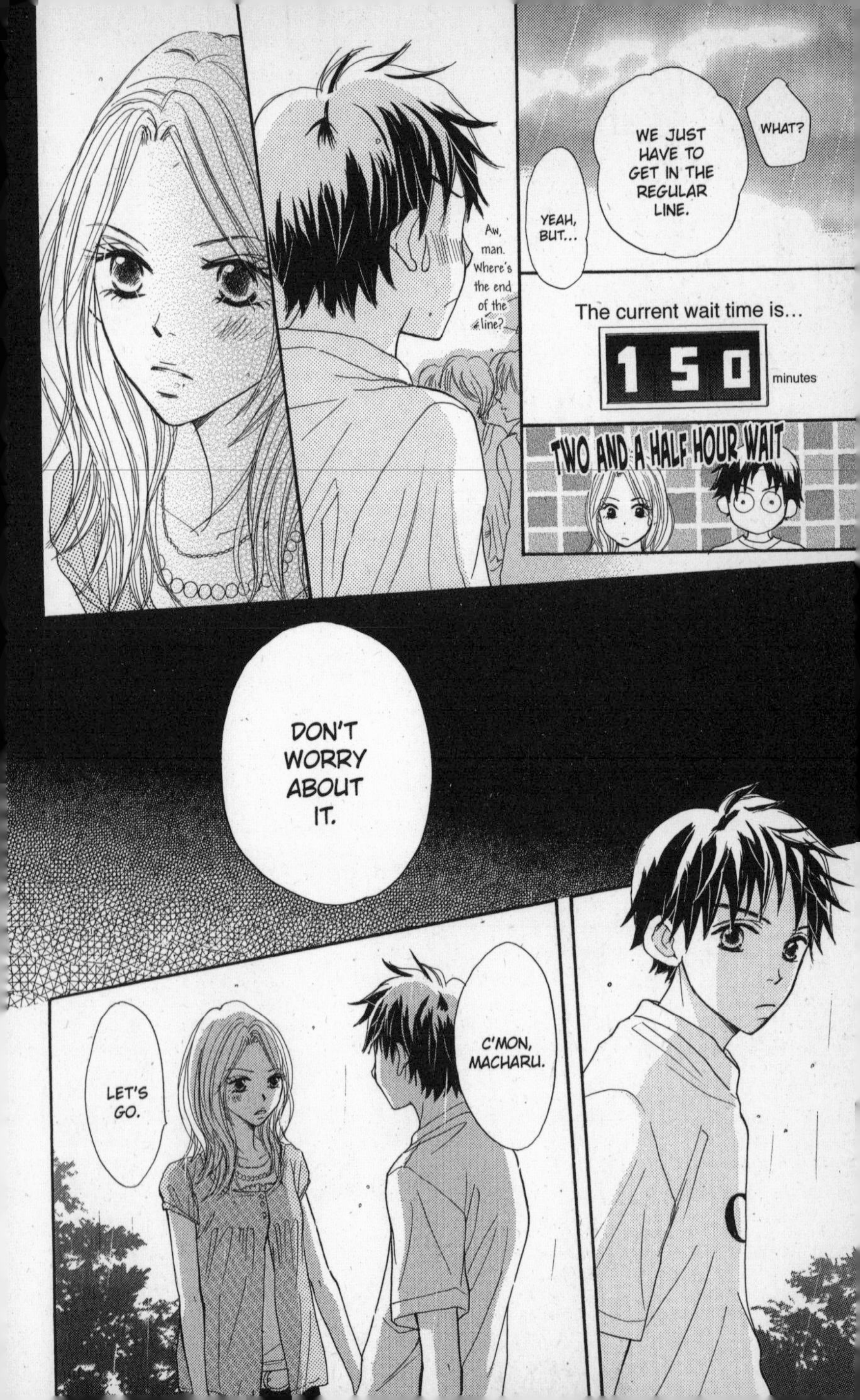
WHAT?
WE JUST HAVE TO GET IN THE REGULAR LINE.
YEAH, BUT...
The current wait time is...
150 minutes
TWO AND A HALF HOUR WAIT
Aw, man. Where's the end of the line?
DON'T WORRY ABOUT IT.
C'MON, MACHARU.
LET'S GO.

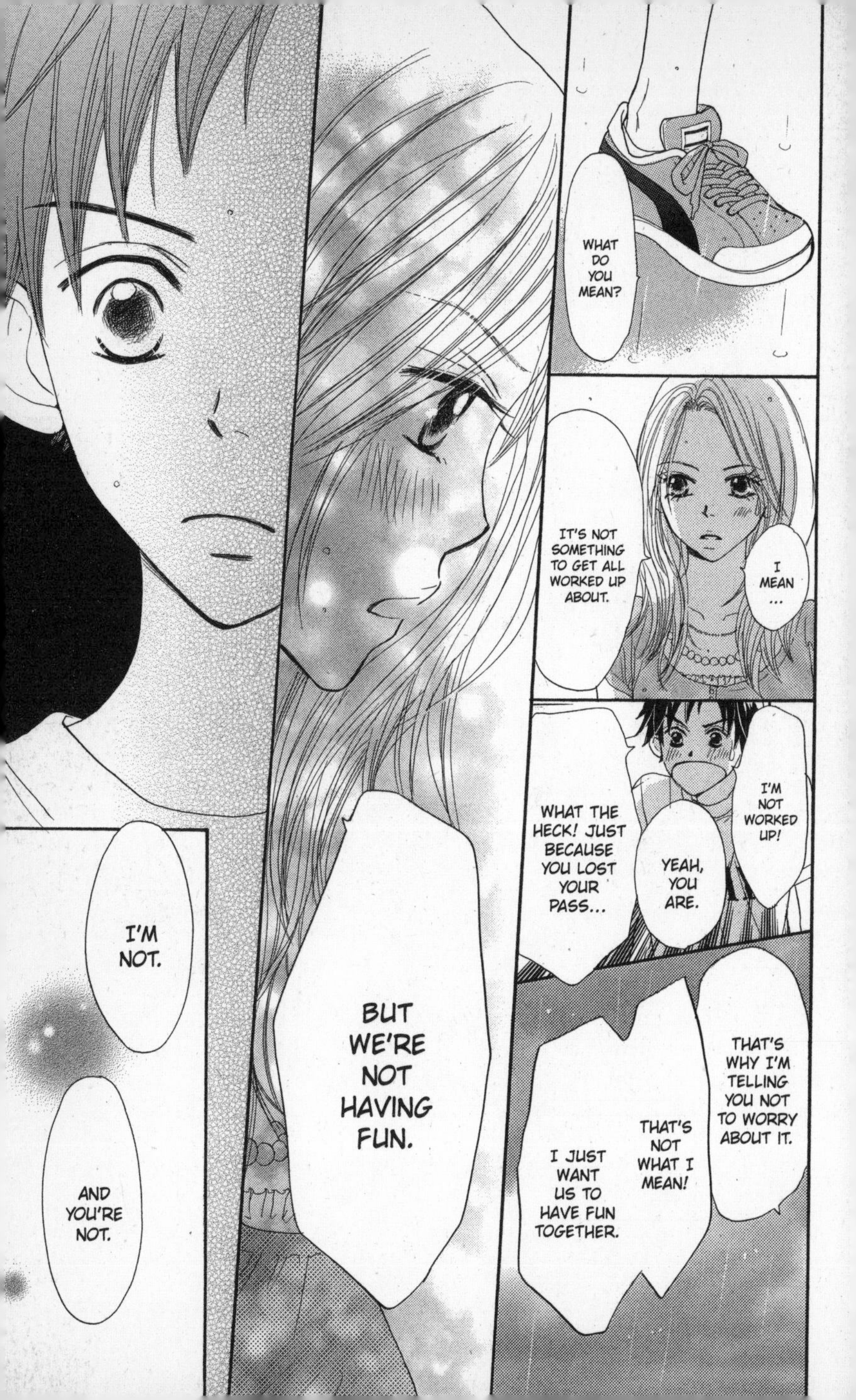
WHAT DO YOU MEAN?
I MEAN...
IT'S NOT SOMETHING TO GET ALL WORKED UP ABOUT.
I'M NOT WORKED UP!
YEAH, YOU ARE.
WHAT THE HECK! JUST BECAUSE YOU LOST YOUR PASS...
THAT'S WHY I'M TELLING YOU NOT TO WORRY ABOUT IT.
THAT'S NOT WHAT I MEAN!
I JUST WANT US TO HAVE FUN TOGETHER.
BUT WE'RE NOT HAVING FUN.
I'M NOT.
AND YOU'RE NOT.

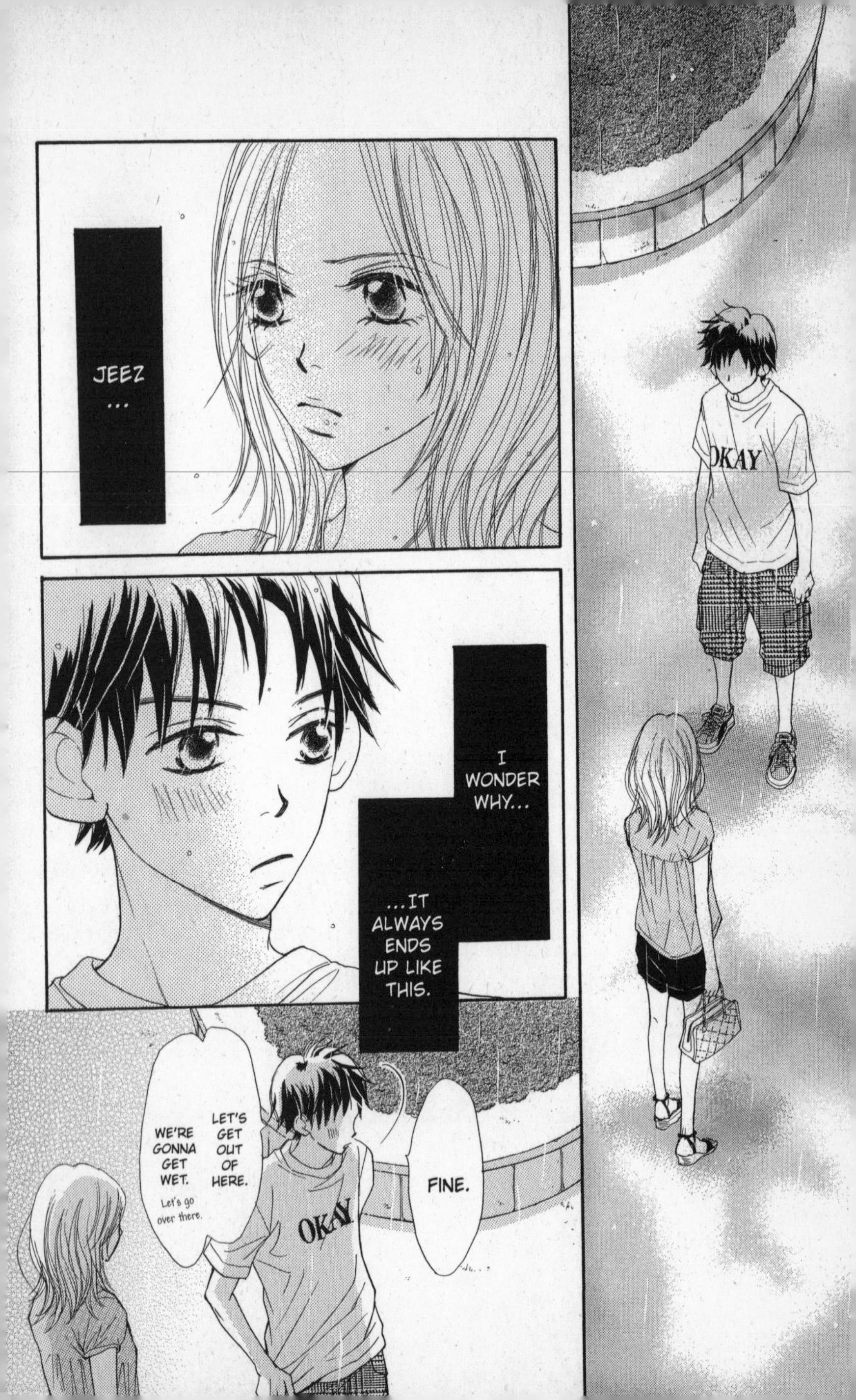
OKAY
JEEZ...
I WONDER WHY...
...IT ALWAYS ENDS UP LIKE THIS.
FINE.
LET'S GET OUT OF HERE.
WE'RE GONNA GET WET.
Let's go over there.
OKAY

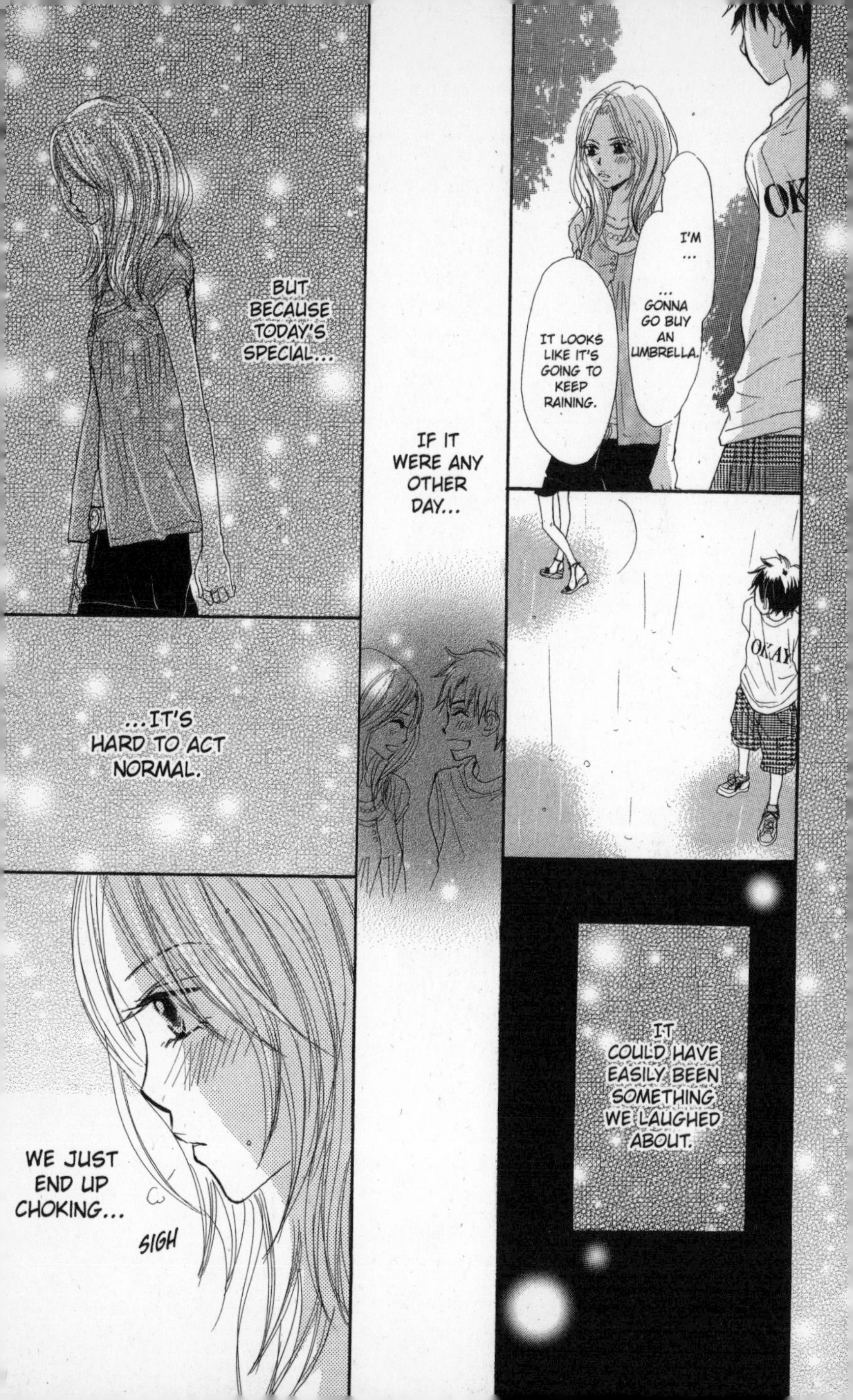
I'M ...
... GONNA GO BUY AN UMBRELLA.
IT LOOKS LIKE IT'S GOING TO KEEP RAINING.
IF IT WERE ANY OTHER DAY...
IT COULD HAVE EASILY BEEN SOMETHING WE LAUGHED ABOUT.
BUT BECAUSE TODAY'S SPECIAL...
...IT'S HARD TO ACT NORMAL.
WE JUST END UP CHOKING...
SIGH

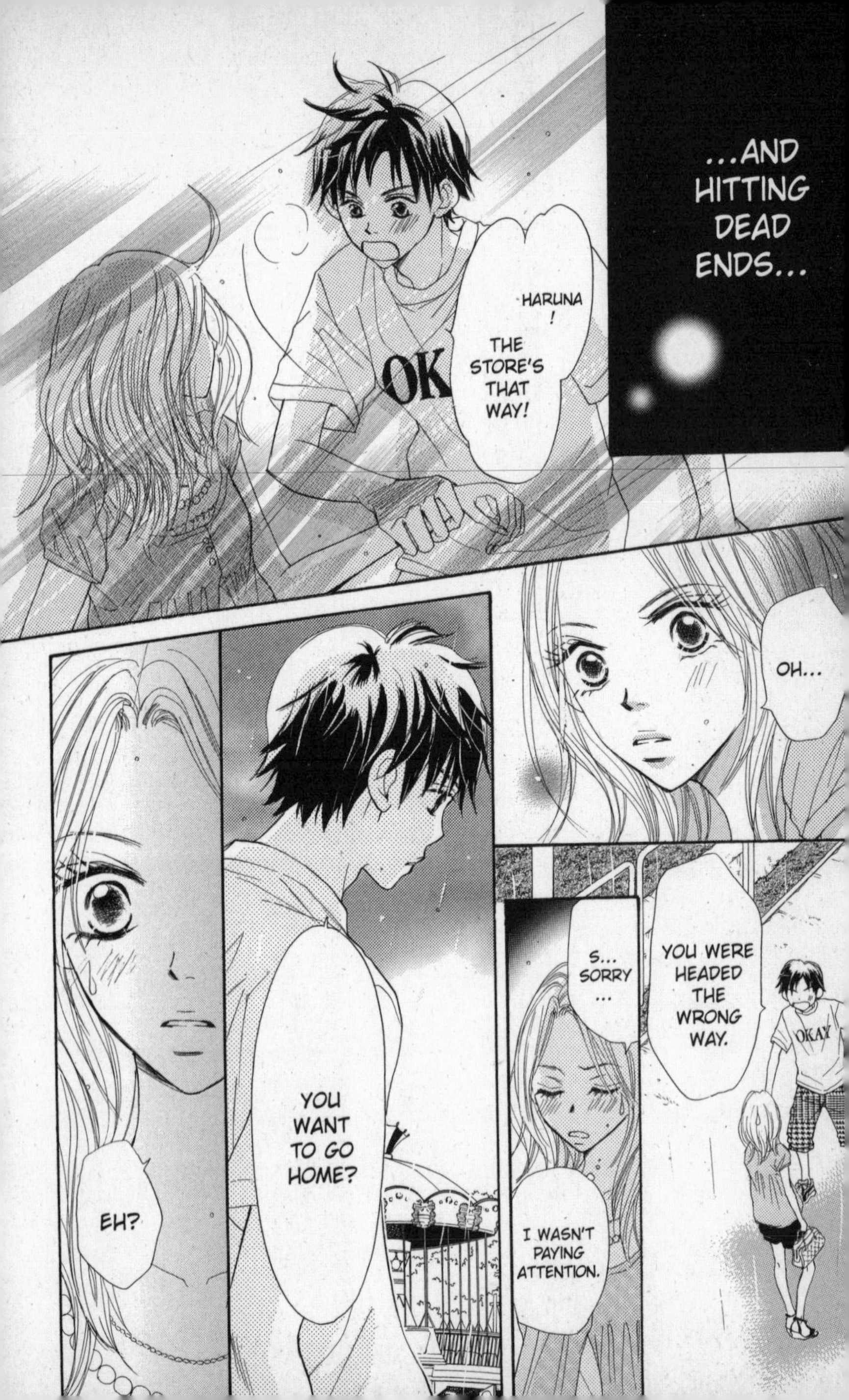

...AND HITTING DEAD ENDS...
OK
HARUNA!
THE STORE'S THAT WAY!
OH...
YOU WERE HEADED THE WRONG WAY.
OKAY
S... SORRY...
I WASN'T PAYING ATTENTION.
YOU WANT TO GO HOME?
EH?

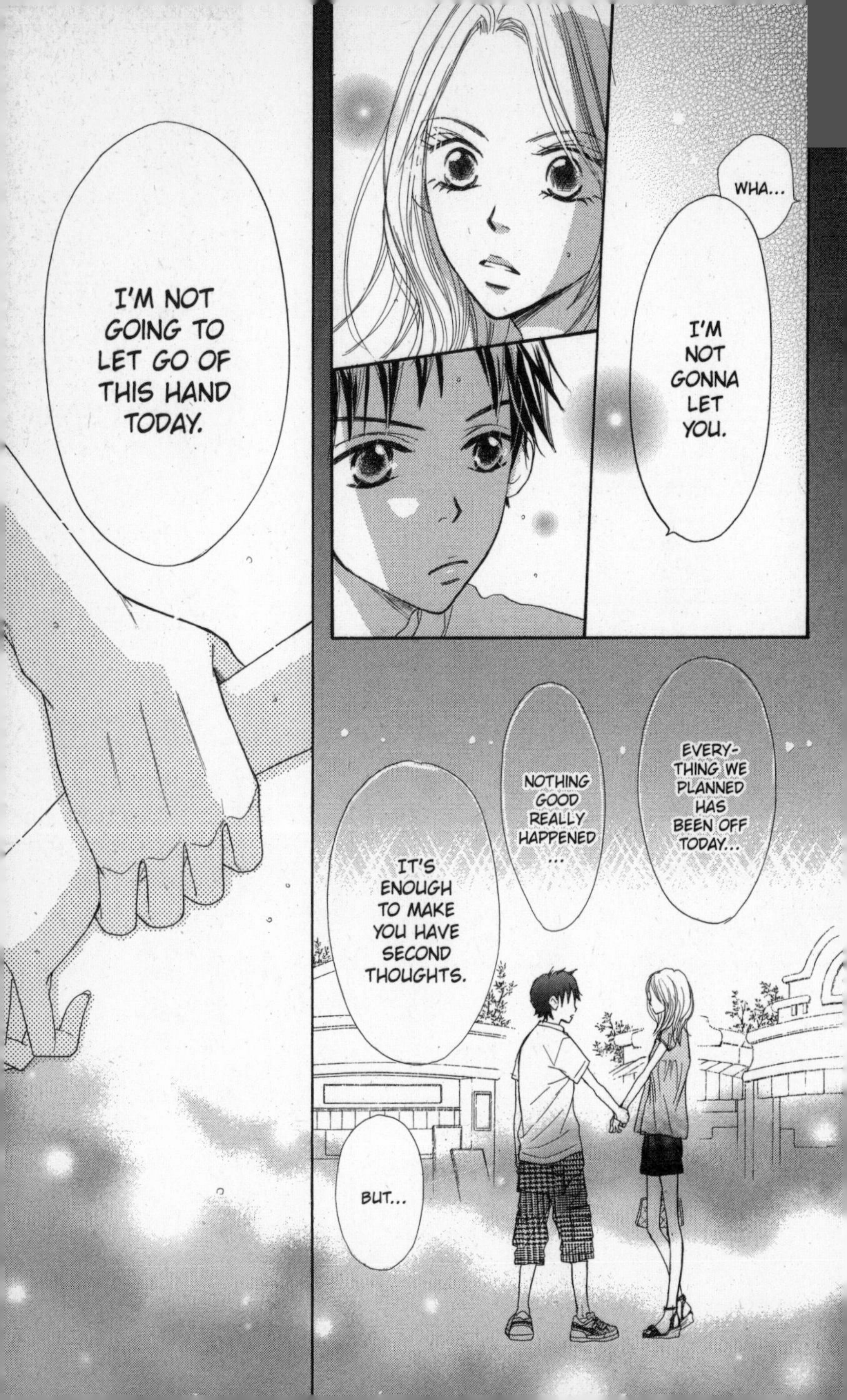
WHA...
I'M NOT GONNA LET YOU.
EVERY-THING WE PLANNED HAS BEEN OFF TODAY...
NOTHING GOOD REALLY HAPPENED...
IT'S ENOUGH TO MAKE YOU HAVE SECOND THOUGHTS.
BUT...
I'M NOT GOING TO LET GO OF THIS HAND TODAY.

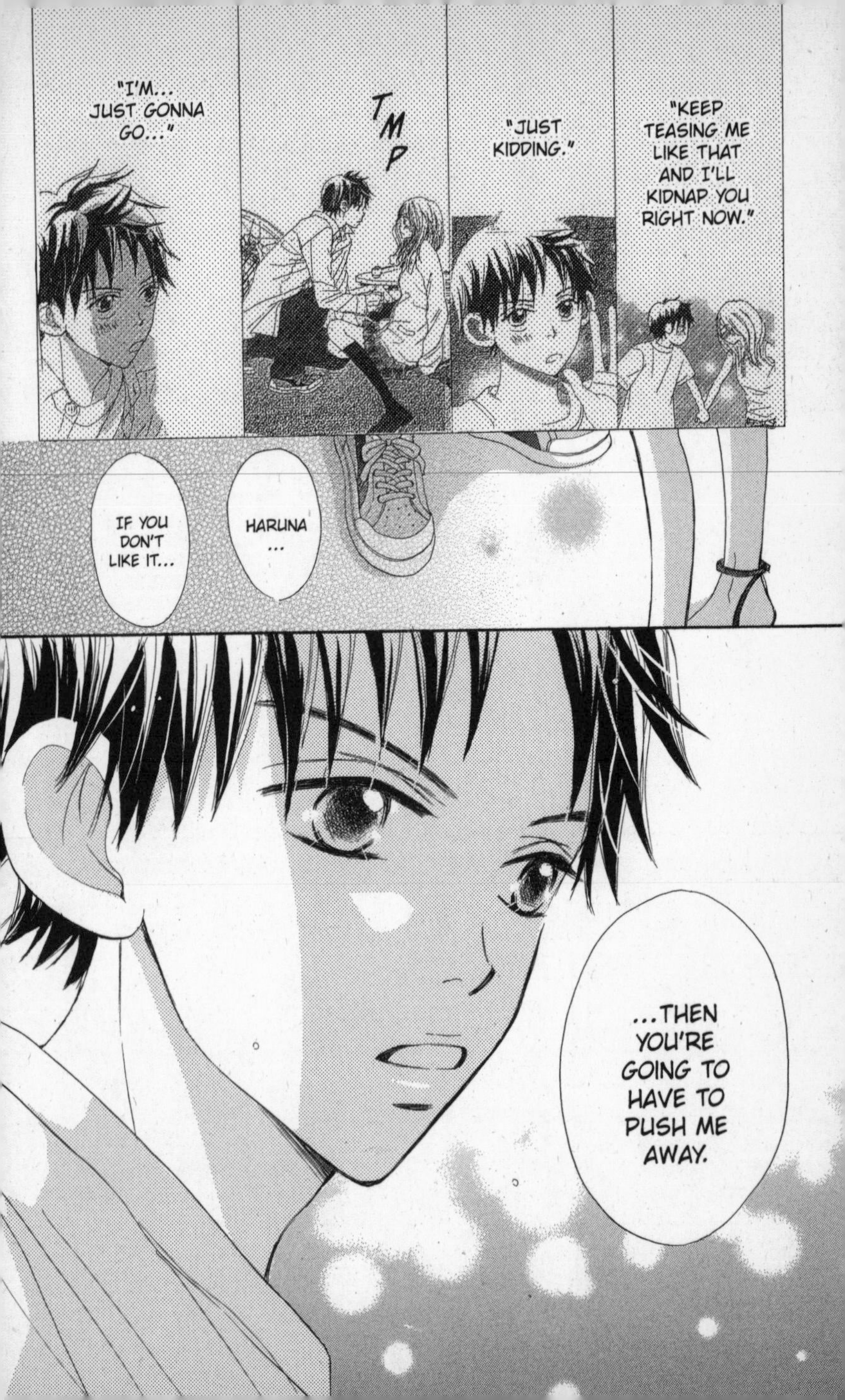
"KEEP TEASING ME LIKE THAT AND I'LL KIDNAP YOU RIGHT NOW."
"JUST KIDDING."
TMP
"I'M... JUST GONNA GO..."
HARUNA ...
IF YOU DON'T LIKE IT...
...THEN YOU'RE GOING TO HAVE TO PUSH ME AWAY.

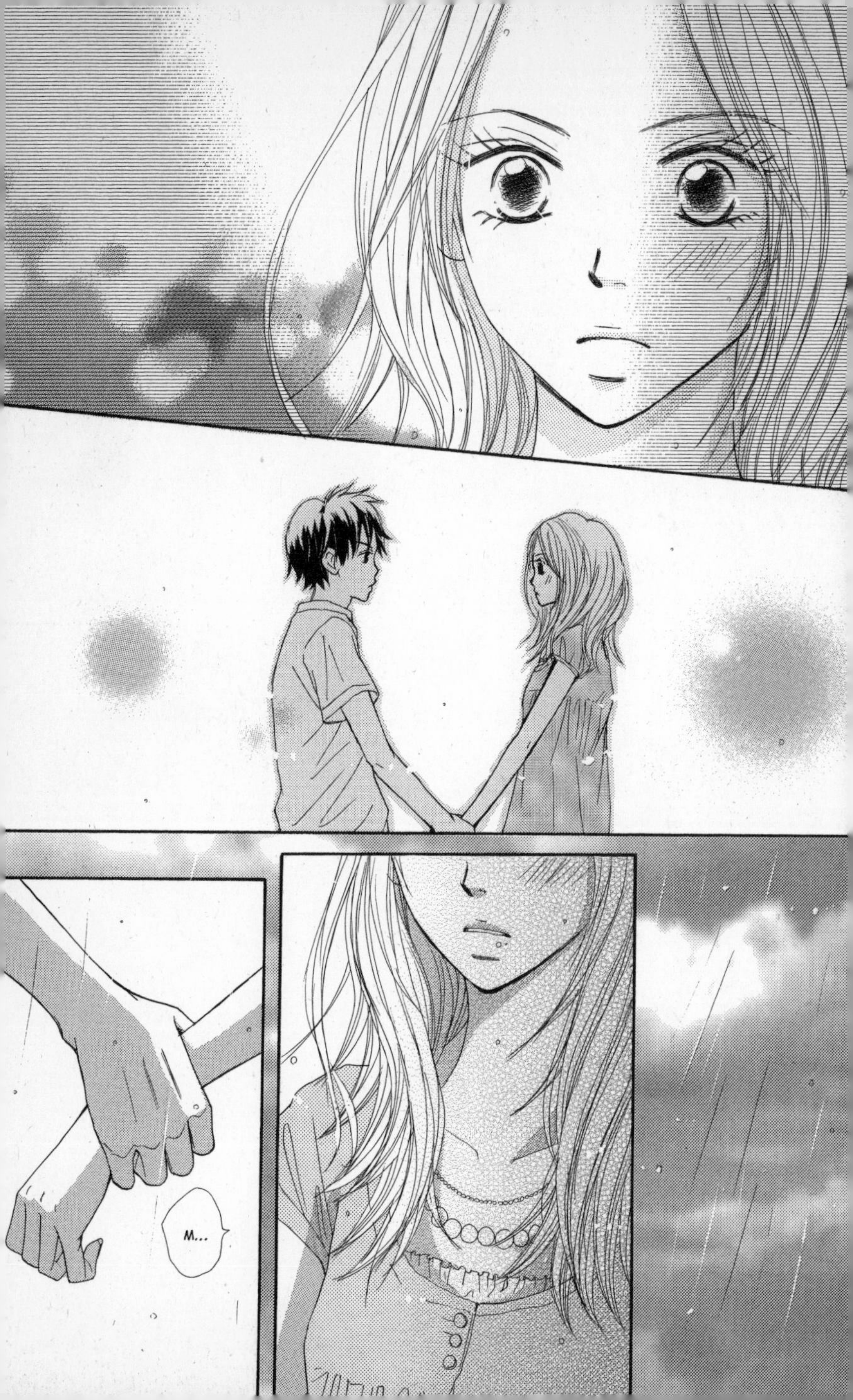
M...

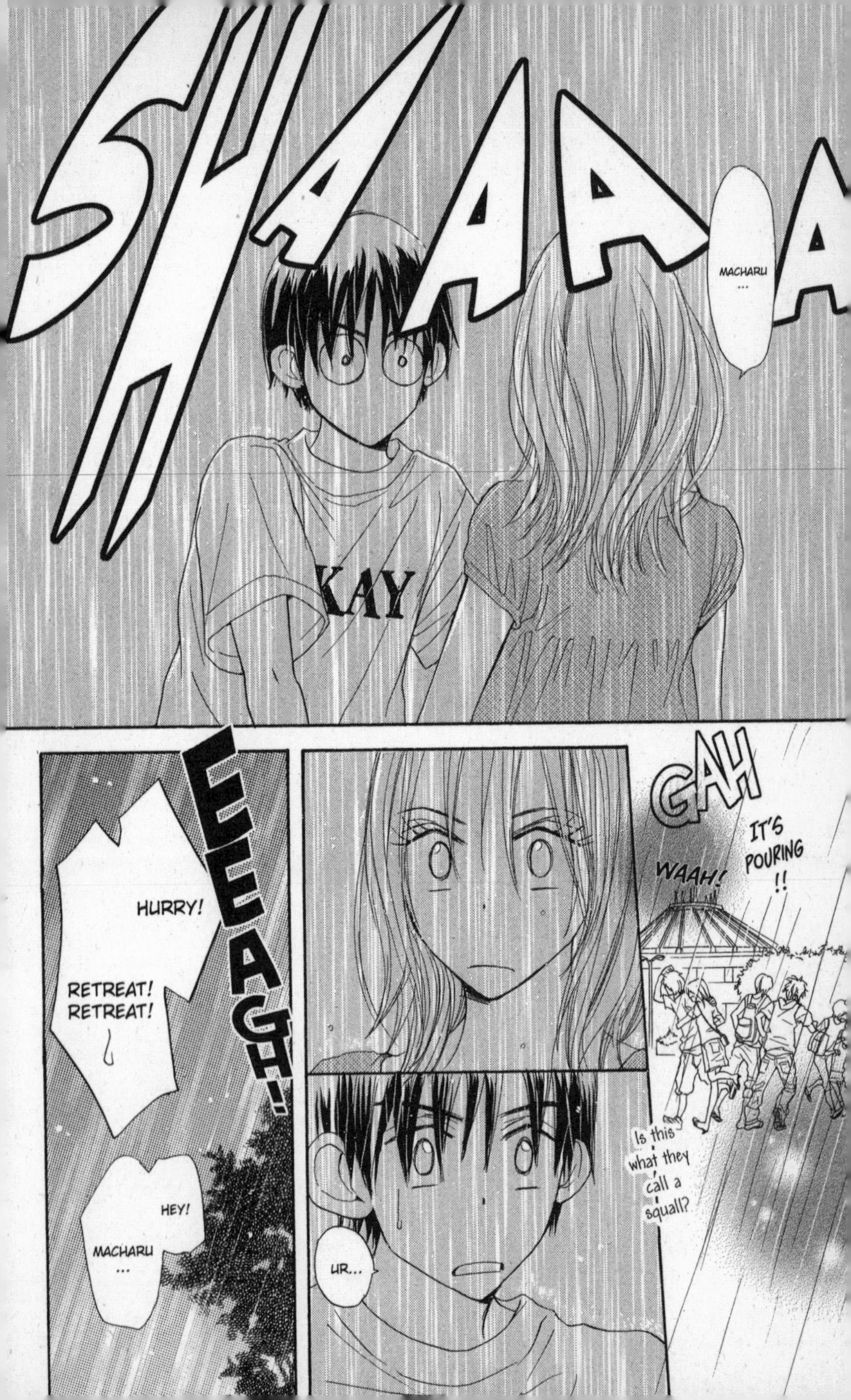
SHAAAAA
MACHARU ...
GAH
IT'S POURING !!
WAAH!
Is this what they call a squall?
EEEAAGH!
HURRY!
RETREAT! RETREAT!
HEY!
MACHARU ...
UR...

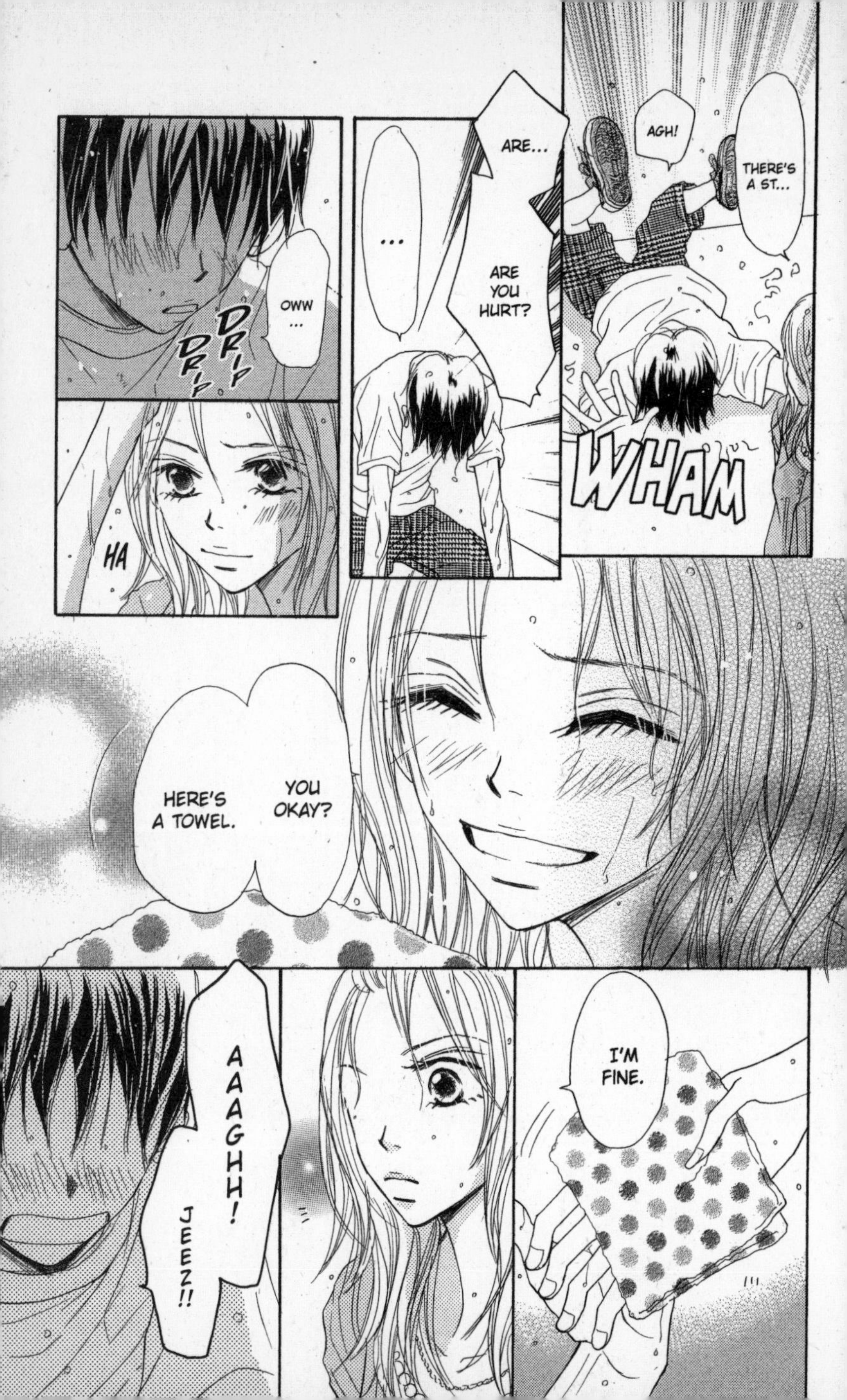
THERE'S A ST...
AGH!
WHAM
ARE...
ARE YOU HURT?
...
OWW ...
DRIP DRIP
HA
YOU OKAY?
HERE'S A TOWEL.
I'M FINE.
AAAAGHH!
JEEZ!!

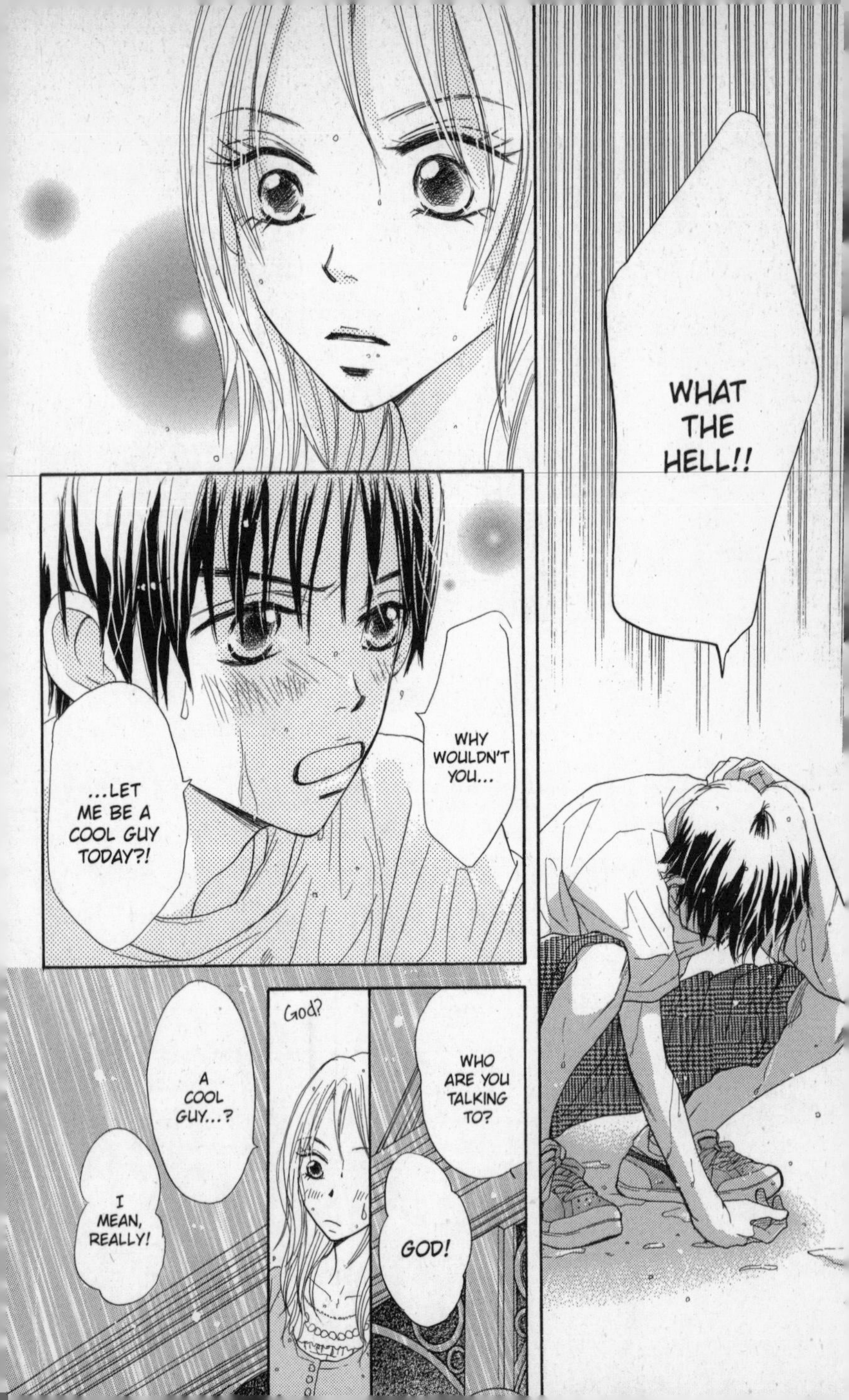
WHAT THE HELL!!
WHY WOULDN'T YOU...
...LET ME BE A COOL GUY TODAY?!
WHO ARE YOU TALKING TO?
GOD!
God?
A COOL GUY...?
I MEAN, REALLY!

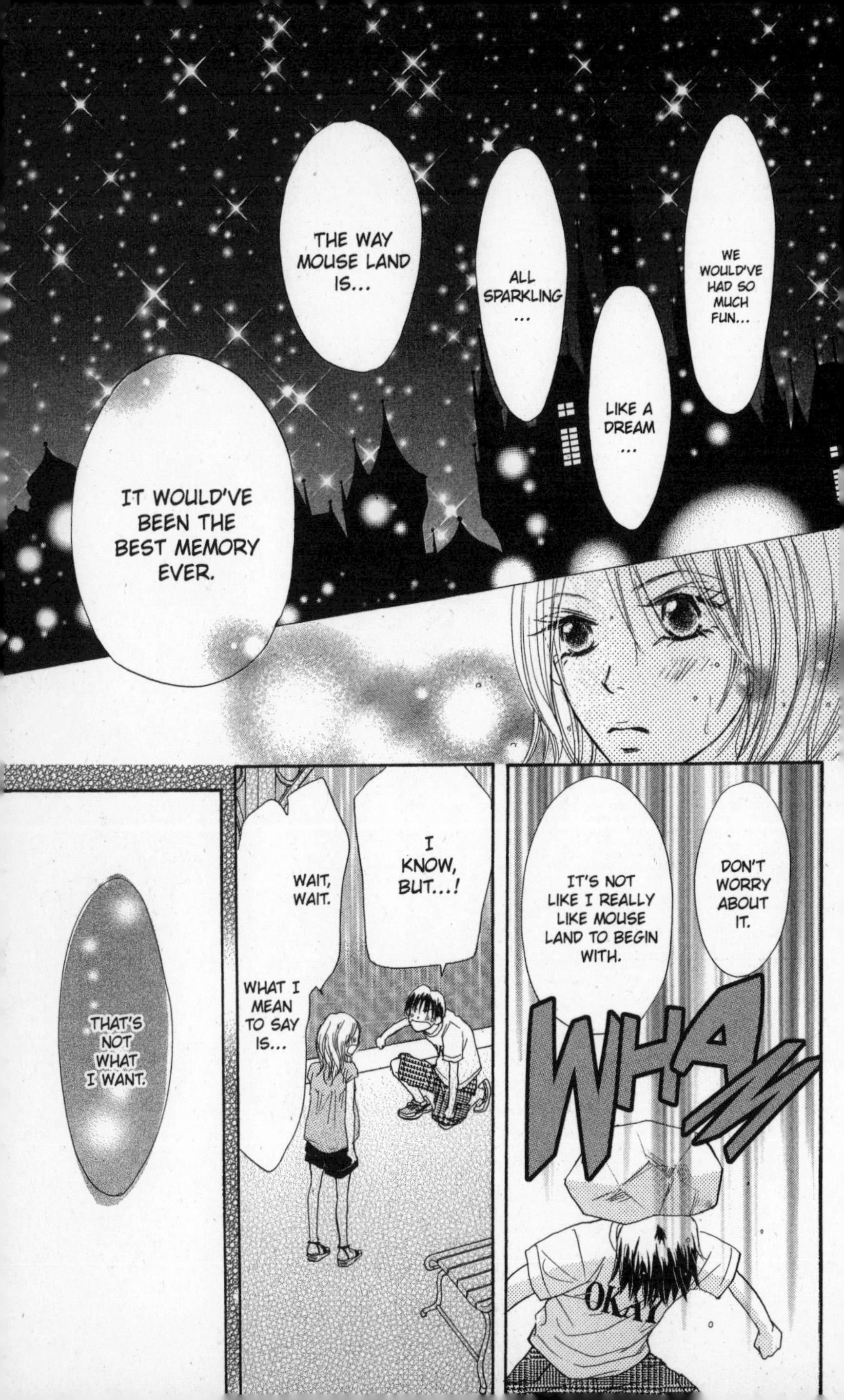
WE WOULD'VE HAD SO MUCH FUN...
LIKE A DREAM...
ALL SPARKLING...
THE WAY MOUSE LAND IS...
IT WOULD'VE BEEN THE BEST MEMORY EVER.
DON'T WORRY ABOUT IT.
IT'S NOT LIKE I REALLY LIKE MOUSE LAND TO BEGIN WITH.
WHAM
OKAY
I KNOW, BUT...!
WAIT, WAIT.
WHAT I MEAN TO SAY IS...
THAT'S NOT WHAT I WANT.

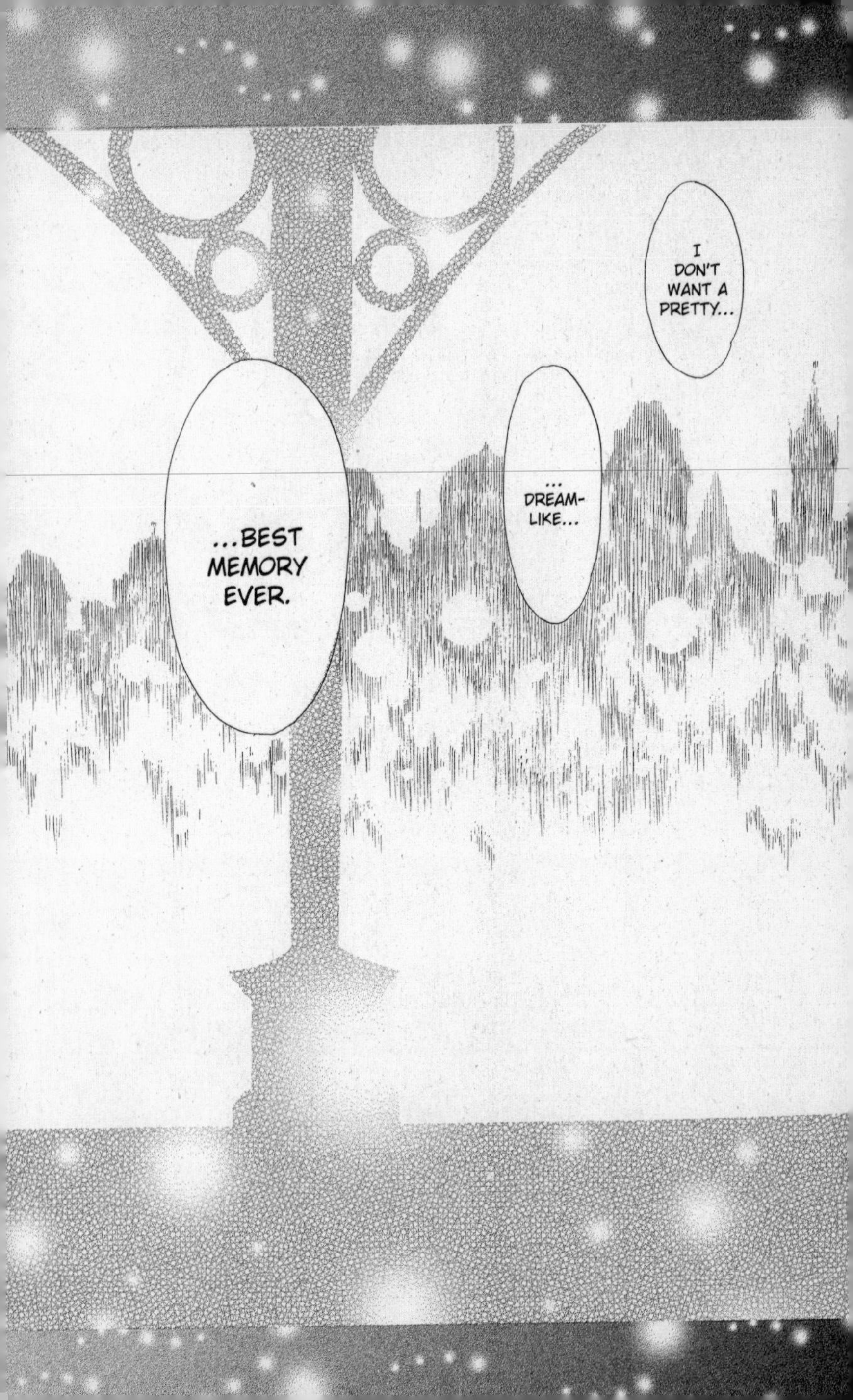
I DON'T WANT A PRETTY...
...DREAM-LIKE...
...BEST MEMORY EVER.

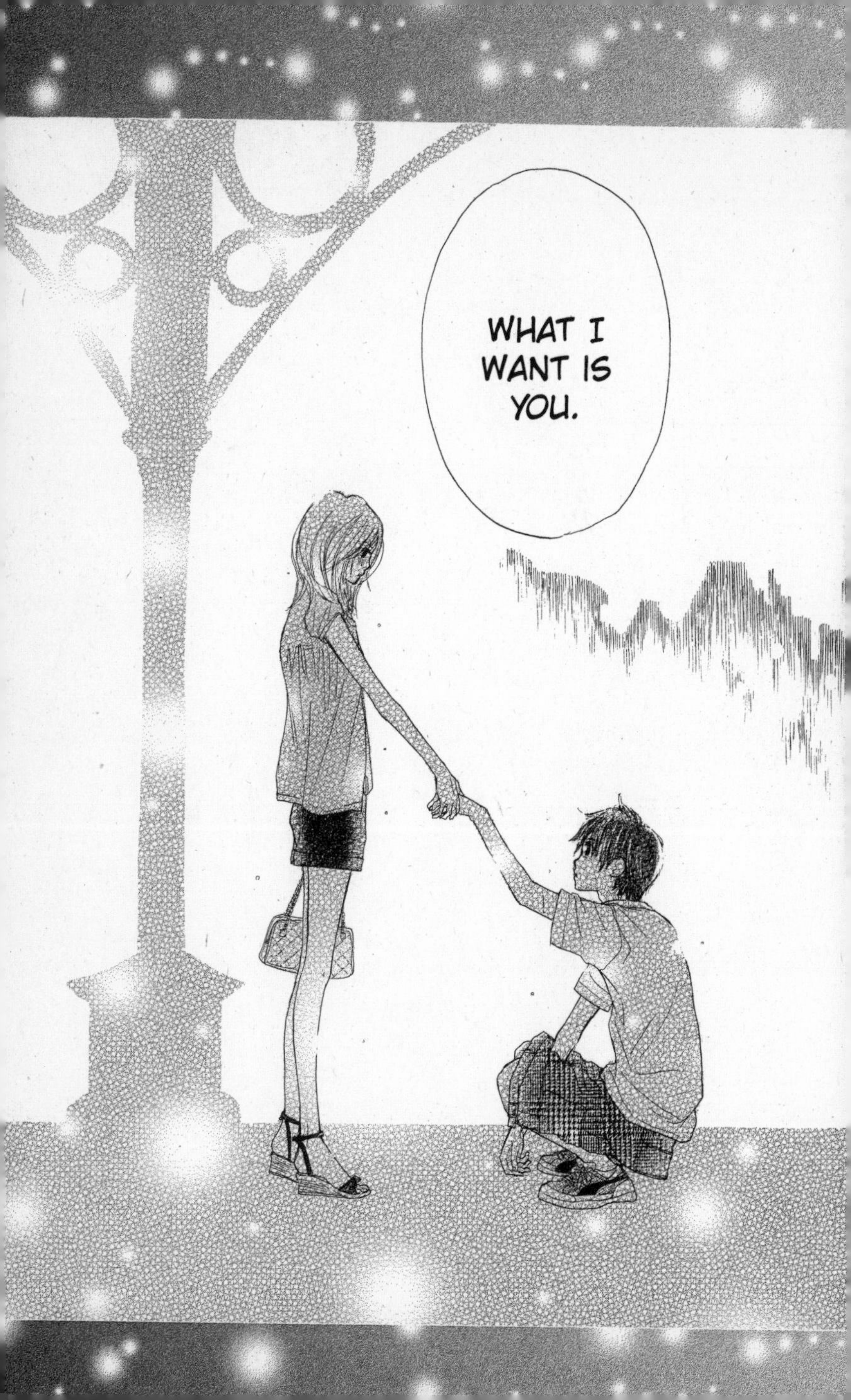
WHAT I WANT IS YOU.

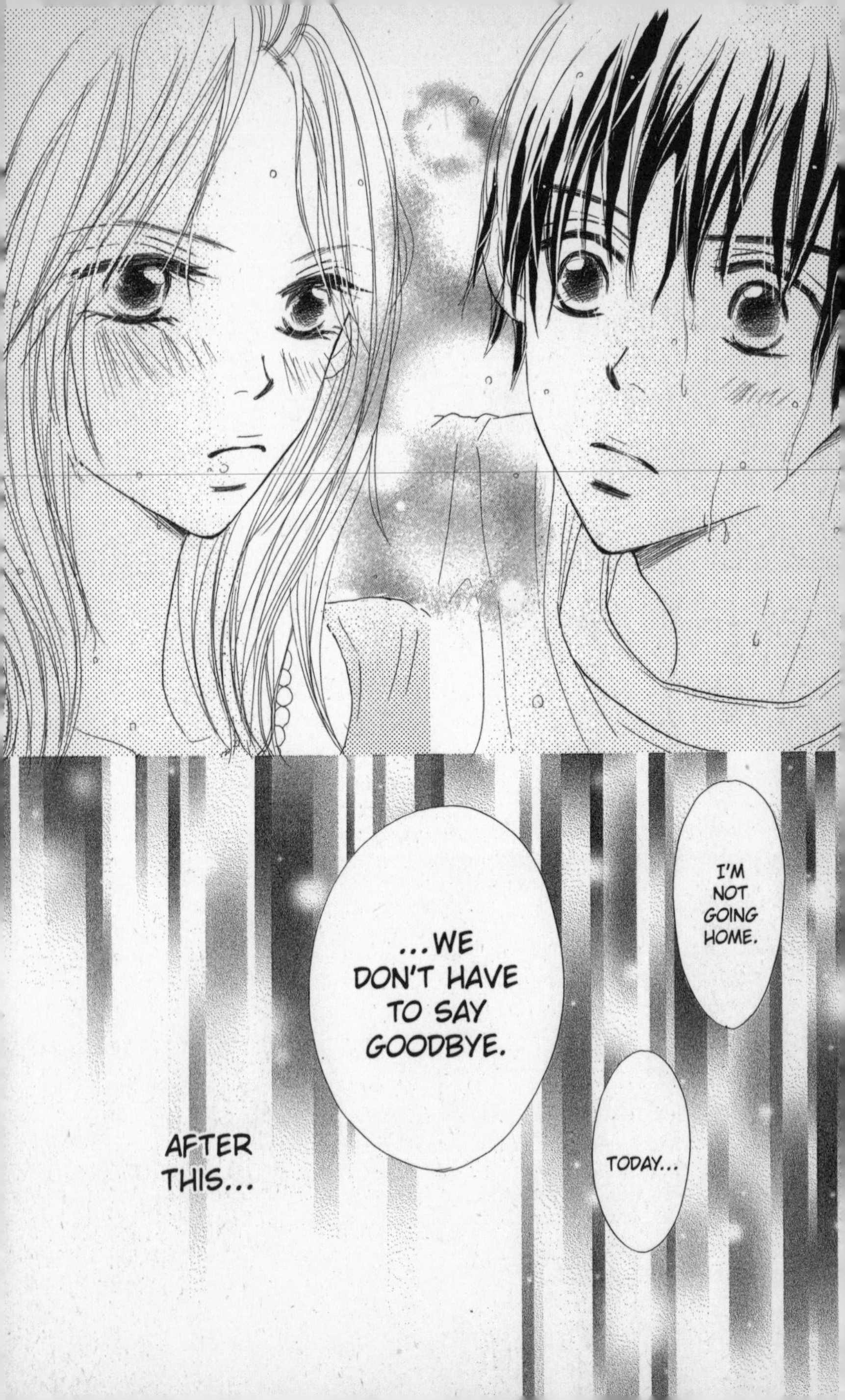
I'M NOT GOING HOME.
TODAY...
...WE DON'T HAVE TO SAY GOODBYE.
AFTER THIS...

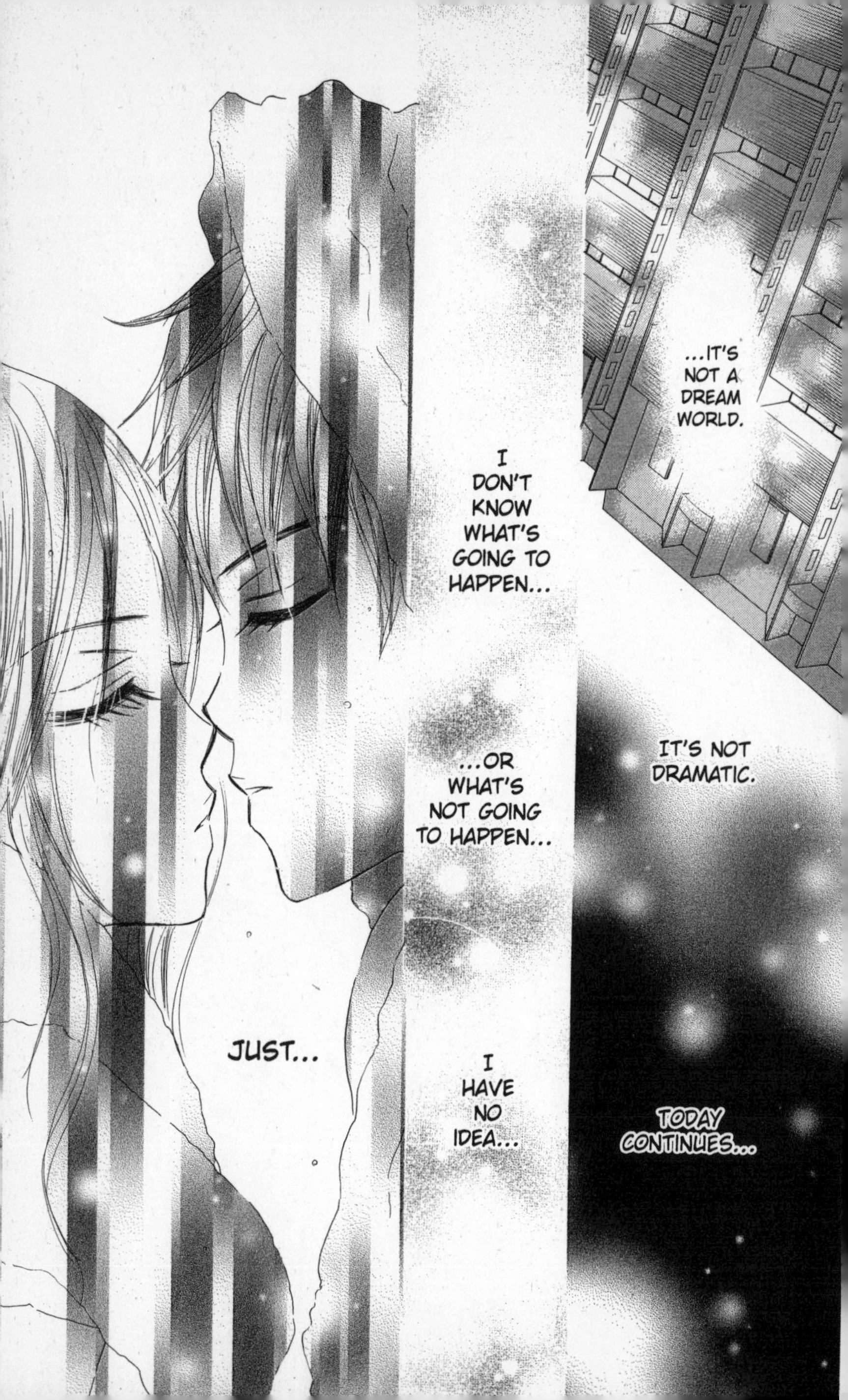
...IT'S NOT A DREAM WORLD.
IT'S NOT DRAMATIC.
TODAY CONTINUES...
I DON'T KNOW WHAT'S GOING TO HAPPEN...
...OR WHAT'S NOT GOING TO HAPPEN...
I HAVE NO IDEA...
JUST...

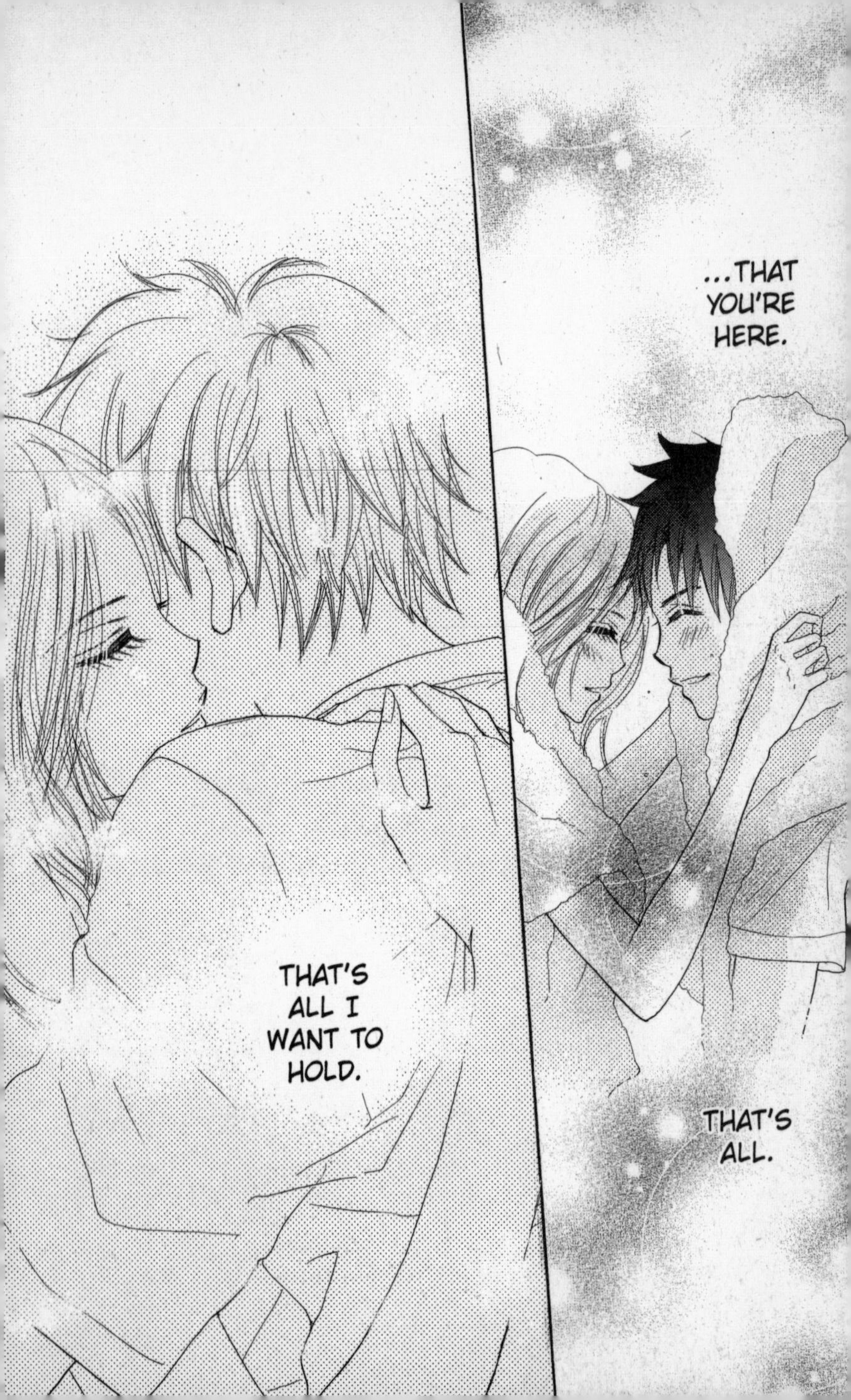
...THAT YOU'RE HERE.
THAT'S ALL.
THAT'S ALL I WANT TO HOLD.

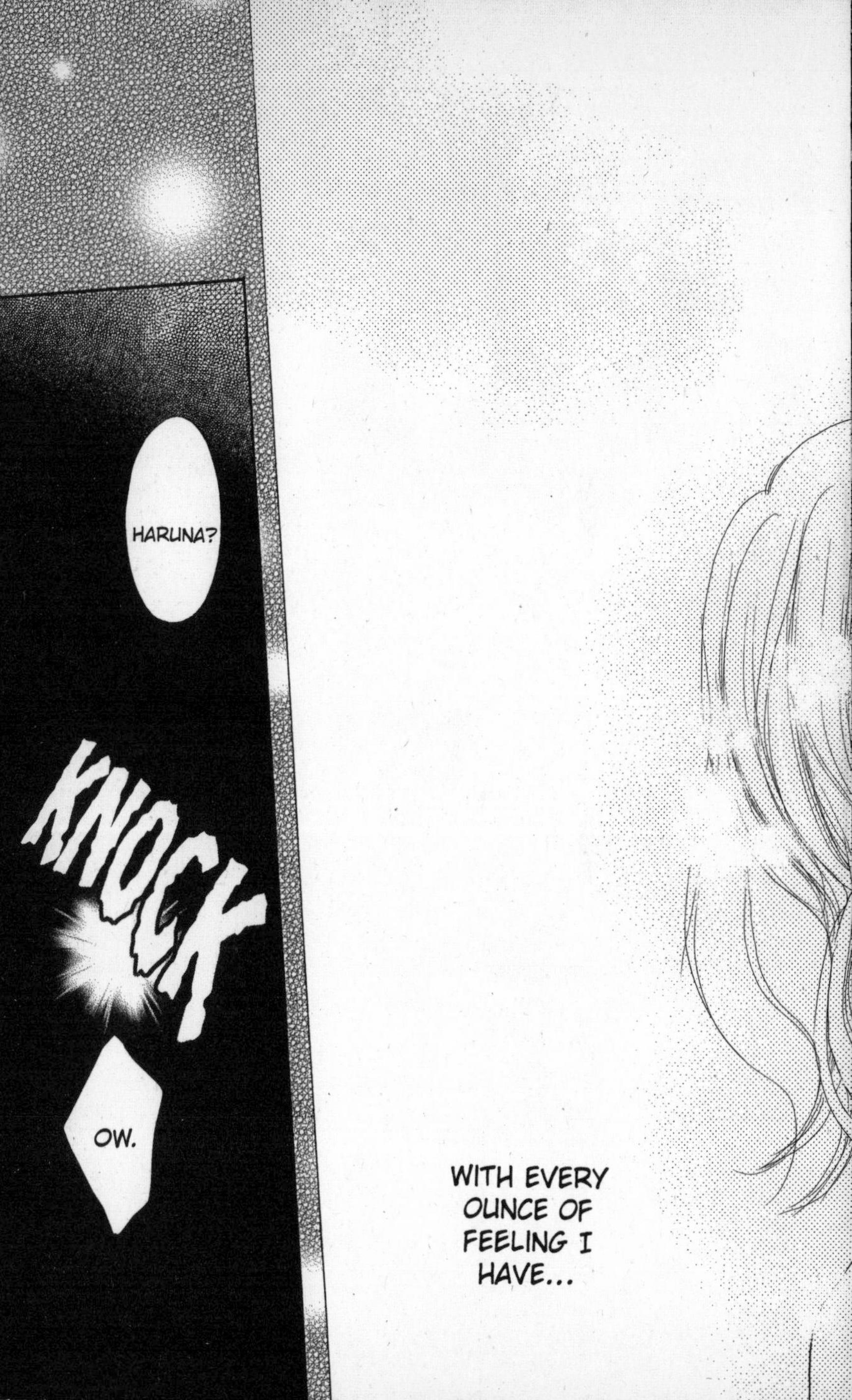
WITH EVERY OUNCE OF FEELING I HAVE...
HARUNA?
KNOCK
OW.

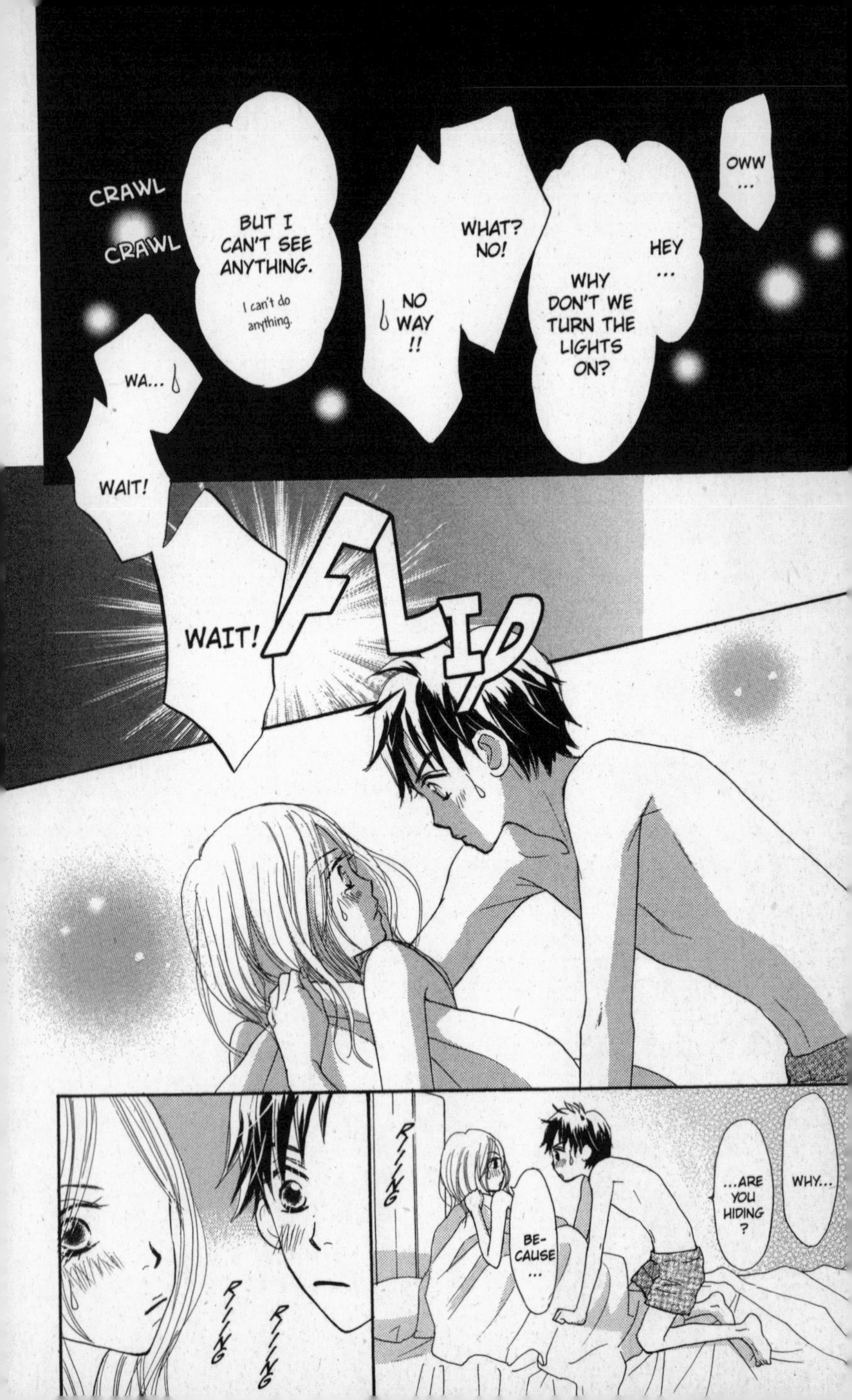
OWW...
HEY...
WHY DON'T WE TURN THE LIGHTS ON?
WHAT? NO!
NO WAY !!
BUT I CAN'T SEE ANYTHING.
I can't do anything.
CRAWL
CRAWL
WA...
WAIT!
WAIT!
FLIP
WHY...
...ARE YOU HIDING?
BE-CAUSE...
RIIING
RIIING
RIIING

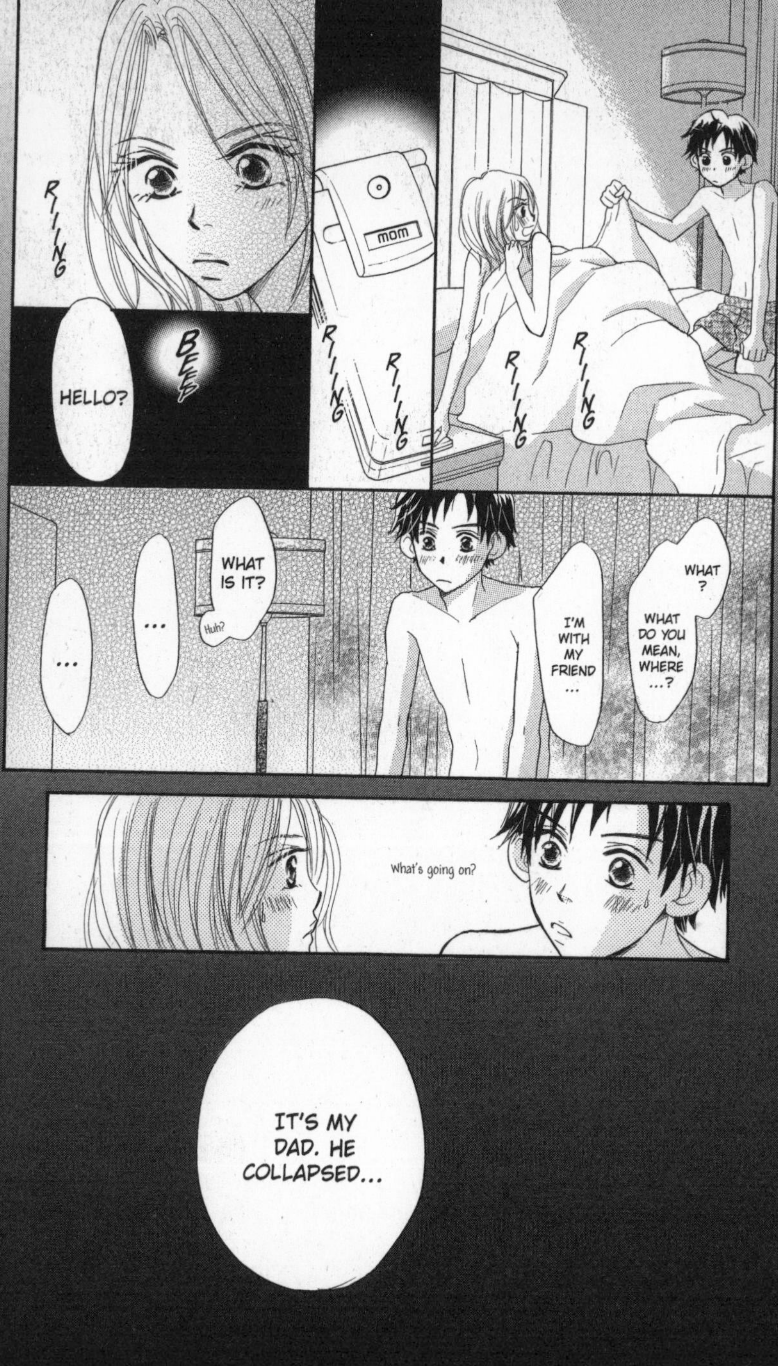
RIIING
RIIING
MOM
RIIING
RIIING
RIIING
BEEP
HELLO?
WHAT?
WHAT DO YOU MEAN, WHERE ...?
I'M WITH MY FRIEND ...
WHAT IS IT?
Huh?
...
...
What's going on?
IT'S MY DAD. HE COLLAPSED...

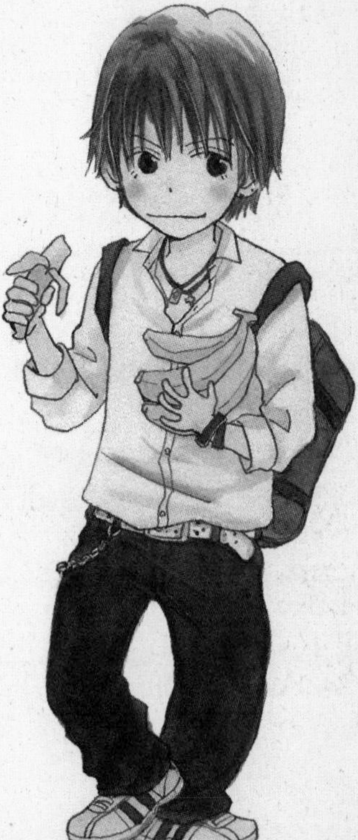
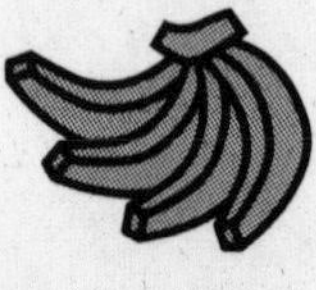

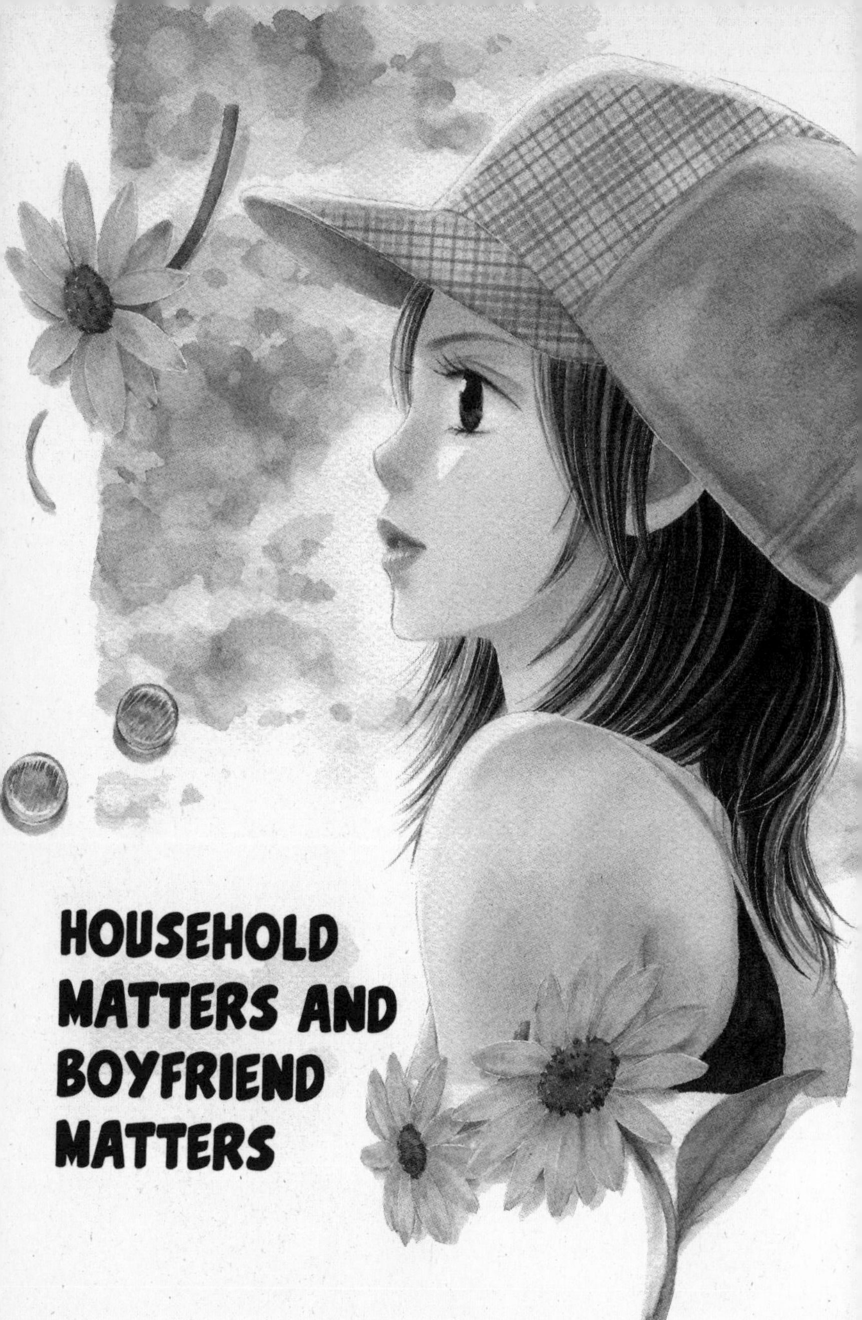

HOUSEHOLD MATTERS AND BOYFRIEND MATTERS

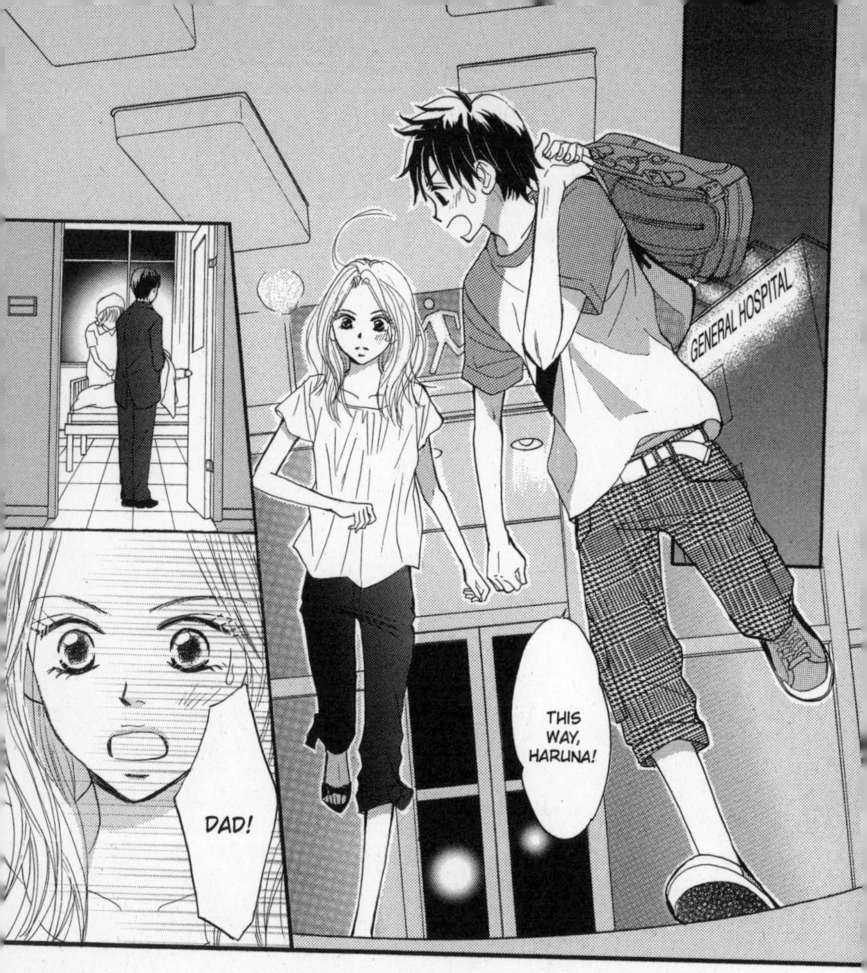
GENERAL HOSPITAL
THIS WAY, HARUNA!
DAD!

Monkey High!

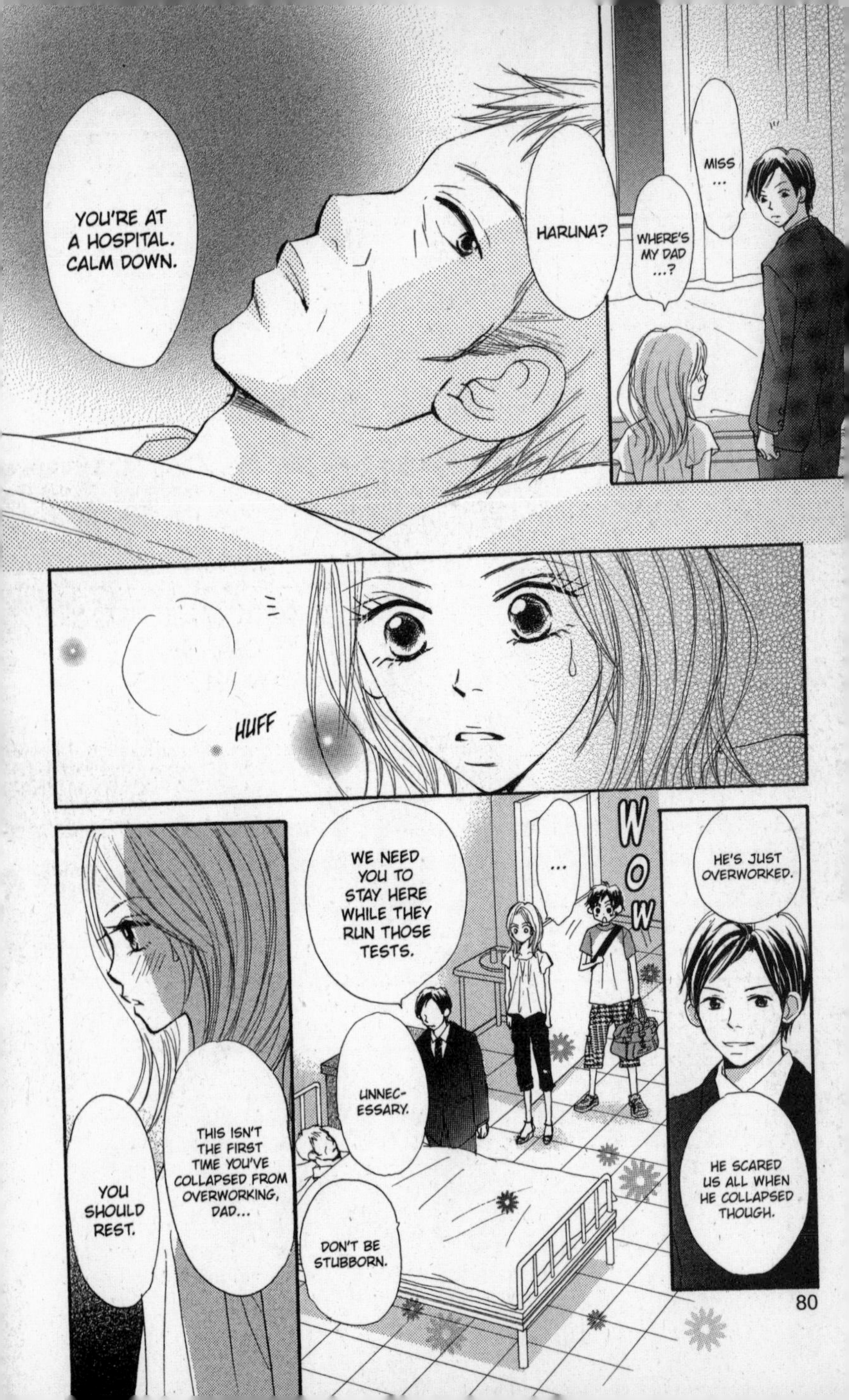
MISS ...
WHERE'S MY DAD ...?
HARUNA?
YOU'RE AT A HOSPITAL. CALM DOWN.
HUFF
HE'S JUST OVERWORKED.
HE SCARED US ALL WHEN HE COLLAPSED THOUGH.
WOW
...
WE NEED YOU TO STAY HERE WHILE THEY RUN THOSE TESTS.
UNNEC-ESSARY.
DON'T BE STUBBORN.
THIS ISN'T THE FIRST TIME YOU'VE COLLAPSED FROM OVERWORKING, DAD...
YOU SHOULD REST.

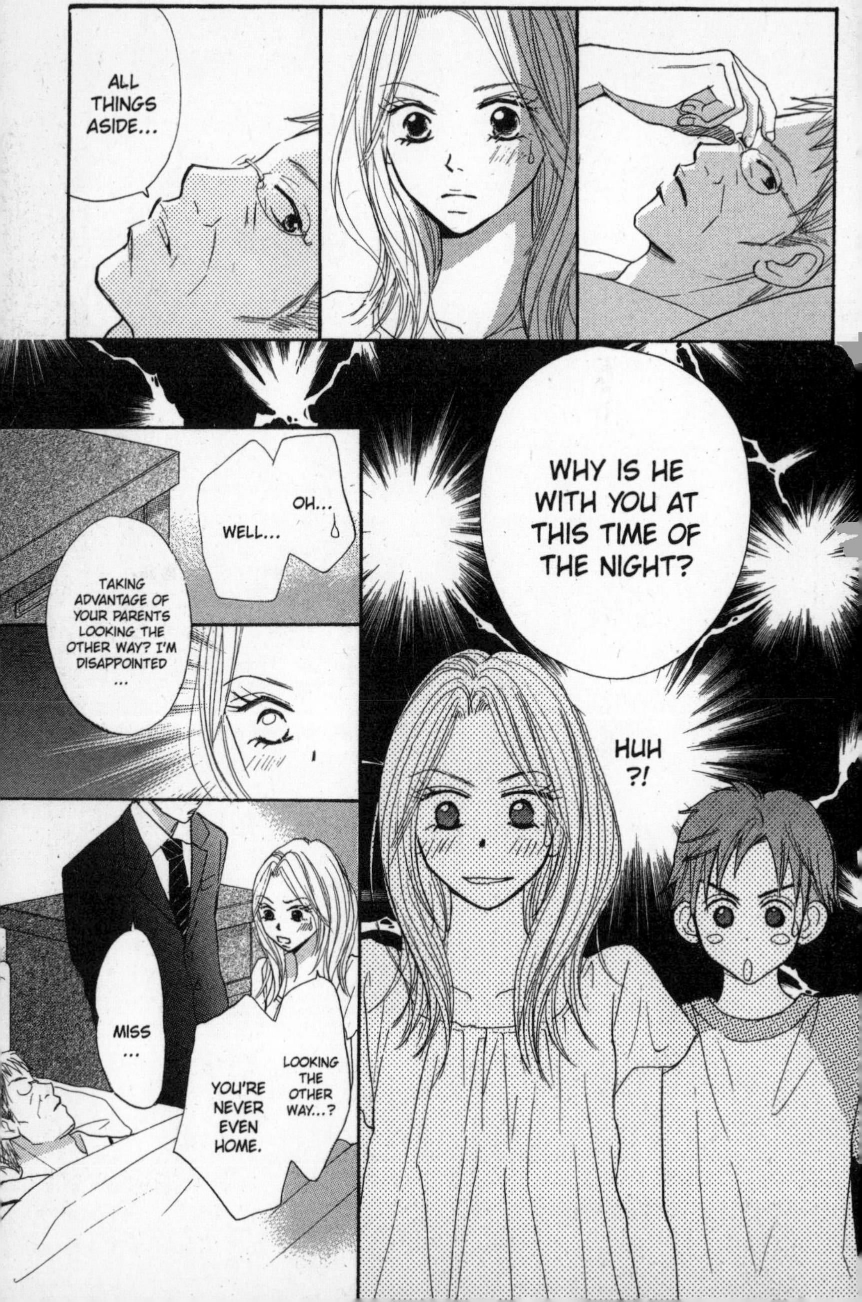
ALL THINGS ASIDE...
WHY IS HE WITH YOU AT THIS TIME OF THE NIGHT?
HUH ?!
OH... WELL...
TAKING ADVANTAGE OF YOUR PARENTS LOOKING THE OTHER WAY? I'M DISAPPOINTED ...
MISS ...
LOOKING THE OTHER WAY...?
YOU'RE NEVER EVEN HOME.

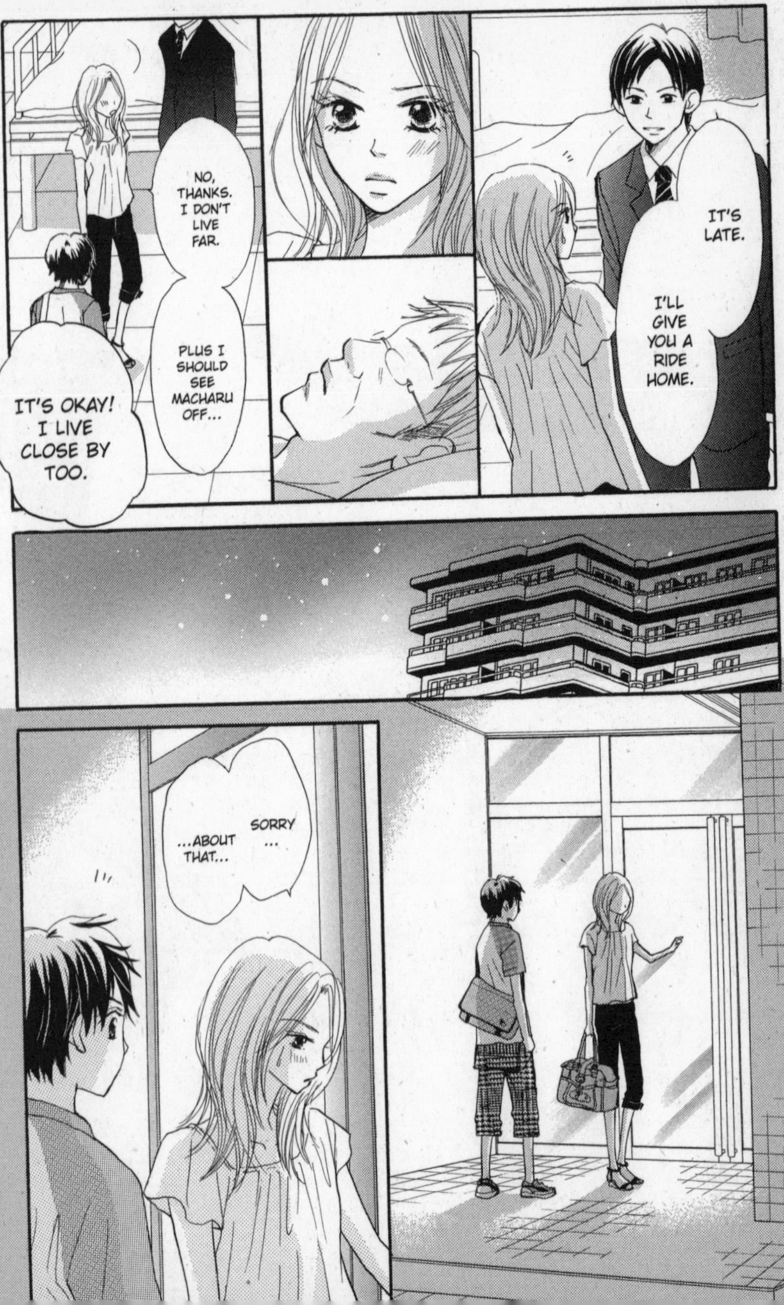
IT'S LATE.
I'LL GIVE YOU A RIDE HOME.
NO, THANKS. I DON'T LIVE FAR.
PLUS I SHOULD SEE MACHARU OFF...
IT'S OKAY! I LIVE CLOSE BY TOO.
SORRY...
...ABOUT THAT...

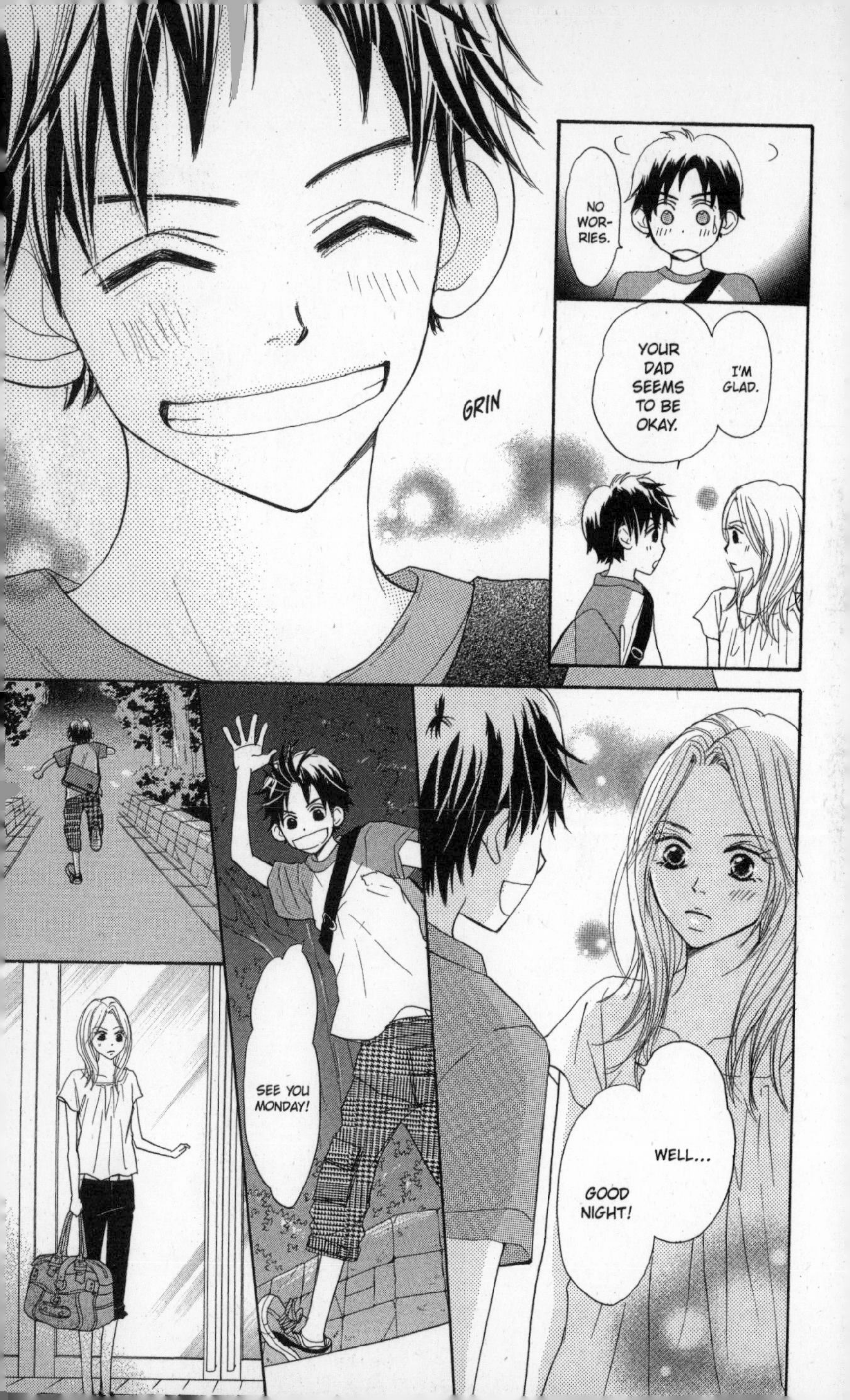
NO WORRIES.
I'M GLAD.
YOUR DAD SEEMS TO BE OKAY.
GRIN
WELL...
GOOD NIGHT!
SEE YOU MONDAY!

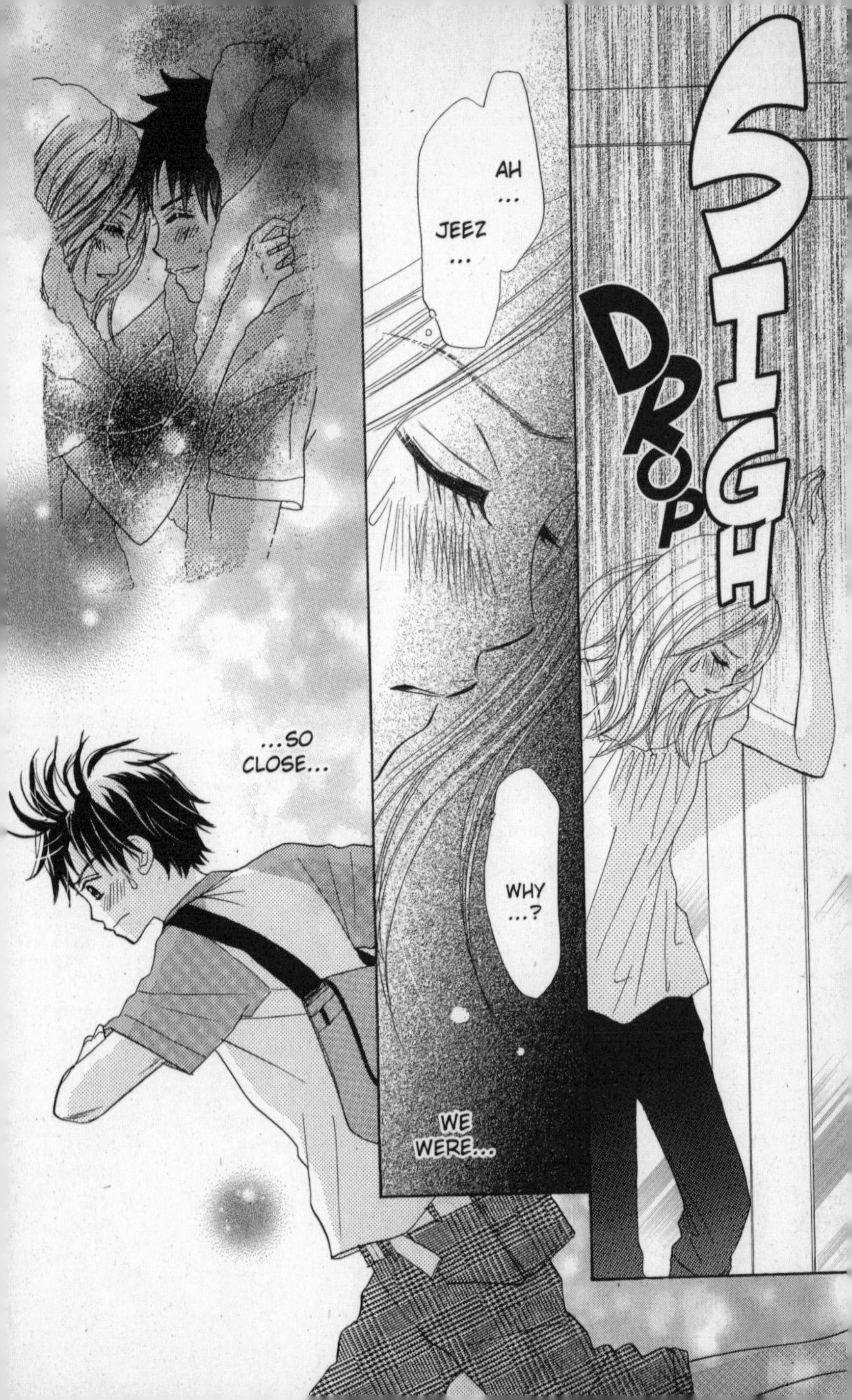
SIGH
DROP
AH... JEEZ...
WHY...?
WE WERE...
...SO CLOSE...

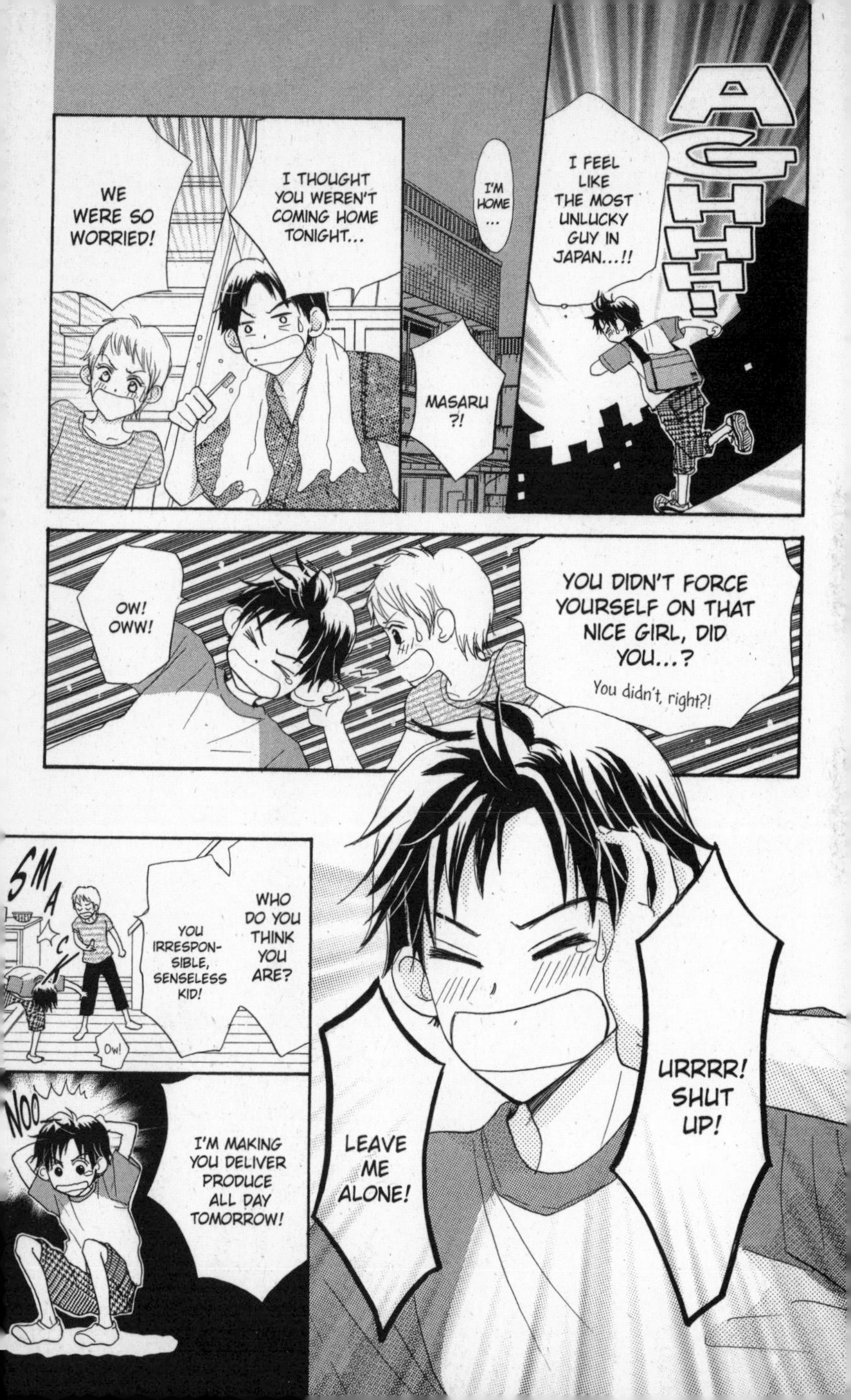
AGHHHH!
I FEEL LIKE THE MOST UNLUCKY GUY IN JAPAN...!!
I'M HOME...
MASARU?!
I THOUGHT YOU WEREN'T COMING HOME TONIGHT...
WE WERE SO WORRIED!
YOU DIDN'T FORCE YOURSELF ON THAT NICE GIRL, DID YOU...?
You didn't, right?!
OW! OWW!
URRRR! SHUT UP!
LEAVE ME ALONE!
WHO DO YOU THINK YOU ARE?
YOU IRRESPONSIBLE, SENSELESS KID!
SMACK
Ow!
I'M MAKING YOU DELIVER PRODUCE ALL DAY TOMORROW!
NOO

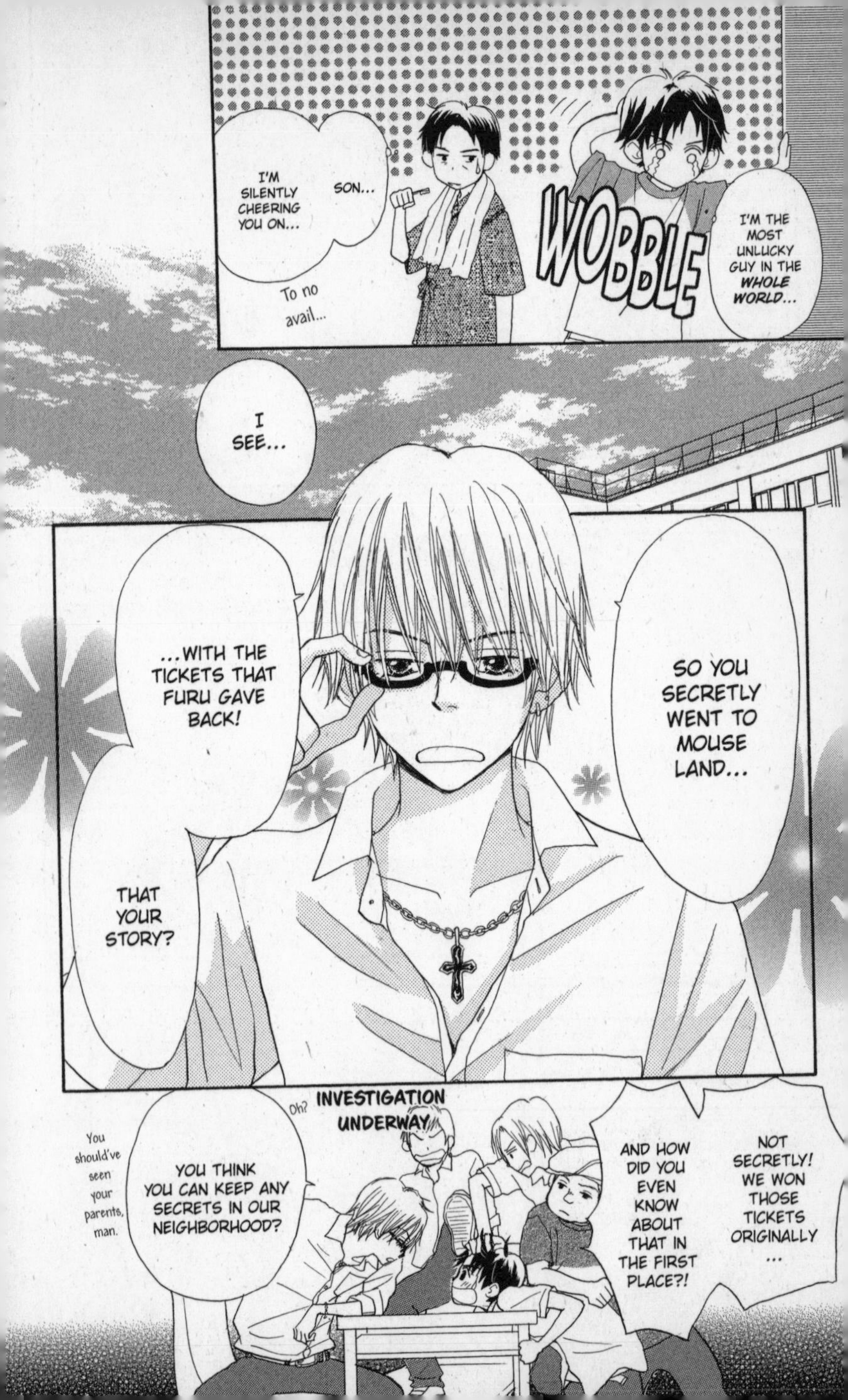
I'M THE MOST UNLUCKY GUY IN THE WHOLE WORLD...
WOBBLE
SON...
I'M SILENTLY CHEERING YOU ON...
To no avail...
I SEE...
SO YOU SECRETLY WENT TO MOUSE LAND...
...WITH THE TICKETS THAT FURU GAVE BACK!
THAT YOUR STORY?
NOT SECRETLY! WE WON THOSE TICKETS ORIGINALLY...
AND HOW DID YOU EVEN KNOW ABOUT THAT IN THE FIRST PLACE?!
INVESTIGATION UNDERWAY
Oh?
YOU THINK YOU CAN KEEP ANY SECRETS IN OUR NEIGHBORHOOD?
You should've seen your parents, man.

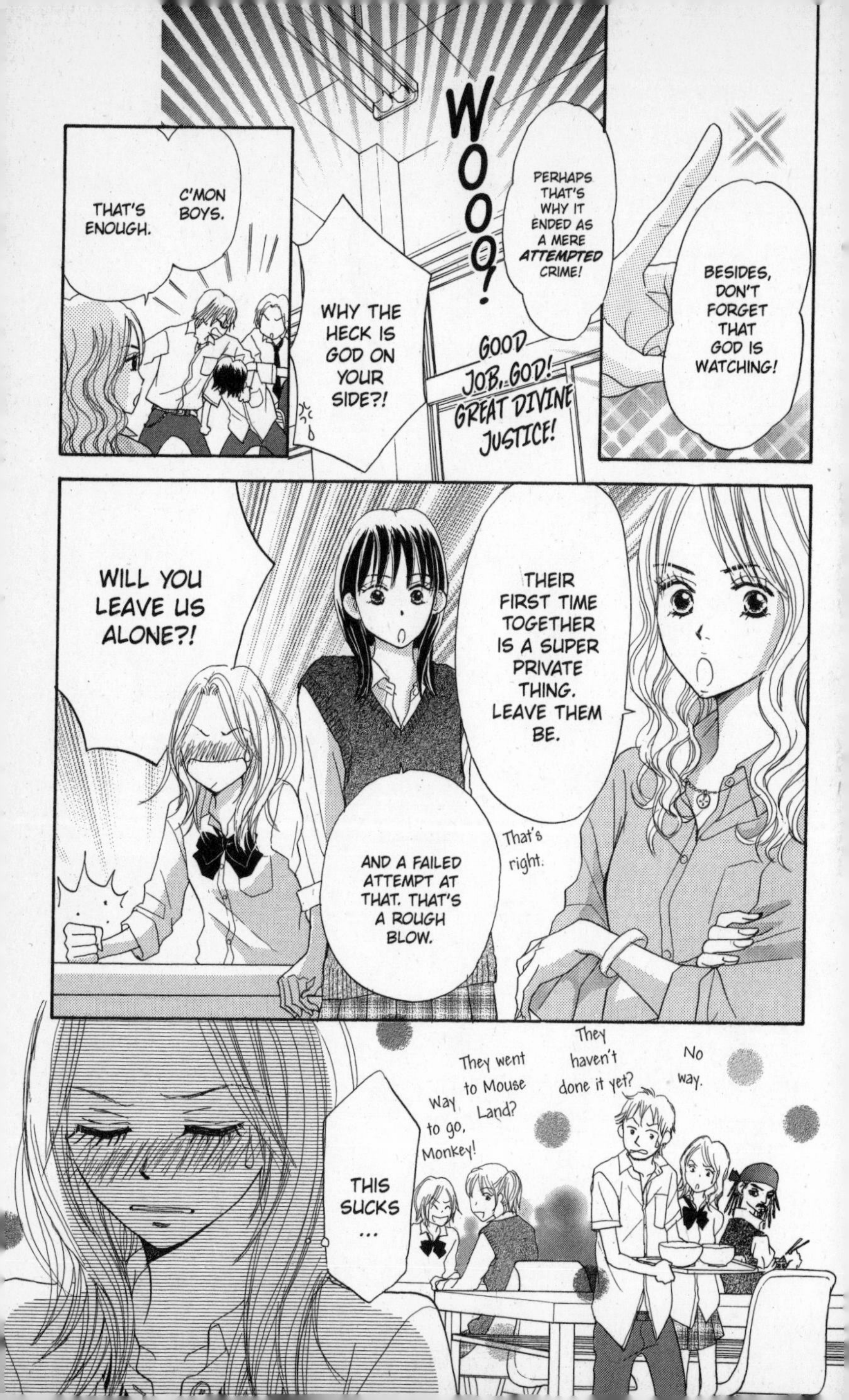
BESIDES, DON'T FORGET THAT GOD IS WATCHING!
PERHAPS THAT'S WHY IT ENDED AS A MERE *ATTEMPTED* CRIME!
WOO?!
GOOD JOB, GOD! GREAT DIVINE JUSTICE!
WHY THE HECK IS GOD ON YOUR SIDE?!
C'MON BOYS.
THAT'S ENOUGH.
THEIR FIRST TIME TOGETHER IS A SUPER PRIVATE THING. LEAVE THEM BE.
That's right.
AND A FAILED ATTEMPT AT THAT. THAT'S A ROUGH BLOW.
WILL YOU LEAVE US ALONE?!
No way.
They haven't done it yet?
They went to Mouse Land?
Way to go, Monkey!
THIS SUCKS...

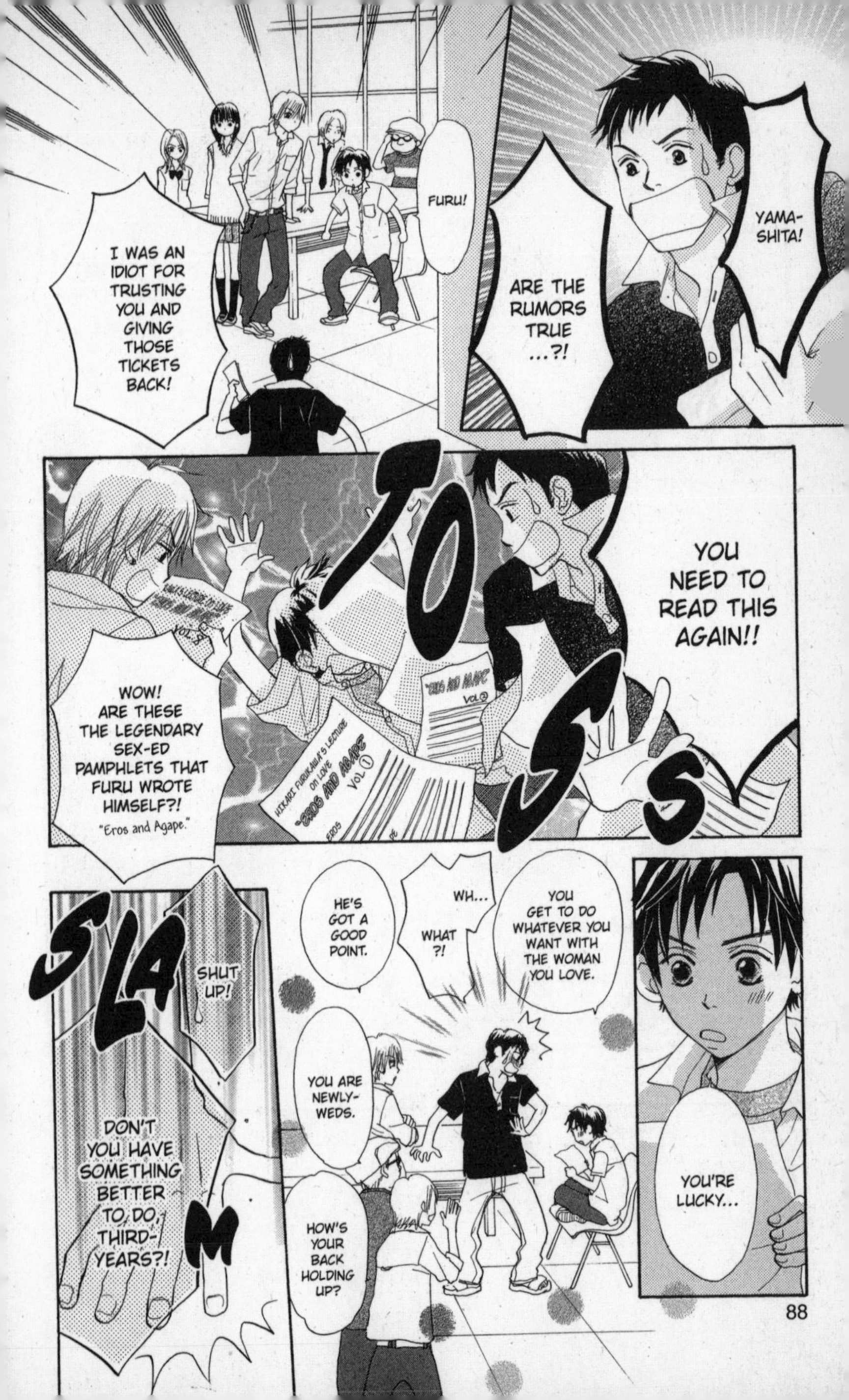
YAMA-SHITA!
ARE THE RUMORS TRUE ...?!
FURU!
I WAS AN IDIOT FOR TRUSTING YOU AND GIVING THOSE TICKETS BACK!
YOU NEED TO READ THIS AGAIN!!
TOSS
HIKARI FURUKAWA'S LECTURE ON LOVE "EROS AND AGAPE" VOL 1
WOW! ARE THESE THE LEGENDARY SEX-ED PAMPHLETS THAT FURU WROTE HIMSELF?!
"Eros and Agape."
YOU'RE LUCKY...
YOU GET TO DO WHATEVER YOU WANT WITH THE WOMAN YOU LOVE.
WH... WHAT?!
HE'S GOT A GOOD POINT.
YOU ARE NEWLY-WEDS.
HOW'S YOUR BACK HOLDING UP?
SLAM
SHUT UP!
DON'T YOU HAVE SOMETHING BETTER TO DO, THIRD-YEARS?!

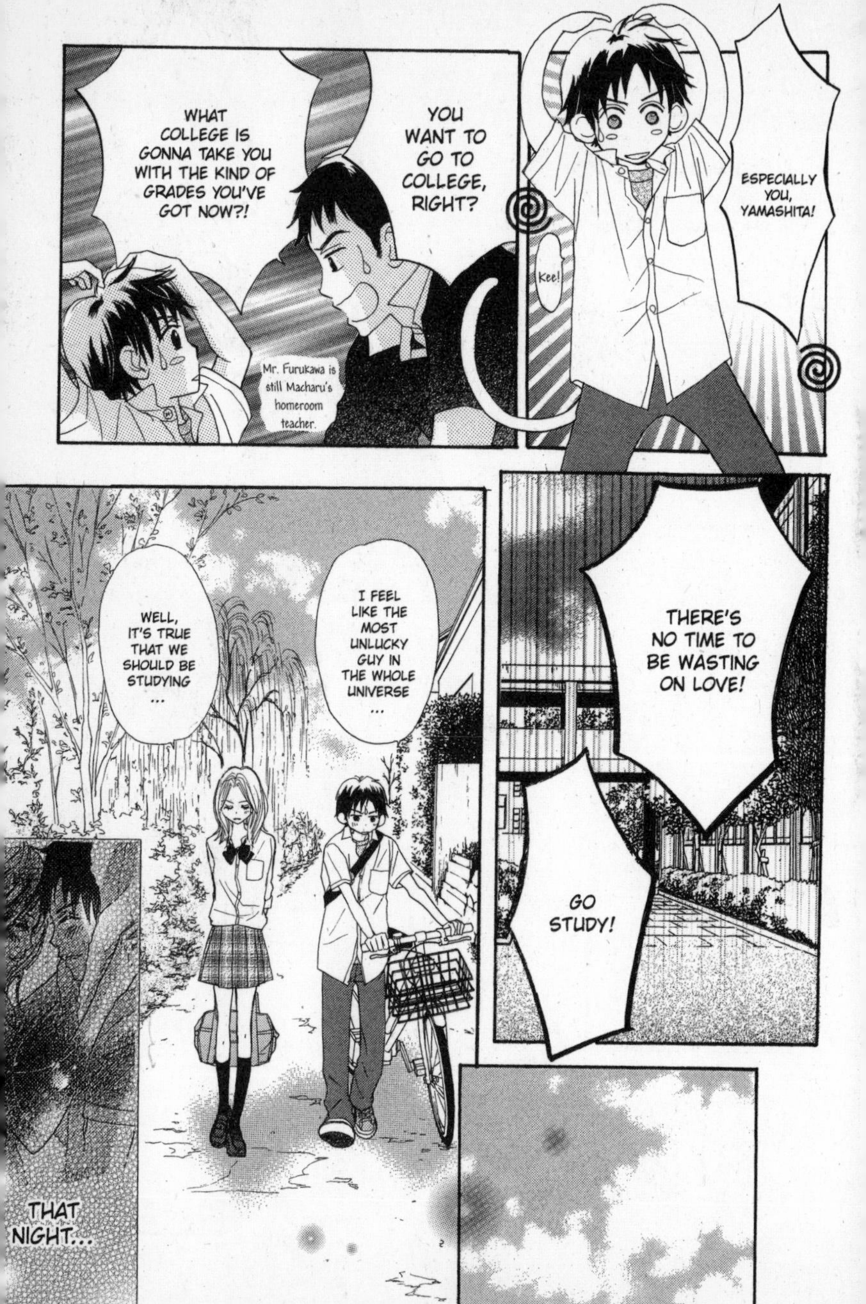
ESPECIALLY YOU, YAMASHITA!
Kee!
YOU WANT TO GO TO COLLEGE, RIGHT?
WHAT COLLEGE IS GONNA TAKE YOU WITH THE KIND OF GRADES YOU'VE GOT NOW?!
Mr. Furukawa is still Macharu's homeroom teacher.
THERE'S NO TIME TO BE WASTING ON LOVE!
GO STUDY!
I FEEL LIKE THE MOST UNLUCKY GUY IN THE WHOLE UNIVERSE ...
WELL, IT'S TRUE THAT WE SHOULD BE STUDYING ...
THAT NIGHT...

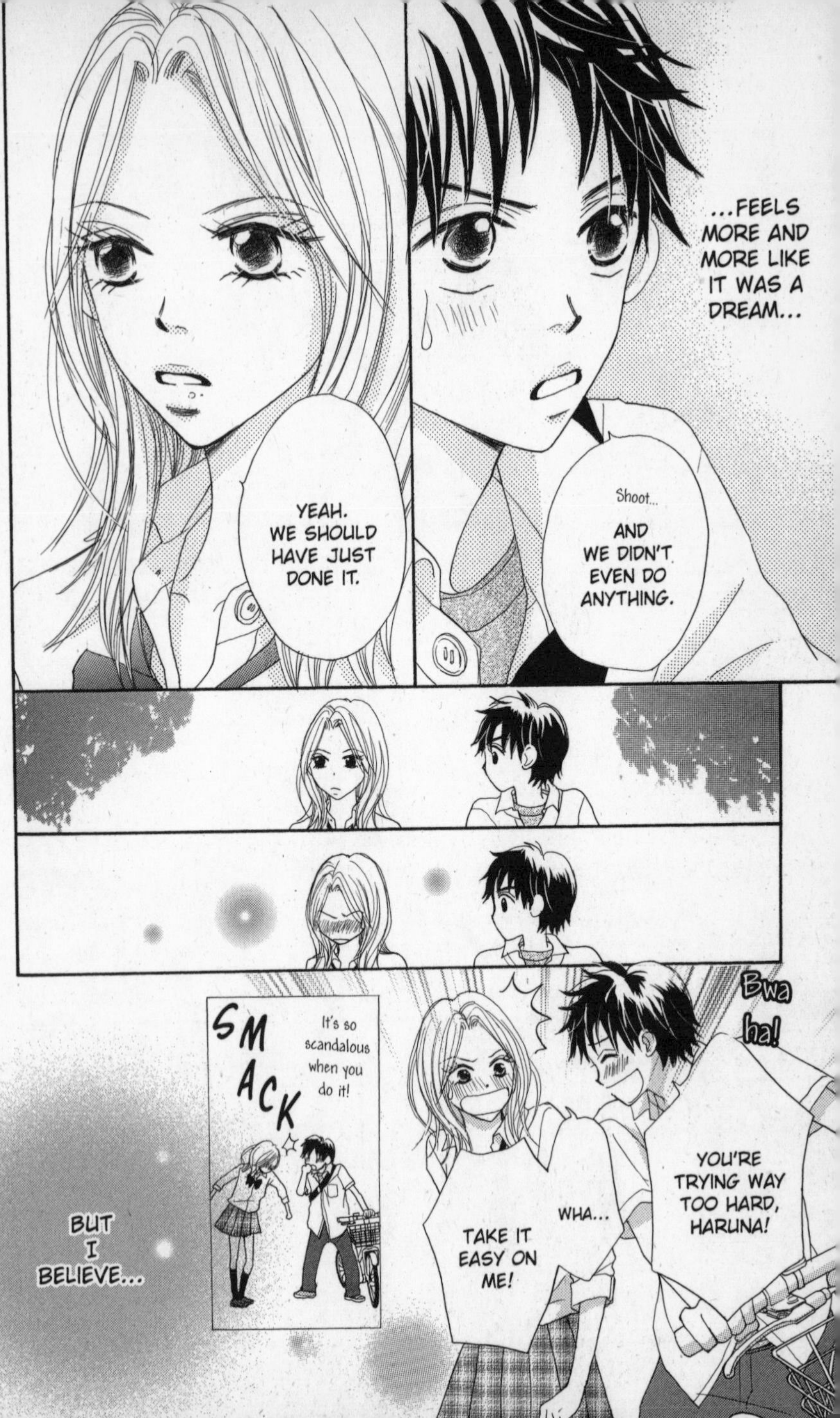
...FEELS MORE AND MORE LIKE IT WAS A DREAM...
Shoot...
AND WE DIDN'T EVEN DO ANYTHING.
YEAH. WE SHOULD HAVE JUST DONE IT.
Bwa ha!
YOU'RE TRYING WAY TOO HARD, HARUNA!
WHA...
TAKE IT EASY ON ME!
SMACK
It's so scandalous when you do it!
BUT I BELIEVE...

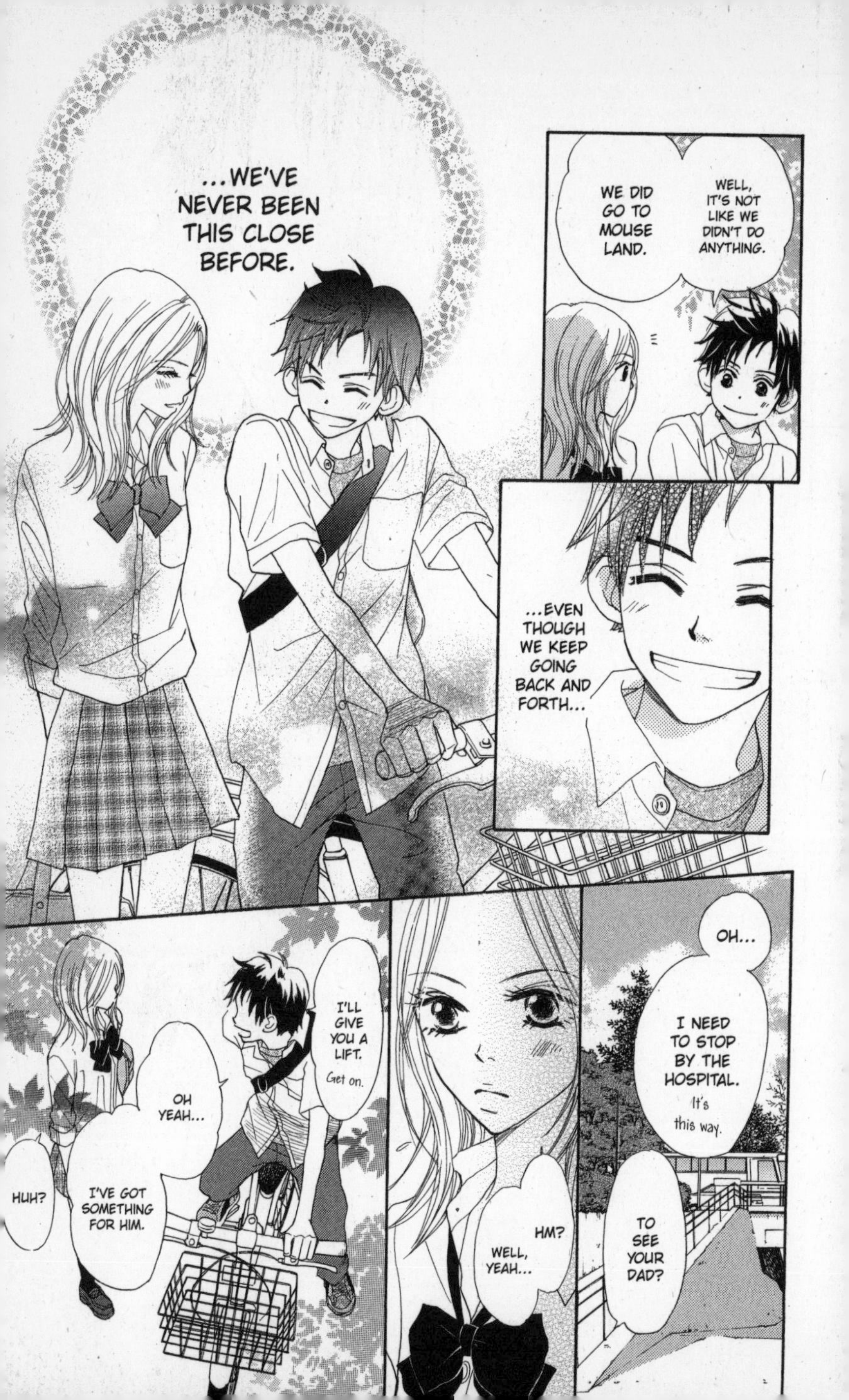
WELL, IT'S NOT LIKE WE DIDN'T DO ANYTHING.
WE DID GO TO MOUSE LAND.
...EVEN THOUGH WE KEEP GOING BACK AND FORTH...
...WE'VE NEVER BEEN THIS CLOSE BEFORE.
OH...
I NEED TO STOP BY THE HOSPITAL.
It's this way.
TO SEE YOUR DAD?
HM?
WELL, YEAH...
I'LL GIVE YOU A LIFT.
Get on.
OH YEAH...
I'VE GOT SOMETHING FOR HIM.
HUH?

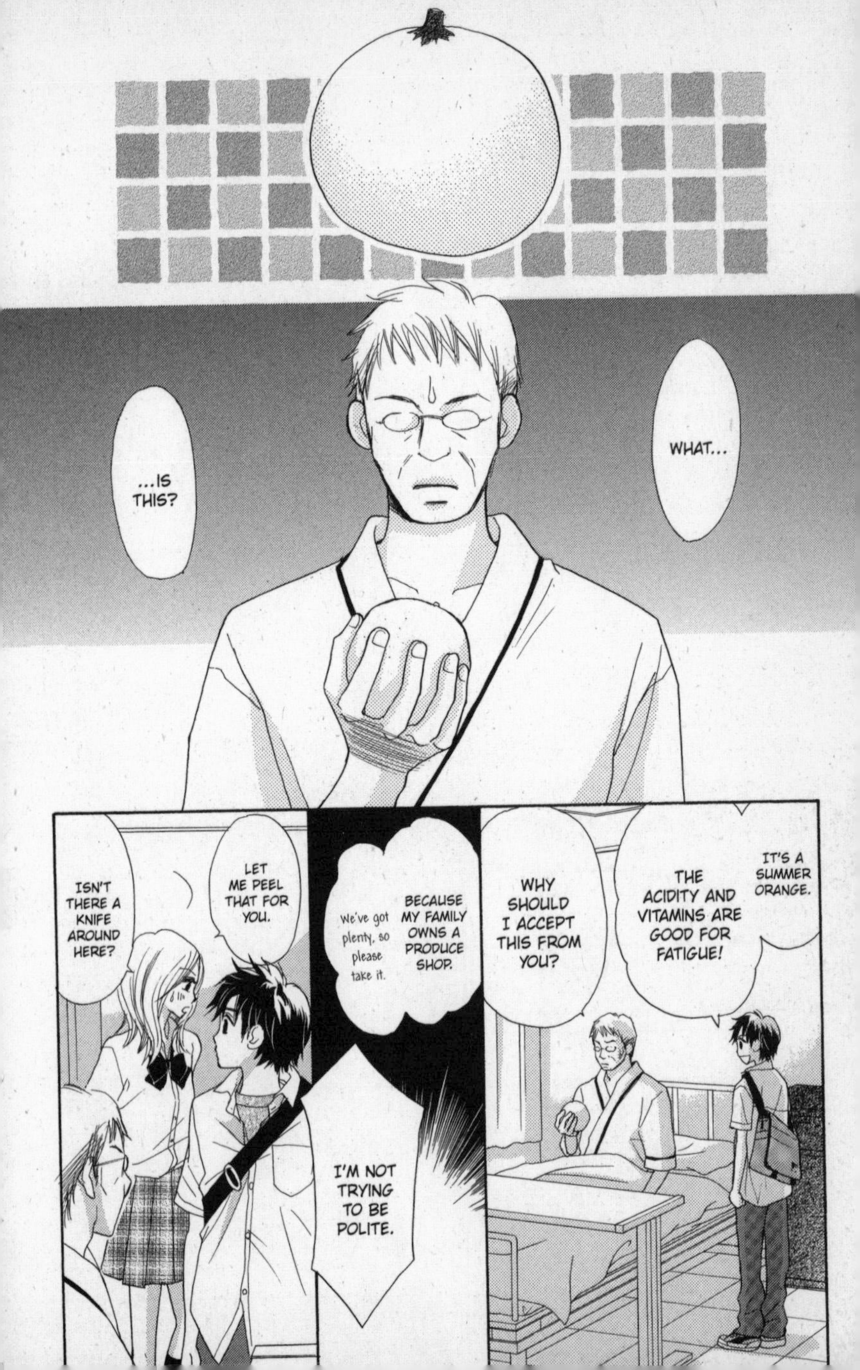
WHAT...
...IS THIS?
IT'S A SUMMER ORANGE.
THE ACIDITY AND VITAMINS ARE GOOD FOR FATIGUE!
WHY SHOULD I ACCEPT THIS FROM YOU?
BECAUSE MY FAMILY OWNS A PRODUCE SHOP.
We've got plenty, so please take it.
I'M NOT TRYING TO BE POLITE.
LET ME PEEL THAT FOR YOU.
ISN'T THERE A KNIFE AROUND HERE?

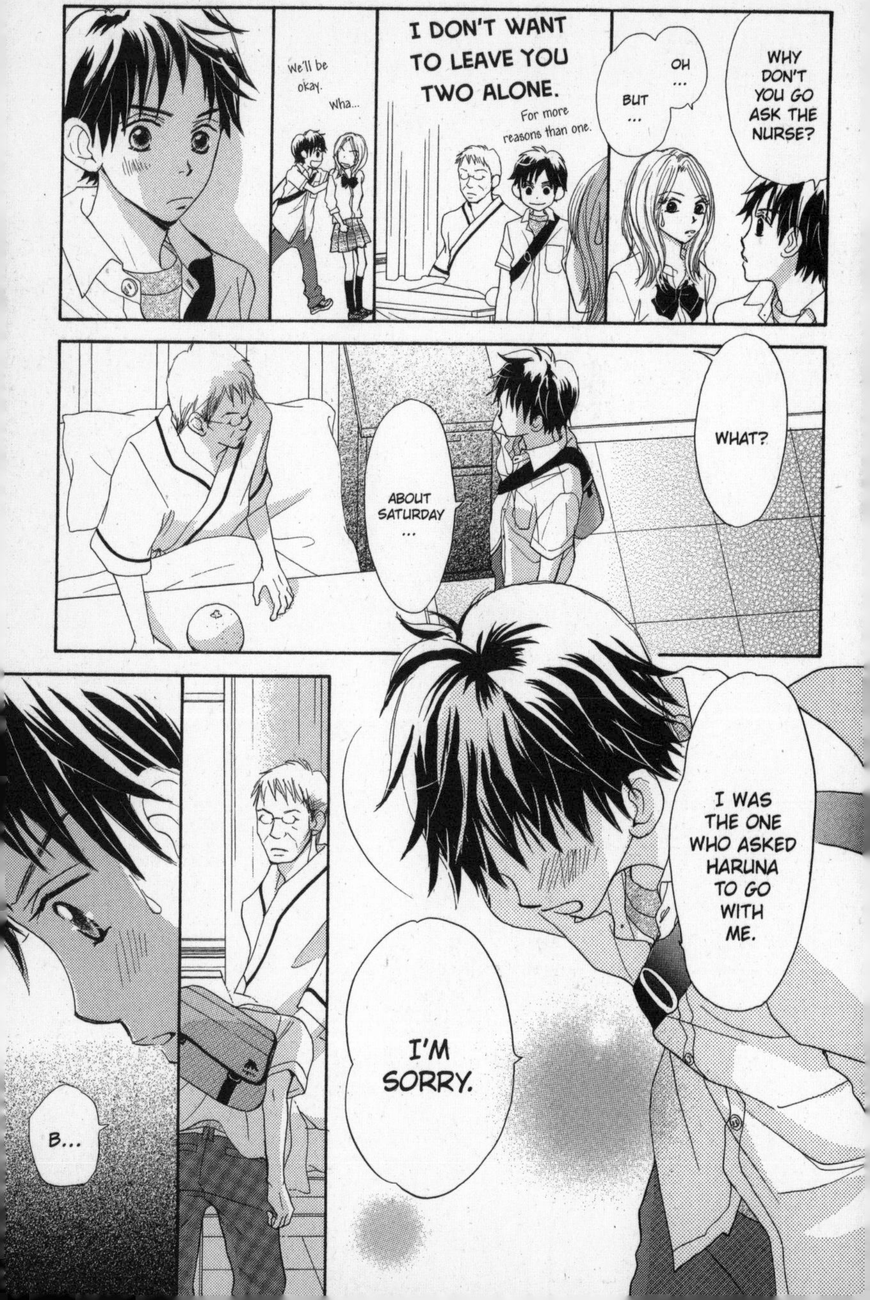
WHY DON'T YOU GO ASK THE NURSE?
OH ...
BUT ...
I DON'T WANT TO LEAVE YOU TWO ALONE.
For more reasons than one.
We'll be okay.
Wha...
WHAT?
ABOUT SATURDAY ...
I WAS THE ONE WHO ASKED HARUNA TO GO WITH ME.
I'M SORRY.
B...

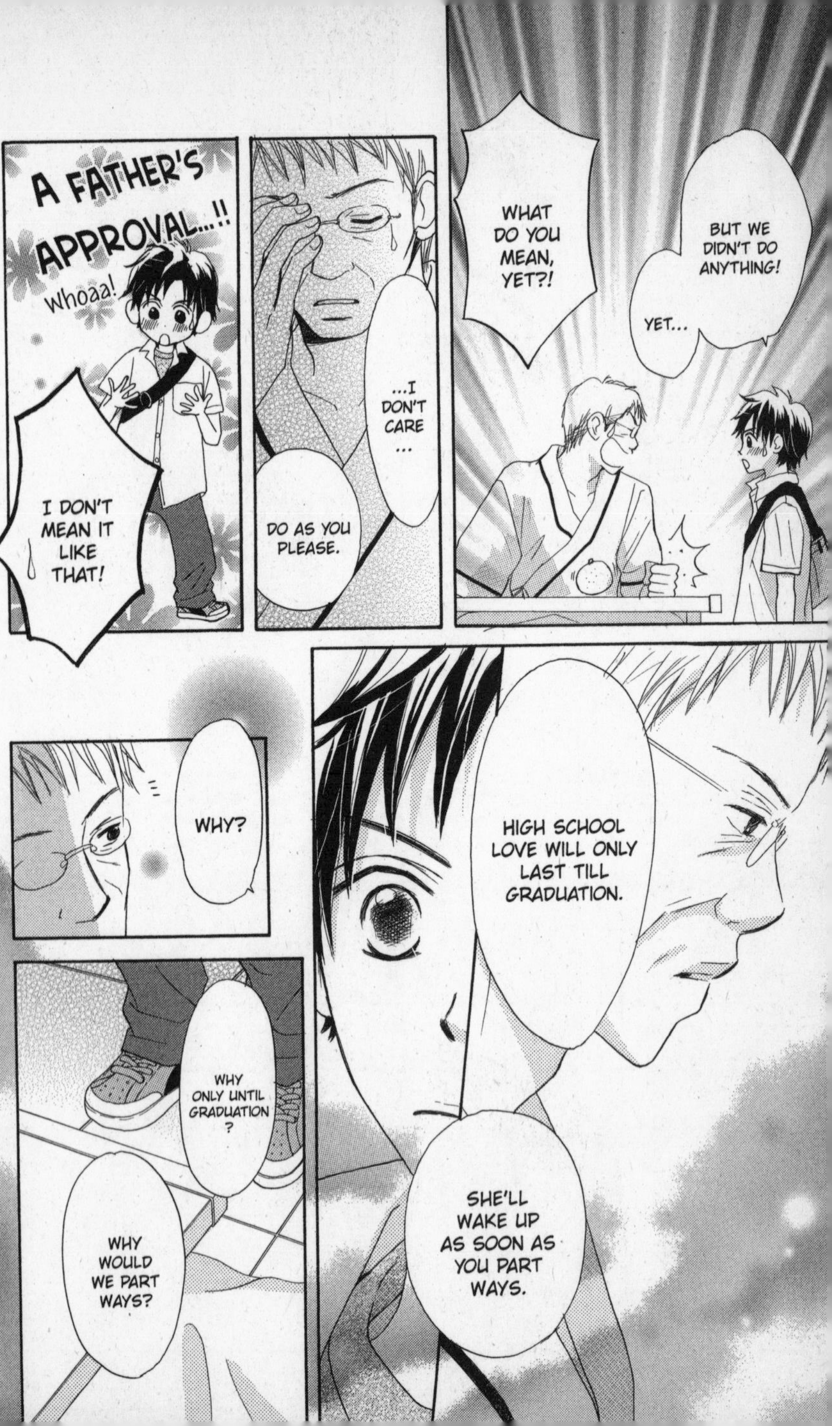
BUT WE DIDN'T DO ANYTHING!
YET...
WHAT DO YOU MEAN, YET?!
...I DON'T CARE ...
DO AS YOU PLEASE.
A FATHER'S APPROVAL...!!
Whoaa!
I DON'T MEAN IT LIKE THAT!
HIGH SCHOOL LOVE WILL ONLY LAST TILL GRADUATION.
SHE'LL WAKE UP AS SOON AS YOU PART WAYS.
WHY?
WHY ONLY UNTIL GRADUATION ?
WHY WOULD WE PART WAYS?

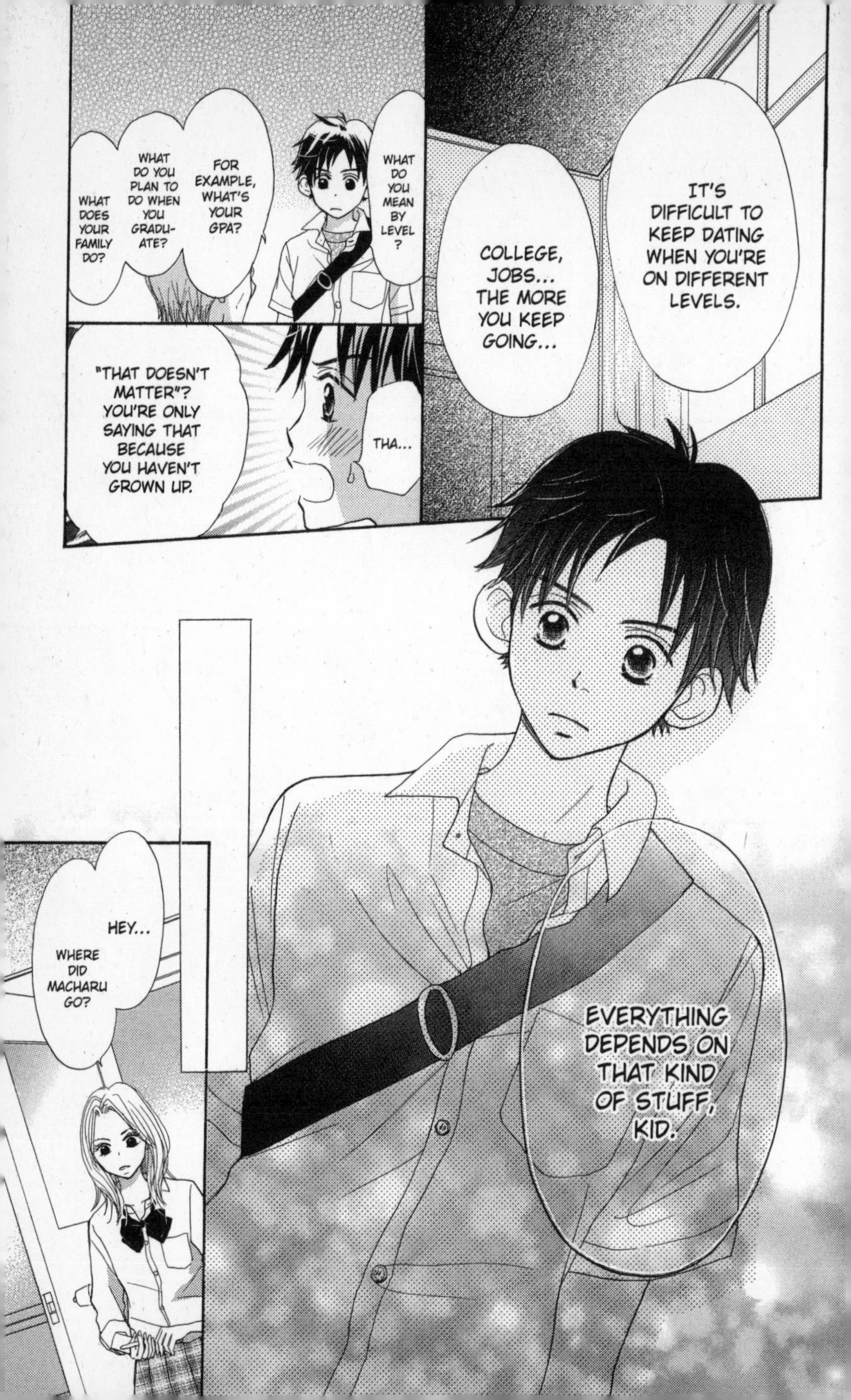

IT'S DIFFICULT TO KEEP DATING WHEN YOU'RE ON DIFFERENT LEVELS.
COLLEGE, JOBS... THE MORE YOU KEEP GOING...
WHAT DO YOU MEAN BY LEVEL?
FOR EXAMPLE, WHAT'S YOUR GPA?
WHAT DO YOU PLAN TO DO WHEN YOU GRADU-ATE?
WHAT DOES YOUR FAMILY DO?
THA...
"THAT DOESN'T MATTER"? YOU'RE ONLY SAYING THAT BECAUSE YOU HAVEN'T GROWN UP.
EVERYTHING DEPENDS ON THAT KIND OF STUFF, KID.
HEY...
WHERE DID MACHARU GO?

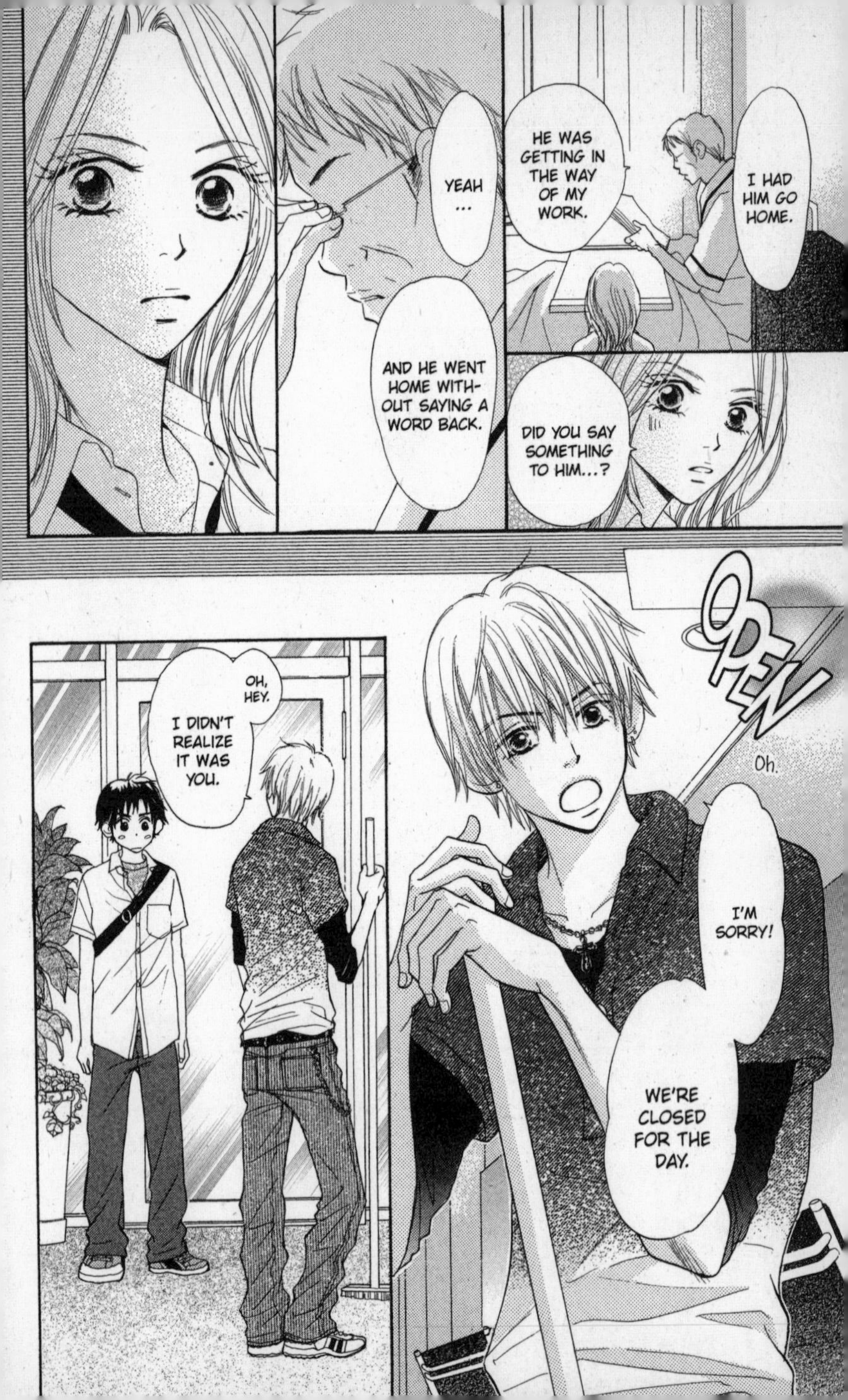
I HAD HIM GO HOME.
HE WAS GETTING IN THE WAY OF MY WORK.
DID YOU SAY SOMETHING TO HIM...?
YEAH...
AND HE WENT HOME WITHOUT SAYING A WORD BACK.
OPEN
Oh.
I'M SORRY!
WE'RE CLOSED FOR THE DAY.
OH, HEY.
I DIDN'T REALIZE IT WAS YOU.

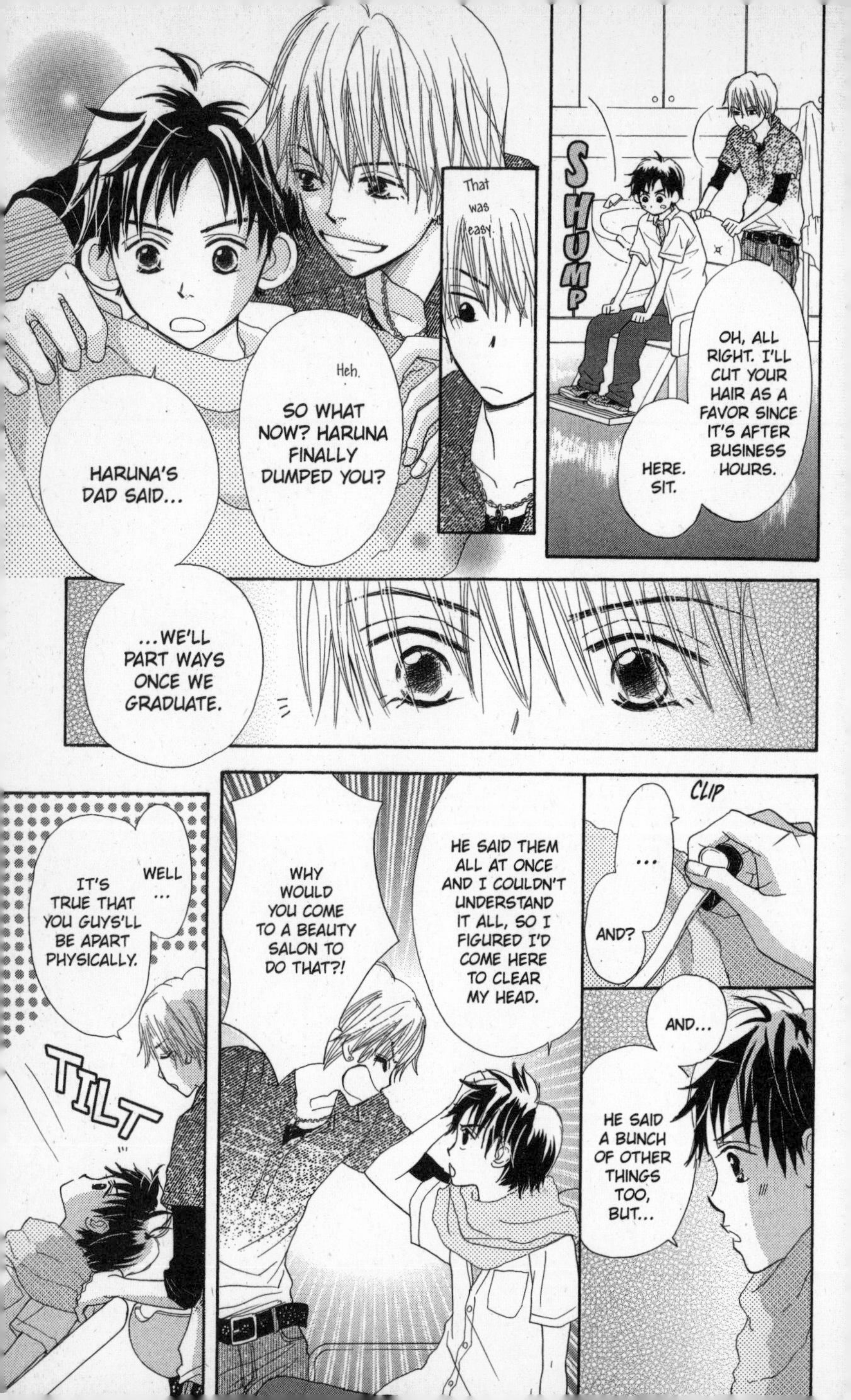
SHUMP
OH, ALL RIGHT. I'LL CUT YOUR HAIR AS A FAVOR SINCE IT'S AFTER BUSINESS HOURS.
HERE. SIT.
That was easy.
Heh.
SO WHAT NOW? HARUNA FINALLY DUMPED YOU?
HARUNA'S DAD SAID...
...WE'LL PART WAYS ONCE WE GRADUATE.
CLIP
...
AND?
AND...
HE SAID A BUNCH OF OTHER THINGS TOO, BUT...
HE SAID THEM ALL AT ONCE AND I COULDN'T UNDERSTAND IT ALL, SO I FIGURED I'D COME HERE TO CLEAR MY HEAD.
WHY WOULD YOU COME TO A BEAUTY SALON TO DO THAT?!
WELL...
IT'S TRUE THAT YOU GUYS'LL BE APART PHYSICALLY.
TILT

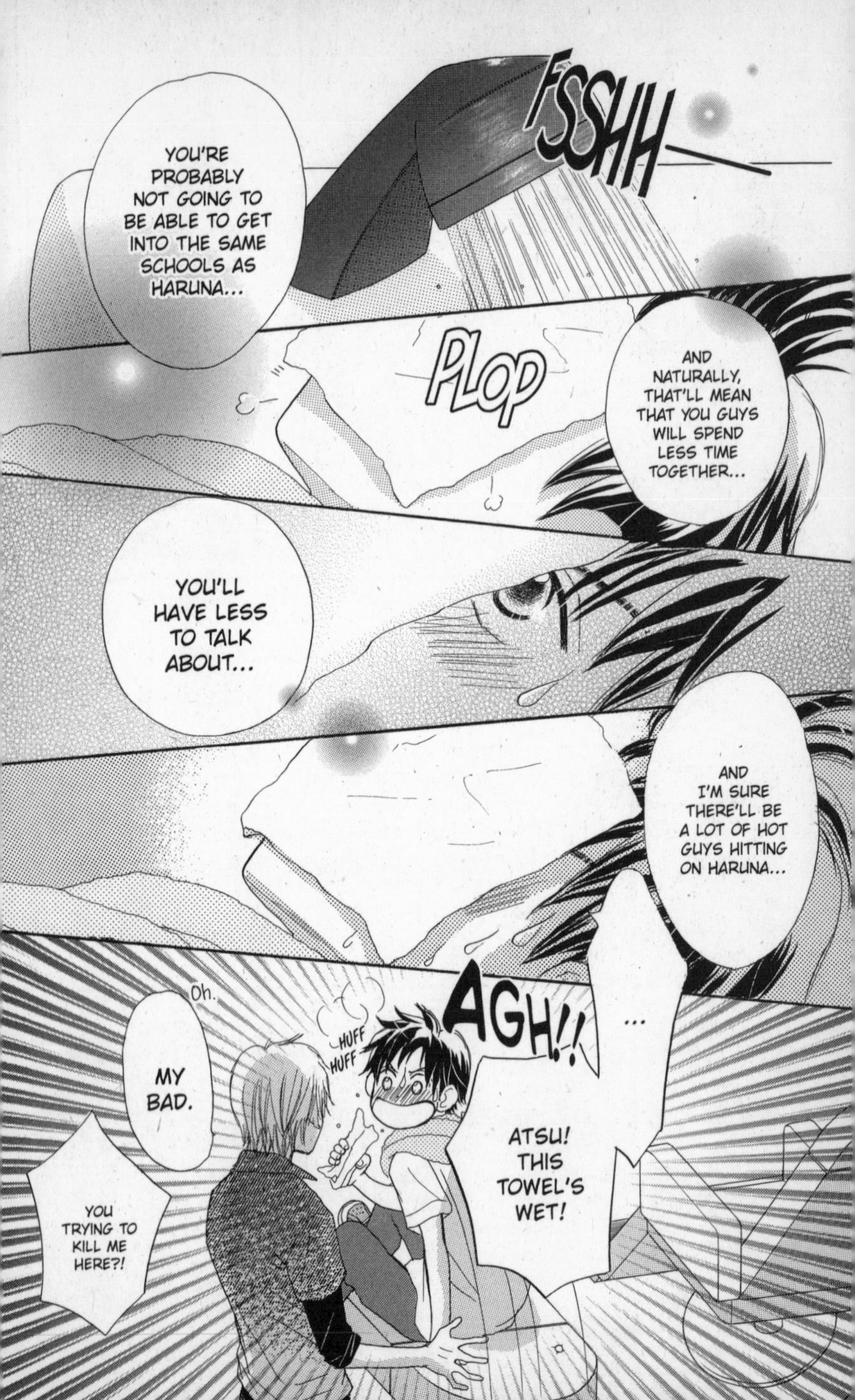
FSSHH
YOU'RE PROBABLY NOT GOING TO BE ABLE TO GET INTO THE SAME SCHOOLS AS HARUNA...
AND NATURALLY, THAT'LL MEAN THAT YOU GUYS WILL SPEND LESS TIME TOGETHER...
PLOP
YOU'LL HAVE LESS TO TALK ABOUT...
AND I'M SURE THERE'LL BE A LOT OF HOT GUYS HITTING ON HARUNA...
...
AGH!!
HUFF HUFF
ATSU! THIS TOWEL'S WET!
YOU TRYING TO KILL ME HERE?!
Oh.
MY BAD.

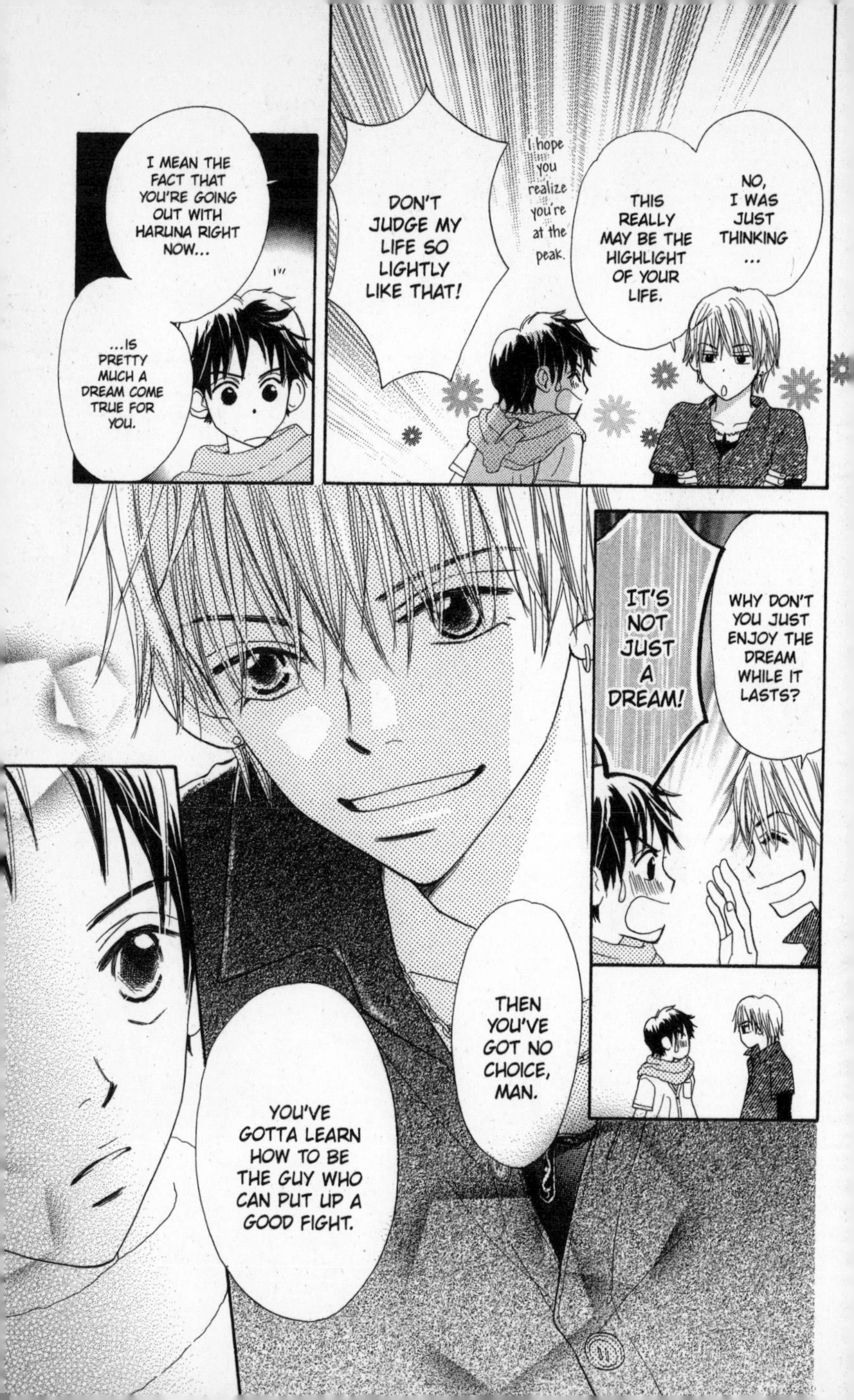
NO, I WAS JUST THINKING ...
THIS REALLY MAY BE THE HIGHLIGHT OF YOUR LIFE.
I hope you realize you're at the peak.
DON'T JUDGE MY LIFE SO LIGHTLY LIKE THAT!
I MEAN THE FACT THAT YOU'RE GOING OUT WITH HARUNA RIGHT NOW...
...IS PRETTY MUCH A DREAM COME TRUE FOR YOU.
WHY DON'T YOU JUST ENJOY THE DREAM WHILE IT LASTS?
IT'S NOT JUST A DREAM!
THEN YOU'VE GOT NO CHOICE, MAN.
YOU'VE GOTTA LEARN HOW TO BE THE GUY WHO CAN PUT UP A GOOD FIGHT.

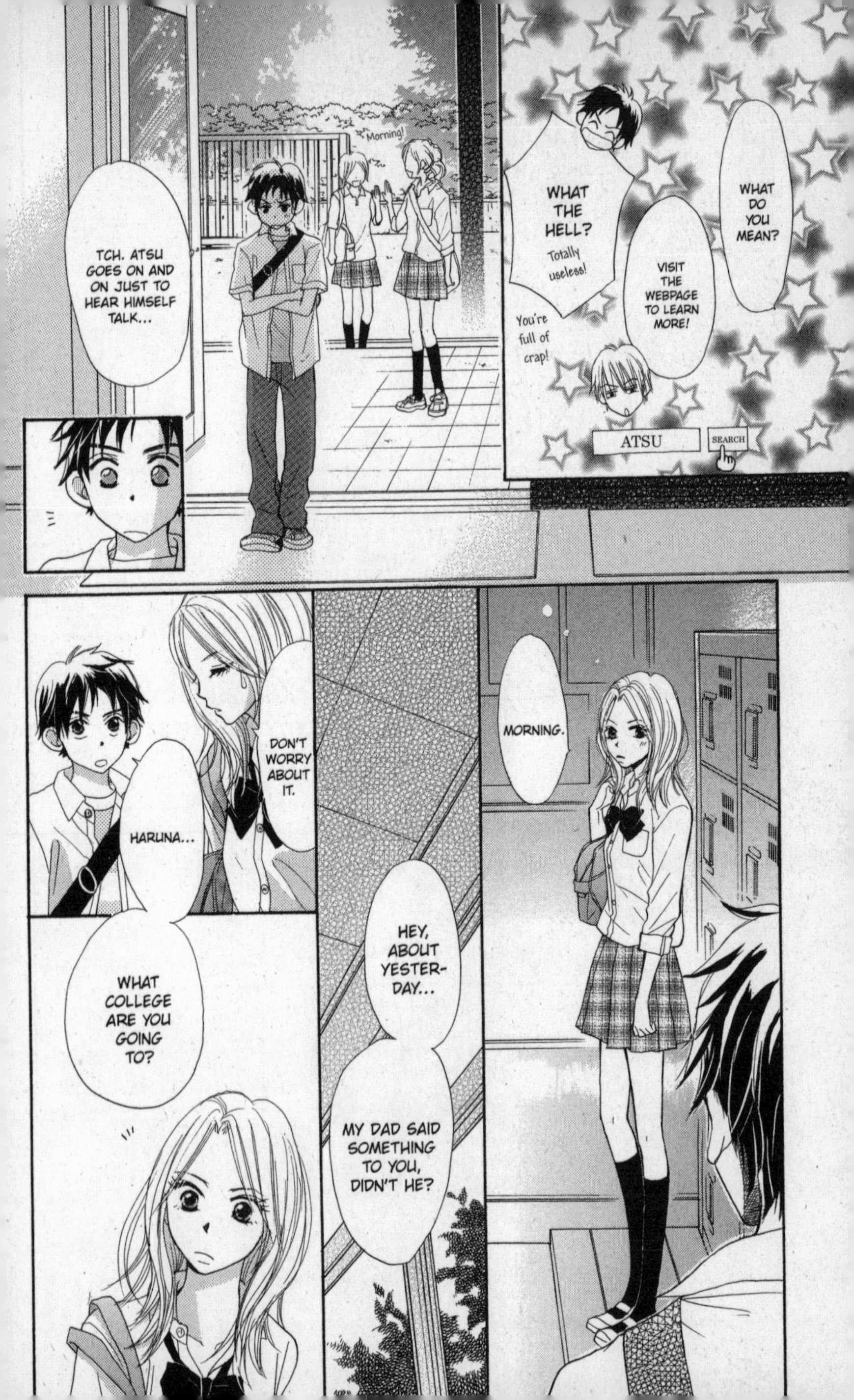
WHAT DO YOU MEAN?
VISIT THE WEBPAGE TO LEARN MORE!
WHAT THE HELL?
Totally useless!
You're full of crap!
ATSU
SEARCH
Morning!
TCH. ATSU GOES ON AND ON JUST TO HEAR HIMSELF TALK...
MORNING.
HEY, ABOUT YESTER-DAY...
MY DAD SAID SOMETHING TO YOU, DIDN'T HE?
DON'T WORRY ABOUT IT.
HARUNA...
WHAT COLLEGE ARE YOU GOING TO?

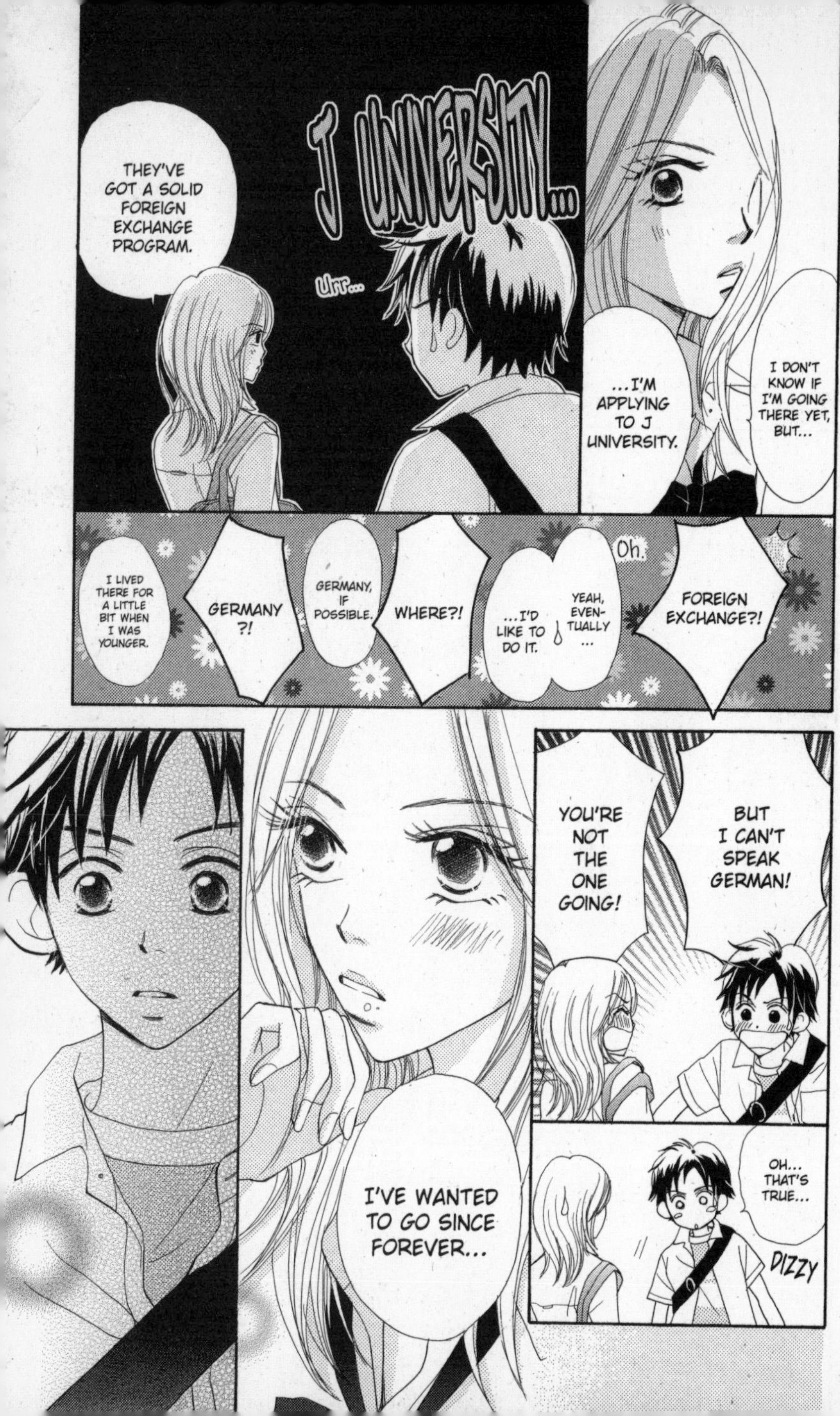
I DON'T KNOW IF I'M GOING THERE YET, BUT...
...I'M APPLYING TO J UNIVERSITY.
J UNIVERSITY...
Urr...
THEY'VE GOT A SOLID FOREIGN EXCHANGE PROGRAM.
FOREIGN EXCHANGE?!
Oh.
YEAH, EVENTUALLY...
...I'D LIKE TO DO IT.
WHERE?!
GERMANY, IF POSSIBLE.
GERMANY?!
I LIVED THERE FOR A LITTLE BIT WHEN I WAS YOUNGER.
BUT I CAN'T SPEAK GERMAN!
YOU'RE NOT THE ONE GOING!
OH... THAT'S TRUE...
DIZZY
I'VE WANTED TO GO SINCE FOREVER...

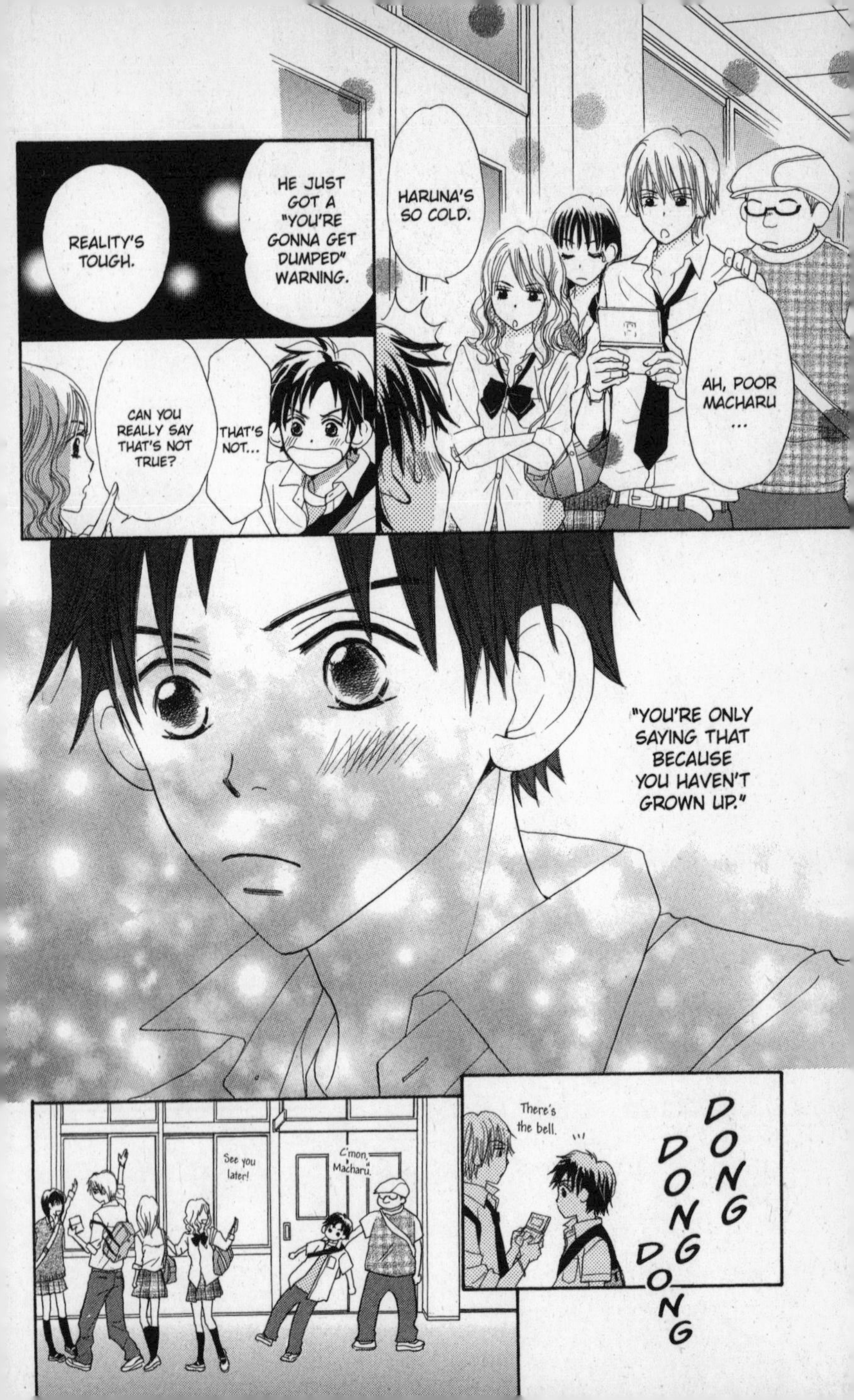
HARUNA'S SO COLD.
AH, POOR MACHARU ...
HE JUST GOT A "YOU'RE GONNA GET DUMPED" WARNING.
REALITY'S TOUGH.
THAT'S NOT...
CAN YOU REALLY SAY THAT'S NOT TRUE?
"YOU'RE ONLY SAYING THAT BECAUSE YOU HAVEN'T GROWN UP."
There's the bell.
DONG DONG DONG DONG
C'mon, Macharu.
See you later!

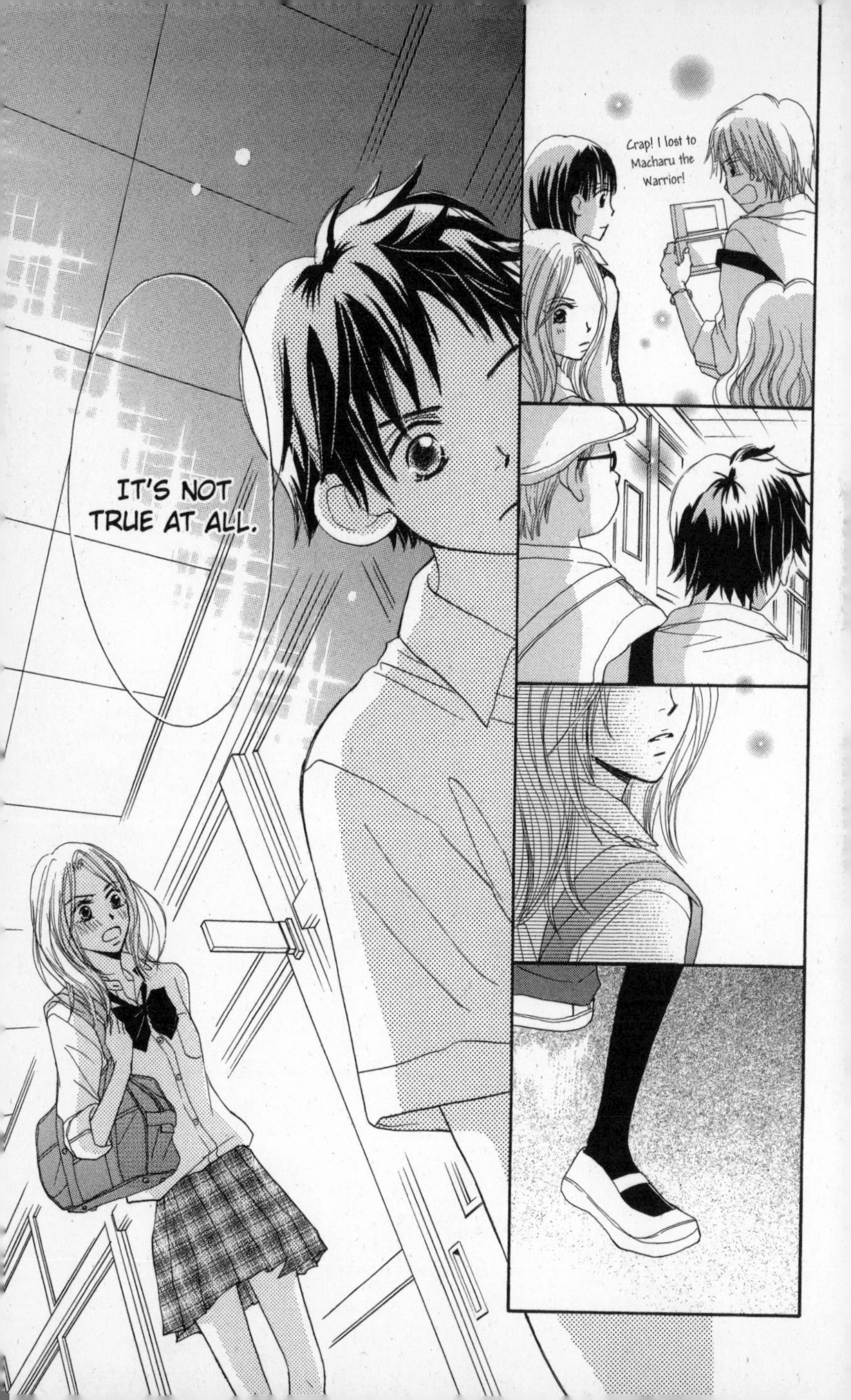
Crap! I lost to Macharu the Warrior!
IT'S NOT TRUE AT ALL.

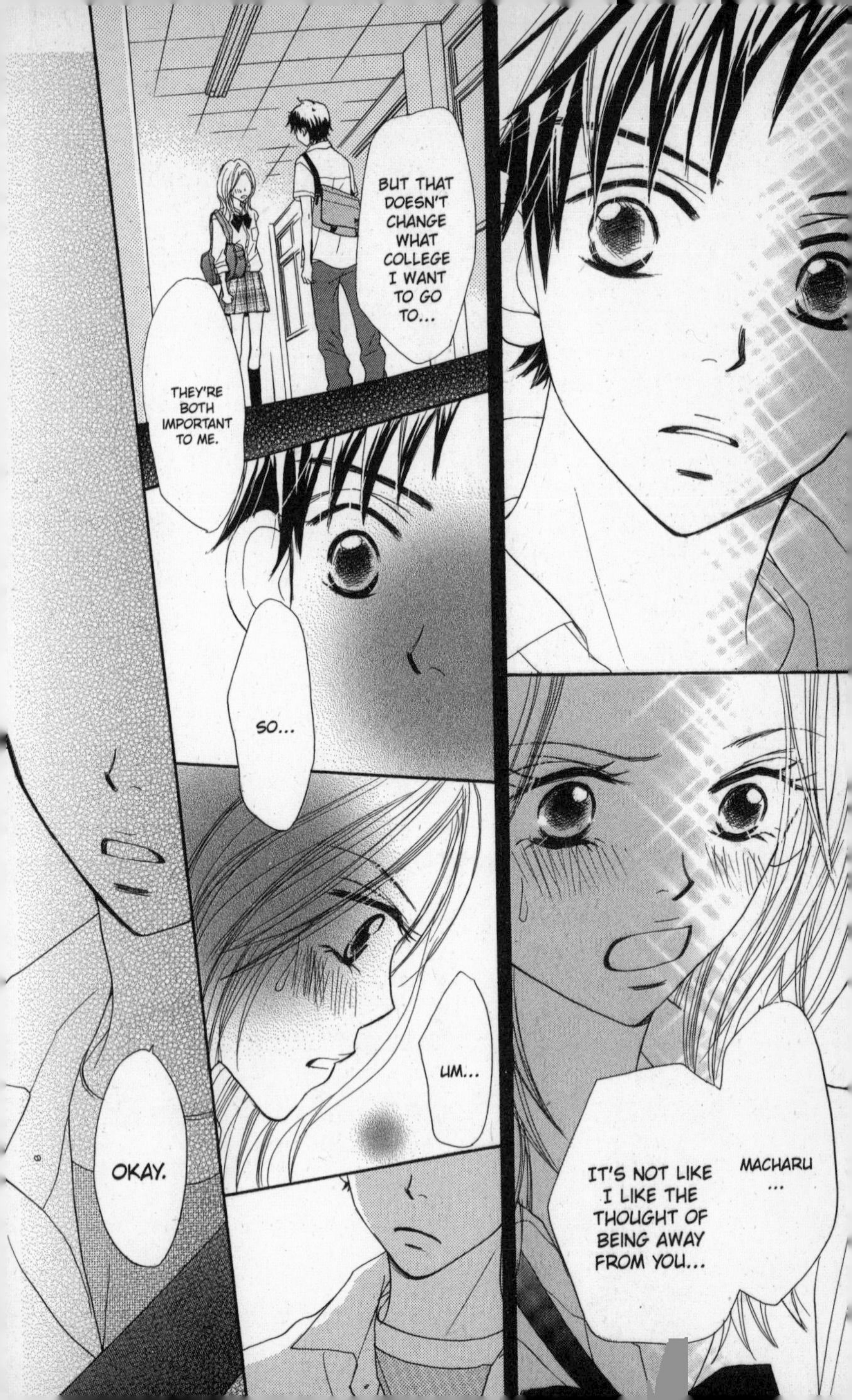
MACHARU...
IT'S NOT LIKE I LIKE THE THOUGHT OF BEING AWAY FROM YOU...
BUT THAT DOESN'T CHANGE WHAT COLLEGE I WANT TO GO TO...
THEY'RE BOTH IMPORTANT TO ME.
SO...
UM...
OKAY.

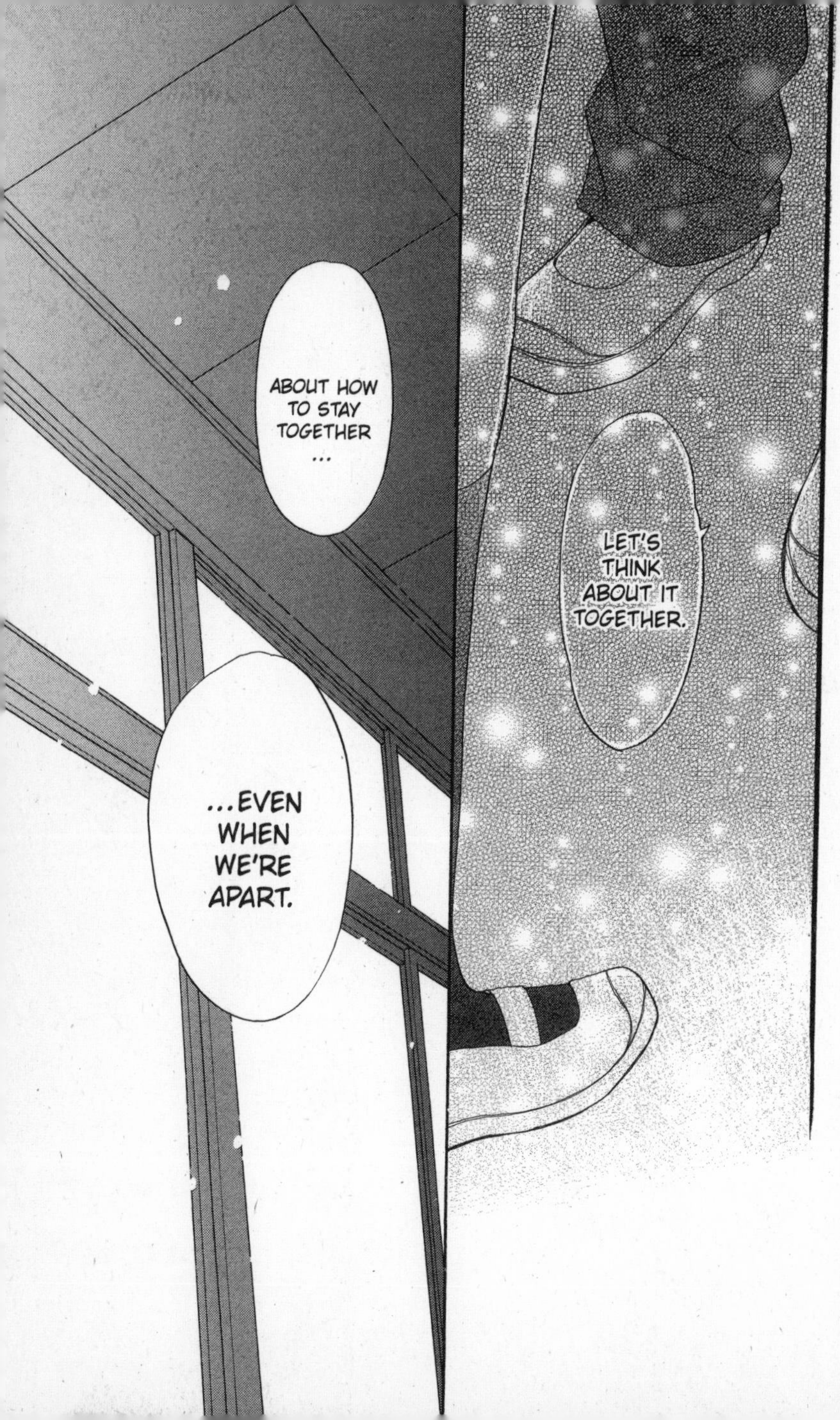
LET'S THINK ABOUT IT TOGETHER.
ABOUT HOW TO STAY TOGETHER ...
...EVEN WHEN WE'RE APART.

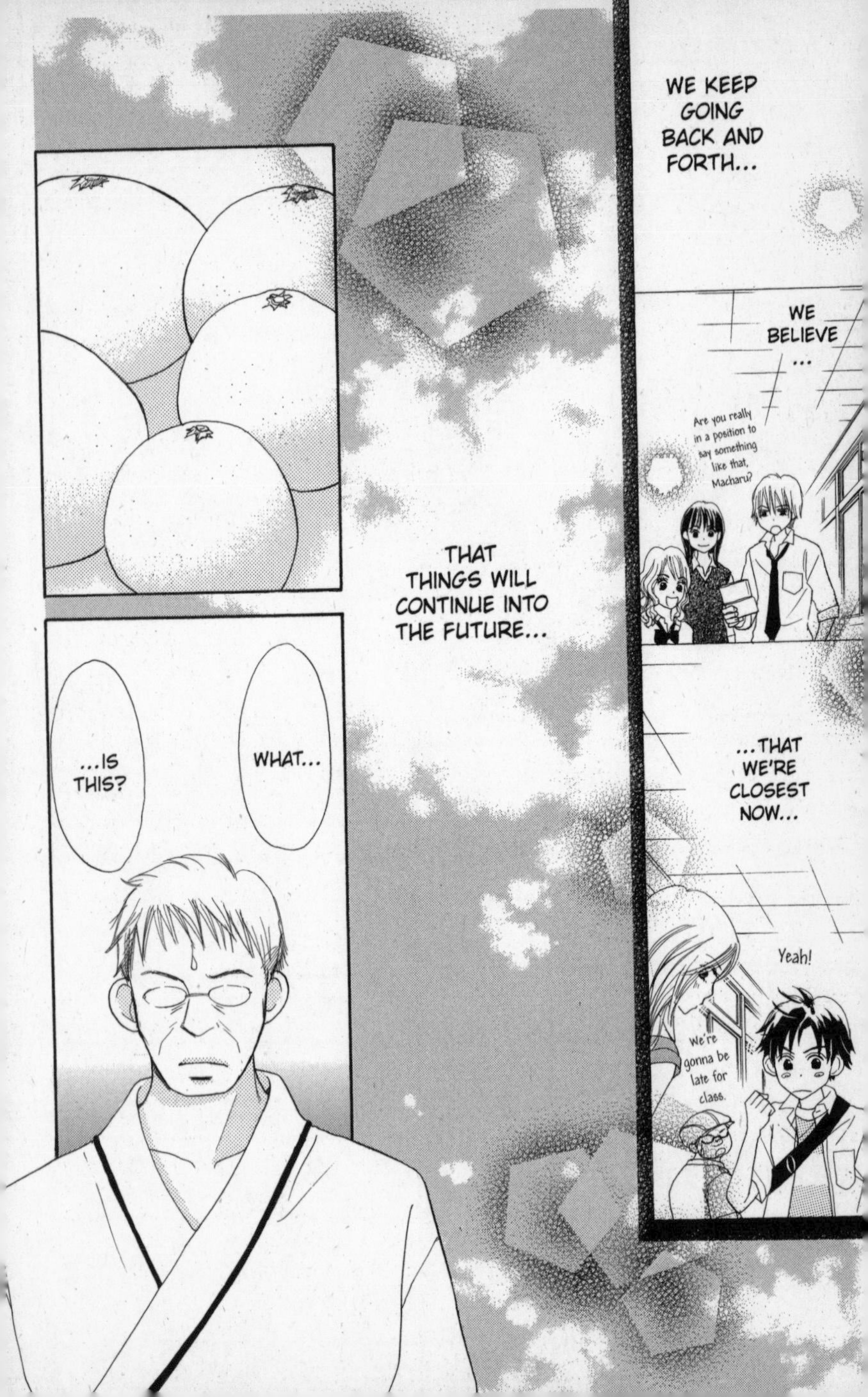
WE KEEP GOING BACK AND FORTH...
WE BELIEVE...
Are you really in a position to say something like that, Macharu?
...THAT WE'RE CLOSEST NOW...
Yeah!
We're gonna be late for class.
THAT THINGS WILL CONTINUE INTO THE FUTURE...
WHAT...
...IS THIS?

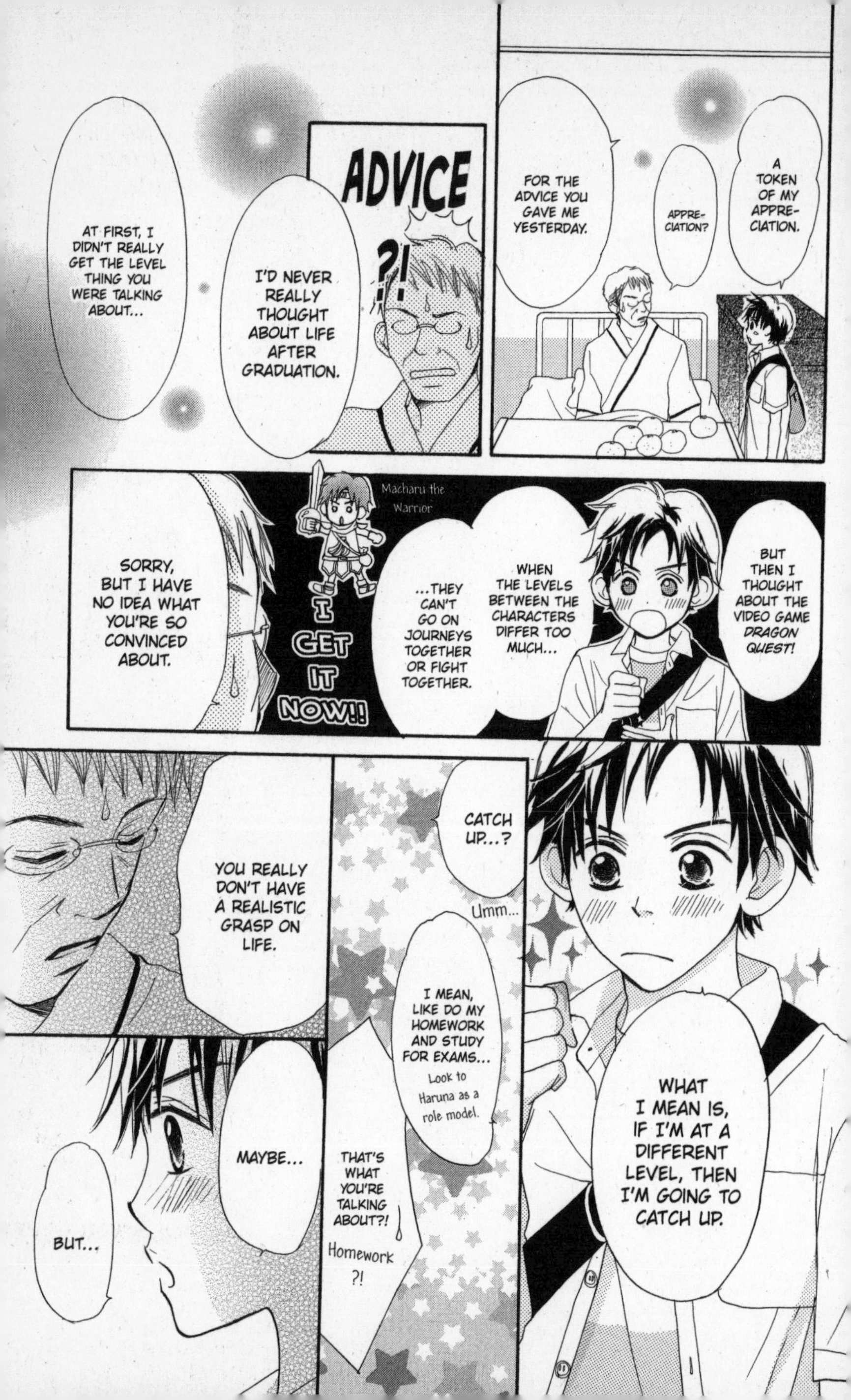
A TOKEN OF MY APPRECIATION.
APPRECIATION?
FOR THE ADVICE YOU GAVE ME YESTERDAY.
ADVICE
?!
I'D NEVER REALLY THOUGHT ABOUT LIFE AFTER GRADUATION.
AT FIRST, I DIDN'T REALLY GET THE LEVEL THING YOU WERE TALKING ABOUT...
BUT THEN I THOUGHT ABOUT THE VIDEO GAME DRAGON QUEST!
WHEN THE LEVELS BETWEEN THE CHARACTERS DIFFER TOO MUCH...
...THEY CAN'T GO ON JOURNEYS TOGETHER OR FIGHT TOGETHER.
Macharu the Warrior
I GET IT NOW!!
SORRY, BUT I HAVE NO IDEA WHAT YOU'RE SO CONVINCED ABOUT.
WHAT I MEAN IS, IF I'M AT A DIFFERENT LEVEL, THEN I'M GOING TO CATCH UP.
CATCH UP...?
Umm...
I MEAN, LIKE DO MY HOMEWORK AND STUDY FOR EXAMS...
Look to Haruna as a role model.
THAT'S WHAT YOU'RE TALKING ABOUT?!
Homework ?!
YOU REALLY DON'T HAVE A REALISTIC GRASP ON LIFE.
MAYBE...
BUT...

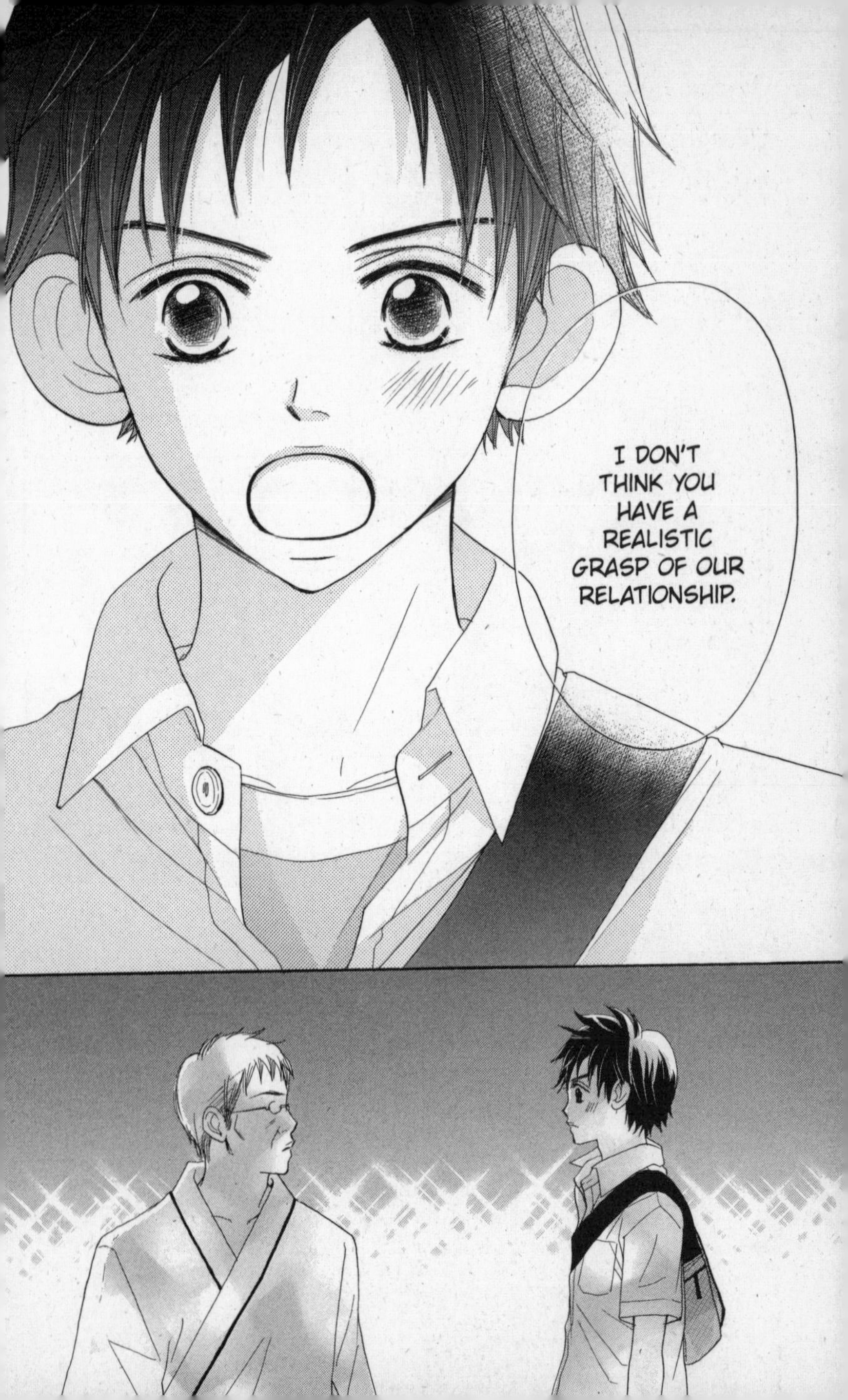
I DON'T THINK YOU HAVE A REALISTIC GRASP OF OUR RELATIONSHIP.

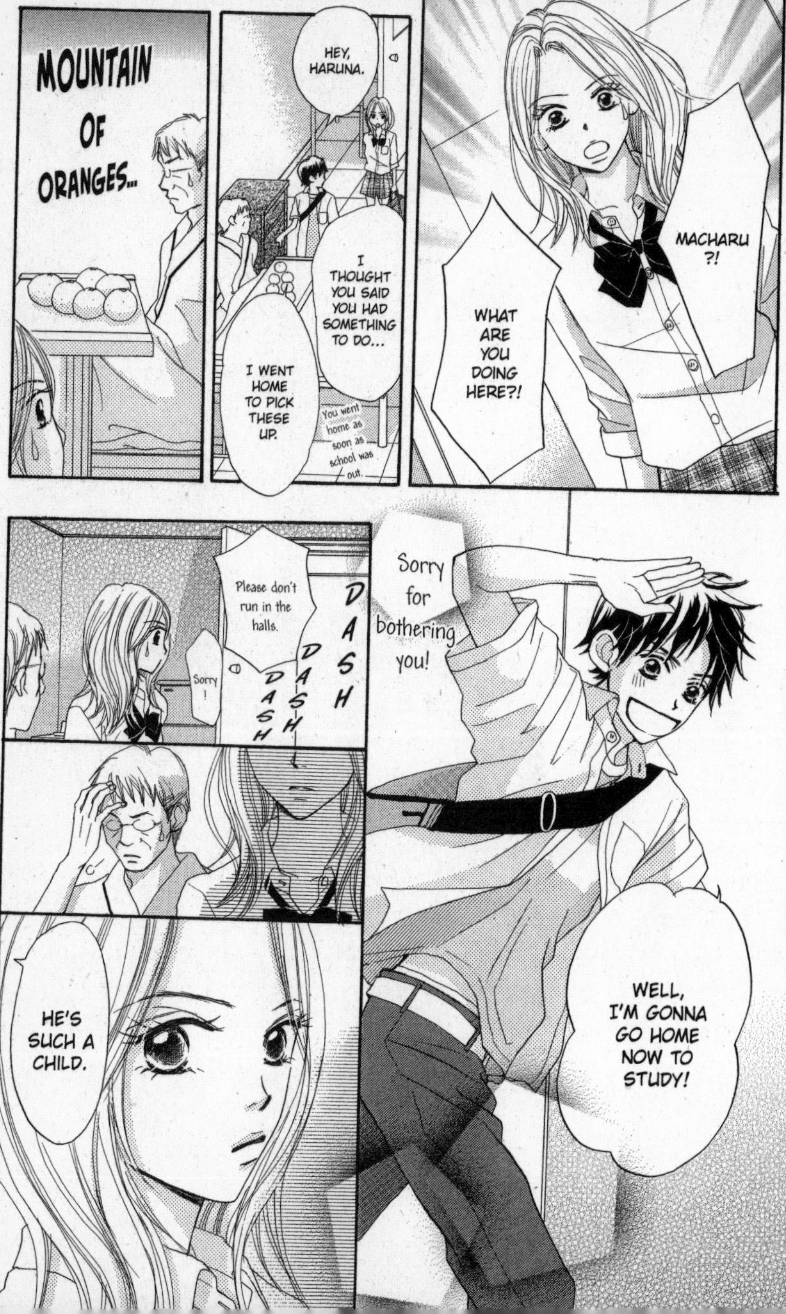
MACHARU ?!
WHAT ARE YOU DOING HERE?!
HEY, HARUNA.
I THOUGHT YOU SAID YOU HAD SOMETHING TO DO...
I WENT HOME TO PICK THESE UP.
You went home as soon as school was out.
MOUNTAIN OF ORANGES...
Sorry for bothering you!
WELL, I'M GONNA GO HOME NOW TO STUDY!
Please don't run in the halls.
DASH
DASH
DASH
Sorry!
HE'S SUCH A CHILD.

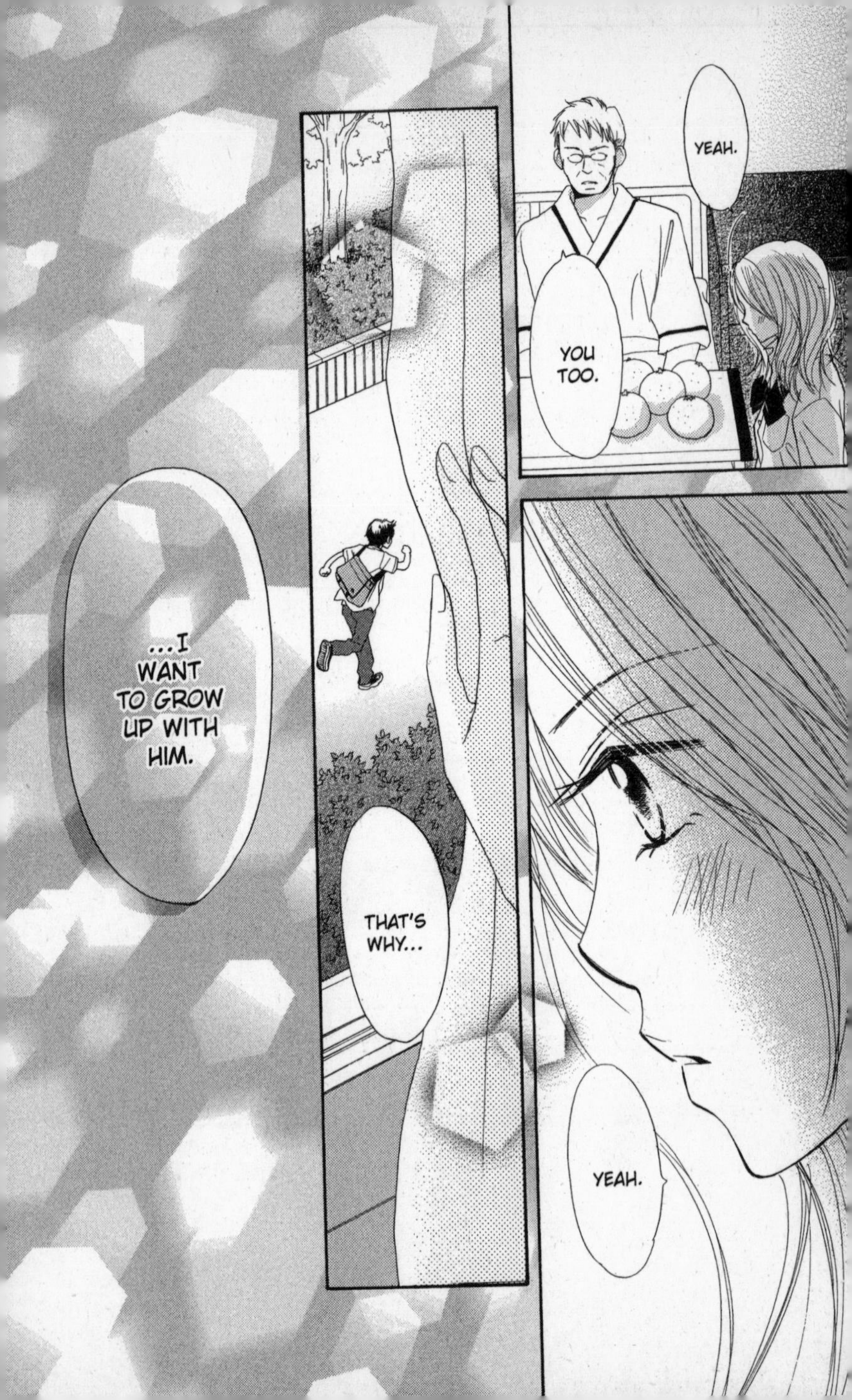
YEAH.
YOU TOO.
YEAH.
THAT'S WHY...
...I WANT TO GROW UP WITH HIM.

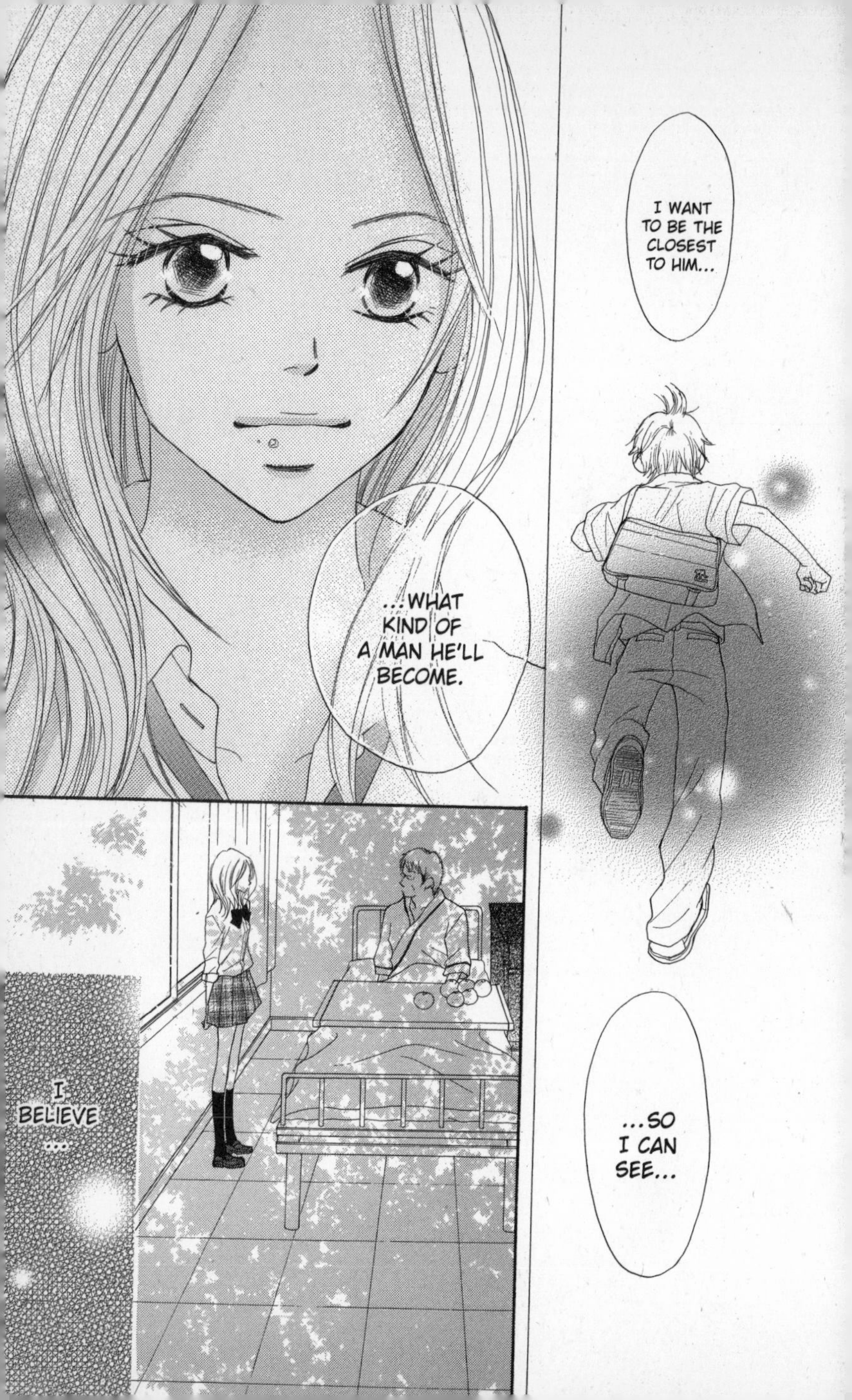
I WANT TO BE THE CLOSEST TO HIM...
...SO I CAN SEE...
...WHAT KIND OF A MAN HE'LL BECOME.
I BELIEVE ...

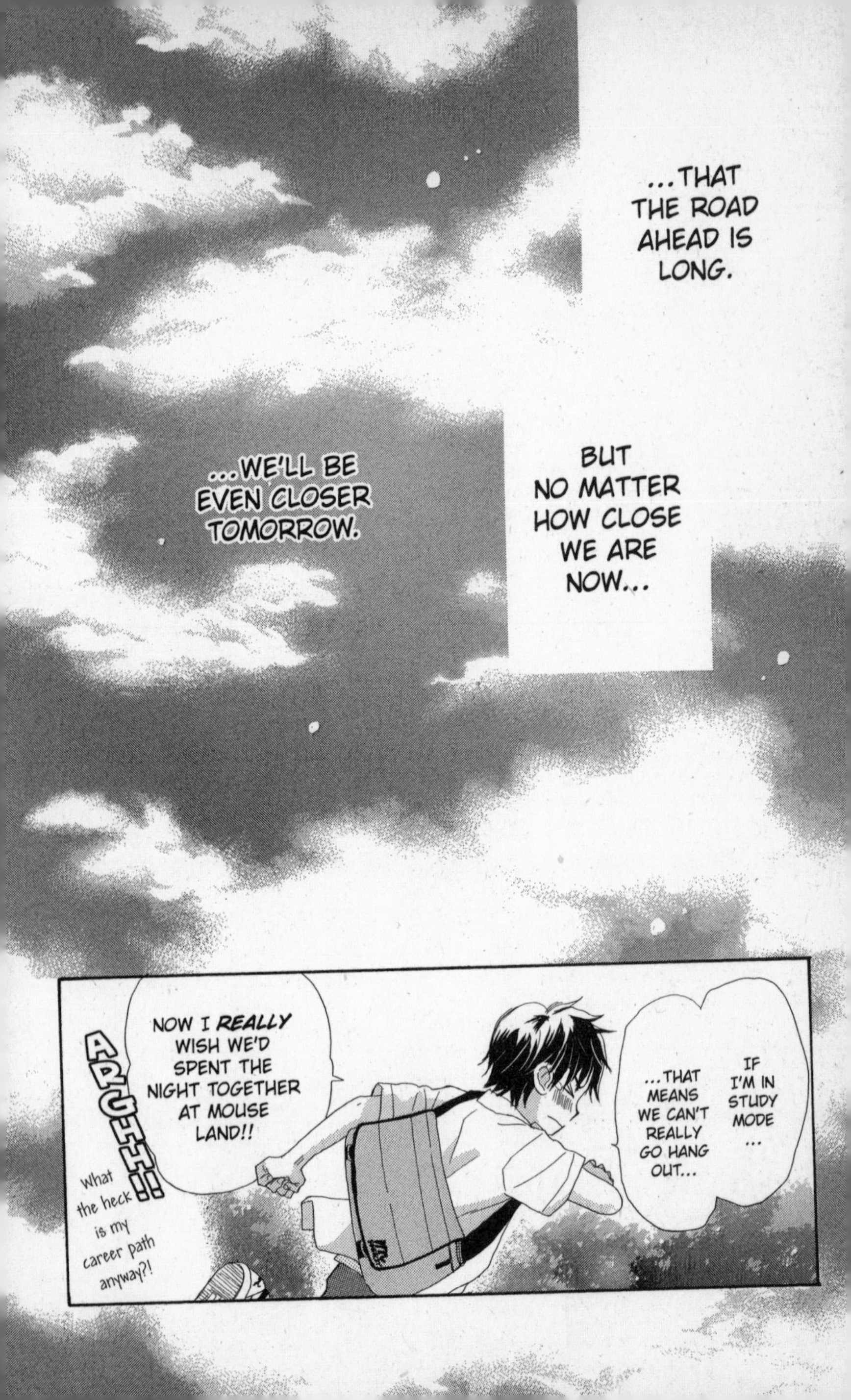
...THAT THE ROAD AHEAD IS LONG.
BUT NO MATTER HOW CLOSE WE ARE NOW...
...WE'LL BE EVEN CLOSER TOMORROW.
IF I'M IN STUDY MODE ...
...THAT MEANS WE CAN'T REALLY GO HANG OUT...
NOW I REALLY WISH WE'D SPENT THE NIGHT TOGETHER AT MOUSE LAND!!
ARGHH!!
What the heck is my career path anyway?!

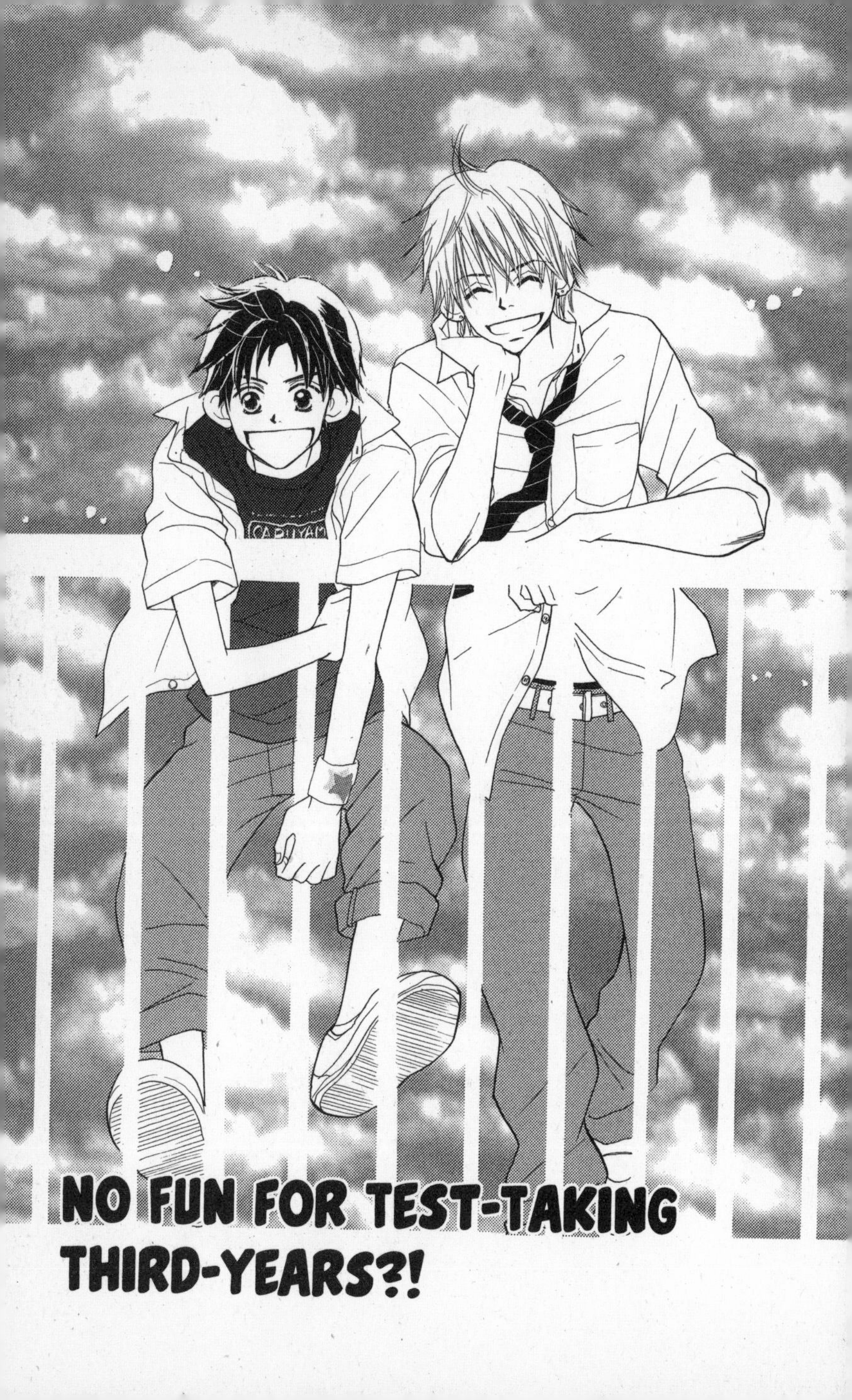
NO FUN FOR TEST-TAKING THIRD-YEARS?!

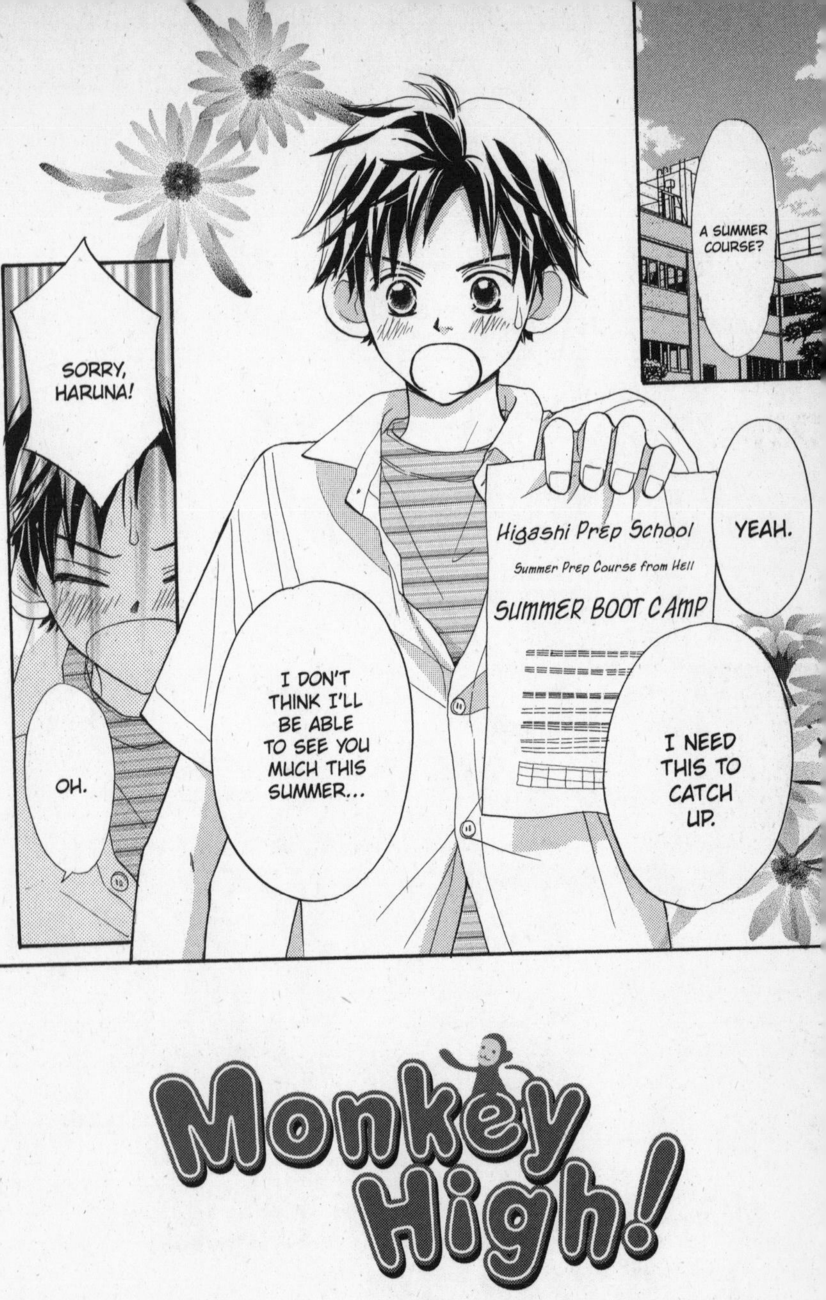
A SUMMER COURSE?
YEAH.
Higashi Prep School
Summer Prep Course from Hell
SUMMER BOOT CAMP
I NEED THIS TO CATCH UP.
I DON'T THINK I'LL BE ABLE TO SEE YOU MUCH THIS SUMMER...
SORRY, HARUNA!
OH.

Monkey High!

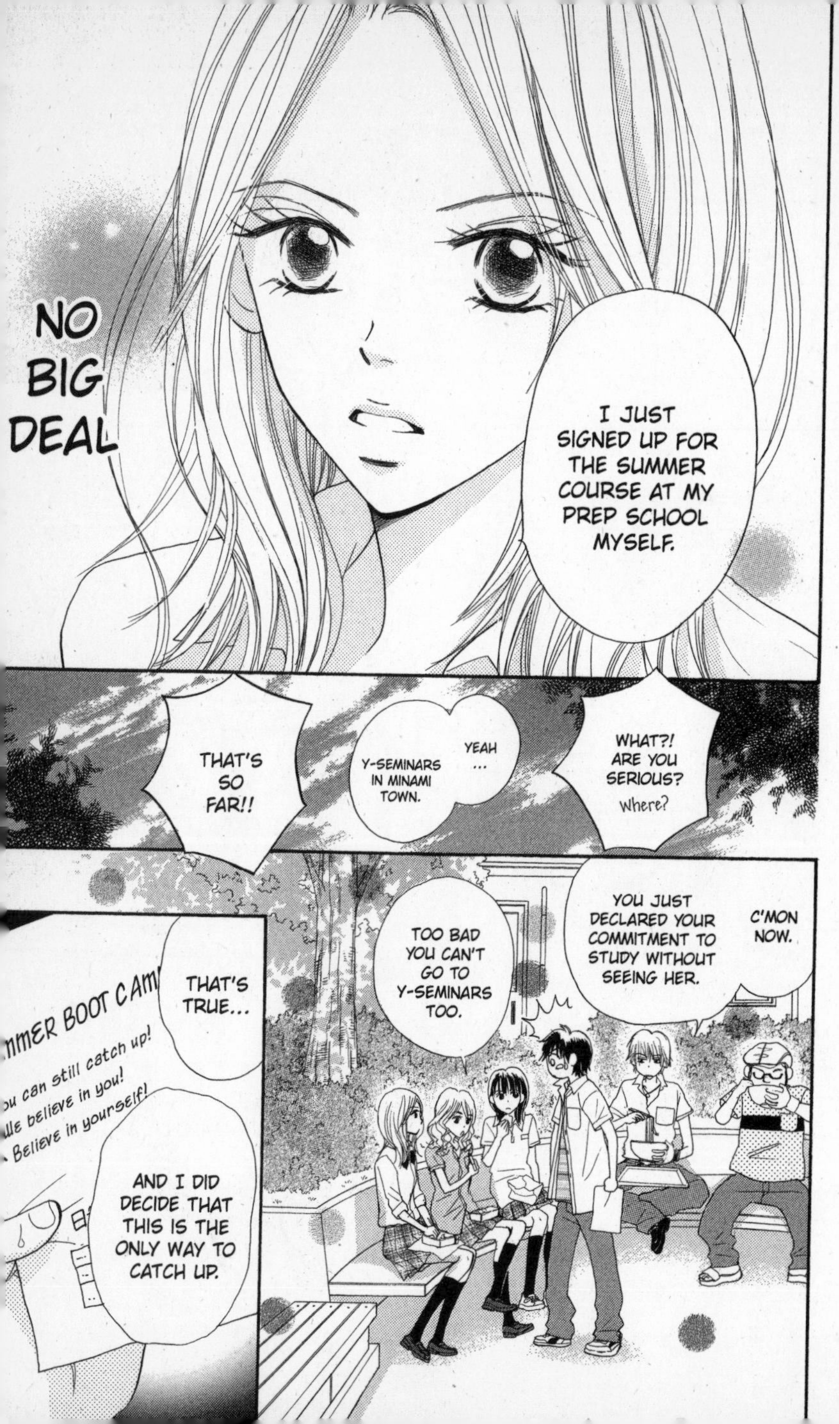

I JUST SIGNED UP FOR THE SUMMER COURSE AT MY PREP SCHOOL MYSELF.
NO BIG DEAL
WHAT?! ARE YOU SERIOUS?
Where?
YEAH ...
Y-SEMINARS IN MINAMI TOWN.
THAT'S SO FAR!!
C'MON NOW.
YOU JUST DECLARED YOUR COMMITMENT TO STUDY WITHOUT SEEING HER.
TOO BAD YOU CAN'T GO TO Y-SEMINARS TOO.
THAT'S TRUE...
mmER BOOT CAM
ou can still catch up!
We believe in you!
Believe in yourself!
AND I DID DECIDE THAT THIS IS THE ONLY WAY TO CATCH UP.

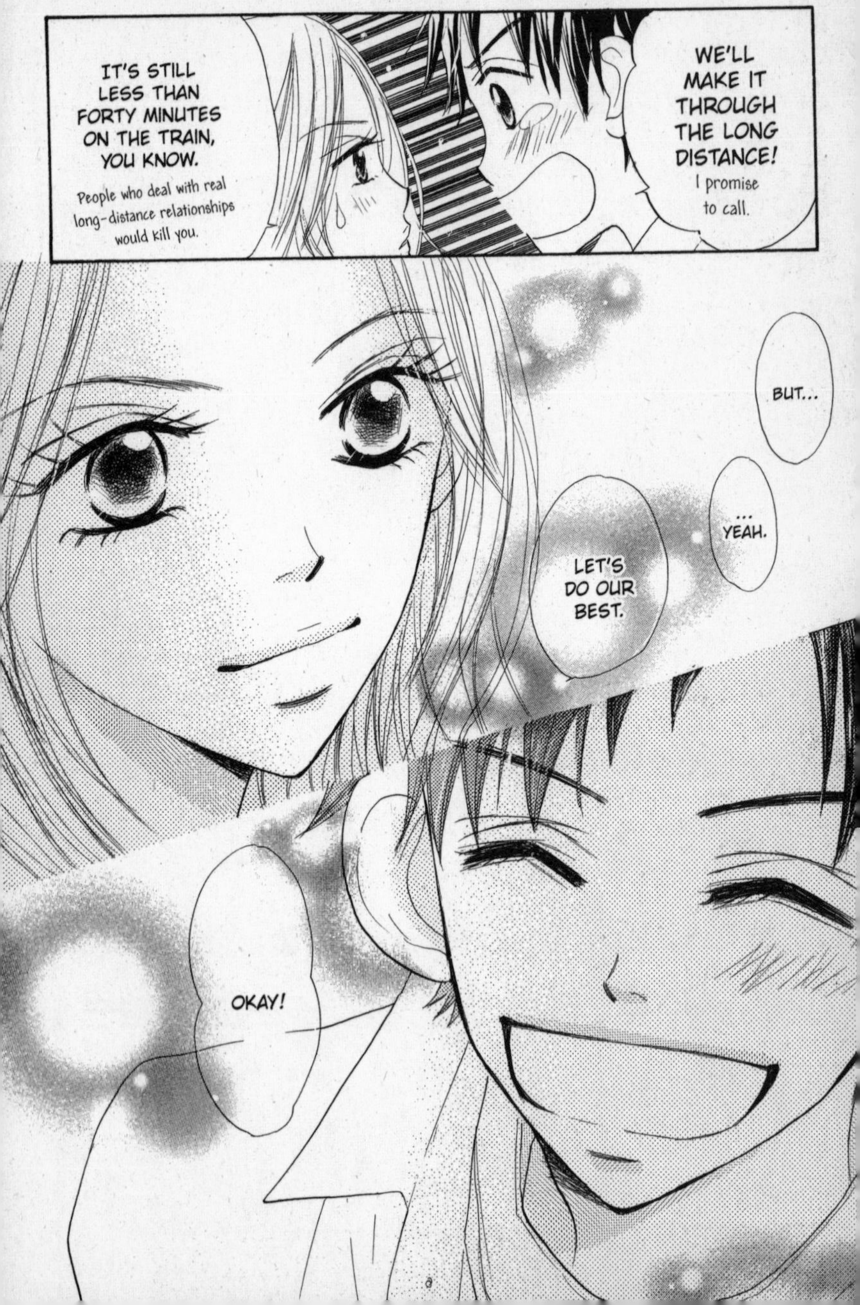

WE'LL MAKE IT THROUGH THE LONG DISTANCE!
I promise to call.
IT'S STILL LESS THAN FORTY MINUTES ON THE TRAIN, YOU KNOW.
People who deal with real long-distance relationships would kill you.
BUT...
...YEAH.
LET'S DO OUR BEST.
OKAY!

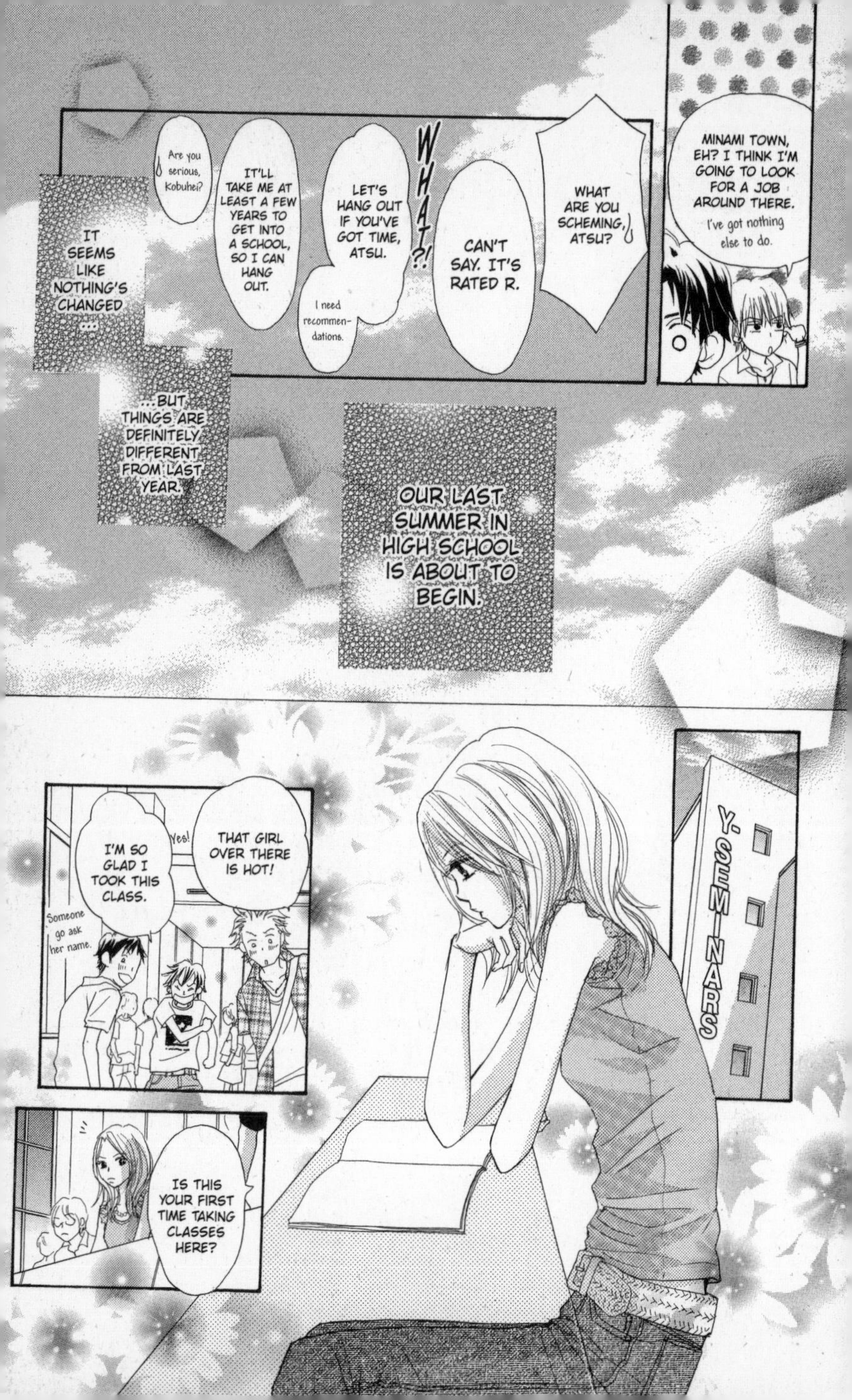
MINAMI TOWN, EH? I THINK I'M GOING TO LOOK FOR A JOB AROUND THERE.
I've got nothing else to do.
WHAT ARE YOU SCHEMING, ATSU?
CAN'T SAY. IT'S RATED R.
WHAT?!
LET'S HANG OUT IF YOU'VE GOT TIME, ATSU.
I need recommendations.
IT'LL TAKE ME AT LEAST A FEW YEARS TO GET INTO A SCHOOL, SO I CAN HANG OUT.
Are you serious, Kobuhei?
IT SEEMS LIKE NOTHING'S CHANGED...
...BUT THINGS ARE DEFINITELY DIFFERENT FROM LAST YEAR.
OUR LAST SUMMER IN HIGH SCHOOL IS ABOUT TO BEGIN.
Y-SEMINARS
THAT GIRL OVER THERE IS HOT!
Yes!
I'M SO GLAD I TOOK THIS CLASS.
Someone go ask her name.
IS THIS YOUR FIRST TIME TAKING CLASSES HERE?

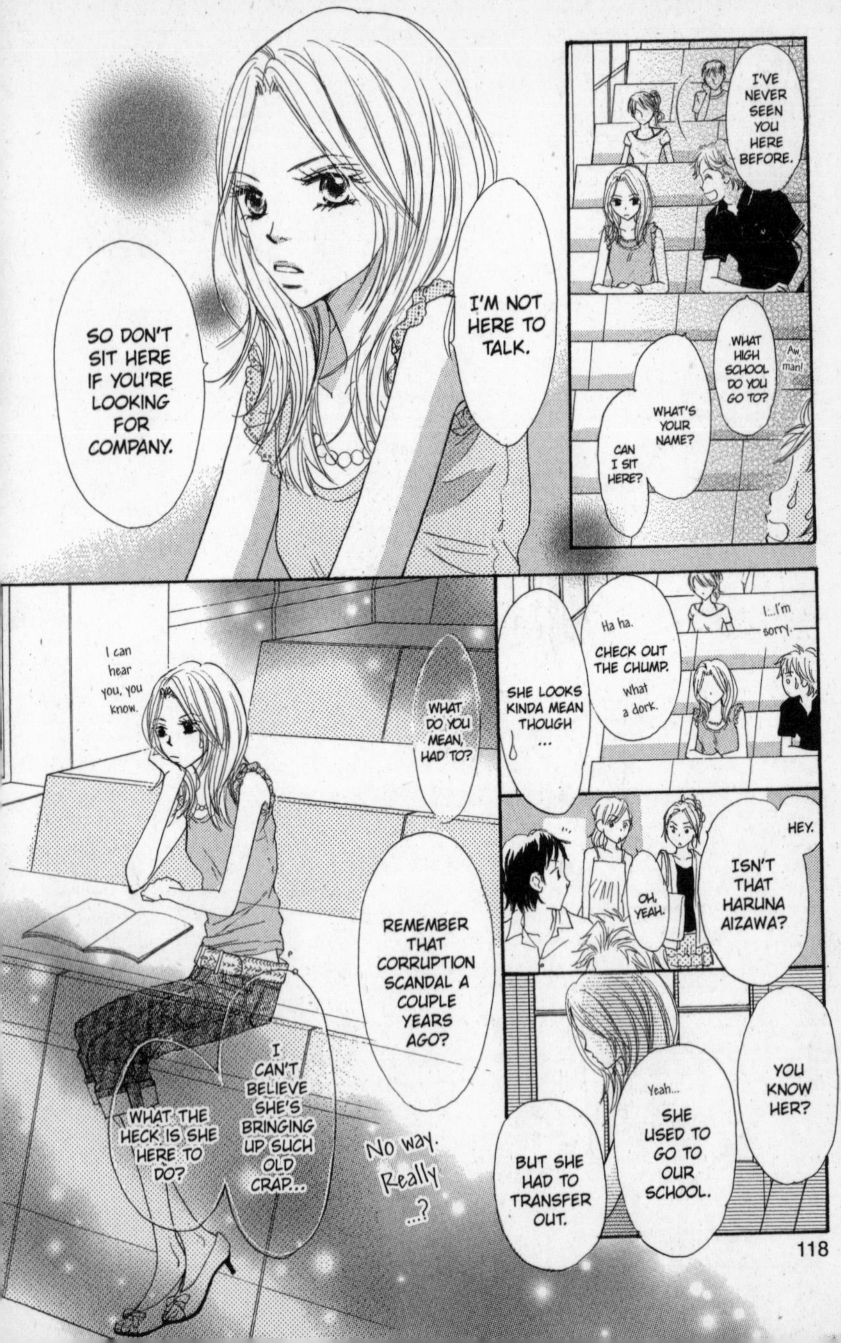
I'VE NEVER SEEN YOU HERE BEFORE.
WHAT HIGH SCHOOL DO YOU GO TO?
Aw, man!
WHAT'S YOUR NAME?
CAN I SIT HERE?
I'M NOT HERE TO TALK.
SO DON'T SIT HERE IF YOU'RE LOOKING FOR COMPANY.
I...I'm sorry.
Ha ha.
CHECK OUT THE CHUMP.
What a dork.
SHE LOOKS KINDA MEAN THOUGH ...
HEY.
ISN'T THAT HARUNA AIZAWA?
...
OH, YEAH.
YOU KNOW HER?
Yeah...
SHE USED TO GO TO OUR SCHOOL.
BUT SHE HAD TO TRANSFER OUT.
WHAT DO YOU MEAN, HAD TO?
REMEMBER THAT CORRUPTION SCANDAL A COUPLE YEARS AGO?
No way. Really ...?
I CAN'T BELIEVE SHE'S BRINGING UP SUCH OLD CRAP...
WHAT THE HECK IS SHE HERE TO DO?
I can hear you, you know.

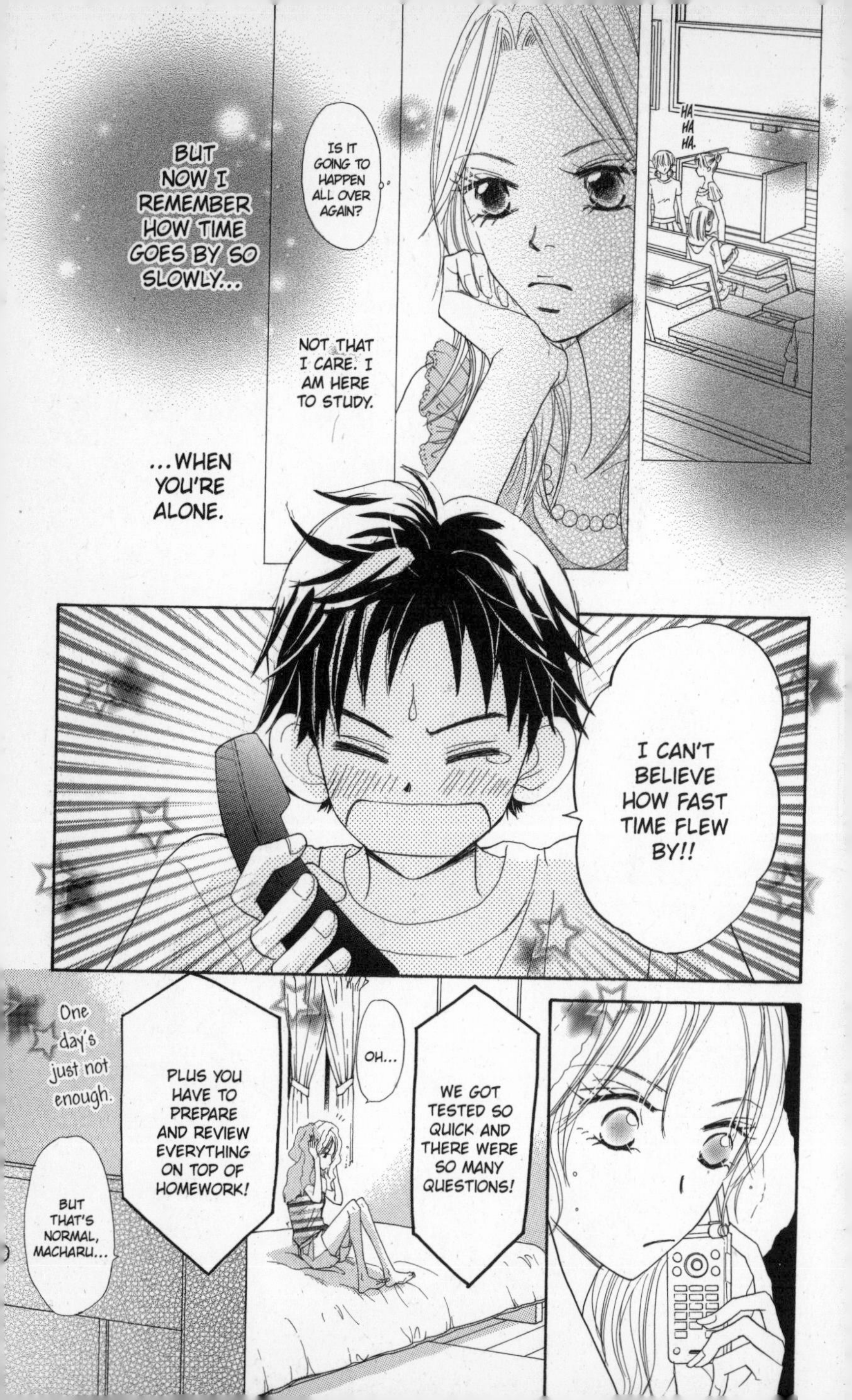
HA HA HA.
IS IT GOING TO HAPPEN ALL OVER AGAIN?
NOT THAT I CARE. I AM HERE TO STUDY.
BUT NOW I REMEMBER HOW TIME GOES BY SO SLOWLY...
...WHEN YOU'RE ALONE.
I CAN'T BELIEVE HOW FAST TIME FLEW BY!!
WE GOT TESTED SO QUICK AND THERE WERE SO MANY QUESTIONS!
OH...
PLUS YOU HAVE TO PREPARE AND REVIEW EVERYTHING ON TOP OF HOMEWORK!
One day's just not enough.
BUT THAT'S NORMAL, MACHARU...

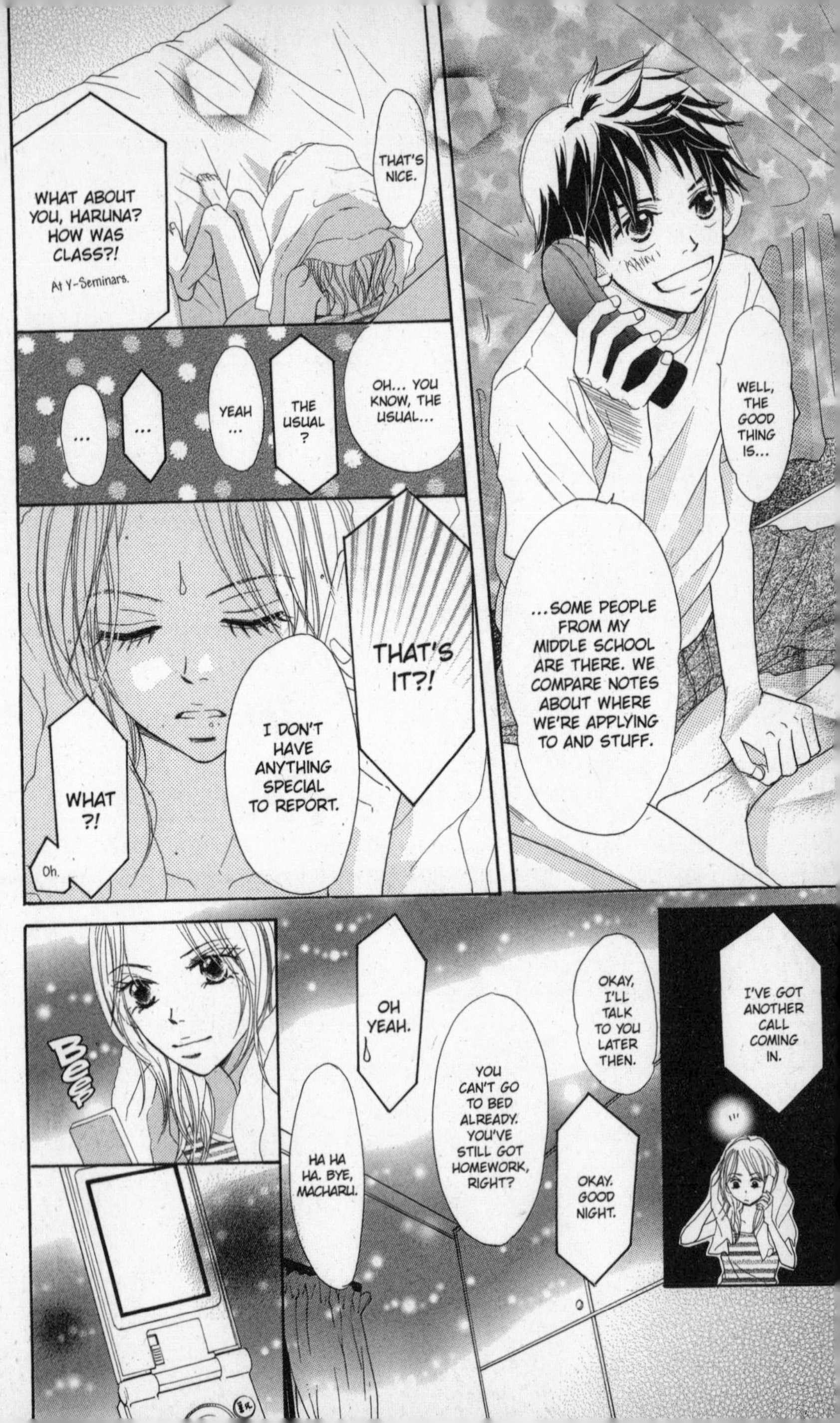

WELL, THE GOOD THING IS...
...SOME PEOPLE FROM MY MIDDLE SCHOOL ARE THERE. WE COMPARE NOTES ABOUT WHERE WE'RE APPLYING TO AND STUFF.
THAT'S NICE.
WHAT ABOUT YOU, HARUNA? HOW WAS CLASS?!
At Y-Seminars.
OH... YOU KNOW, THE USUAL...
THE USUAL ?
YEAH ...
...
...
THAT'S IT?!
I DON'T HAVE ANYTHING SPECIAL TO REPORT.
WHAT ?!
Oh.
I'VE GOT ANOTHER CALL COMING IN.
OKAY, I'LL TALK TO YOU LATER THEN.
OKAY. GOOD NIGHT.
YOU CAN'T GO TO BED ALREADY. YOU'VE STILL GOT HOMEWORK, RIGHT?
OH YEAH.
HA HA HA. BYE, MACHARU.
Beep

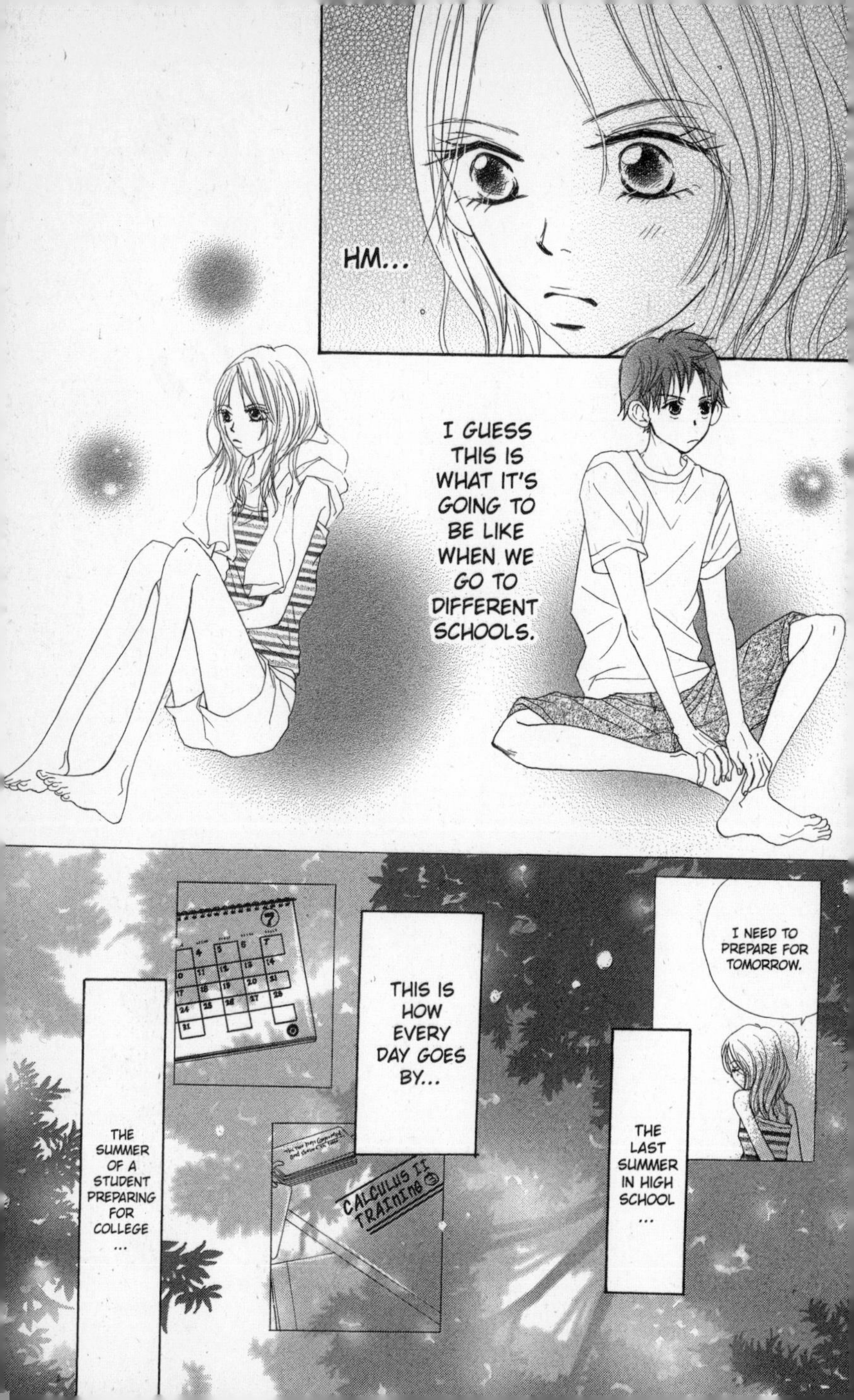
HM...
I GUESS THIS IS WHAT IT'S GOING TO BE LIKE WHEN WE GO TO DIFFERENT SCHOOLS.
I NEED TO PREPARE FOR TOMORROW.
THE LAST SUMMER IN HIGH SCHOOL ...
THIS IS HOW EVERY DAY GOES BY...
CALCULUS II TRAINING
THE SUMMER OF A STUDENT PREPARING FOR COLLEGE ...

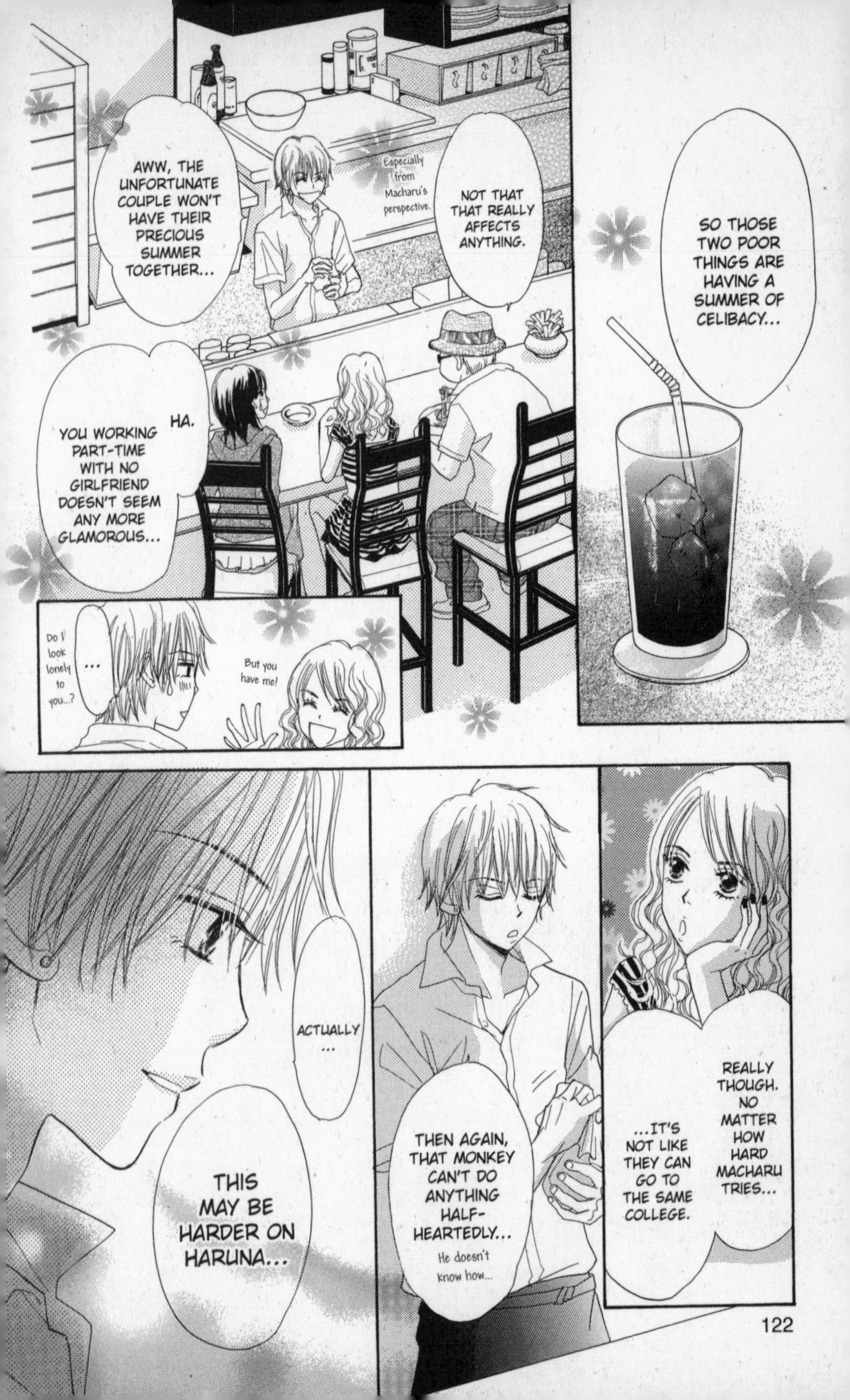

SO THOSE TWO POOR THINGS ARE HAVING A SUMMER OF CELIBACY...
AWW, THE UNFORTUNATE COUPLE WON'T HAVE THEIR PRECIOUS SUMMER TOGETHER...
NOT THAT THAT REALLY AFFECTS ANYTHING.
Especially from Macharu's perspective.
HA.
YOU WORKING PART-TIME WITH NO GIRLFRIEND DOESN'T SEEM ANY MORE GLAMOROUS...
But you have me!
...
Do I look lonely to you...?
REALLY THOUGH. NO MATTER HOW HARD MACHARU TRIES...
...IT'S NOT LIKE THEY CAN GO TO THE SAME COLLEGE.
THEN AGAIN, THAT MONKEY CAN'T DO ANYTHING HALF-HEARTEDLY...
He doesn't know how...
ACTUALLY...
THIS MAY BE HARDER ON HARUNA...

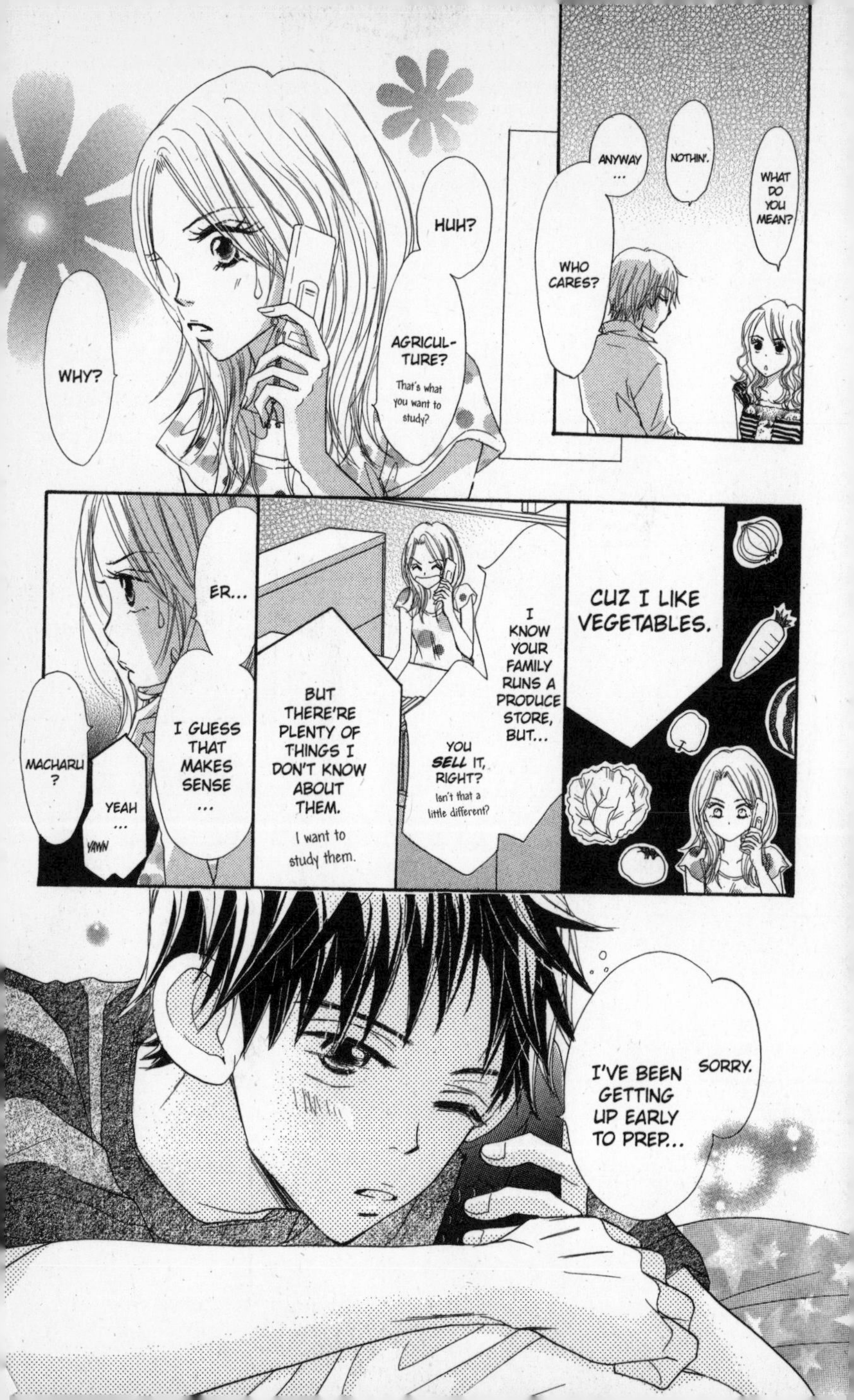
WHAT DO YOU MEAN?
NOTHIN'.
ANYWAY...
WHO CARES?
HUH?
AGRICUL-TURE?
That's what you want to study?
WHY?
CUZ I LIKE VEGETABLES.
I KNOW YOUR FAMILY RUNS A PRODUCE STORE, BUT...
YOU SELL IT, RIGHT?
Isn't that a little different?
BUT THERE'RE PLENTY OF THINGS I DON'T KNOW ABOUT THEM.
I want to study them.
ER...
I GUESS THAT MAKES SENSE...
MACHARU?
YEAH...
YAWN
SORRY.
I'VE BEEN GETTING UP EARLY TO PREP...

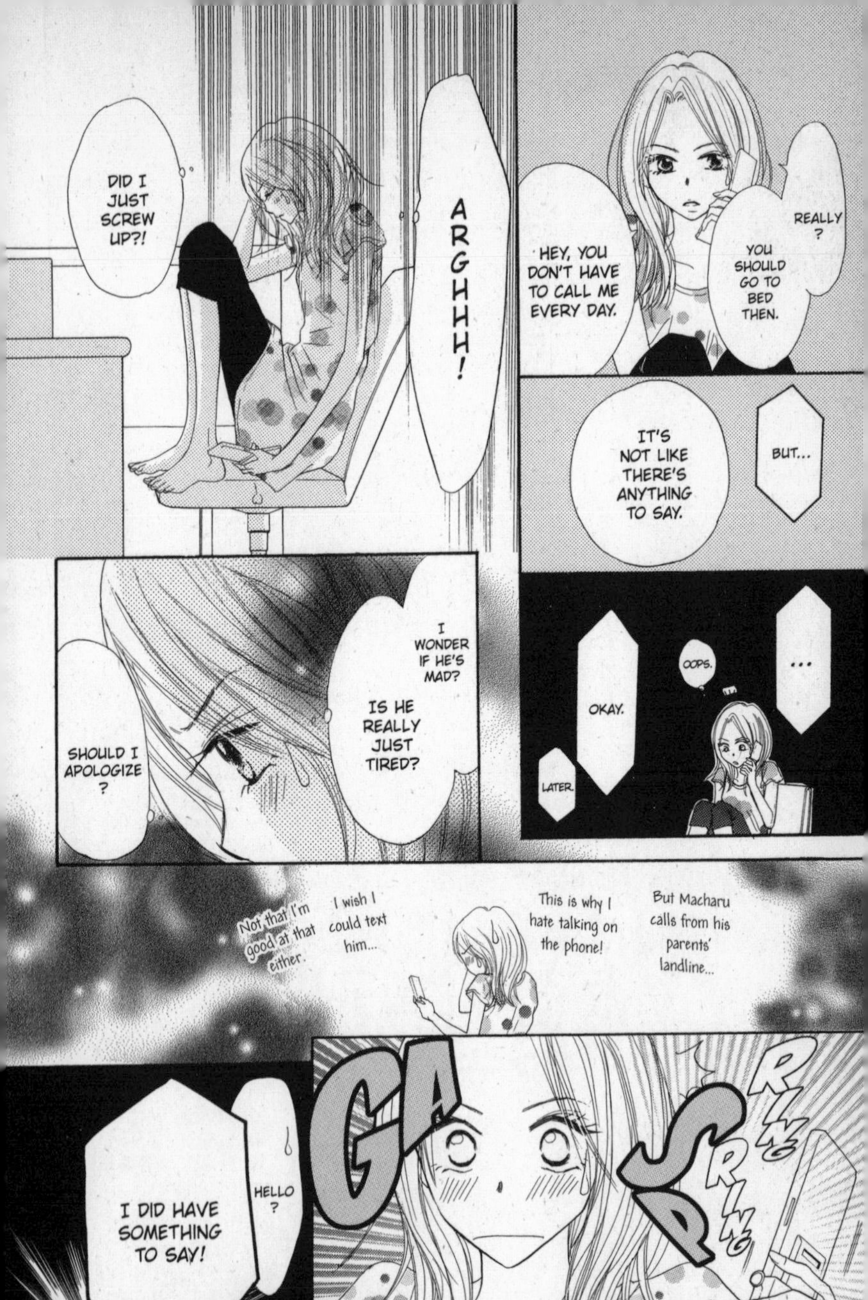
REALLY?
YOU SHOULD GO TO BED THEN.
HEY, YOU DON'T HAVE TO CALL ME EVERY DAY.
BUT...
IT'S NOT LIKE THERE'S ANYTHING TO SAY.
ARGHHH!
DID I JUST SCREW UP?!
...
OOPS.
OKAY.
LATER.
I WONDER IF HE'S MAD?
IS HE REALLY JUST TIRED?
SHOULD I APOLOGIZE?
But Macharu calls from his parents' landline...
This is why I hate talking on the phone!
I wish I could text him...
Not that I'm good at that either.
RING RING
GASP
HELLO?
I DID HAVE SOMETHING TO SAY!

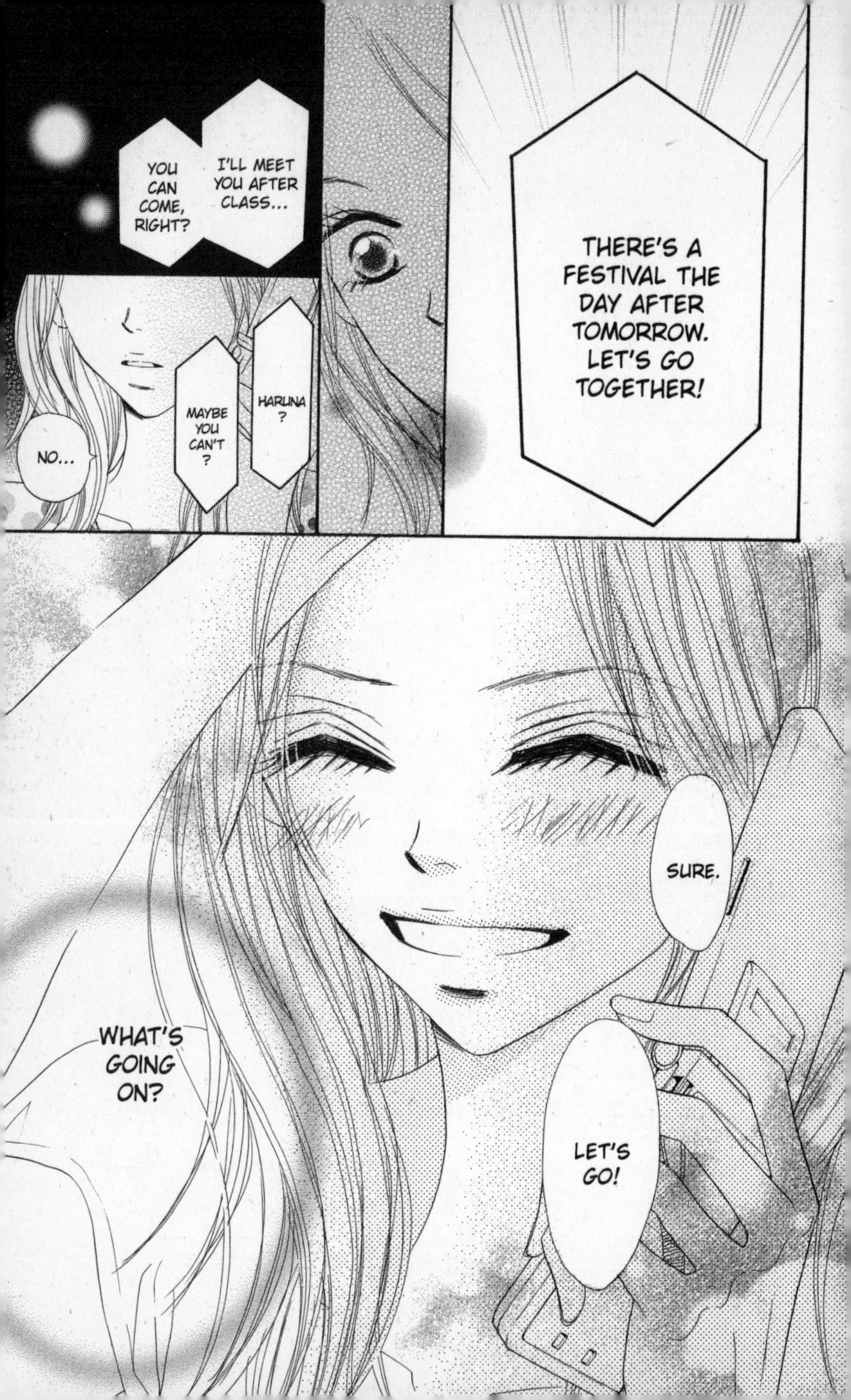
THERE'S A FESTIVAL THE DAY AFTER TOMORROW. LET'S GO TOGETHER!
I'LL MEET YOU AFTER CLASS...
YOU CAN COME, RIGHT?
HARUNA?
MAYBE YOU CAN'T?
NO...
SURE.
LET'S GO!
WHAT'S GOING ON?

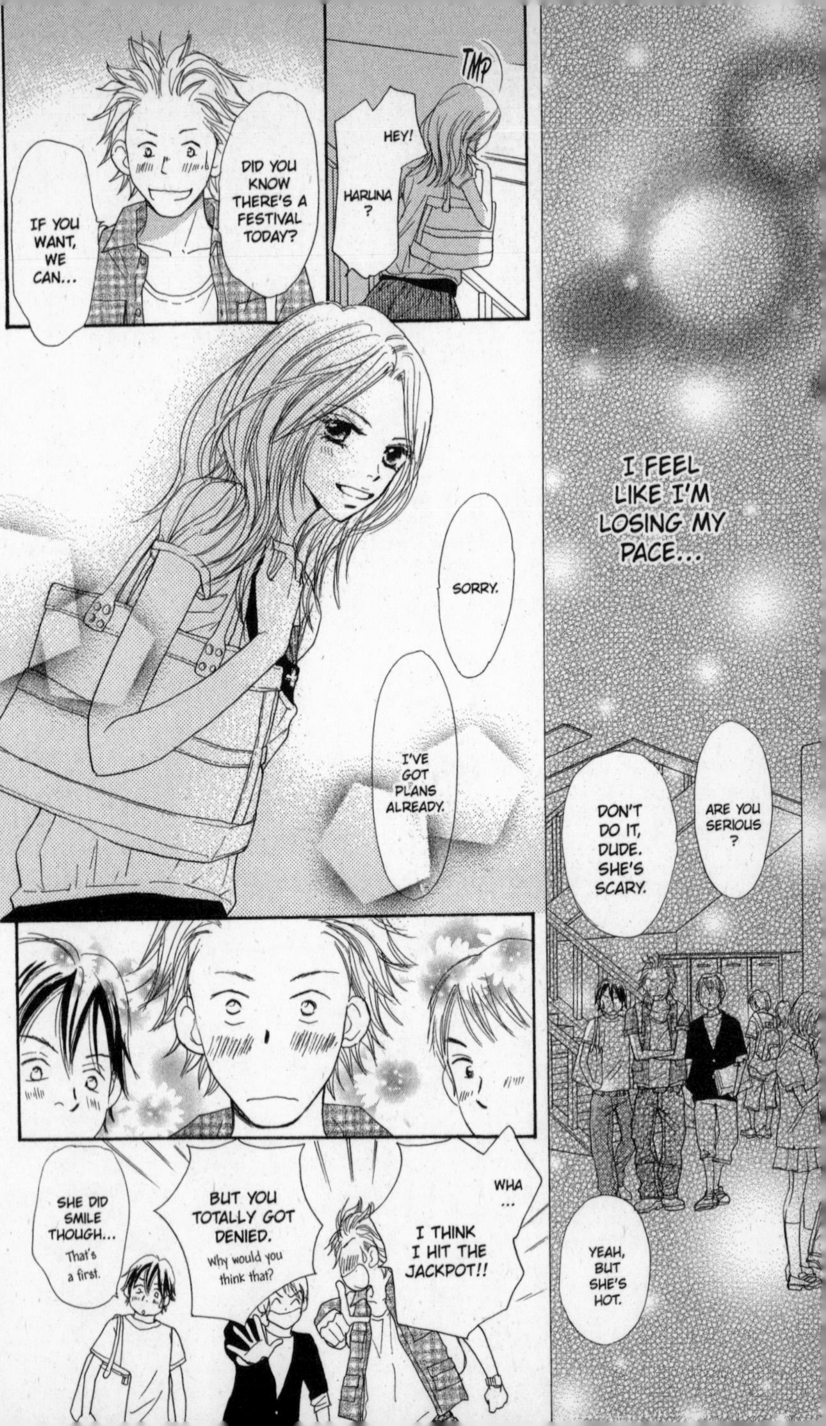
I FEEL LIKE I'M LOSING MY PACE...
ARE YOU SERIOUS?
DON'T DO IT, DUDE. SHE'S SCARY.
YEAH, BUT SHE'S HOT.
TMP
HEY!
HARUNA?
DID YOU KNOW THERE'S A FESTIVAL TODAY?
IF YOU WANT, WE CAN...
SORRY.
I'VE GOT PLANS ALREADY.
WHA...
I THINK I HIT THE JACKPOT!!
BUT YOU TOTALLY GOT DENIED.
Why would you think that?
SHE DID SMILE THOUGH...
That's a first.

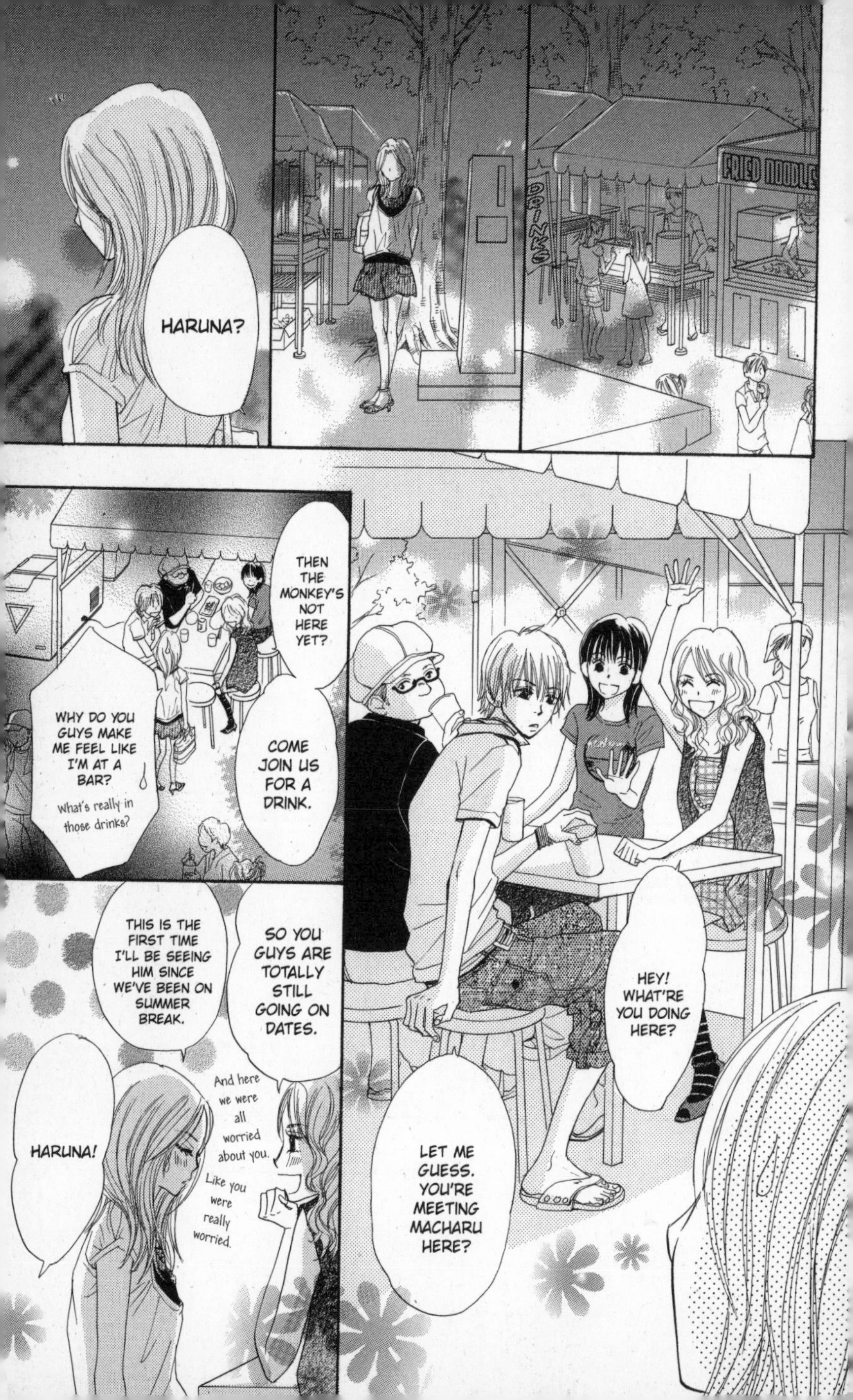
FRIED NOODLES
DRINKS
HARUNA?
HEY! WHAT'RE YOU DOING HERE?
LET ME GUESS. YOU'RE MEETING MACHARU HERE?
THEN THE MONKEY'S NOT HERE YET?
COME JOIN US FOR A DRINK.
WHY DO YOU GUYS MAKE ME FEEL LIKE I'M AT A BAR?
What's really in those drinks?
SO YOU GUYS ARE TOTALLY STILL GOING ON DATES.
THIS IS THE FIRST TIME I'LL BE SEEING HIM SINCE WE'VE BEEN ON SUMMER BREAK.
And here we were all worried about you.
Like you were really worried.
HARUNA!

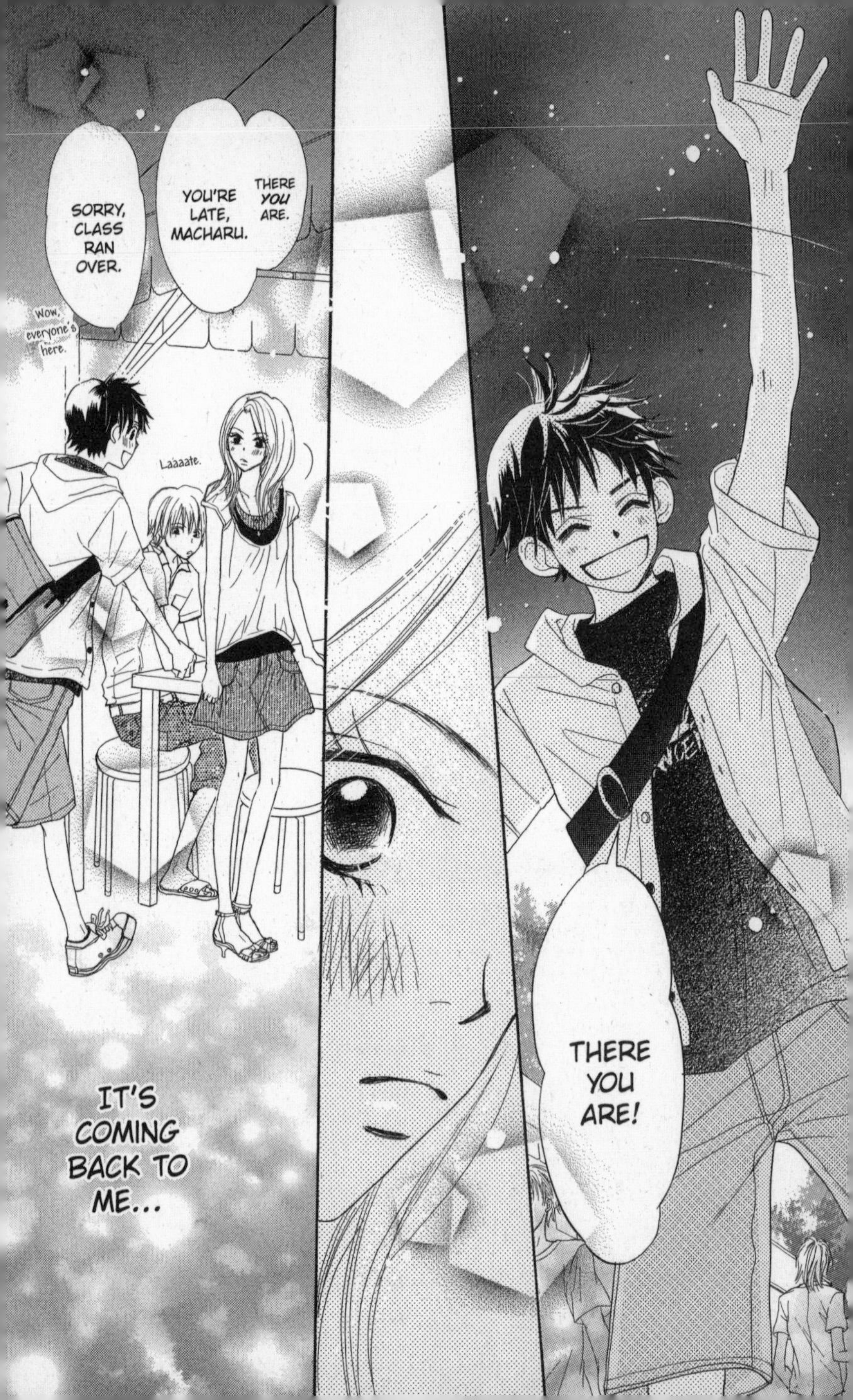
THERE YOU ARE!
THERE YOU ARE.
YOU'RE LATE, MACHARU.
SORRY, CLASS RAN OVER.
Wow, everyone's here.
Laaaate.
IT'S COMING BACK TO ME...

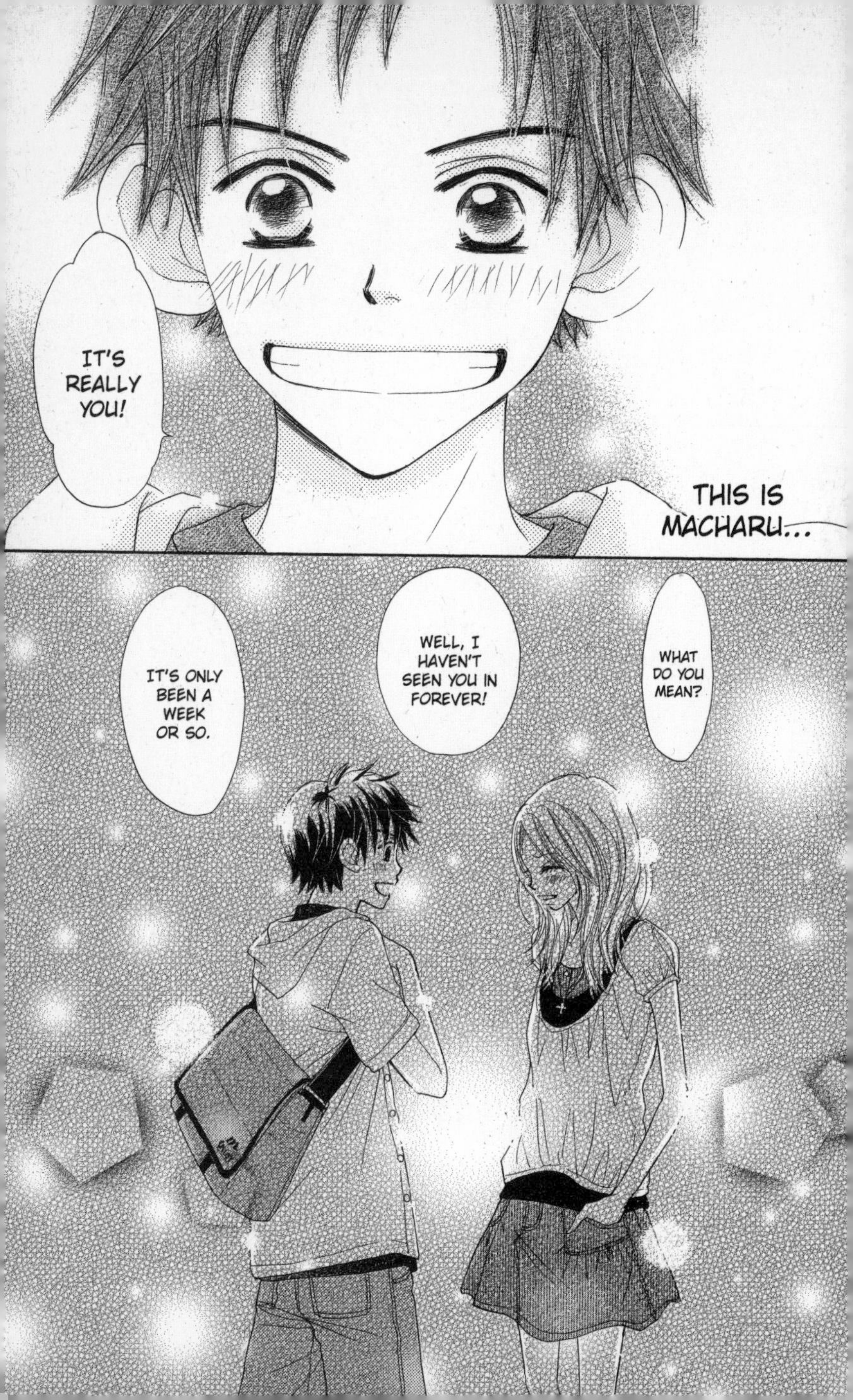
IT'S REALLY YOU!
THIS IS MACHARU...
WHAT DO YOU MEAN?
WELL, I HAVEN'T SEEN YOU IN FOREVER!
IT'S ONLY BEEN A WEEK OR SO.

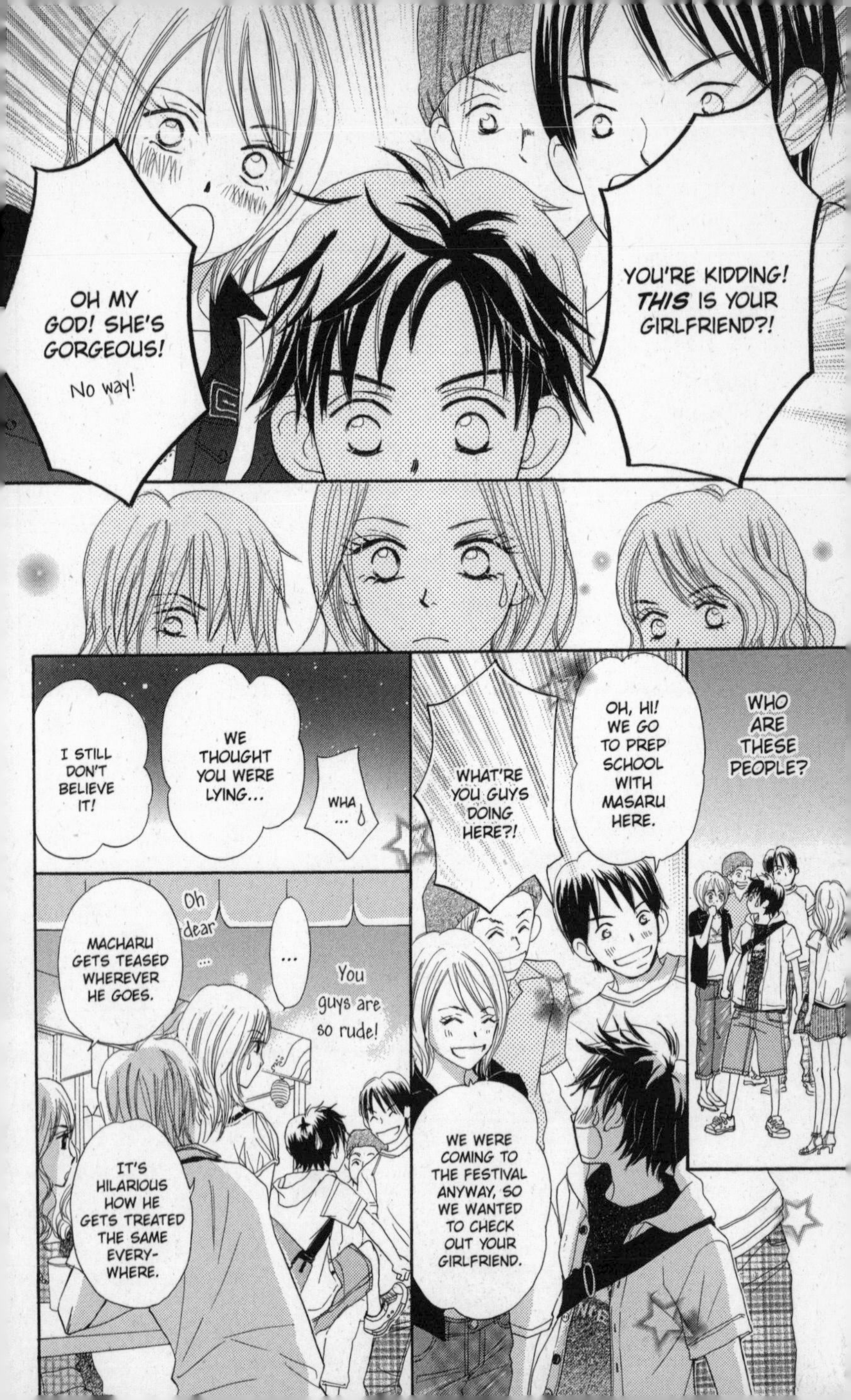
YOU'RE KIDDING! *THIS* IS YOUR GIRLFRIEND?!
OH MY GOD! SHE'S GORGEOUS!
No way!
WHO ARE THESE PEOPLE?
OH, HI! WE GO TO PREP SCHOOL WITH MASARU HERE.
WHAT'RE YOU GUYS DOING HERE?!
WE WERE COMING TO THE FESTIVAL ANYWAY, SO WE WANTED TO CHECK OUT YOUR GIRLFRIEND.
WHA ...
WE THOUGHT YOU WERE LYING...
I STILL DON'T BELIEVE IT!
...
Oh dear ...
You guys are so rude!
MACHARU GETS TEASED WHEREVER HE GOES.
IT'S HILARIOUS HOW HE GETS TREATED THE SAME EVERY-WHERE.

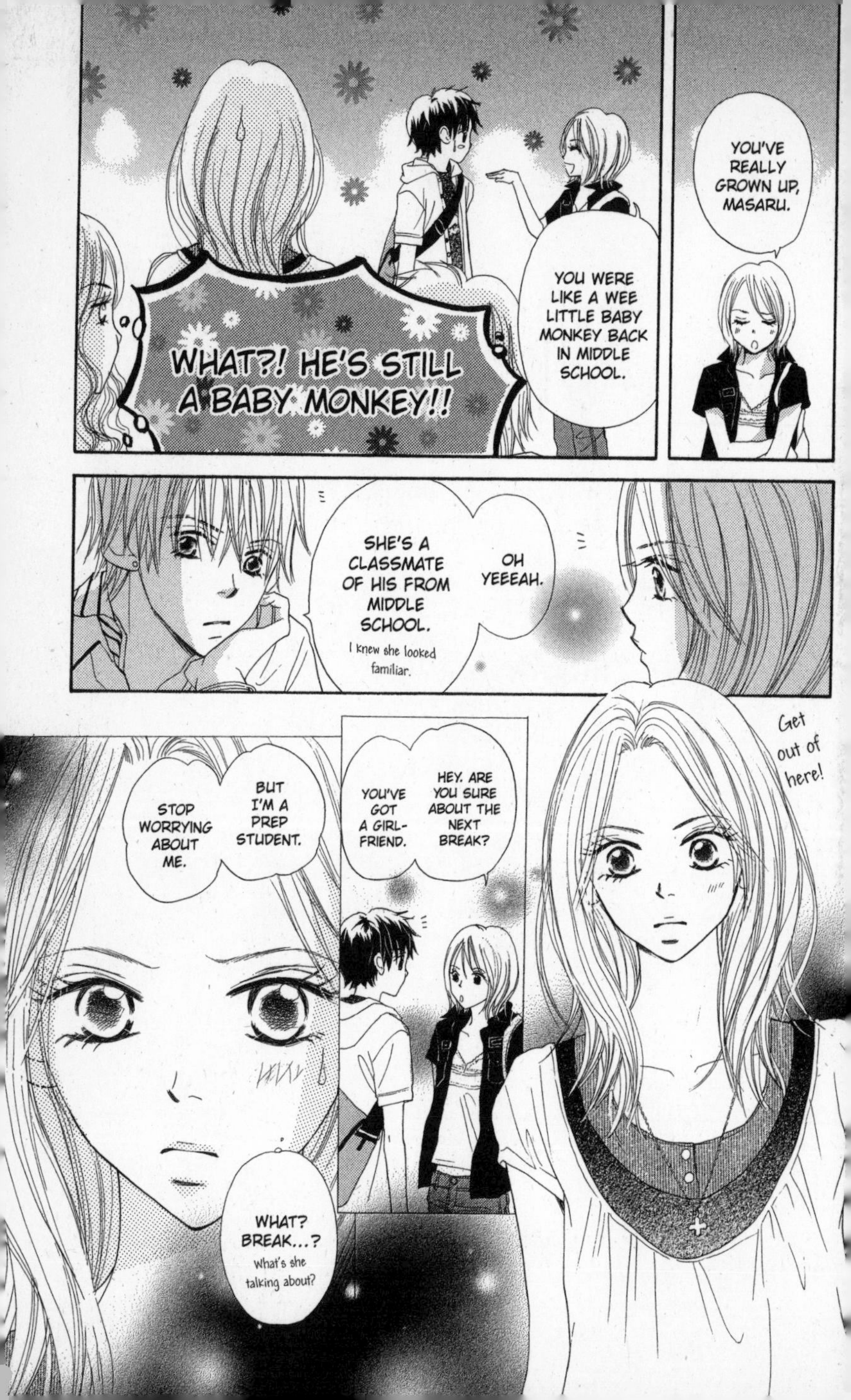

YOU'VE REALLY GROWN UP, MASARU.
YOU WERE LIKE A WEE LITTLE BABY MONKEY BACK IN MIDDLE SCHOOL.
WHAT?! HE'S STILL A BABY MONKEY!!
OH YEEEAH.
SHE'S A CLASSMATE OF HIS FROM MIDDLE SCHOOL.
I knew she looked familiar.
Get out of here!
HEY. ARE YOU SURE ABOUT THE NEXT BREAK?
YOU'VE GOT A GIRL-FRIEND.
BUT I'M A PREP STUDENT.
STOP WORRYING ABOUT ME.
WHAT? BREAK...?
What's she talking about?

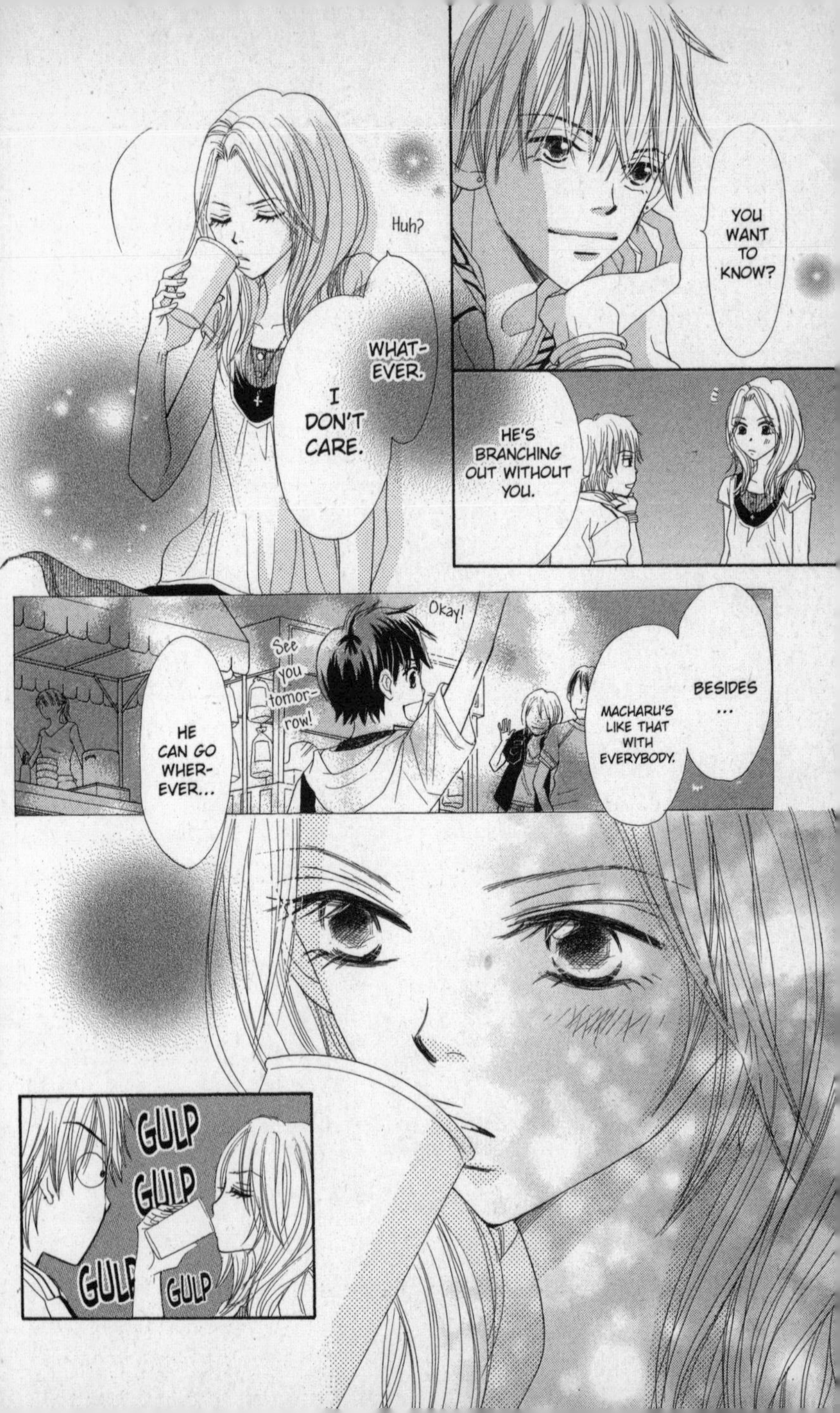
YOU WANT TO KNOW?
HE'S BRANCHING OUT WITHOUT YOU.
Huh?
WHAT-EVER.
I DON'T CARE.
BESIDES...
MACHARU'S LIKE THAT WITH EVERYBODY.
Okay!
See you tomor-row!
HE CAN GO WHER-EVER...
GULP
GULP
GULP
GULP

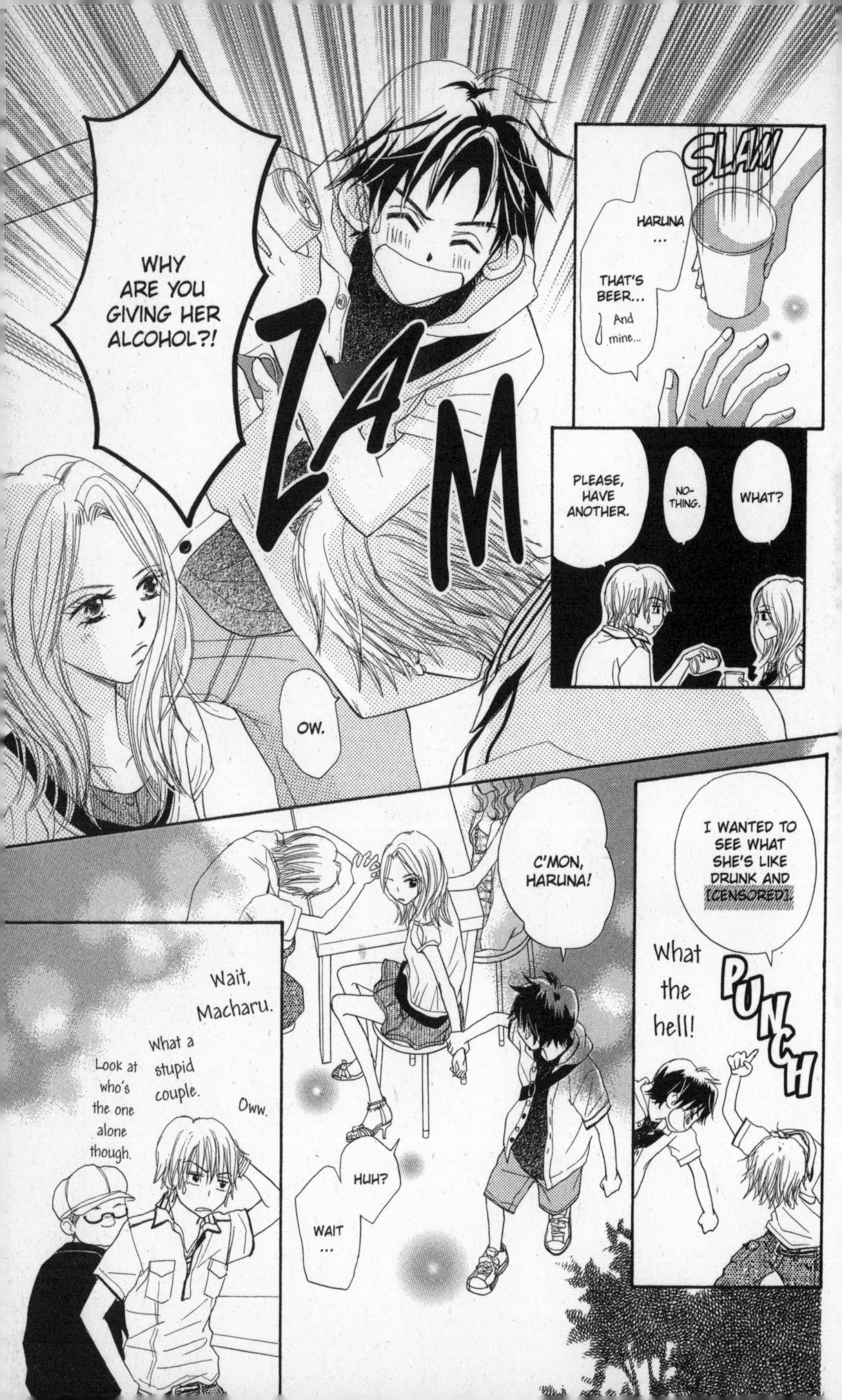

SLAM
HARUNA ...
THAT'S BEER...
And mine...
WHAT?
NO-THING.
PLEASE, HAVE ANOTHER.
WHY ARE YOU GIVING HER ALCOHOL?!
ZAM
OW.
I WANTED TO SEE WHAT SHE'S LIKE DRUNK AND [CENSORED].
What the hell!
PUNCH
C'MON, HARUNA!
HUH?
WAIT ...
Wait, Macharu.
Oww.
What a stupid couple.
Look at who's the one alone though.

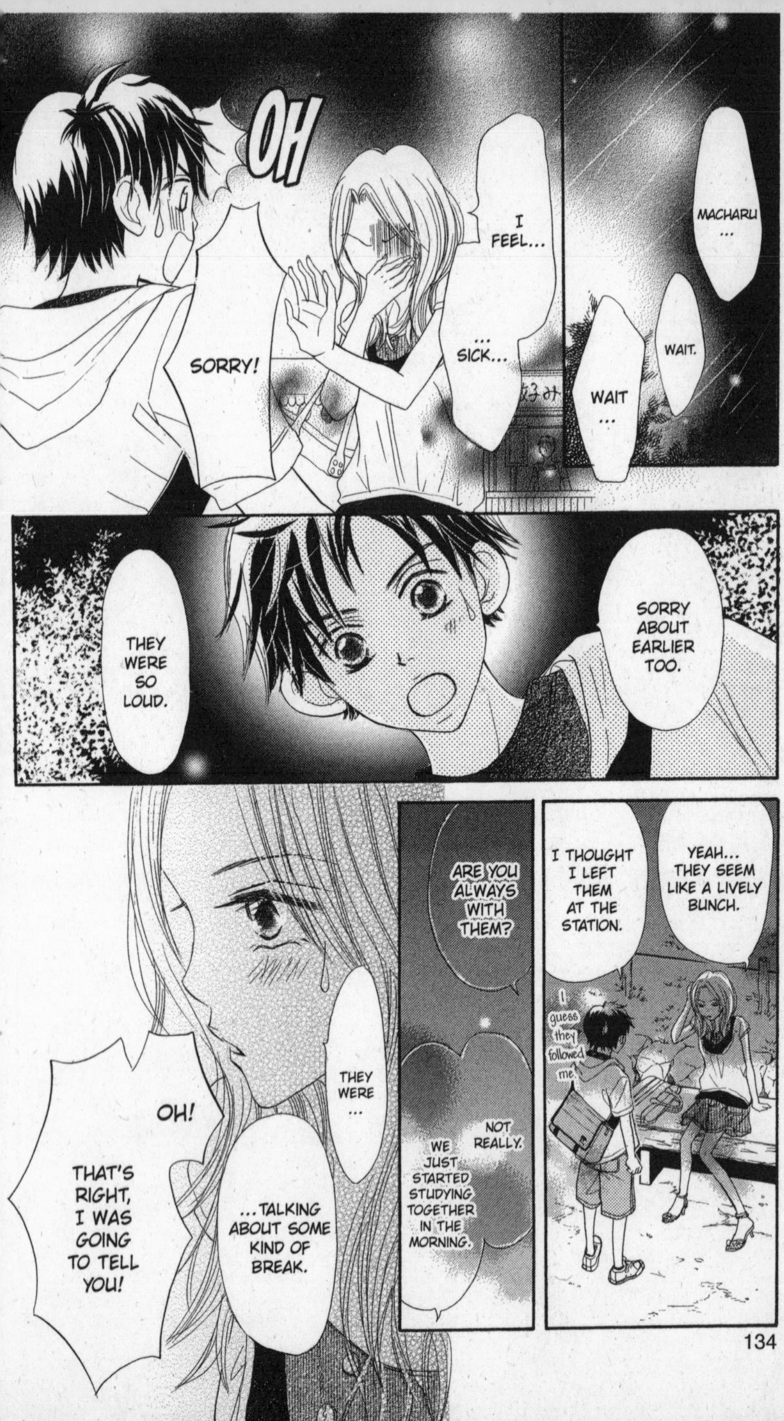
MACHARU ...
WAIT.
WAIT ...
I FEEL...
... SICK...
OH
SORRY!
SORRY ABOUT EARLIER TOO.
THEY WERE SO LOUD.
YEAH... THEY SEEM LIKE A LIVELY BUNCH.
I THOUGHT I LEFT THEM AT THE STATION.
I guess they followed me.
ARE YOU ALWAYS WITH THEM?
NOT REALLY.
WE JUST STARTED STUDYING TOGETHER IN THE MORNING.
THEY WERE ...
...TALKING ABOUT SOME KIND OF BREAK.
OH!
THAT'S RIGHT, I WAS GOING TO TELL YOU!

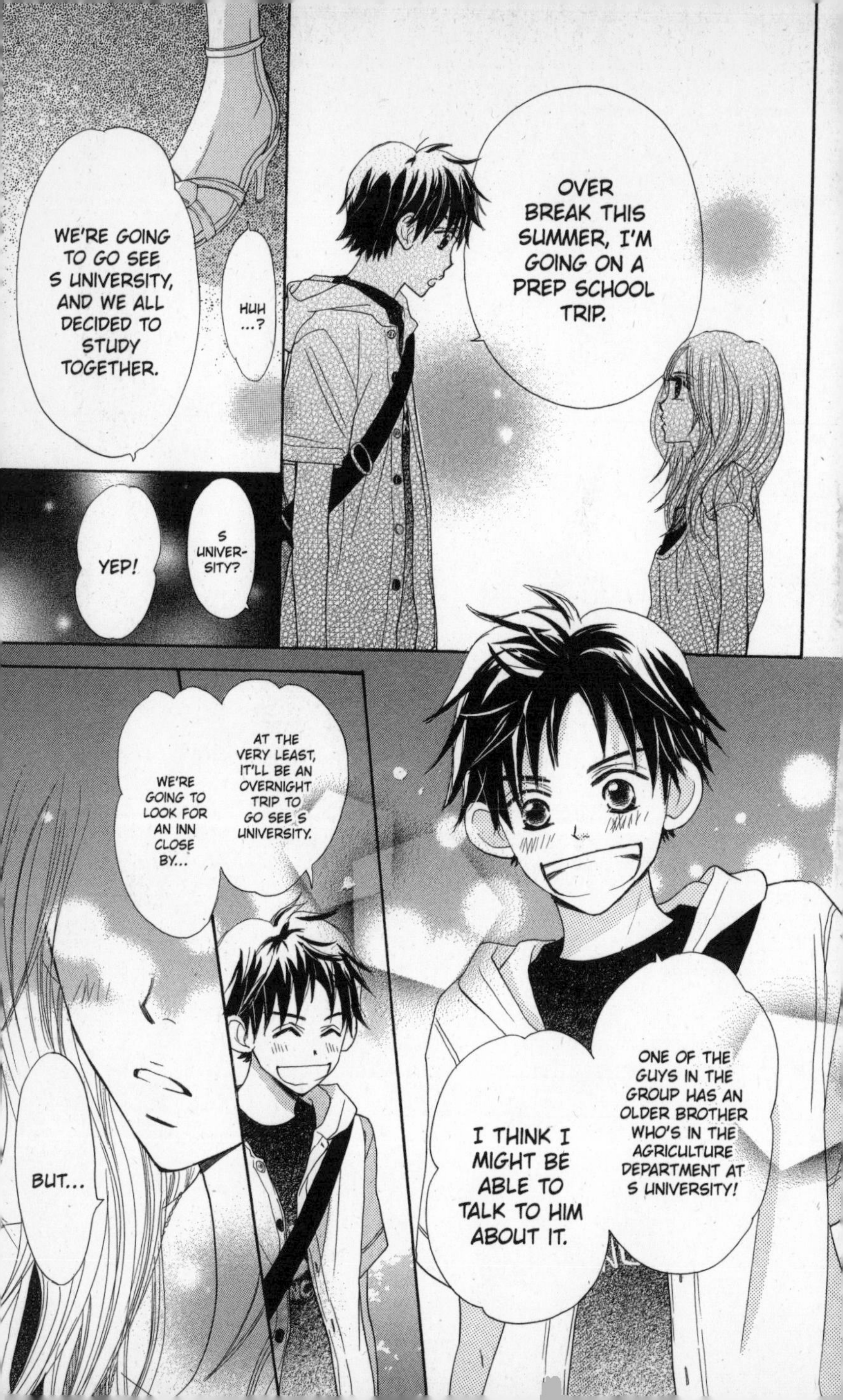
OVER BREAK THIS SUMMER, I'M GOING ON A PREP SCHOOL TRIP.
HUH ...?
WE'RE GOING TO GO SEE S UNIVERSITY, AND WE ALL DECIDED TO STUDY TOGETHER.
S UNIVER-SITY?
YEP!
ONE OF THE GUYS IN THE GROUP HAS AN OLDER BROTHER WHO'S IN THE AGRICULTURE DEPARTMENT AT S UNIVERSITY!
I THINK I MIGHT BE ABLE TO TALK TO HIM ABOUT IT.
AT THE VERY LEAST, IT'LL BE AN OVERNIGHT TRIP TO GO SEE S UNIVERSITY.
WE'RE GOING TO LOOK FOR AN INN CLOSE BY...
BUT...

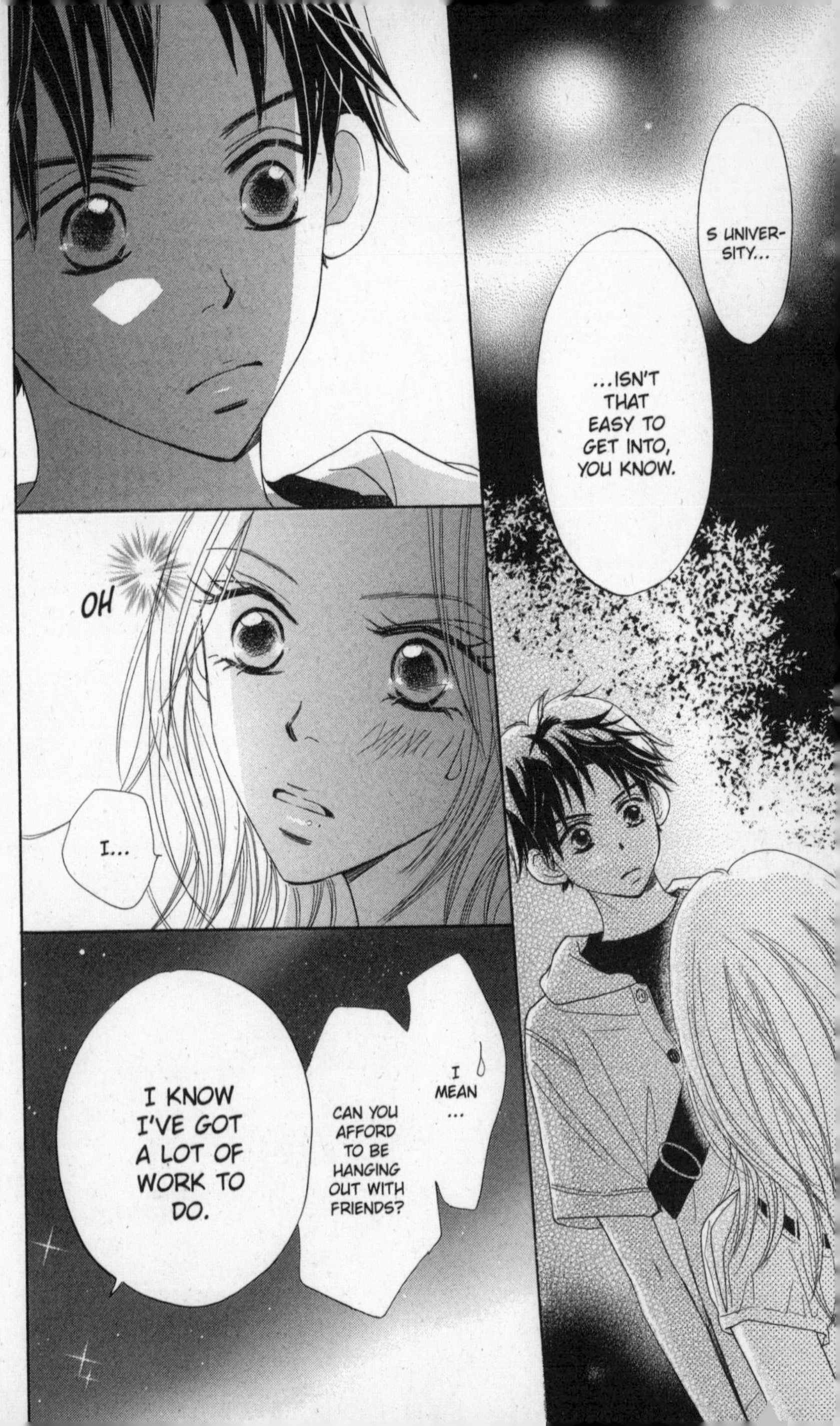
S UNIVER-SITY...
...ISN'T THAT EASY TO GET INTO, YOU KNOW.
OH
I...
I MEAN ...
CAN YOU AFFORD TO BE HANGING OUT WITH FRIENDS?
I KNOW I'VE GOT A LOT OF WORK TO DO.

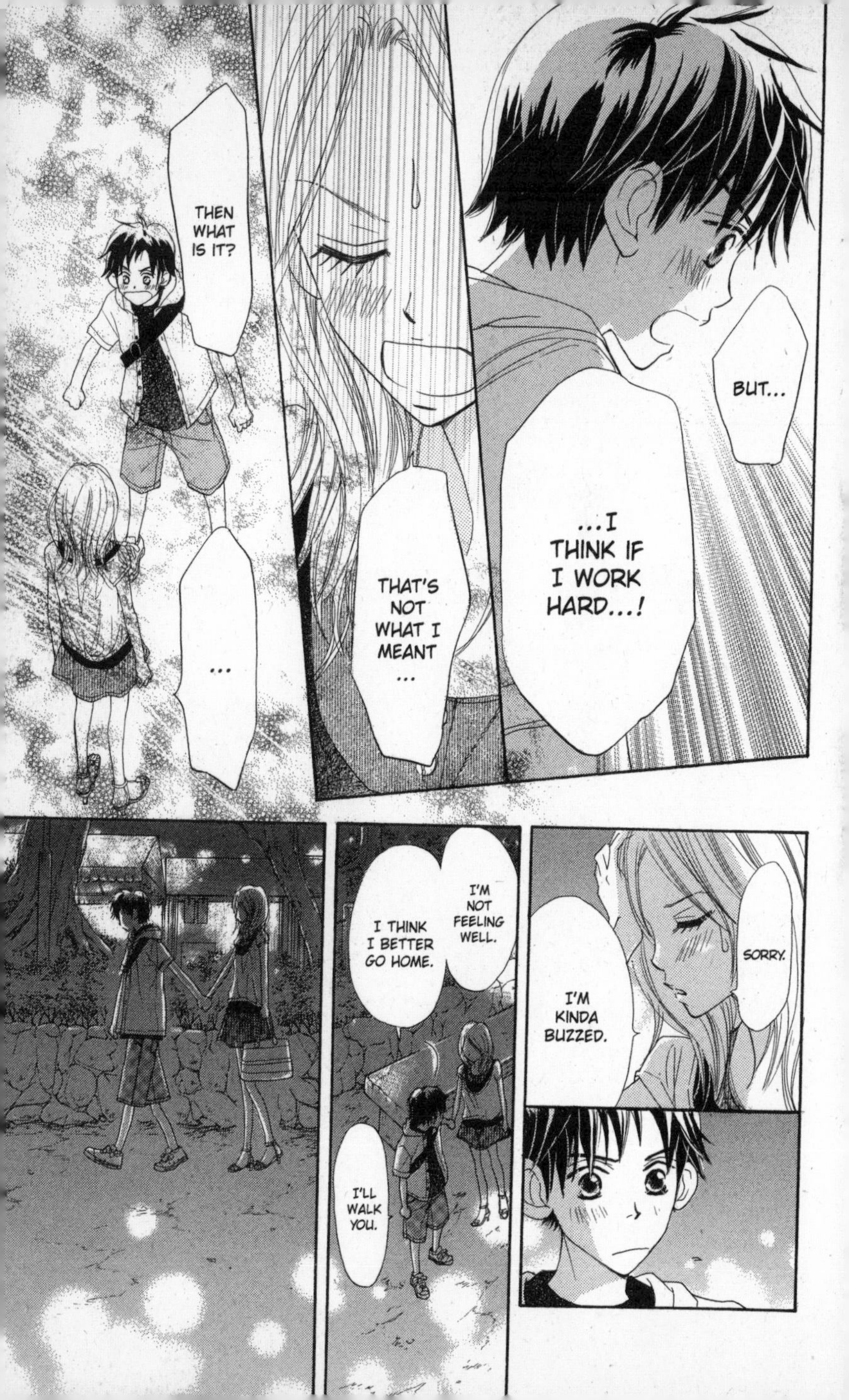
BUT...
...I THINK IF I WORK HARD...!
THAT'S NOT WHAT I MEANT...
THEN WHAT IS IT?
...
SORRY.
I'M KINDA BUZZED.
I'M NOT FEELING WELL.
I THINK I BETTER GO HOME.
I'LL WALK YOU.

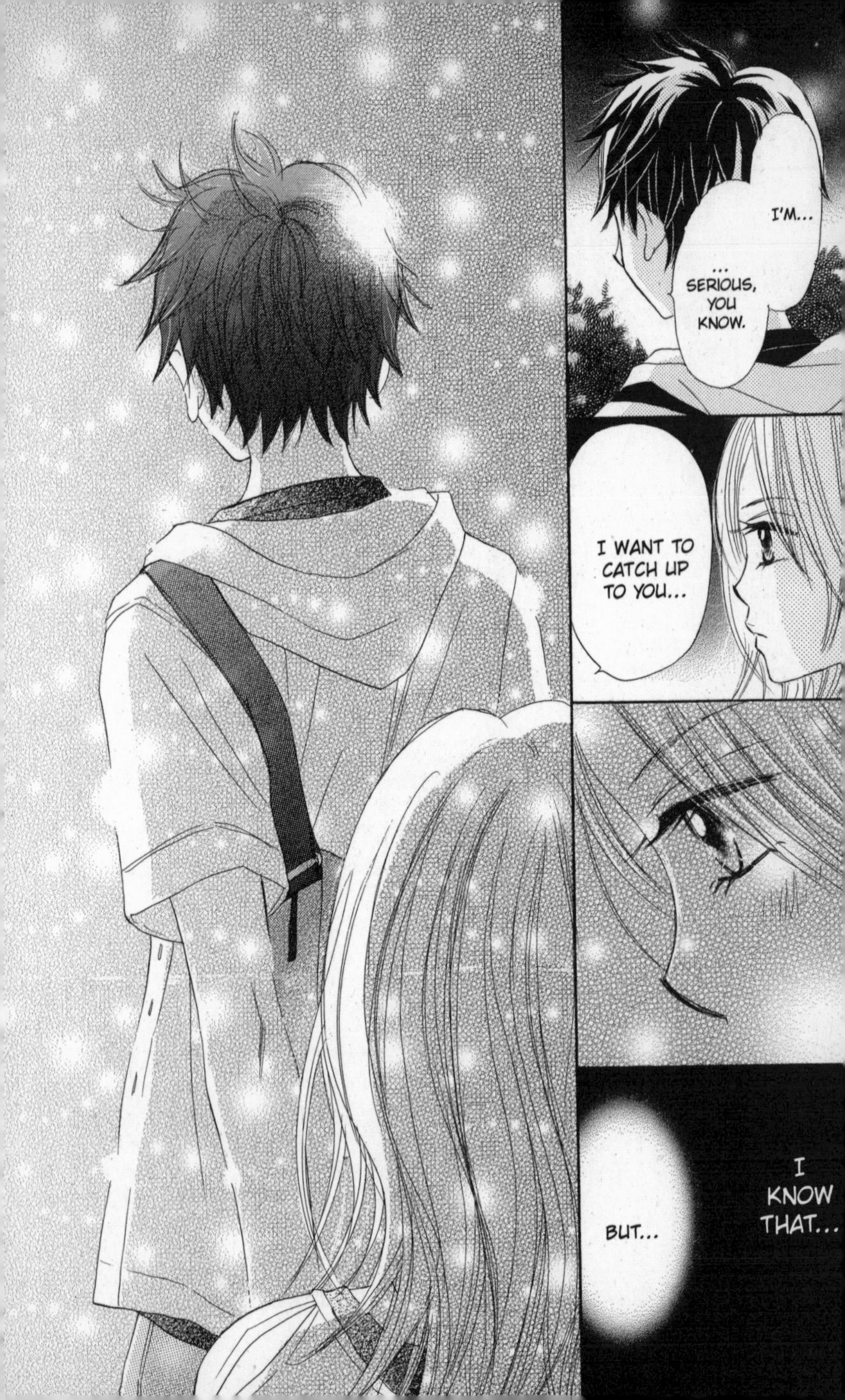
I'M...
... SERIOUS, YOU KNOW.
I WANT TO CATCH UP TO YOU...
I KNOW THAT...
BUT...

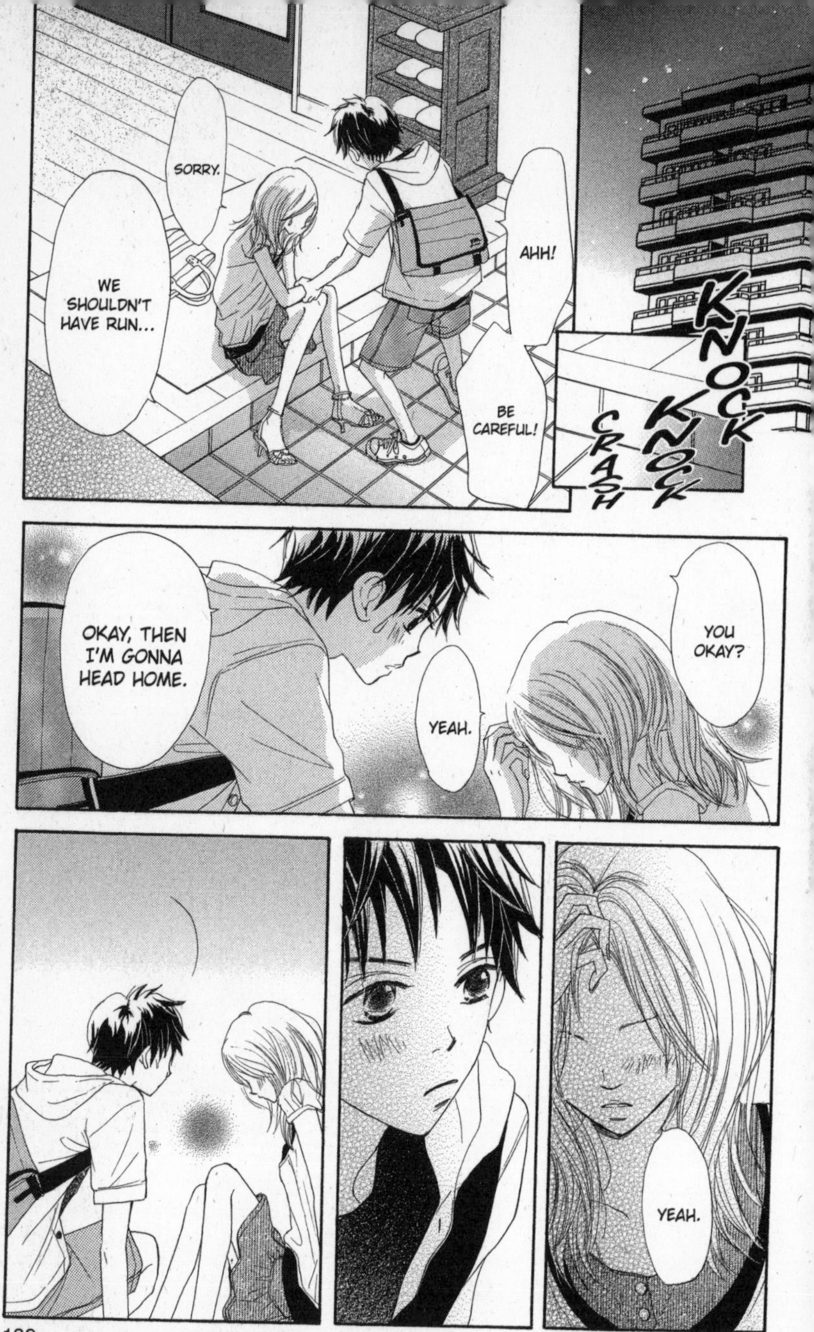
KNOCK
KNOCK
CRASH
AHH!
BE CAREFUL!
SORRY.
WE SHOULDN'T HAVE RUN...
YOU OKAY?
YEAH.
OKAY, THEN I'M GONNA HEAD HOME.
YEAH.

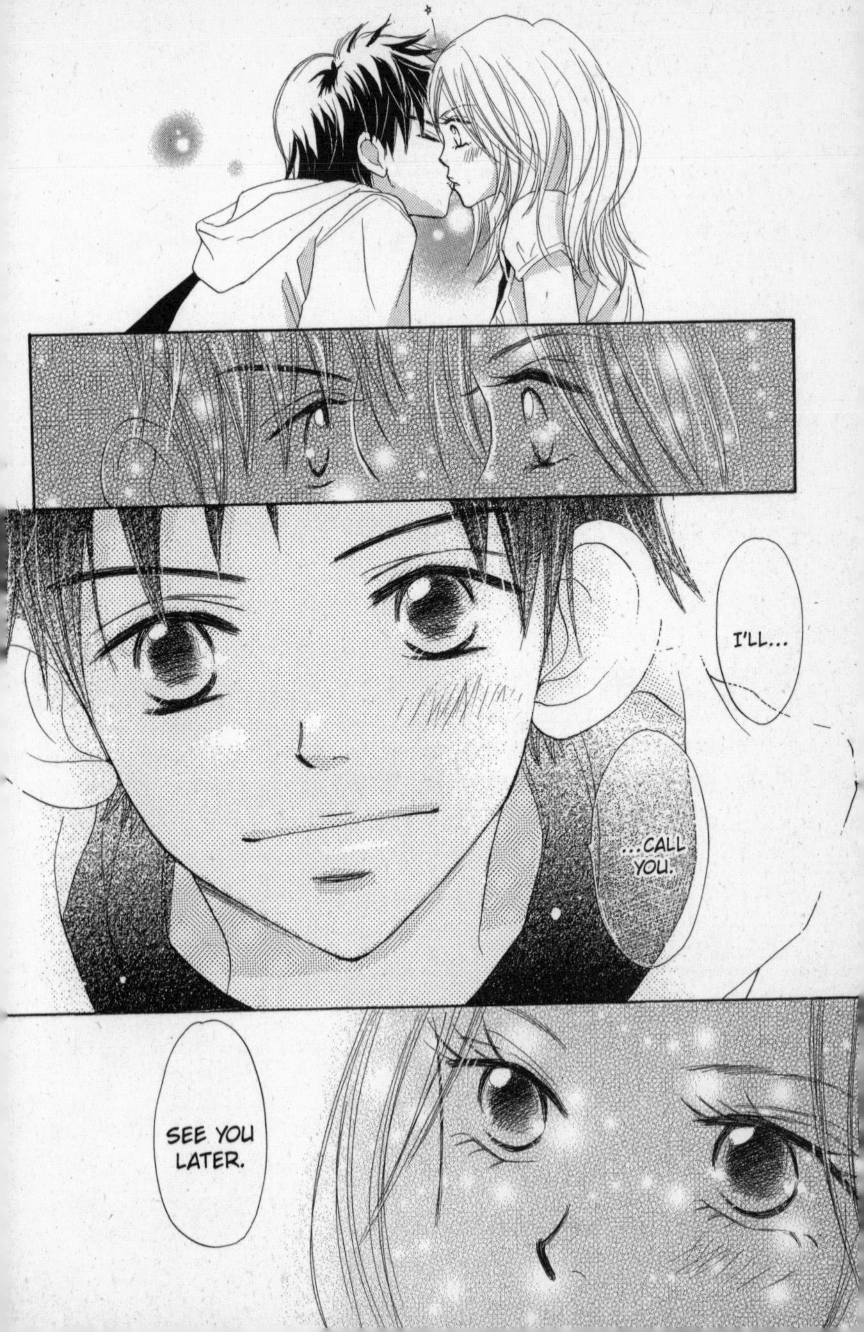
I'LL...
...CALL YOU.
SEE YOU LATER.

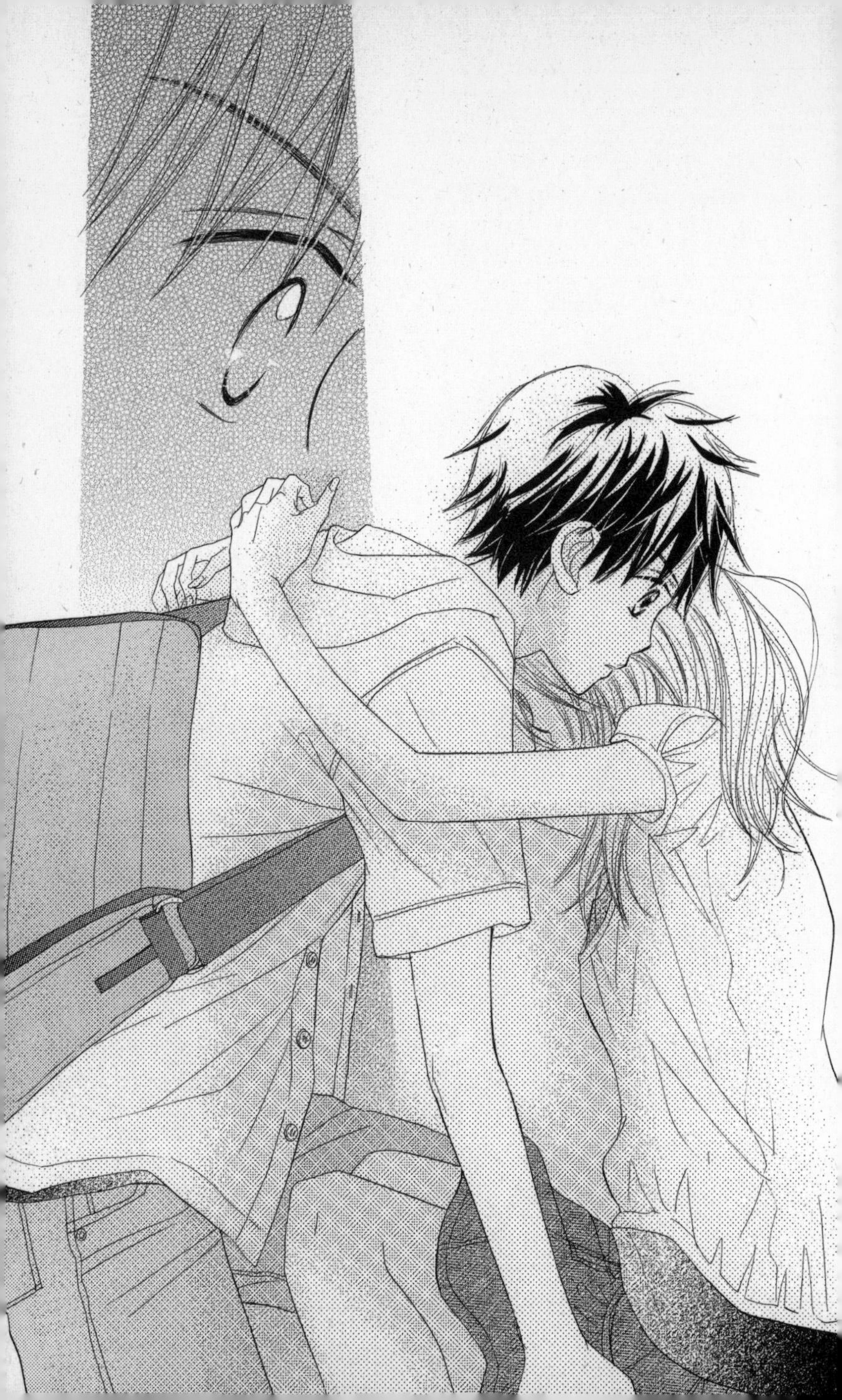

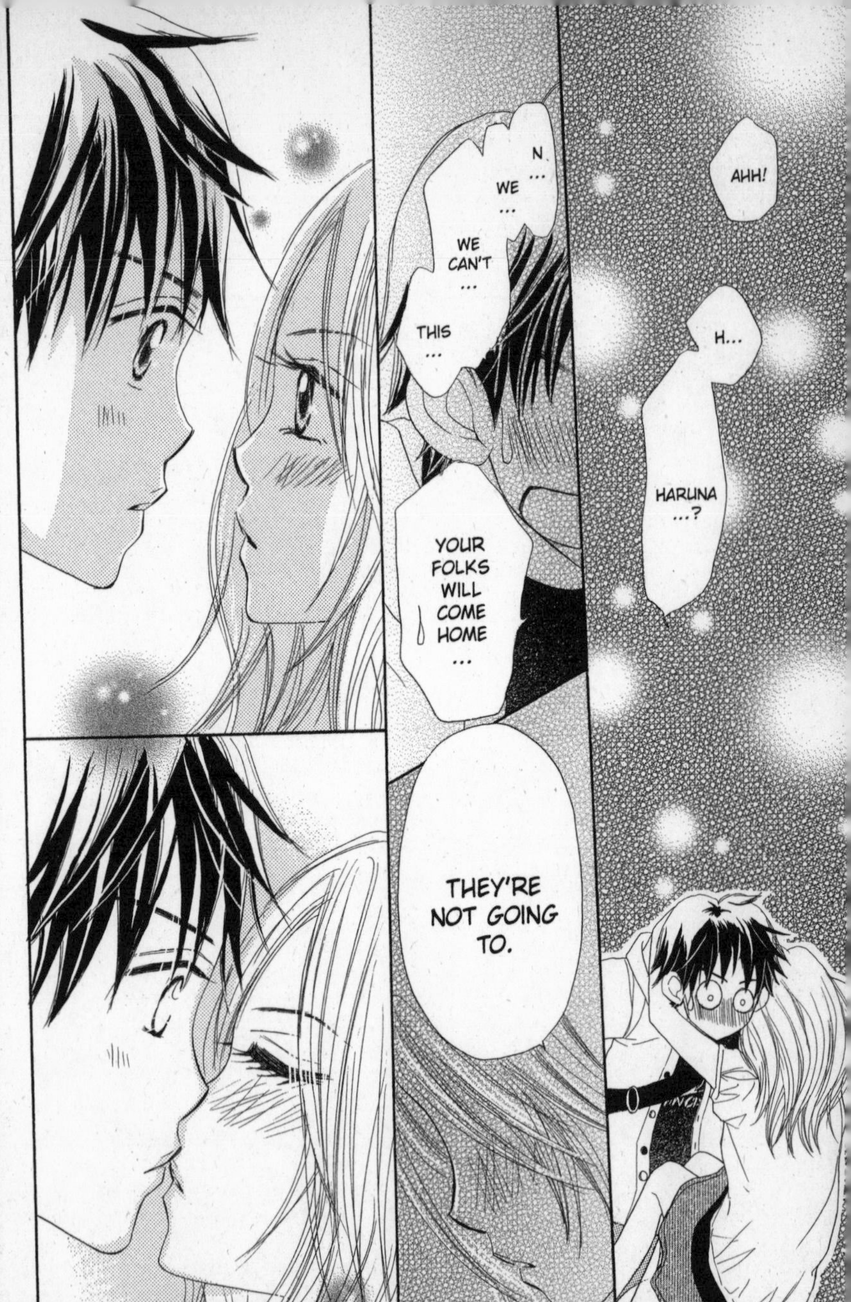
AHH!
H...
HARUNA ...?
N ... WE ... WE CAN'T ... THIS ...
YOUR FOLKS WILL COME HOME ...
THEY'RE NOT GOING TO.

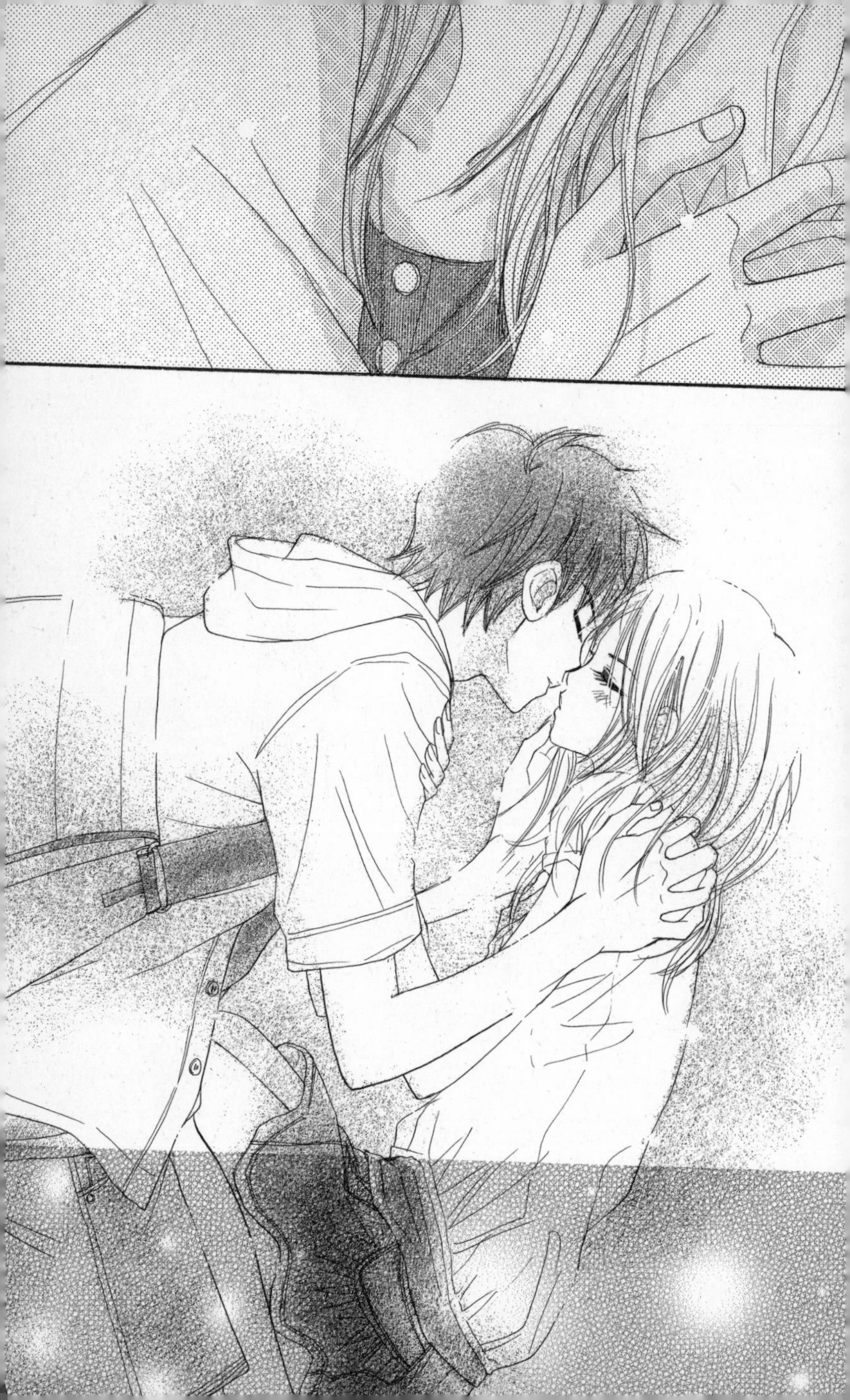

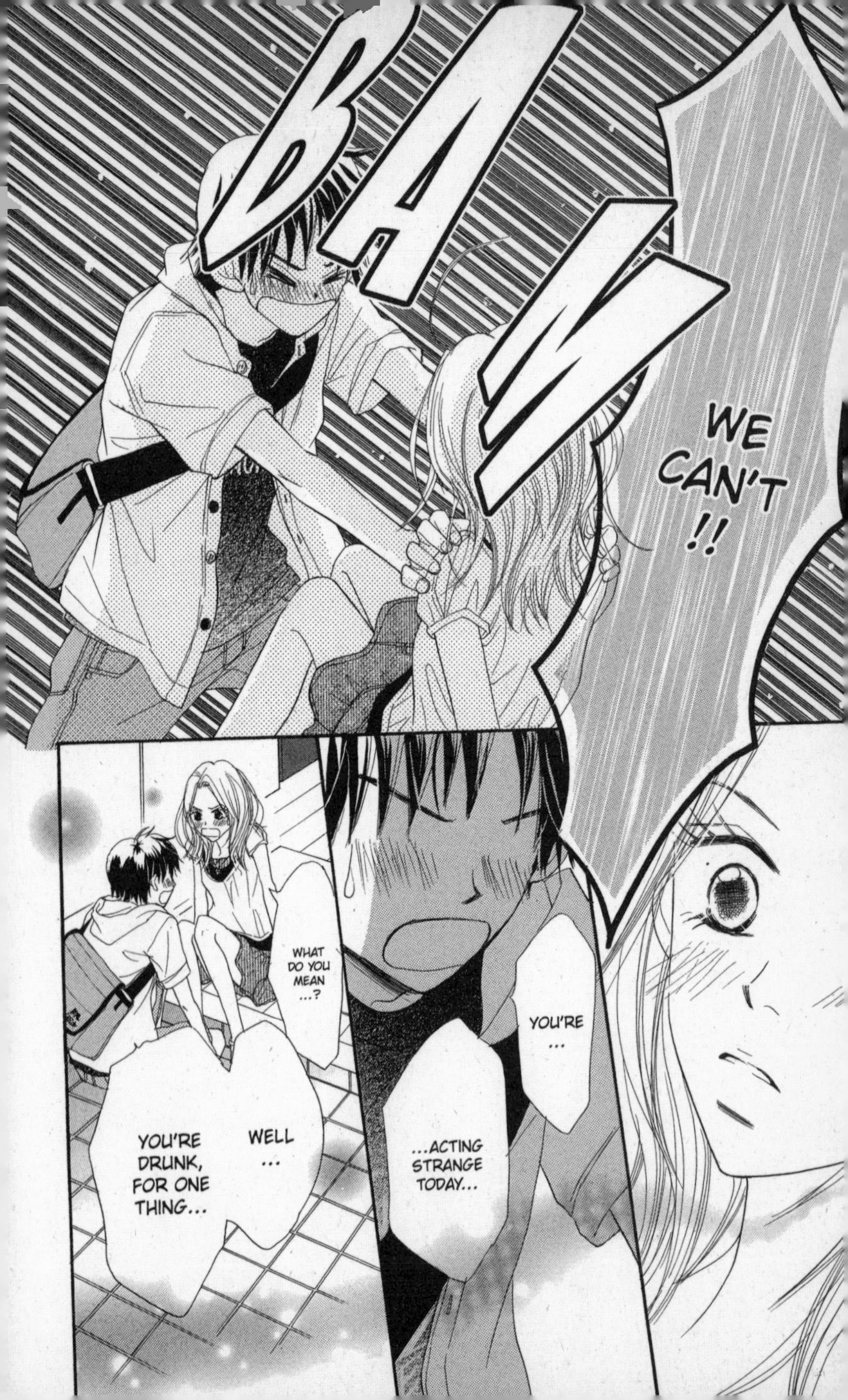
BAM
WE CAN'T!!
YOU'RE...
...ACTING STRANGE TODAY...
WHAT DO YOU MEAN...?
WELL...
YOU'RE DRUNK, FOR ONE THING...

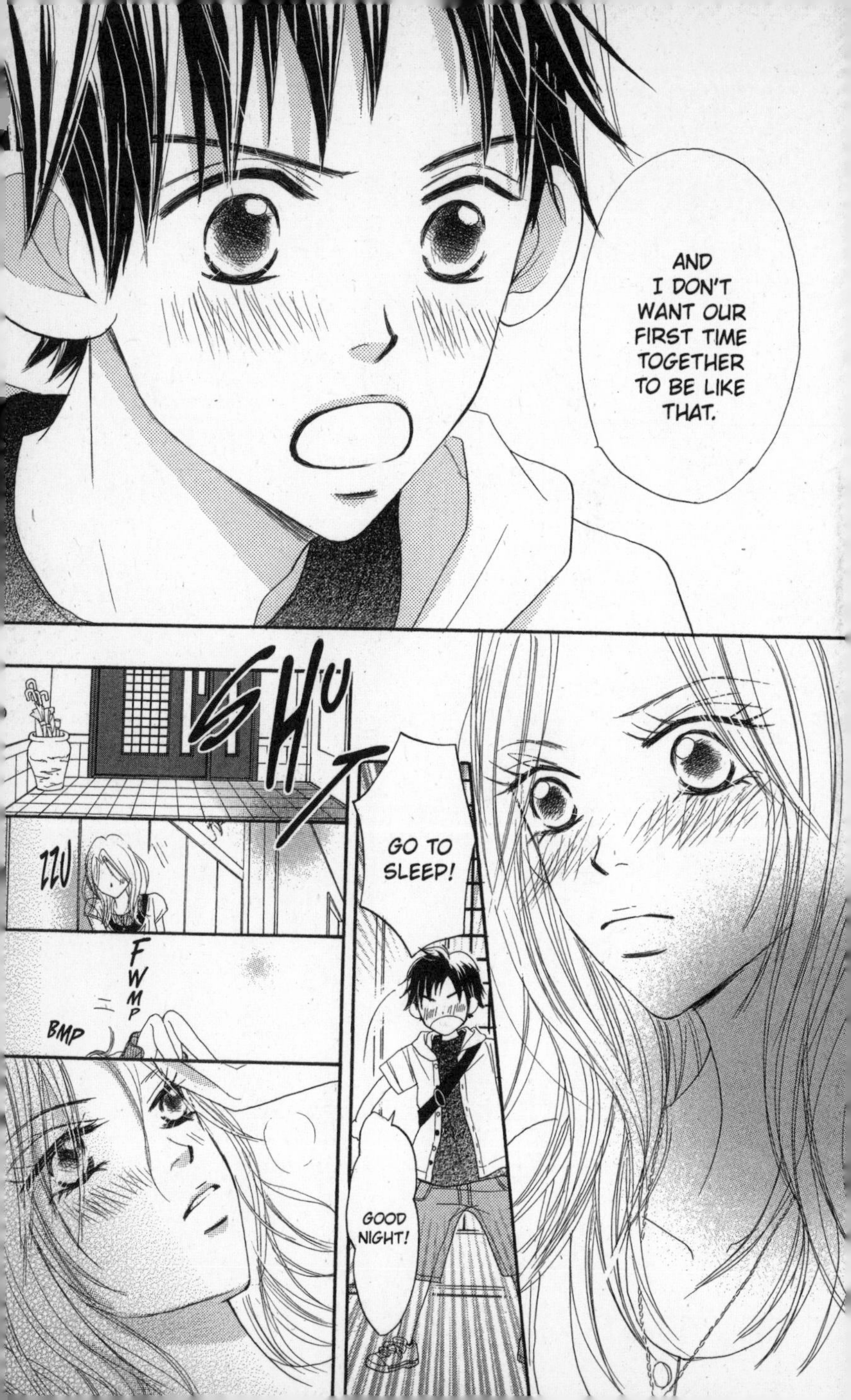
AND I DON'T WANT OUR FIRST TIME TOGETHER TO BE LIKE THAT.
GO TO SLEEP!
GOOD NIGHT!
SHUT
ZZU
FWMP
BMP

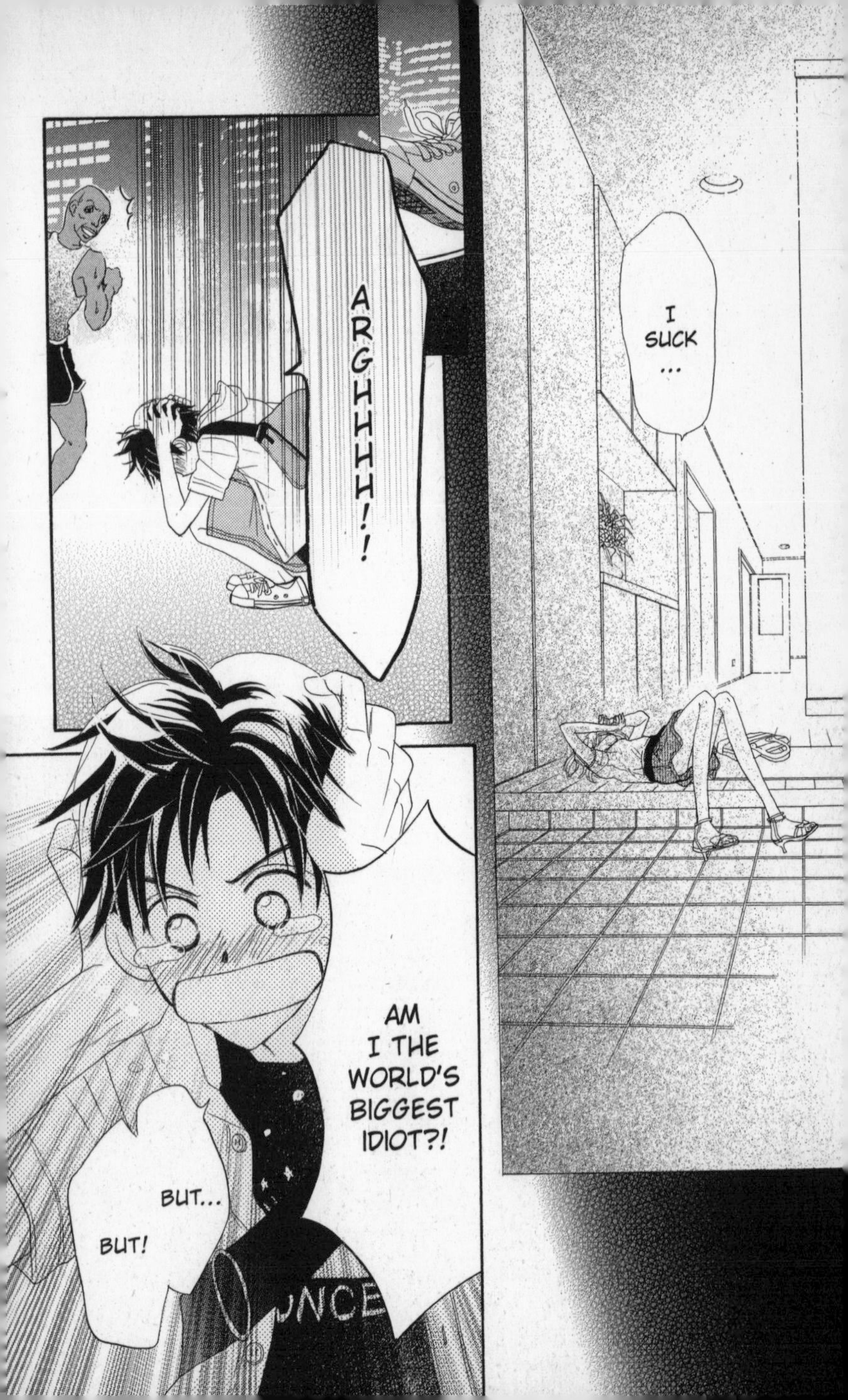
I SUCK...
ARGHHHH!!
AM I THE WORLD'S BIGGEST IDIOT?!
BUT...
BUT!

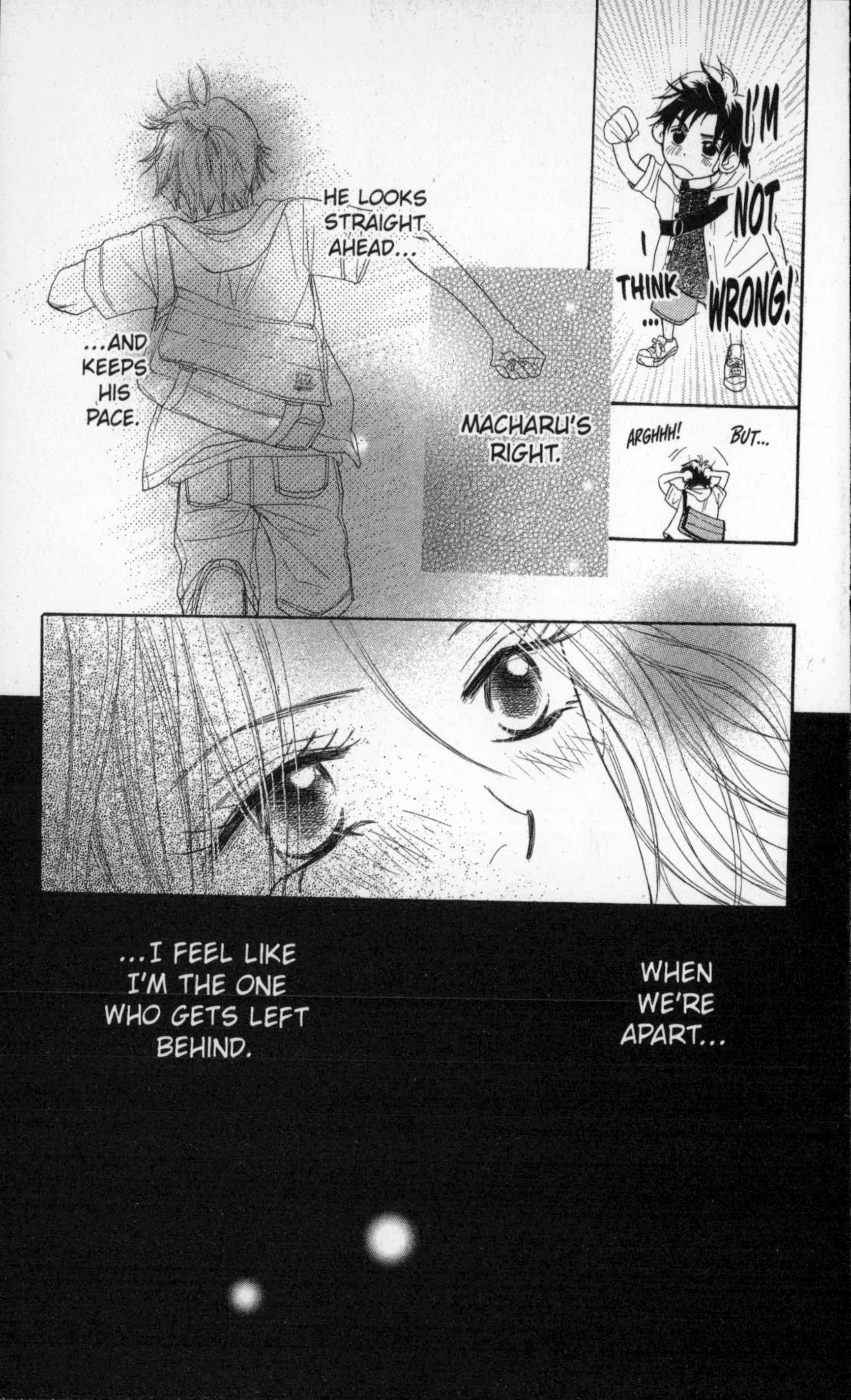
I'M NOT WRONG!
I THINK...
BUT...
ARGHHH!
MACHARU'S RIGHT.
HE LOOKS STRAIGHT AHEAD...
...AND KEEPS HIS PACE.
WHEN WE'RE APART...
...I FEEL LIKE I'M THE ONE WHO GETS LEFT BEHIND.

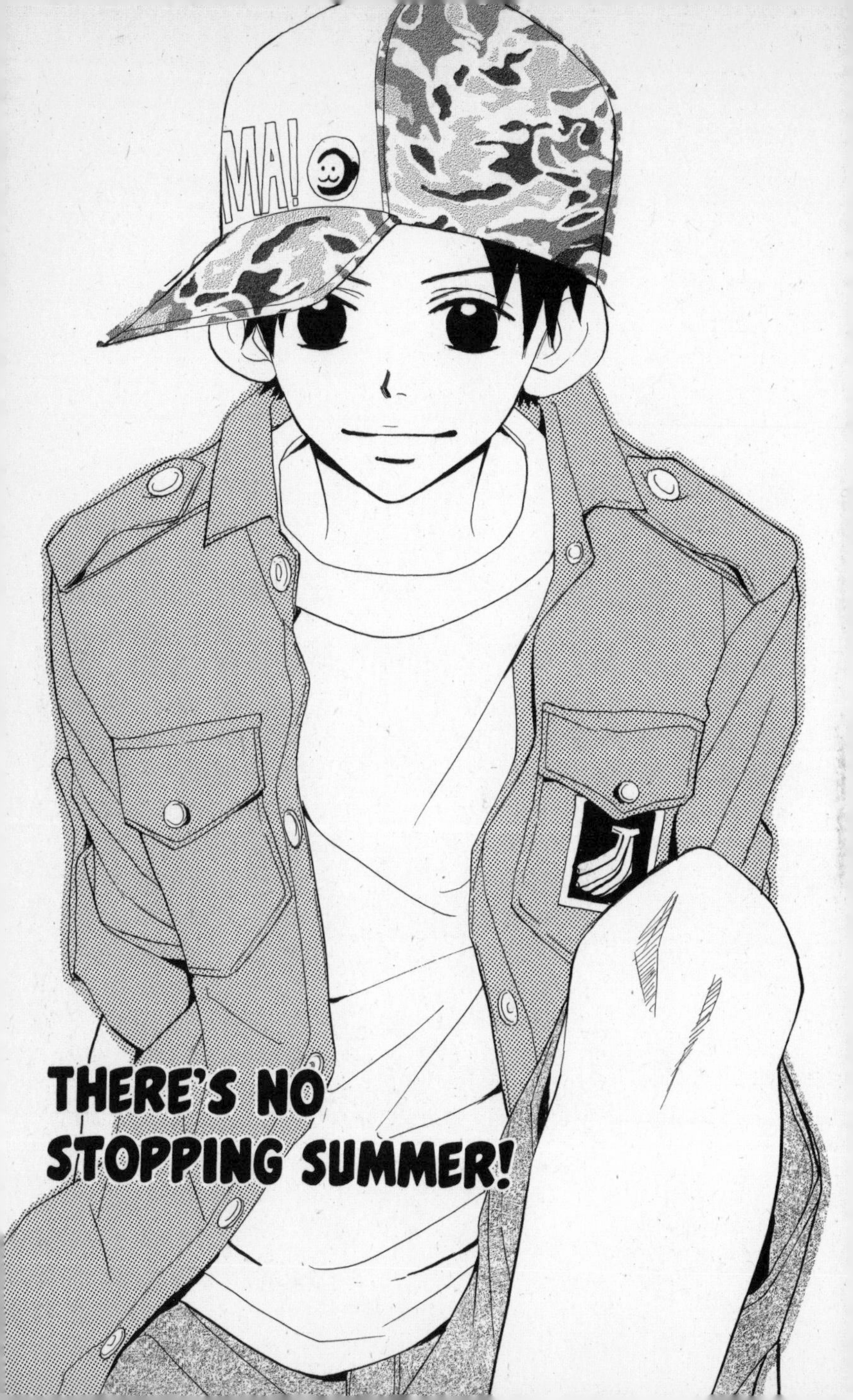
MA!
THERE'S NO STOPPING SUMMER!

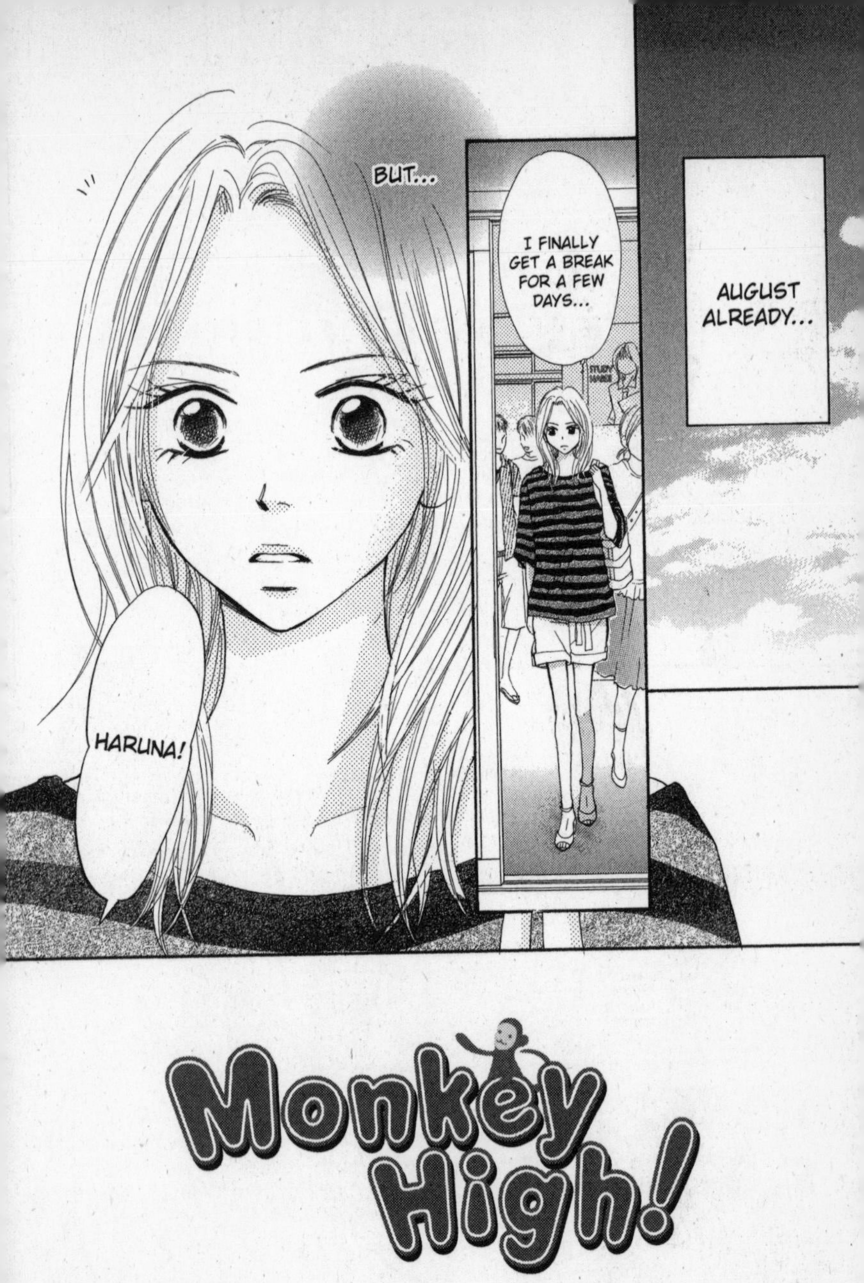
AUGUST ALREADY...
I FINALLY GET A BREAK FOR A FEW DAYS...
BUT...
HARUNA!

Monkey High!

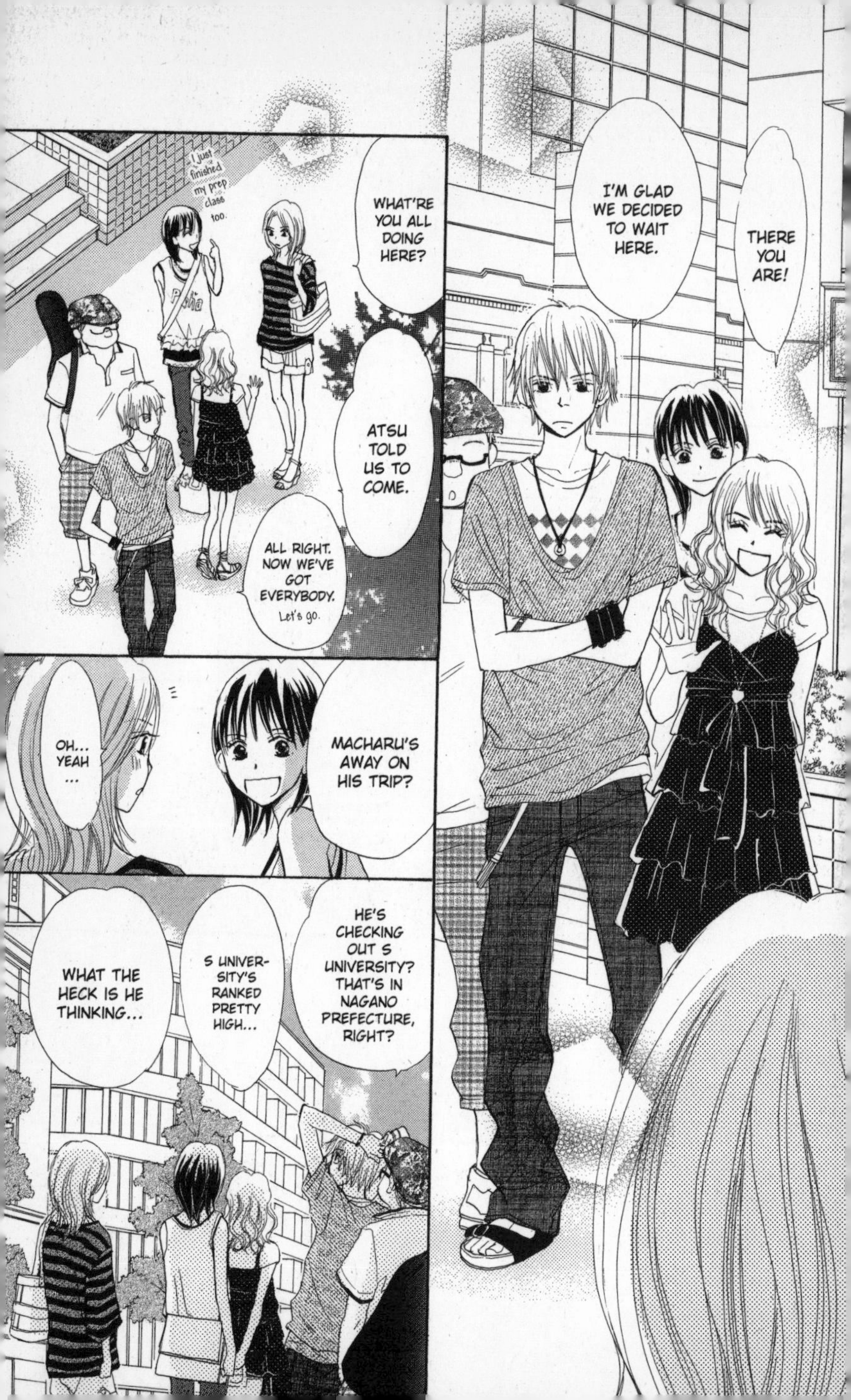
THERE YOU ARE!
I'M GLAD WE DECIDED TO WAIT HERE.
WHAT'RE YOU ALL DOING HERE?
I just finished my prep class too.
ATSU TOLD US TO COME.
ALL RIGHT. NOW WE'VE GOT EVERYBODY.
Let's go.
MACHARU'S AWAY ON HIS TRIP?
OH... YEAH ...
HE'S CHECKING OUT S UNIVERSITY? THAT'S IN NAGANO PREFECTURE, RIGHT?
S UNIVERSITY'S RANKED PRETTY HIGH...
WHAT THE HECK IS HE THINKING...

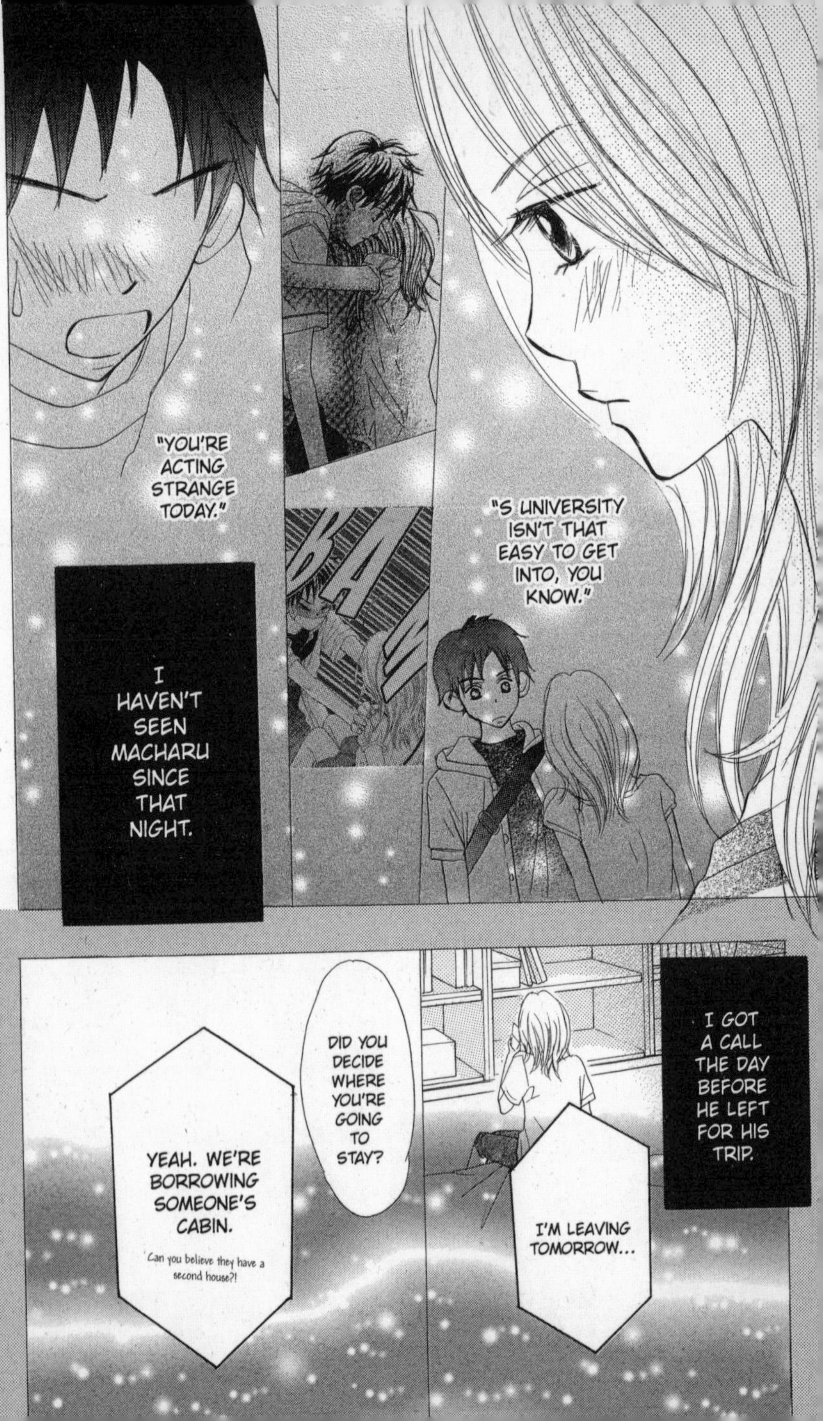
"S UNIVERSITY ISN'T THAT EASY TO GET INTO, YOU KNOW."
"YOU'RE ACTING STRANGE TODAY."
I HAVEN'T SEEN MACHARU SINCE THAT NIGHT.
I GOT A CALL THE DAY BEFORE HE LEFT FOR HIS TRIP.
I'M LEAVING TOMORROW...
DID YOU DECIDE WHERE YOU'RE GOING TO STAY?
YEAH. WE'RE BORROWING SOMEONE'S CABIN.
Can you believe they have a second house?!

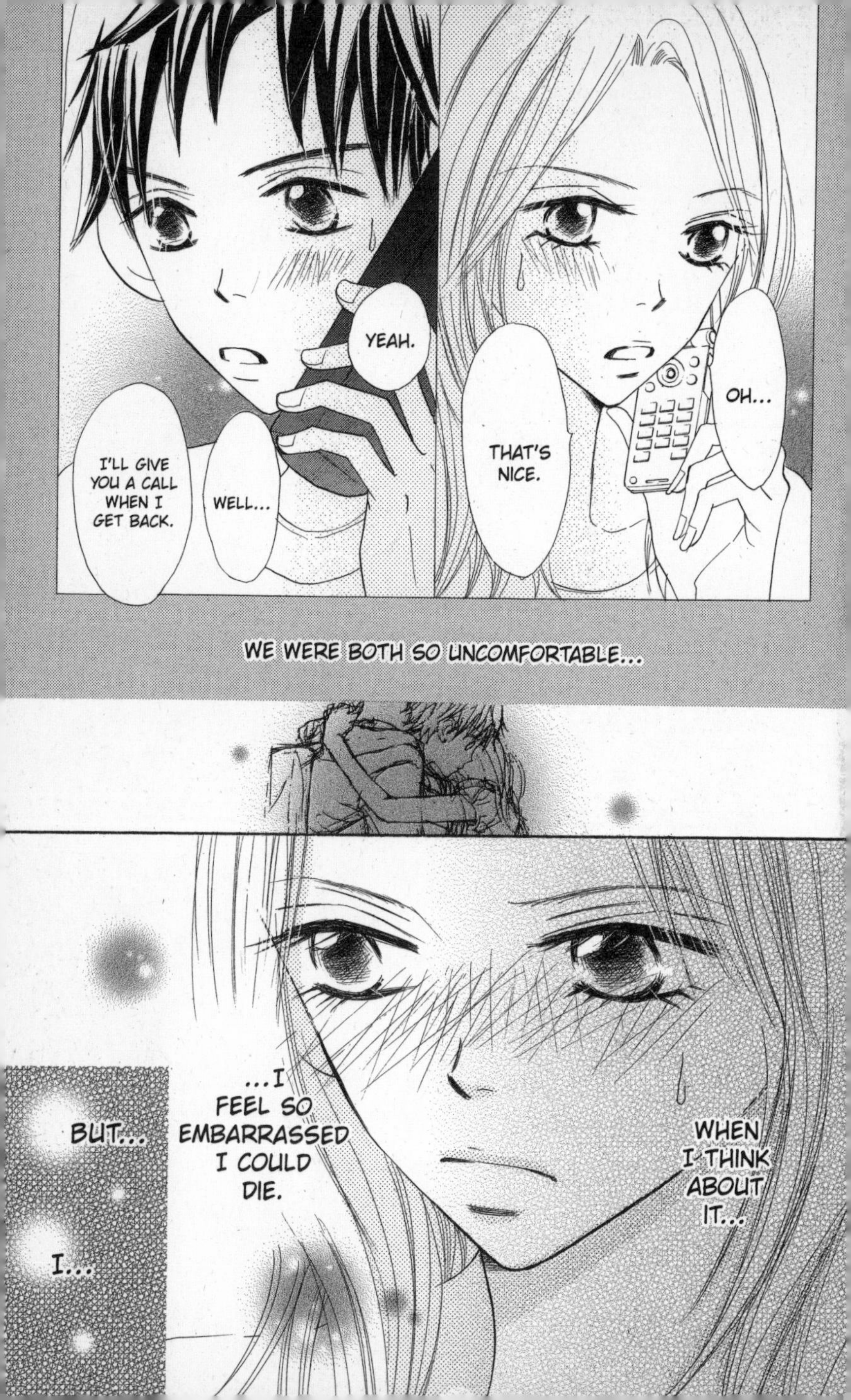
OH...
THAT'S NICE.
YEAH.
WELL...
I'LL GIVE YOU A CALL WHEN I GET BACK.
WE WERE BOTH SO UNCOMFORTABLE...
WHEN I THINK ABOUT IT...
...I FEEL SO EMBARRASSED I COULD DIE.
BUT...
I...

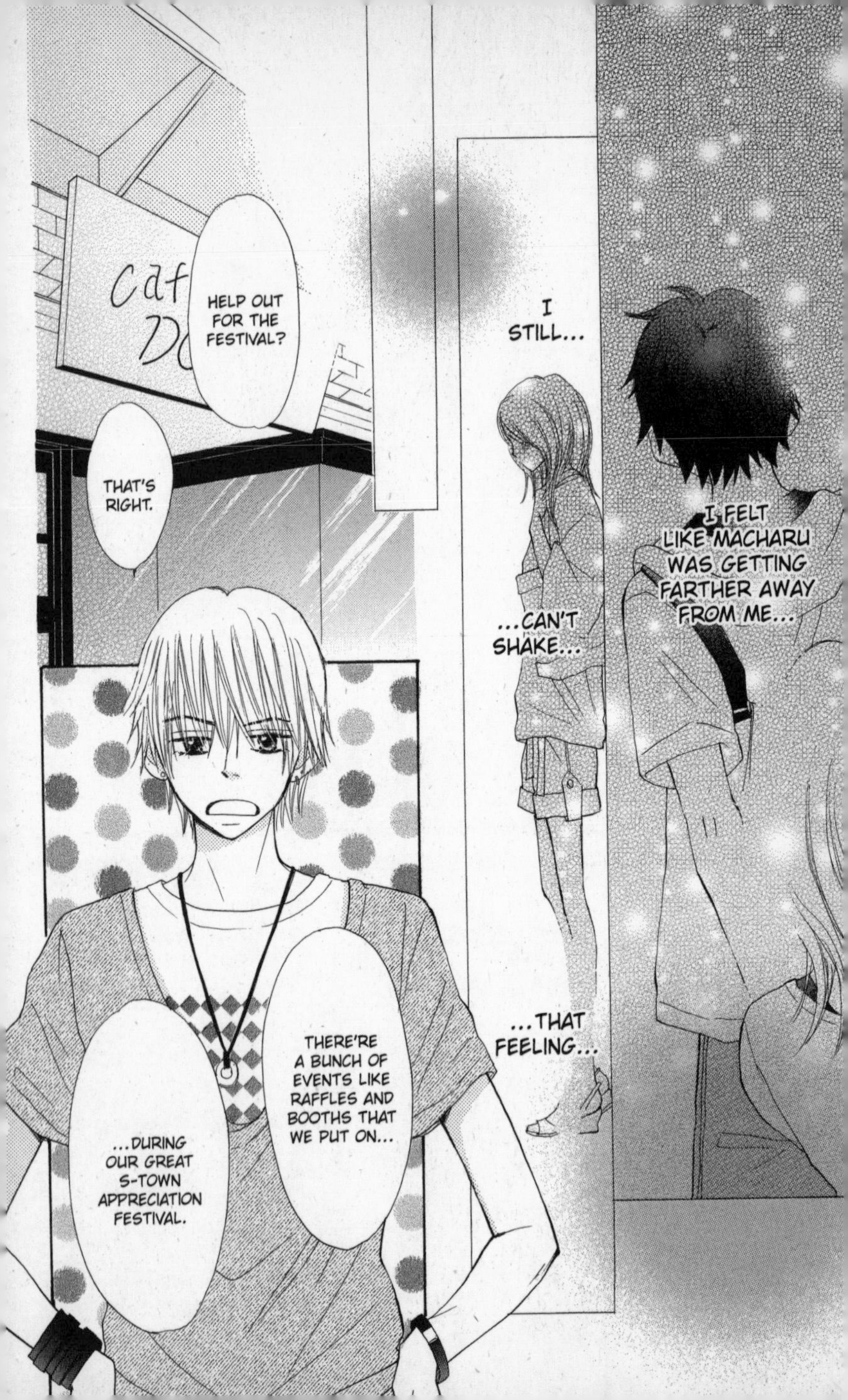
I FELT LIKE MACHARU WAS GETTING FARTHER AWAY FROM ME...
I STILL...
...CAN'T SHAKE...
...THAT FEELING...
HELP OUT FOR THE FESTIVAL?
THAT'S RIGHT.
THERE'RE A BUNCH OF EVENTS LIKE RAFFLES AND BOOTHS THAT WE PUT ON...
...DURING OUR GREAT S-TOWN APPRECIATION FESTIVAL.

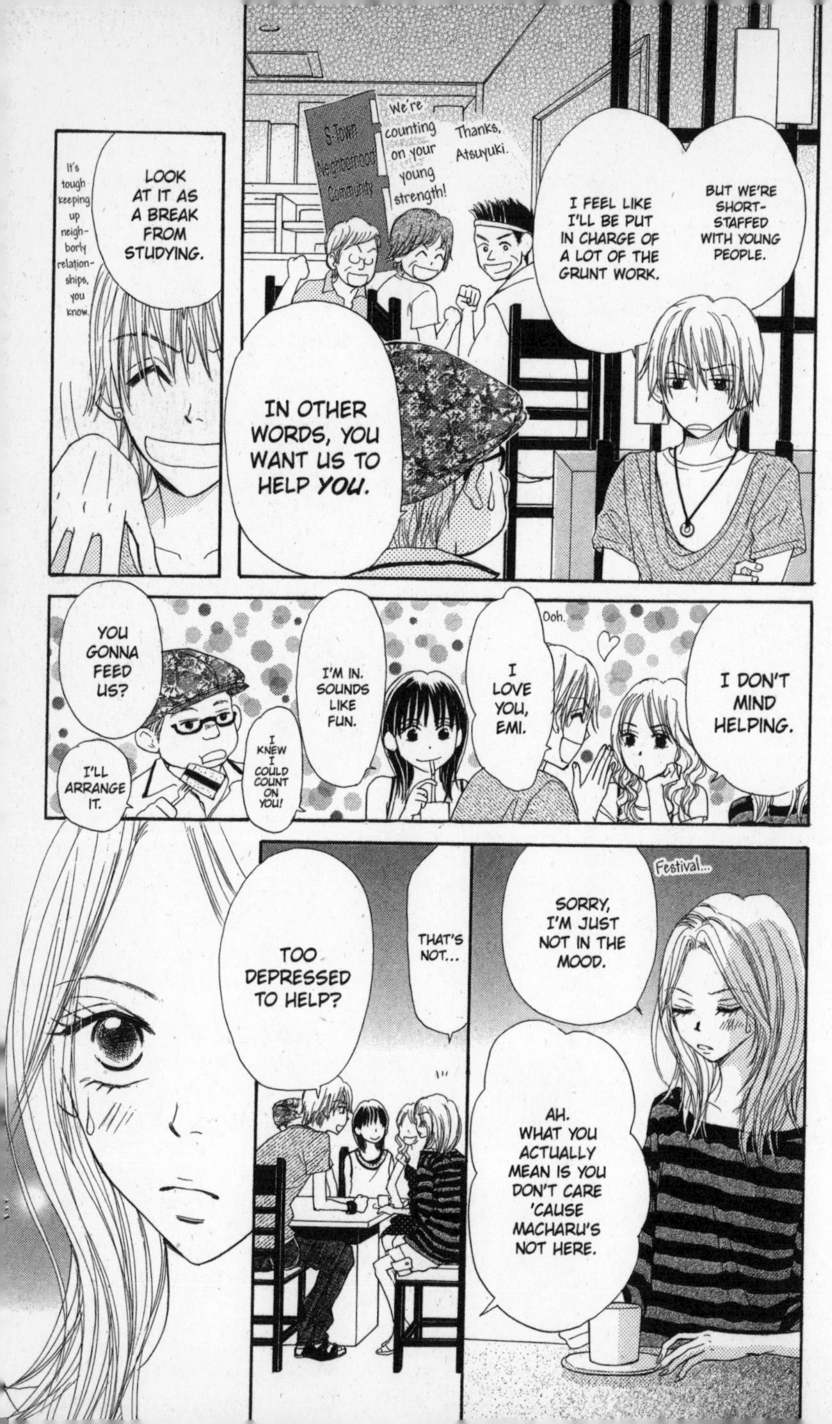
BUT WE'RE SHORT-STAFFED WITH YOUNG PEOPLE.
I FEEL LIKE I'LL BE PUT IN CHARGE OF A LOT OF THE GRUNT WORK.
Thanks, Atsuyuki.
We're counting on your young strength!
S-Town Neighborhood Community
IN OTHER WORDS, YOU WANT US TO HELP *YOU*.
LOOK AT IT AS A BREAK FROM STUDYING.
It's tough keeping up neighborly relationships, you know.
I DON'T MIND HELPING.
Ooh.
I LOVE YOU, EMI.
I'M IN. SOUNDS LIKE FUN.
I KNEW I COULD COUNT ON YOU!
YOU GONNA FEED US?
I'LL ARRANGE IT.
Festival...
SORRY, I'M JUST NOT IN THE MOOD.
AH. WHAT YOU ACTUALLY MEAN IS YOU DON'T CARE 'CAUSE MACHARU'S NOT HERE.
THAT'S NOT...
TOO DEPRESSED TO HELP?

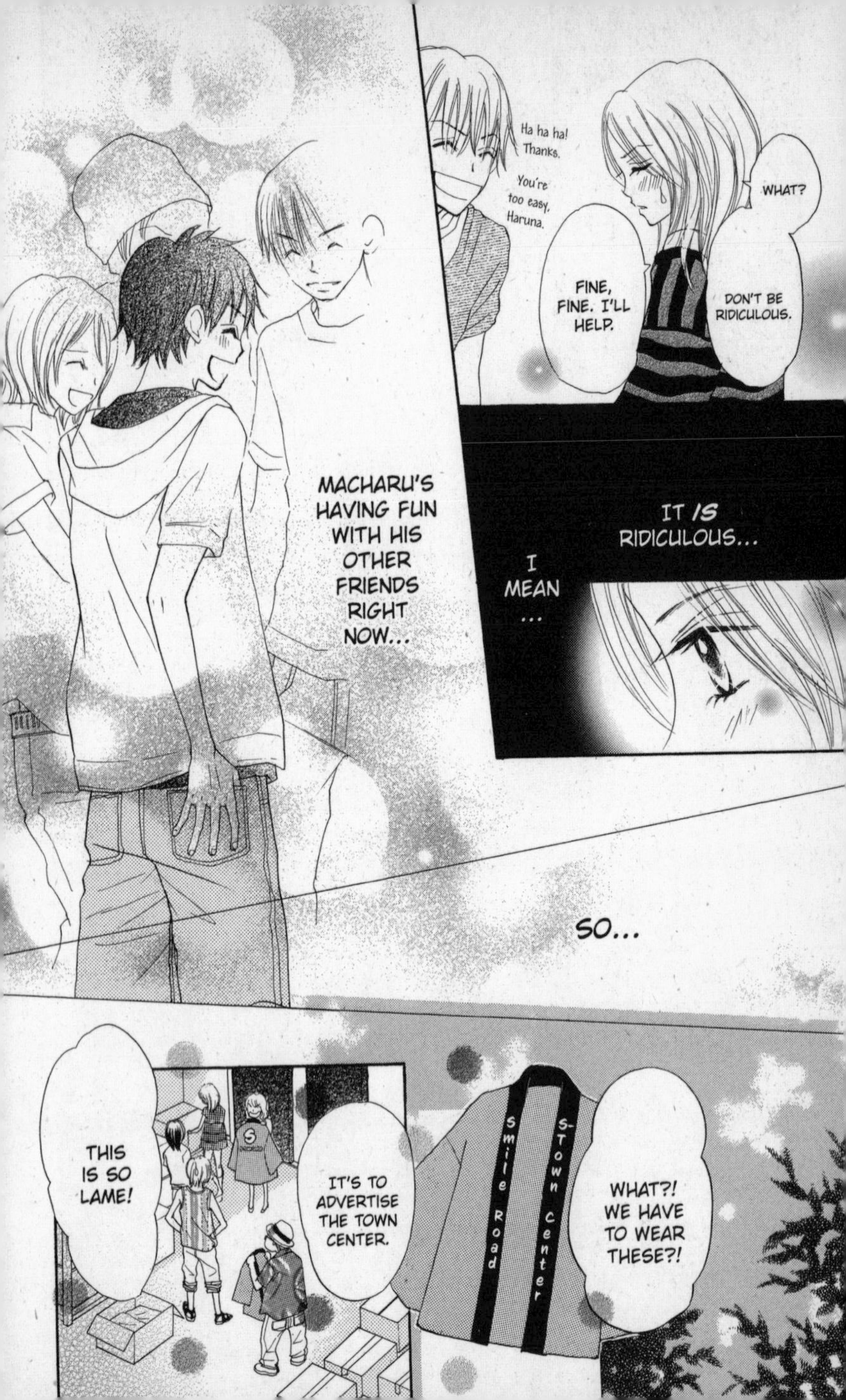
WHAT?
DON'T BE RIDICULOUS.
Ha ha ha! Thanks.
You're too easy, Haruna.
FINE, FINE. I'LL HELP.
IT *IS* RIDICULOUS...
I MEAN...
MACHARU'S HAVING FUN WITH HIS OTHER FRIENDS RIGHT NOW...
SO...
WHAT?! WE HAVE TO WEAR THESE?!
S-Town center
Smile Road
IT'S TO ADVERTISE THE TOWN CENTER.
THIS IS SO LAME!

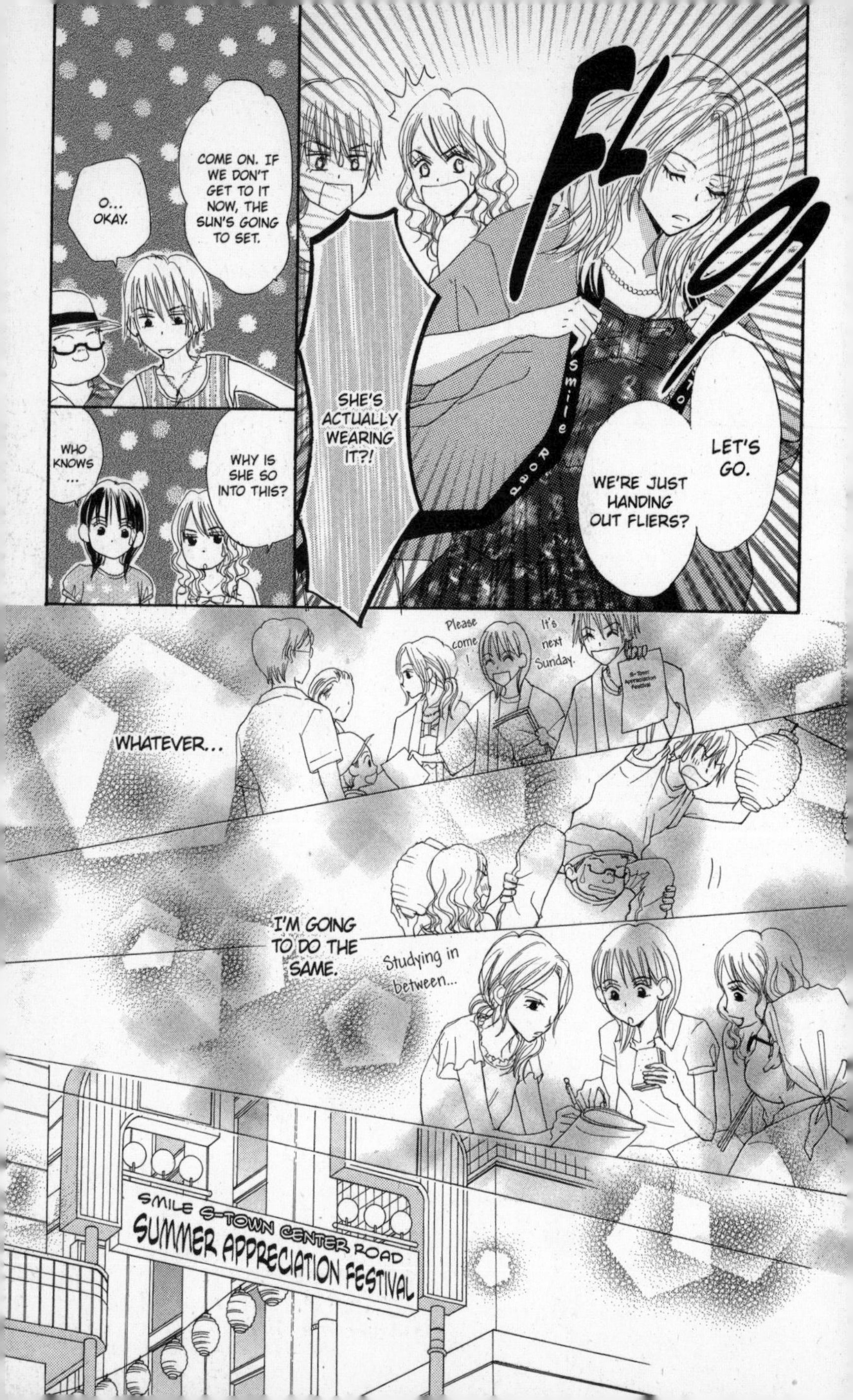
FLOP
Smile Road
LET'S GO.
WE'RE JUST HANDING OUT FLIERS?
SHE'S ACTUALLY WEARING IT?!
COME ON. IF WE DON'T GET TO IT NOW, THE SUN'S GOING TO SET.
O... OKAY.
WHY IS SHE SO INTO THIS?
WHO KNOWS ...
It's next Sunday.
Please come!
WHATEVER...
I'M GOING TO DO THE SAME.
Studying in between...
SMILE S-TOWN CENTER ROAD
SUMMER APPRECIATION FESTIVAL

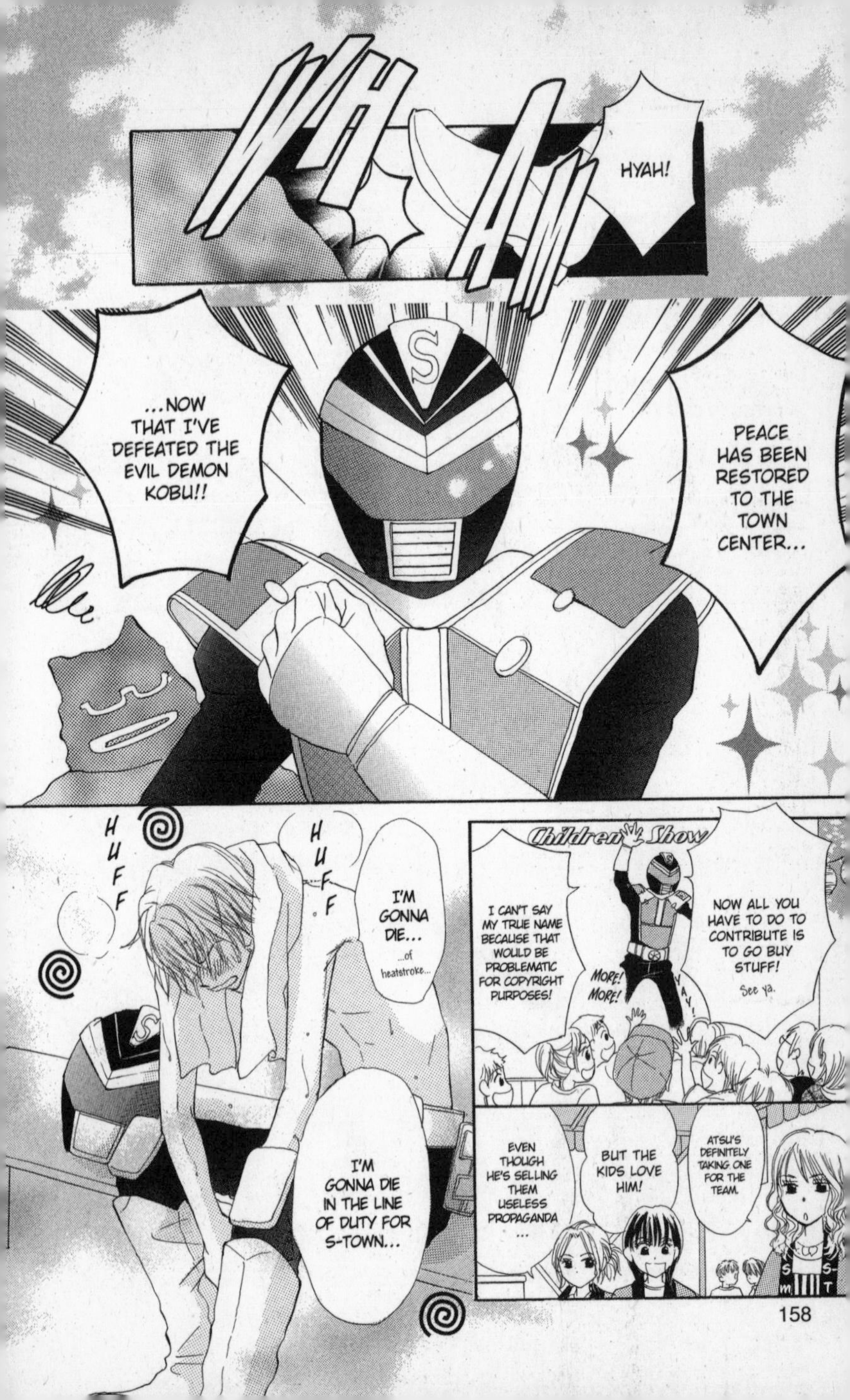
WHAM
HYAH!
PEACE HAS BEEN RESTORED TO THE TOWN CENTER...
...NOW THAT I'VE DEFEATED THE EVIL DEMON KOBU!!
Children Show
NOW ALL YOU HAVE TO DO TO CONTRIBUTE IS TO GO BUY STUFF!
See ya.
YAY!
MORE! MORE!
I CAN'T SAY MY TRUE NAME BECAUSE THAT WOULD BE PROBLEMATIC FOR COPYRIGHT PURPOSES!
ATSU'S DEFINITELY TAKING ONE FOR THE TEAM.
BUT THE KIDS LOVE HIM!
EVEN THOUGH HE'S SELLING THEM USELESS PROPAGANDA ...
HUFF
HUFF
I'M GONNA DIE...
...of heatstroke...
I'M GONNA DIE IN THE LINE OF DUTY FOR S-TOWN...

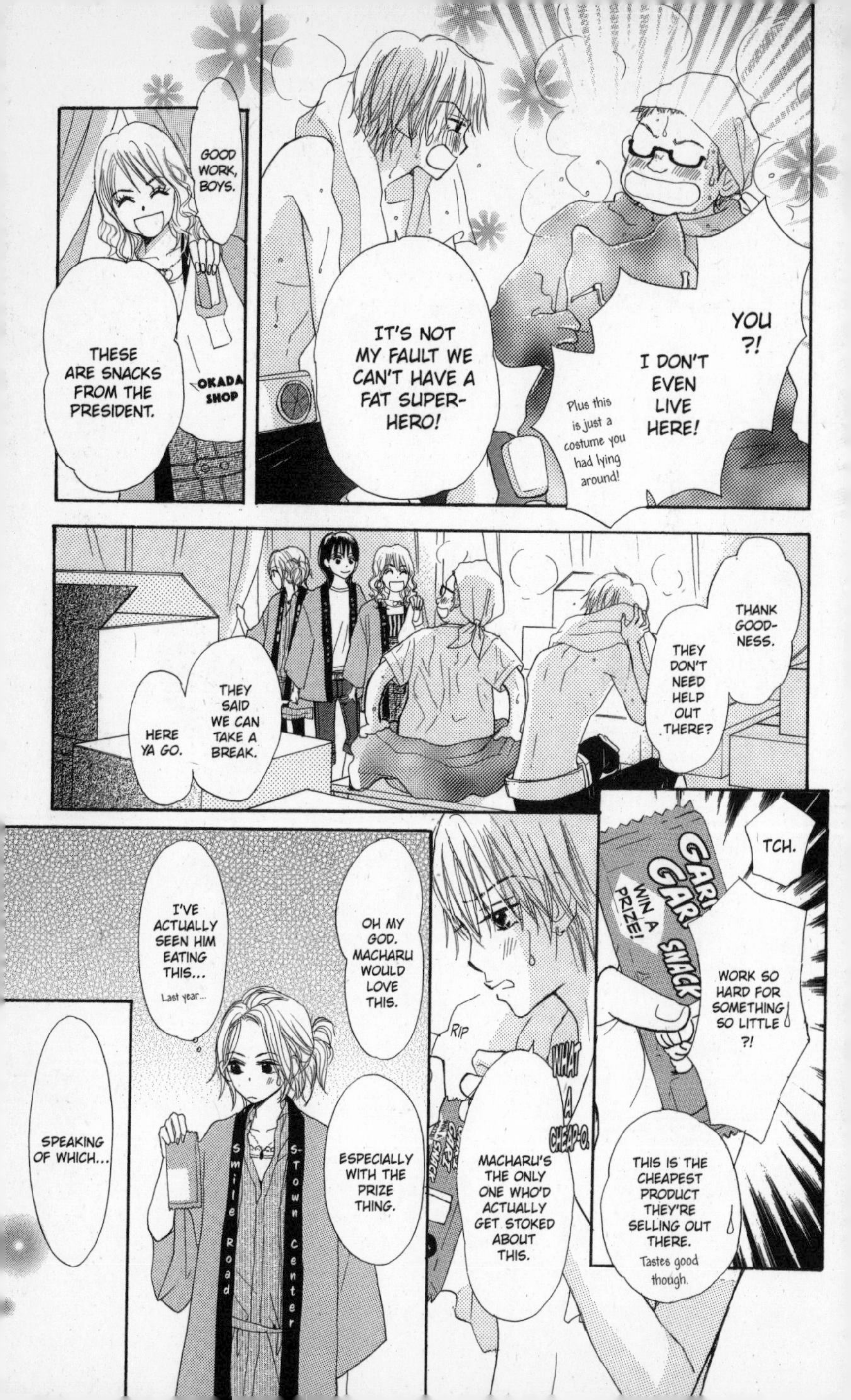
YOU ?!
I DON'T EVEN LIVE HERE!
Plus this is just a costume you had lying around!
IT'S NOT MY FAULT WE CAN'T HAVE A FAT SUPER-HERO!
GOOD WORK, BOYS.
THESE ARE SNACKS FROM THE PRESIDENT.
OKADA SHOP
THANK GOOD-NESS.
THEY DON'T NEED HELP OUT THERE?
THEY SAID WE CAN TAKE A BREAK.
HERE YA GO.
TCH.
WIN A PRIZE!
SNACK
WORK SO HARD FOR SOMETHING SO LITTLE ?!
THIS IS THE CHEAPEST PRODUCT THEY'RE SELLING OUT THERE.
Tastes good though.
RIP
WHAT A CHEAP-O.
MACHARU'S THE ONLY ONE WHO'D ACTUALLY GET STOKED ABOUT THIS.
OH MY GOD. MACHARU WOULD LOVE THIS.
I'VE ACTUALLY SEEN HIM EATING THIS...
Last year...
ESPECIALLY WITH THE PRIZE THING.
SPEAKING OF WHICH...
Smile Road
S-Town Center

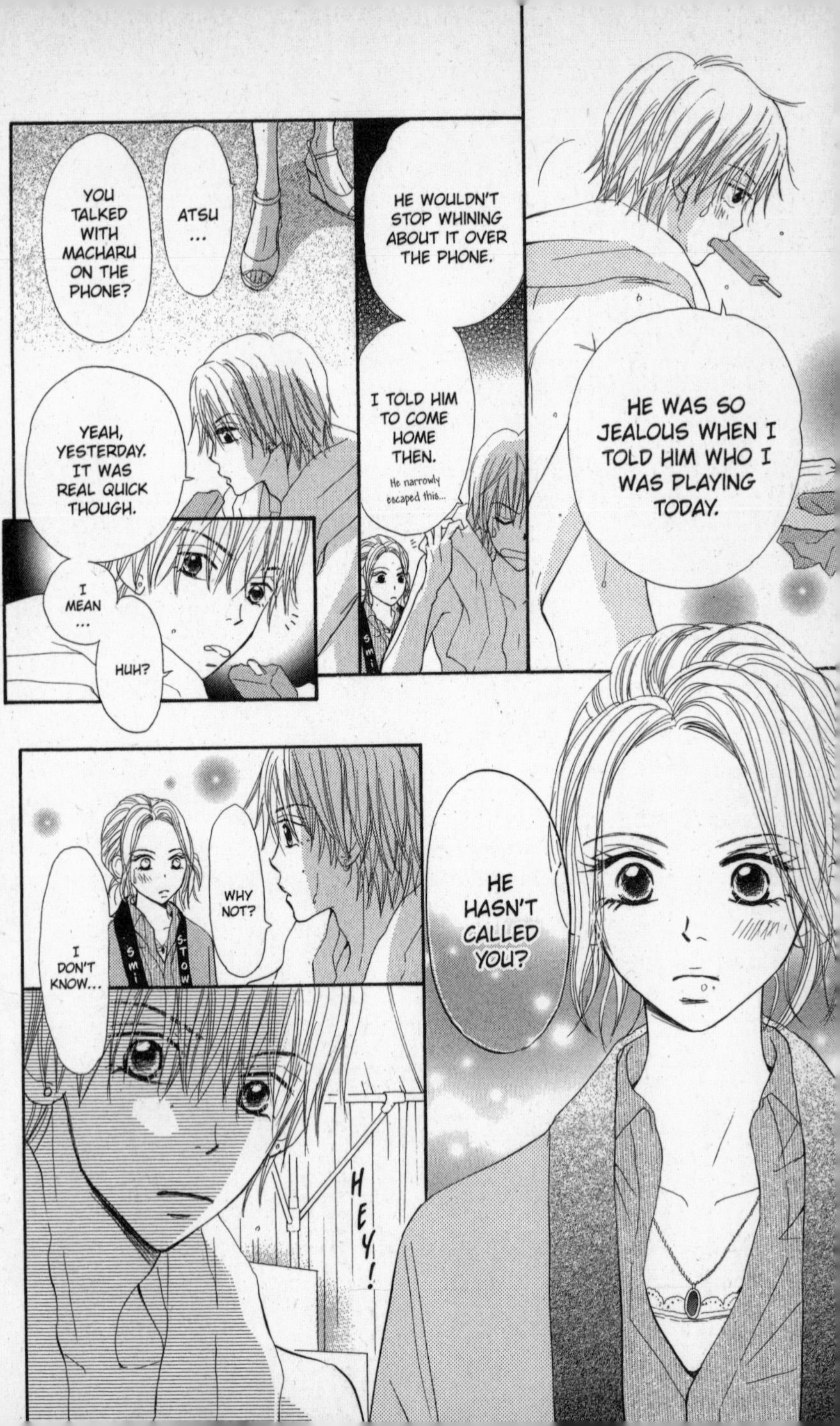
HE WAS SO JEALOUS WHEN I TOLD HIM WHO I WAS PLAYING TODAY.
HE WOULDN'T STOP WHINING ABOUT IT OVER THE PHONE.
I TOLD HIM TO COME HOME THEN.
He narrowly escaped this...
ATSU ...
YOU TALKED WITH MACHARU ON THE PHONE?
YEAH, YESTERDAY. IT WAS REAL QUICK THOUGH.
I MEAN ...
HUH?
HE HASN'T CALLED YOU?
WHY NOT?
I DON'T KNOW...
HEY!

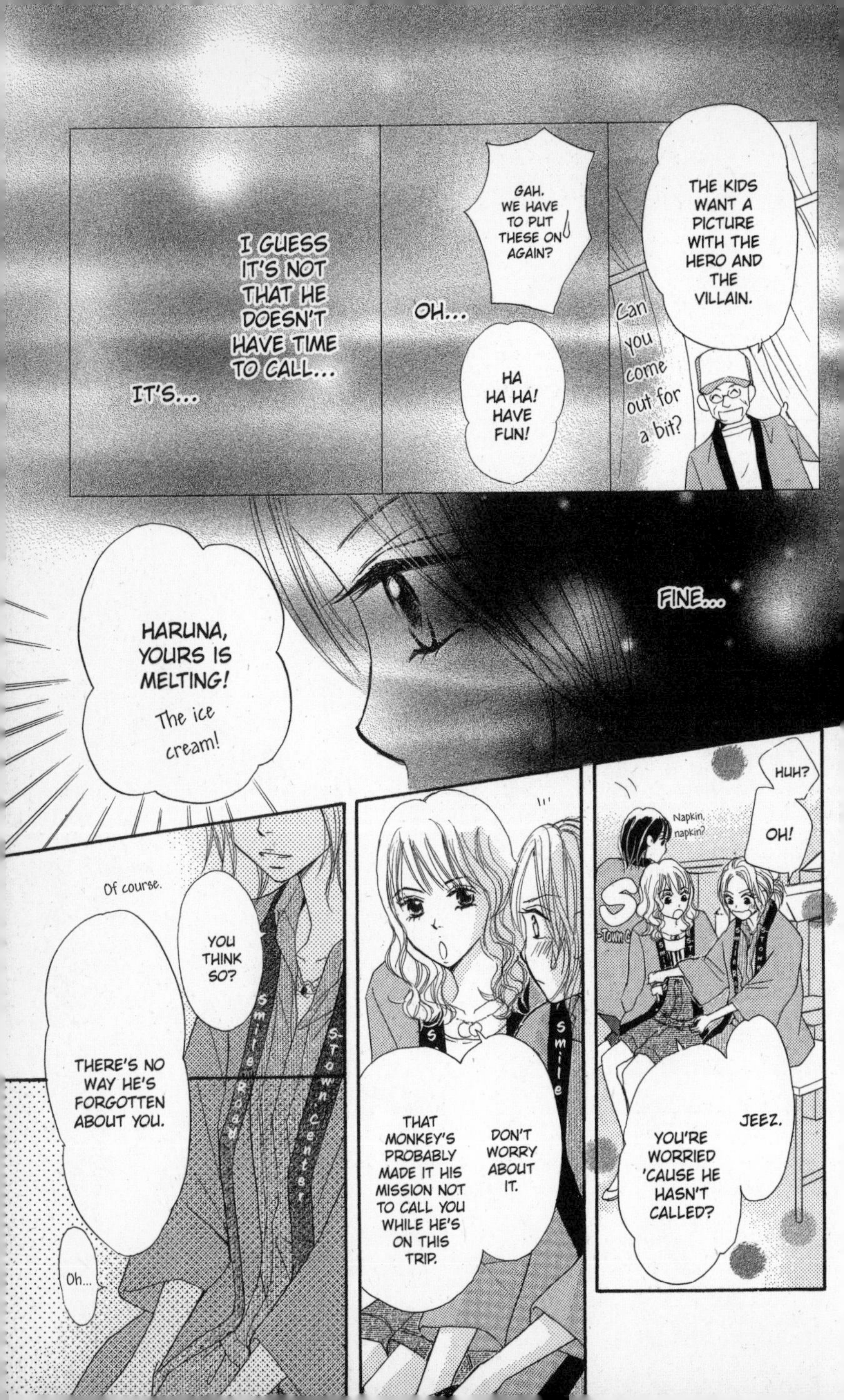
THE KIDS WANT A PICTURE WITH THE HERO AND THE VILLAIN.
Can you come out for a bit?
GAH. WE HAVE TO PUT THESE ON AGAIN?
OH...
HA HA HA! HAVE FUN!
I GUESS IT'S NOT THAT HE DOESN'T HAVE TIME TO CALL...
IT'S...
FINE...
HARUNA, YOURS IS MELTING!
The ice cream!
HUH?
OH!
Napkin, napkin?
JEEZ.
YOU'RE WORRIED 'CAUSE HE HASN'T CALLED?
DON'T WORRY ABOUT IT.
THAT MONKEY'S PROBABLY MADE IT HIS MISSION NOT TO CALL YOU WHILE HE'S ON THIS TRIP.
YOU THINK SO?
Of course.
THERE'S NO WAY HE'S FORGOTTEN ABOUT YOU.
Oh...

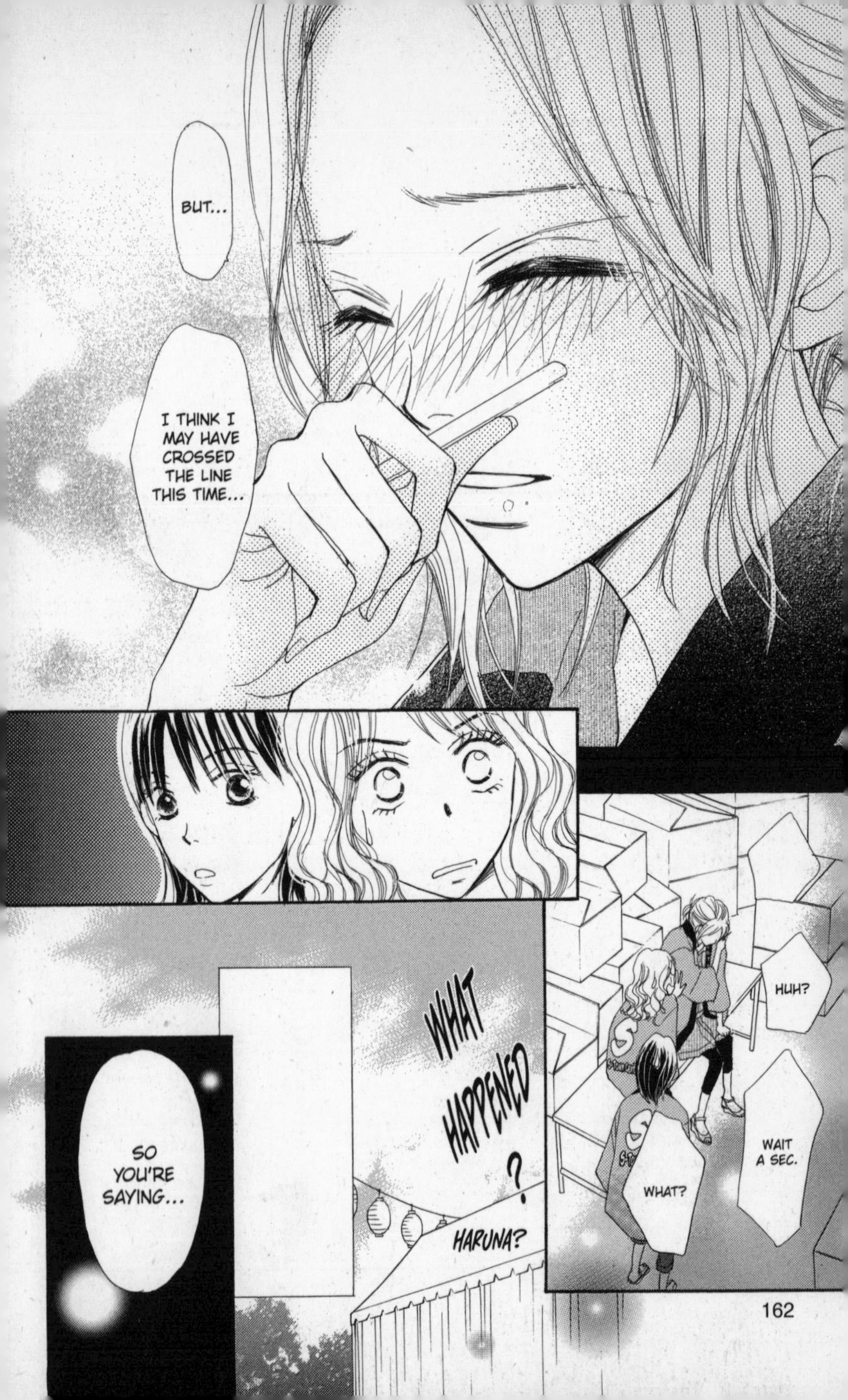
BUT...
I THINK I MAY HAVE CROSSED THE LINE THIS TIME...
HUH?
WAIT A SEC.
WHAT?
WHAT HAPPENED?
HARUNA?
SO YOU'RE SAYING...

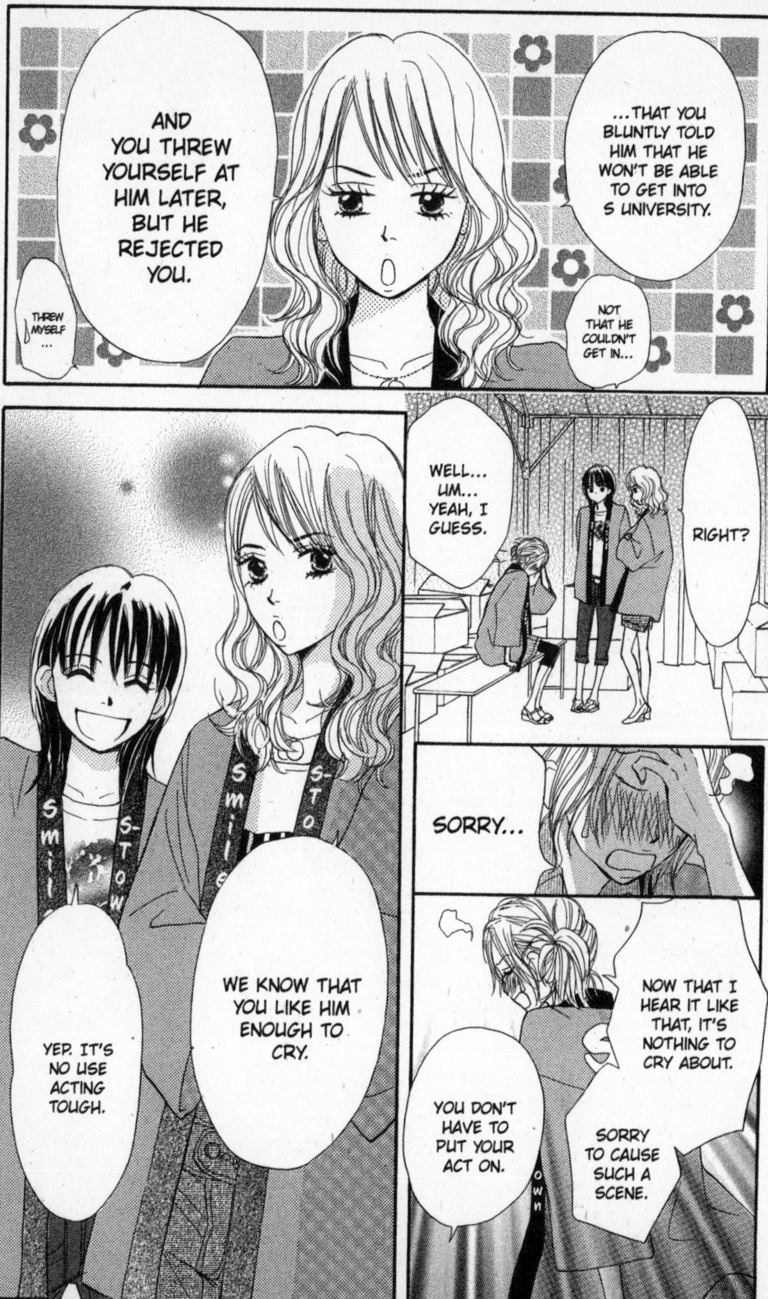
...THAT YOU BLUNTLY TOLD HIM THAT HE WON'T BE ABLE TO GET INTO S UNIVERSITY.
NOT THAT HE COULDN'T GET IN...
AND YOU THREW YOURSELF AT HIM LATER, BUT HE REJECTED YOU.
THREW MYSELF...
RIGHT?
WELL... UM... YEAH, I GUESS.
SORRY...
NOW THAT I HEAR IT LIKE THAT, IT'S NOTHING TO CRY ABOUT.
SORRY TO CAUSE SUCH A SCENE.
YOU DON'T HAVE TO PUT YOUR ACT ON.
WE KNOW THAT YOU LIKE HIM ENOUGH TO CRY.
YEP. IT'S NO USE ACTING TOUGH.

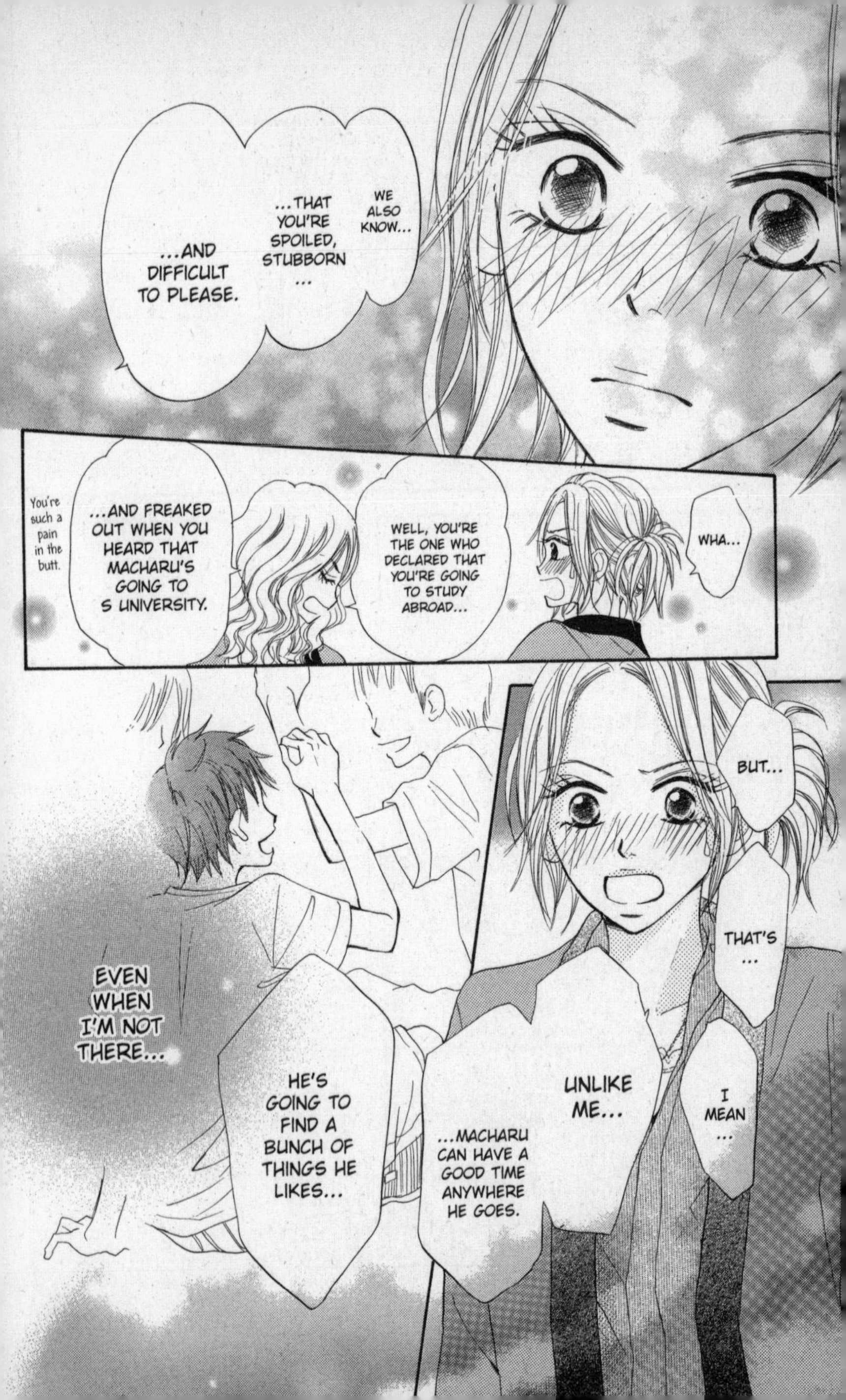
WE ALSO KNOW...
...THAT YOU'RE SPOILED, STUBBORN...
...AND DIFFICULT TO PLEASE.
WHA...
WELL, YOU'RE THE ONE WHO DECLARED THAT YOU'RE GOING TO STUDY ABROAD...
...AND FREAKED OUT WHEN YOU HEARD THAT MACHARU'S GOING TO S UNIVERSITY.
You're such a pain in the butt.
BUT...
THAT'S...
I MEAN...
UNLIKE ME...
...MACHARU CAN HAVE A GOOD TIME ANYWHERE HE GOES.
HE'S GOING TO FIND A BUNCH OF THINGS HE LIKES...
EVEN WHEN I'M NOT THERE...

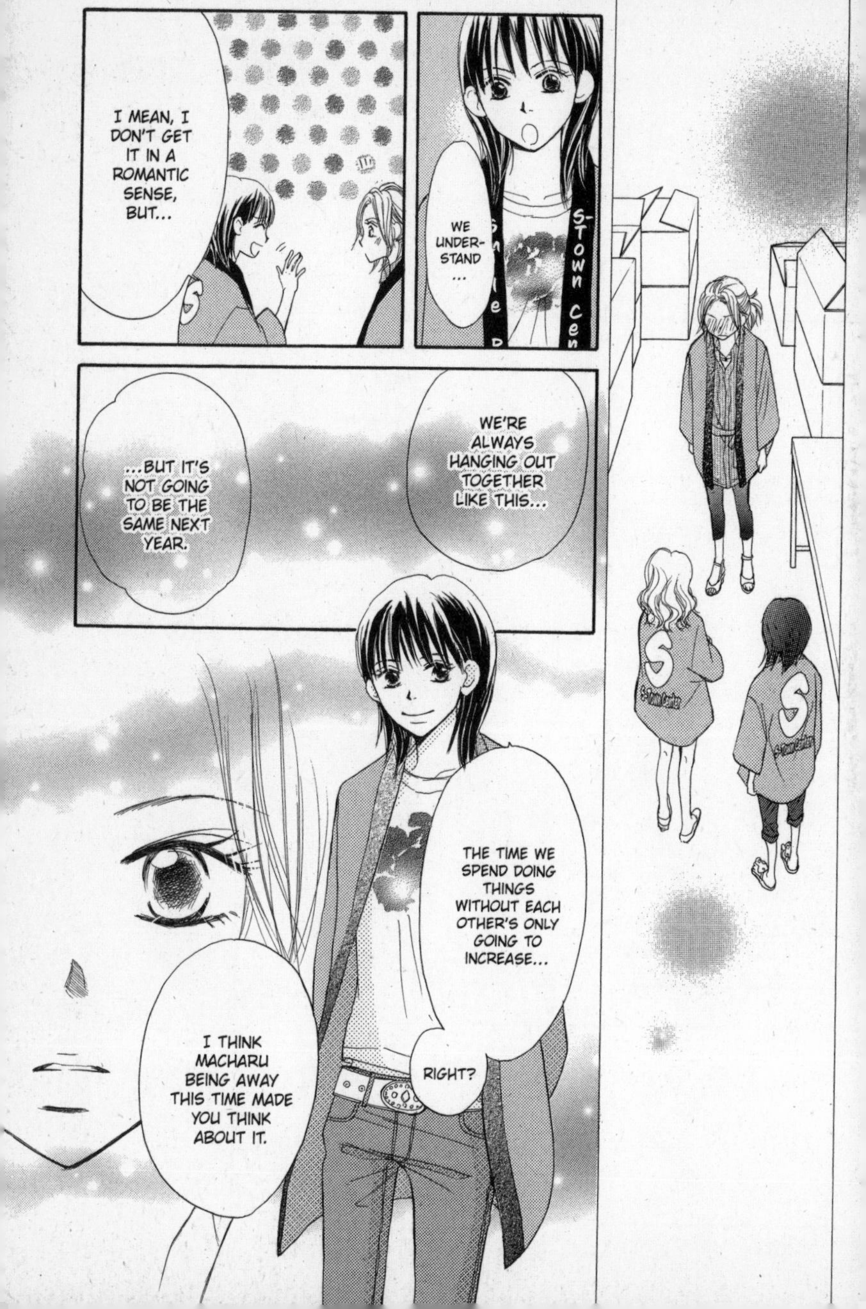
WE UNDERSTAND...
I MEAN, I DON'T GET IT IN A ROMANTIC SENSE, BUT...
WE'RE ALWAYS HANGING OUT TOGETHER LIKE THIS...
...BUT IT'S NOT GOING TO BE THE SAME NEXT YEAR.
THE TIME WE SPEND DOING THINGS WITHOUT EACH OTHER'S ONLY GOING TO INCREASE...
RIGHT?
I THINK MACHARU BEING AWAY THIS TIME MADE YOU THINK ABOUT IT.

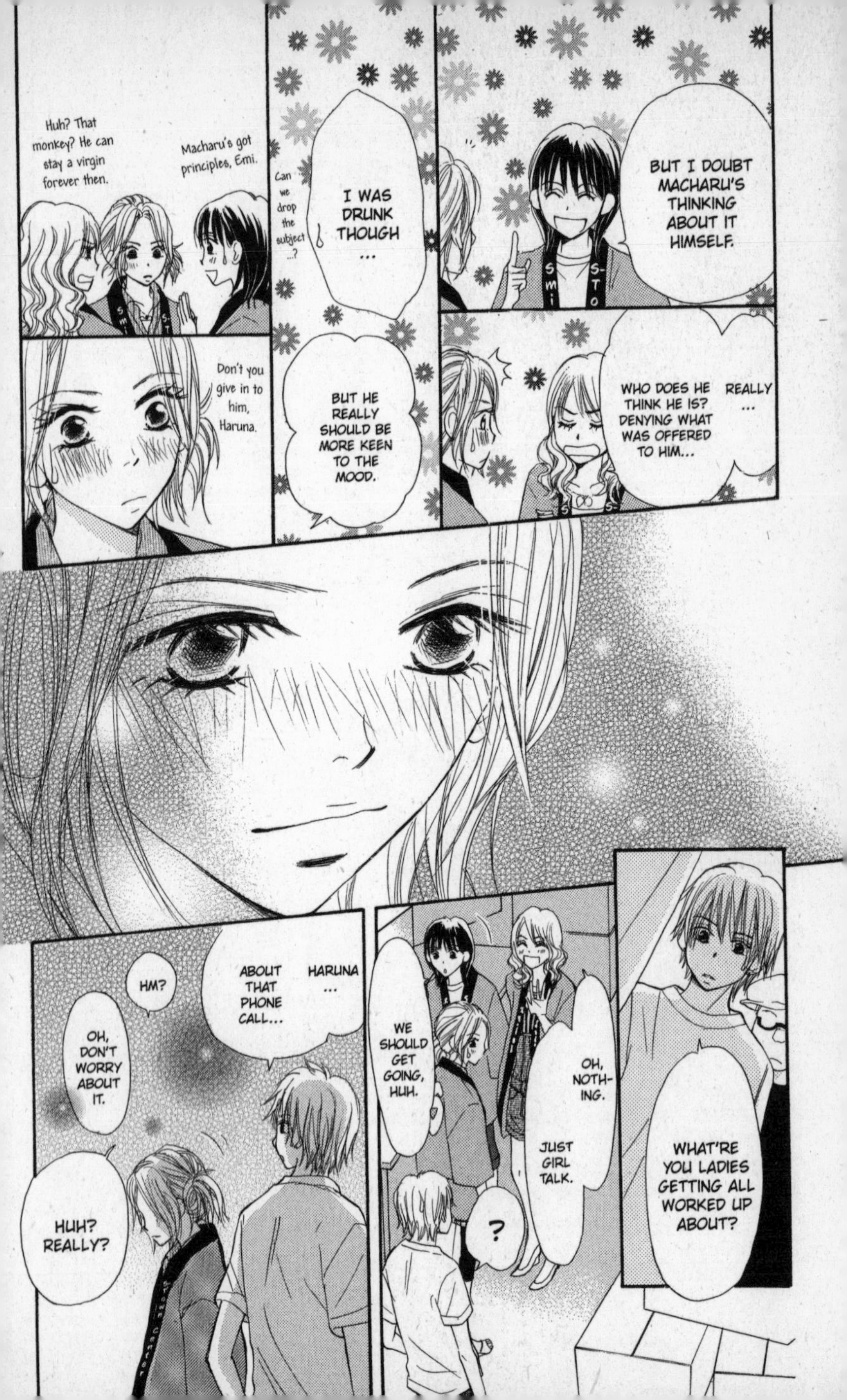
BUT I DOUBT MACHARU'S THINKING ABOUT IT HIMSELF.
I WAS DRUNK THOUGH...
Can we drop the subject...?
Macharu's got principles, Emi.
Huh? That monkey? He can stay a virgin forever then.
REALLY...
WHO DOES HE THINK HE IS? DENYING WHAT WAS OFFERED TO HIM...
BUT HE REALLY SHOULD BE MORE KEEN TO THE MOOD.
Don't you give in to him, Haruna.
WHAT'RE YOU LADIES GETTING ALL WORKED UP ABOUT?
OH, NOTHING.
JUST GIRL TALK.
WE SHOULD GET GOING, HUH.
?
HARUNA...
ABOUT THAT PHONE CALL...
HM?
OH, DON'T WORRY ABOUT IT.
HUH? REALLY?

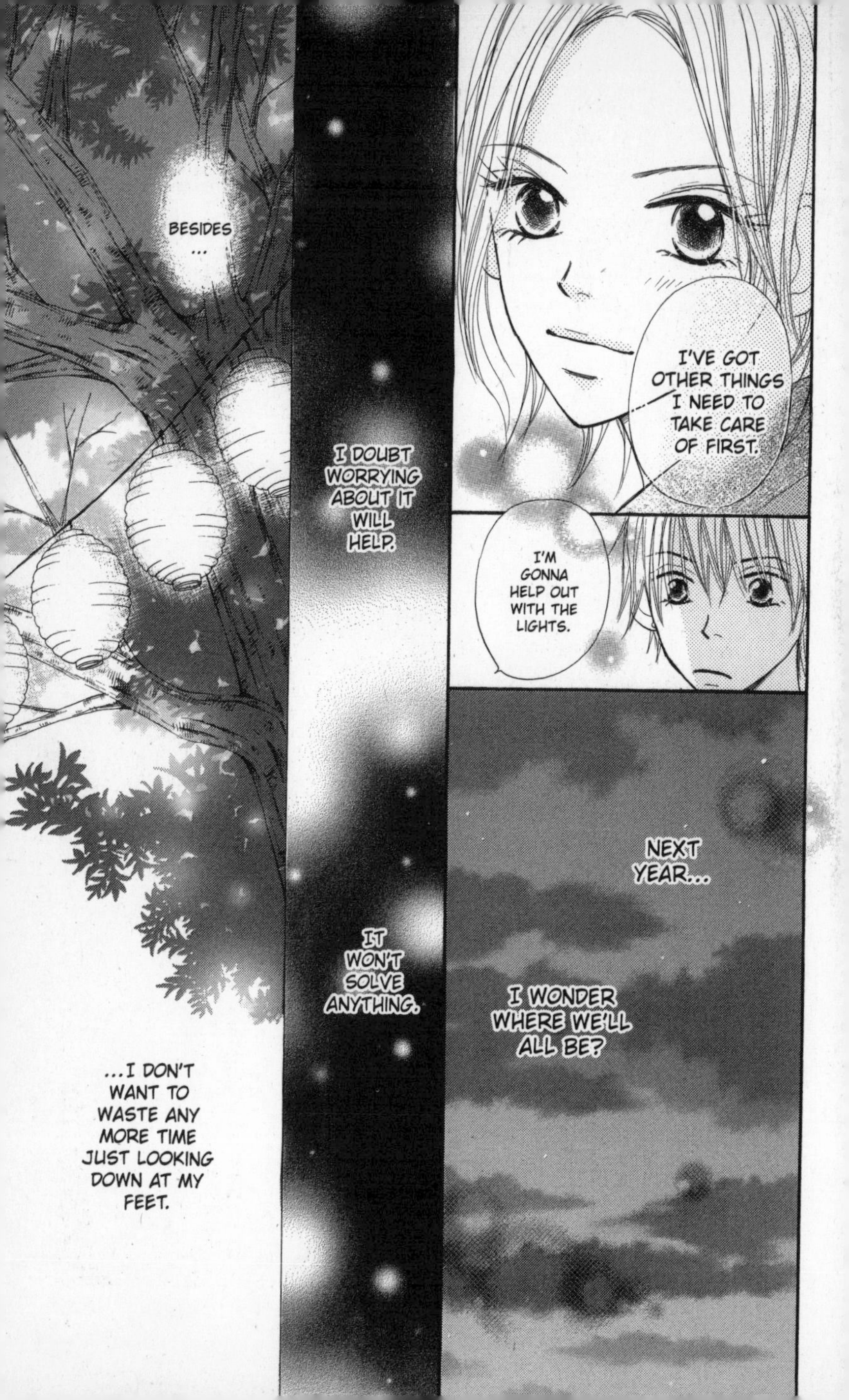
I'VE GOT OTHER THINGS I NEED TO TAKE CARE OF FIRST.
I'M GONNA HELP OUT WITH THE LIGHTS.
NEXT YEAR...
I WONDER WHERE WE'LL ALL BE?
I DOUBT WORRYING ABOUT IT WILL HELP.
IT WON'T SOLVE ANYTHING.
BESIDES...
...I DON'T WANT TO WASTE ANY MORE TIME JUST LOOKING DOWN AT MY FEET.

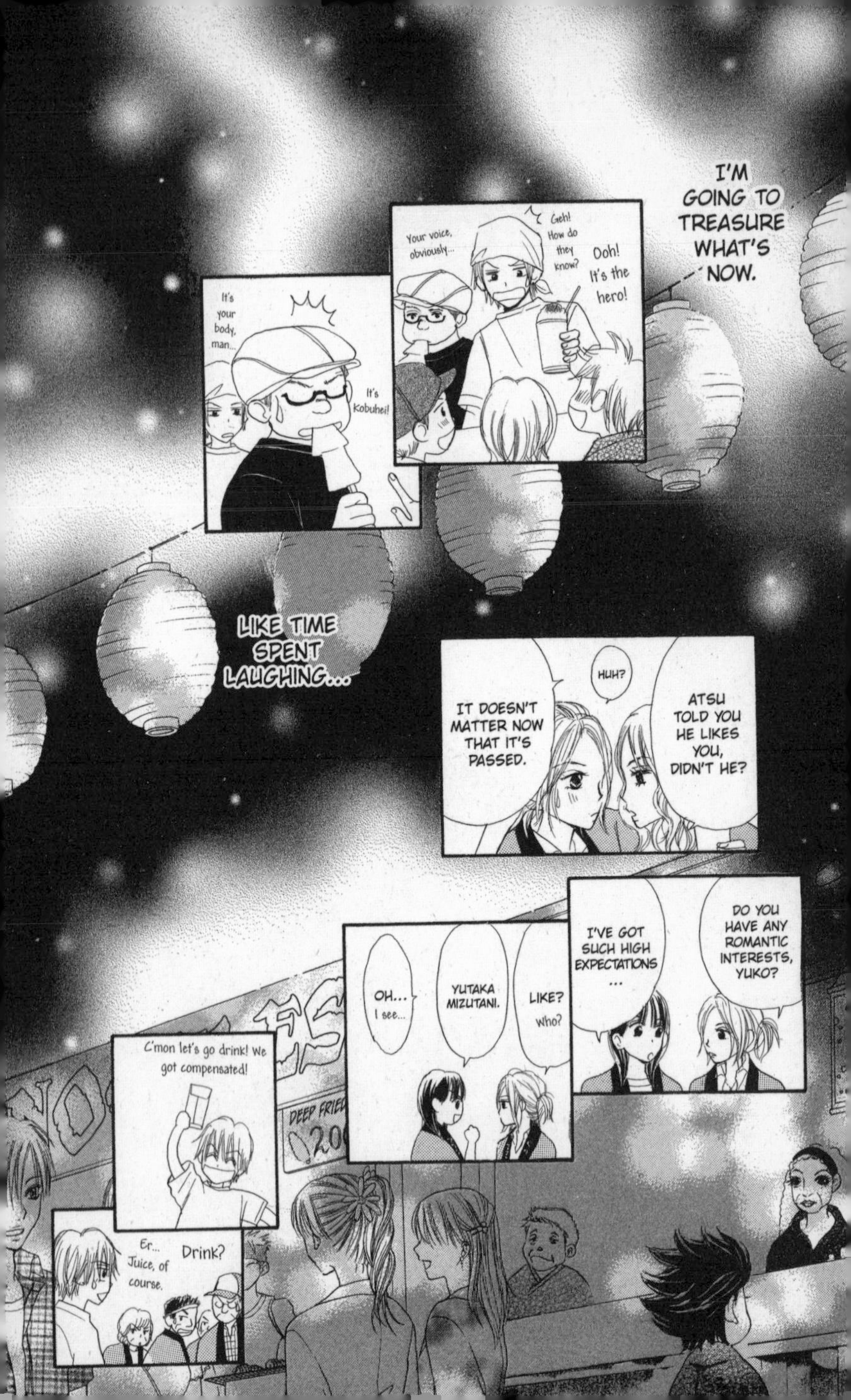

I'M GOING TO TREASURE WHAT'S NOW.
Ooh! It's the hero!
Geh! How do they know?
Your voice, obviously...
It's Kobuhei!
It's your body, man...
LIKE TIME SPENT LAUGHING...
ATSU TOLD YOU HE LIKES YOU, DIDN'T HE?
HUH?
IT DOESN'T MATTER NOW THAT IT'S PASSED.
DO YOU HAVE ANY ROMANTIC INTERESTS, YUKO?
I'VE GOT SUCH HIGH EXPECTATIONS ...
LIKE? Who?
YUTAKA MIZUTANI.
OH... I see...
C'mon let's go drink! We got compensated!
Drink?
Er... Juice, of course.
DEEP FRIED

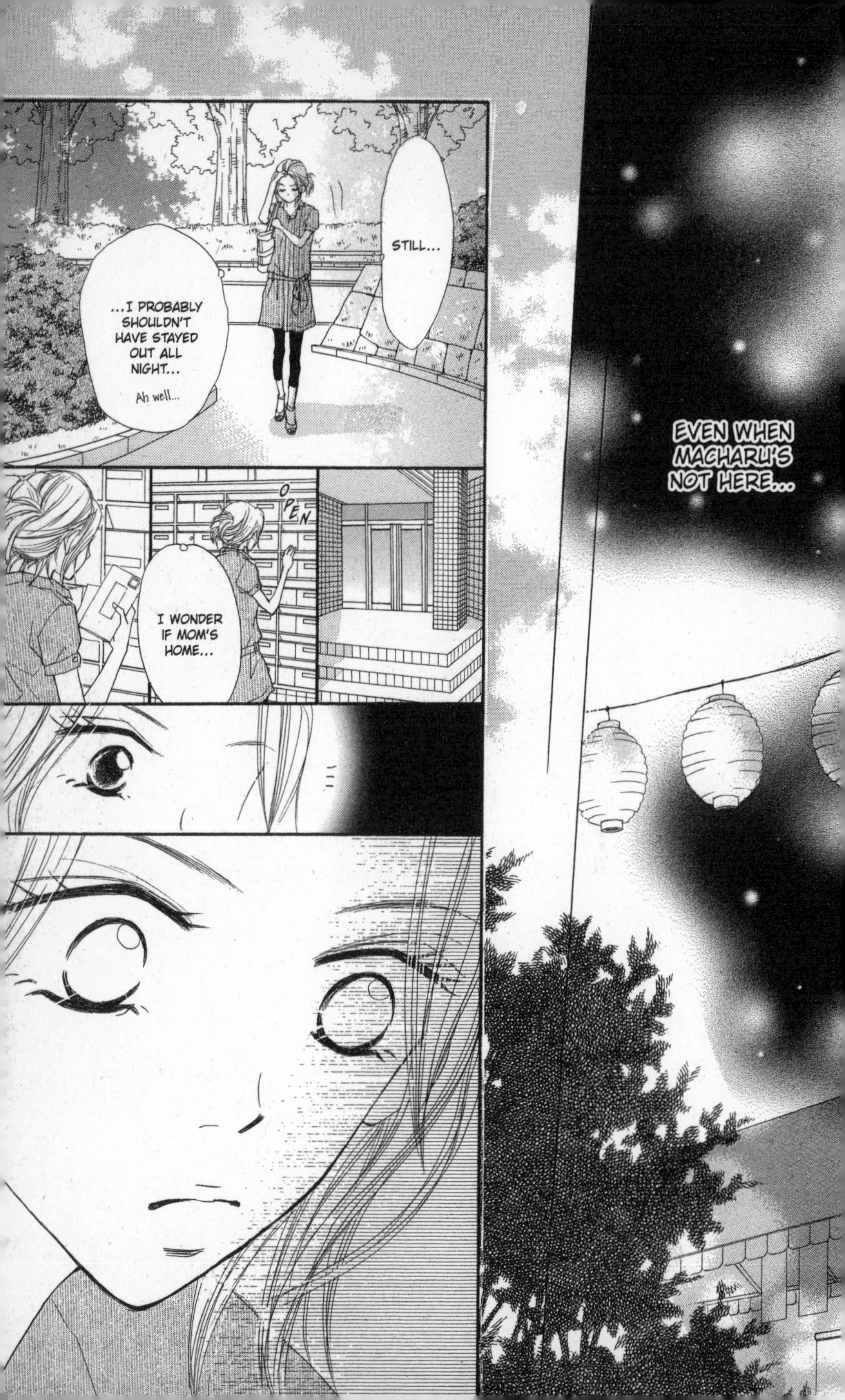
EVEN WHEN MACHARU'S NOT HERE...
STILL...
...I PROBABLY SHOULDN'T HAVE STAYED OUT ALL NIGHT...
Ah well...
OPEN
I WONDER IF MOM'S HOME...

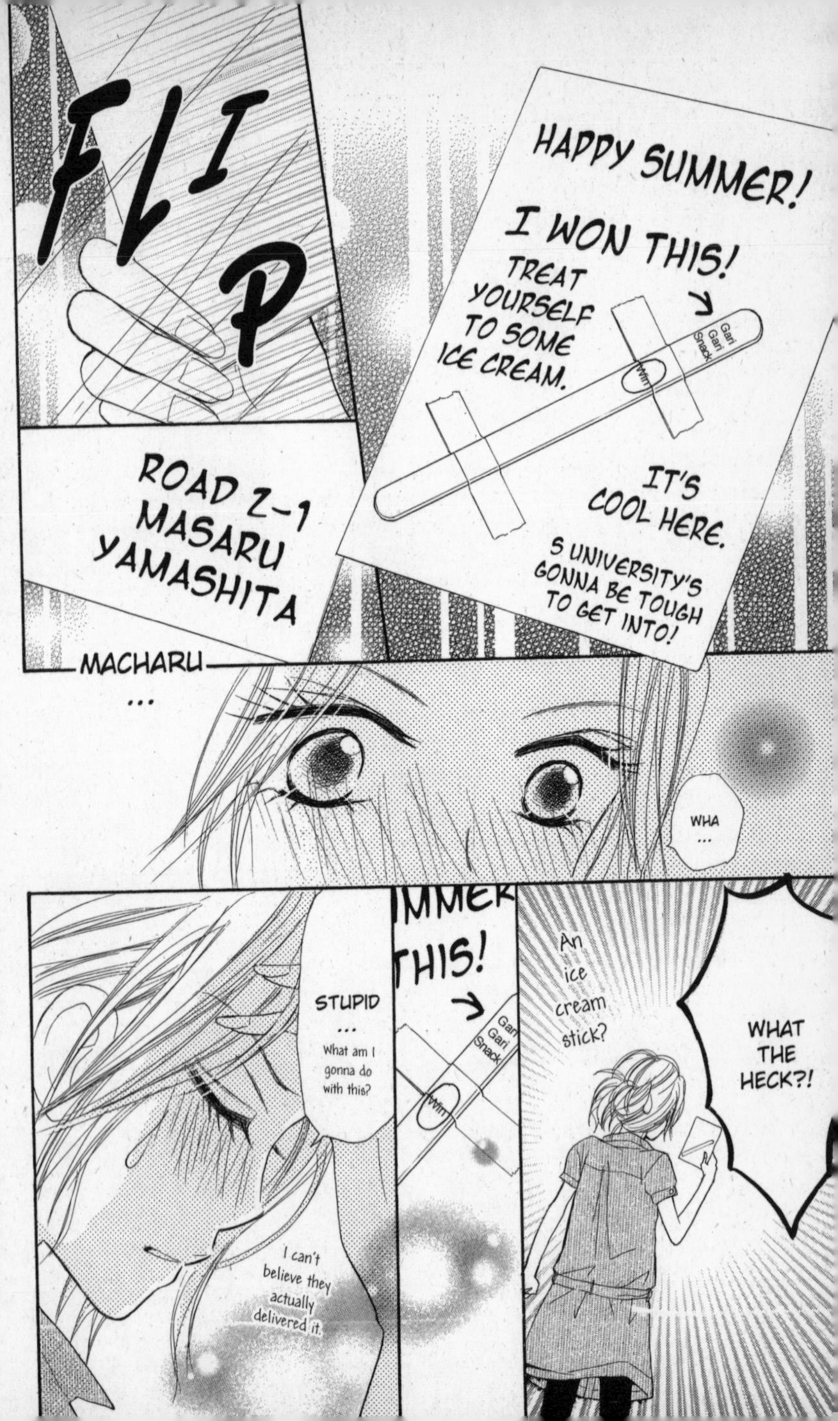
HAPPY SUMMER!
I WON THIS!
TREAT YOURSELF TO SOME ICE CREAM.
Gari Gari Snack
IT'S COOL HERE.
S UNIVERSITY'S GONNA BE TOUGH TO GET INTO!
FLIP
ROAD Z-1 MASARU YAMASHITA
MACHARU...
WHA...
WHAT THE HECK?!
An ice cream stick?
THIS!
Gari Gari Snack
STUPID...
What am I gonna do with this?
I can't believe they actually delivered it.

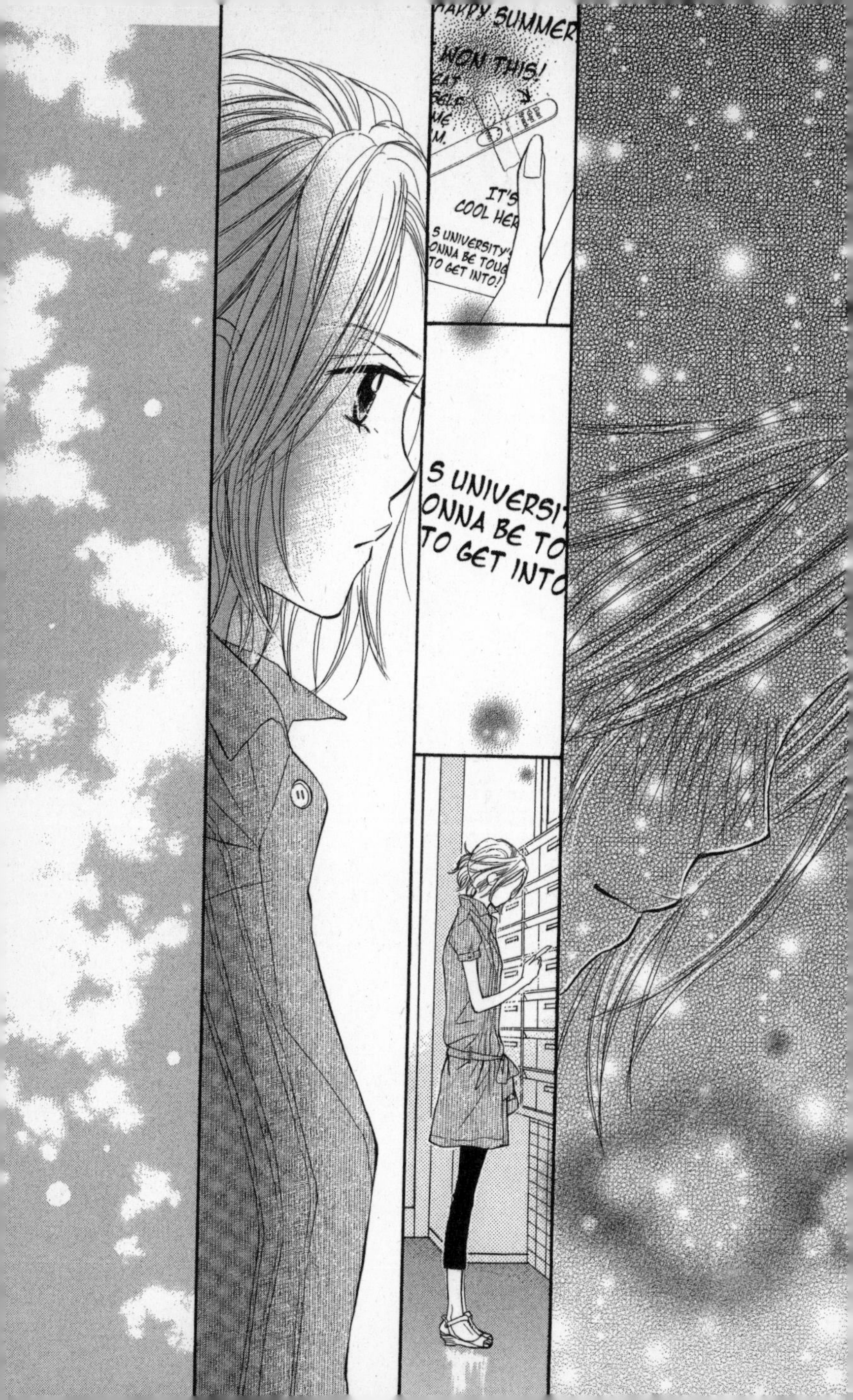
HAPPY SUMMER
WON THIS!
IT'S COOL HER
S UNIVERSITY'S ONNA BE TOUG TO GET INTO!
S UNIVERSIT ONNA BE TO TO GET INTO

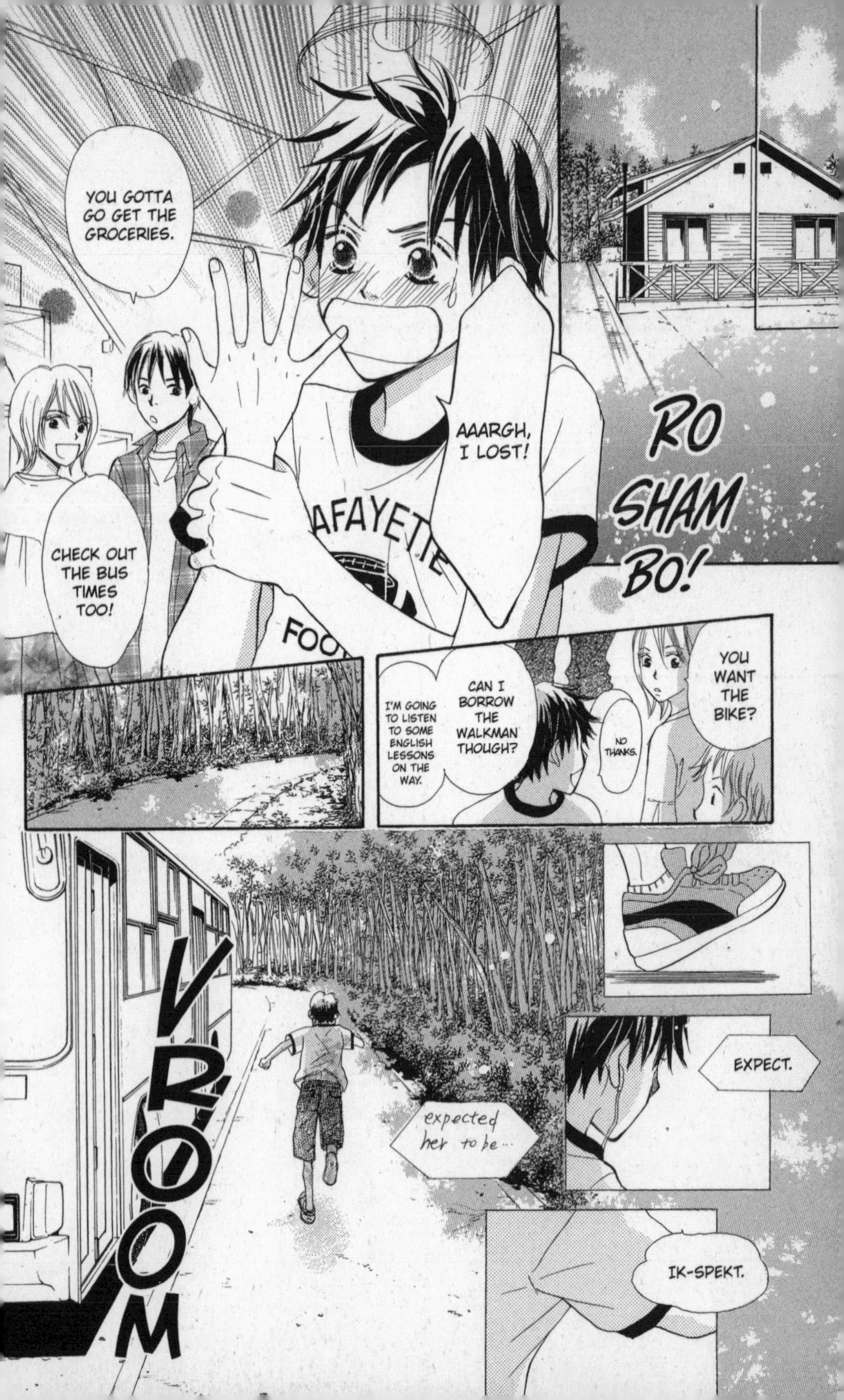
RO SHAM BO!
AAARGH, I LOST!
YOU GOTTA GO GET THE GROCERIES.
CHECK OUT THE BUS TIMES TOO!
YOU WANT THE BIKE?
NO THANKS.
CAN I BORROW THE WALKMAN THOUGH?
I'M GOING TO LISTEN TO SOME ENGLISH LESSONS ON THE WAY.
EXPECT.
IK-SPEKT.
expected her to be...
VROOOM

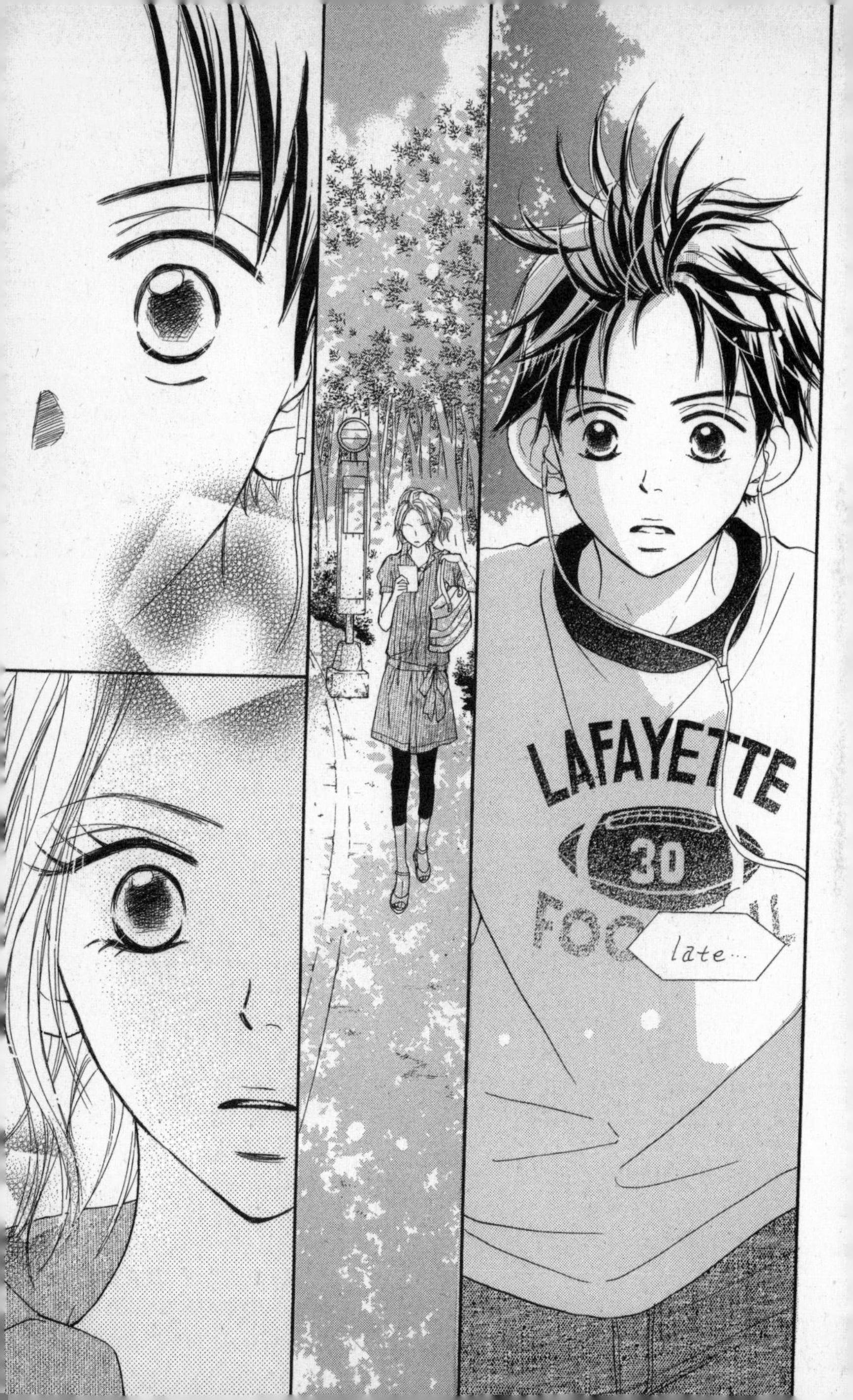
LAFAYETTE
30
late...

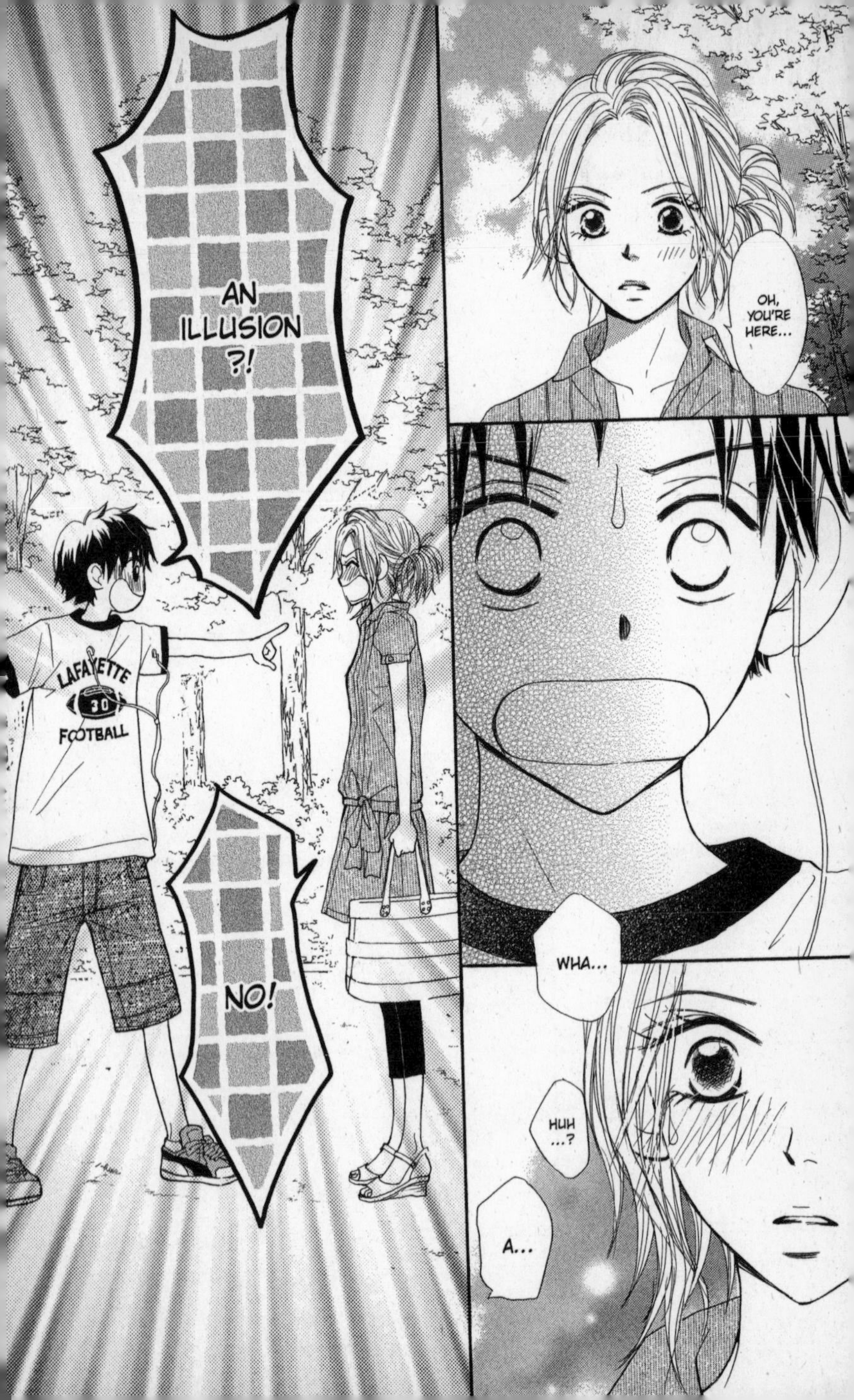
OH, YOU'RE HERE...
WHA...
HUH ...?
A...
AN ILLUSION ?!
LAFAYETTE
30
FOOTBALL
NO!

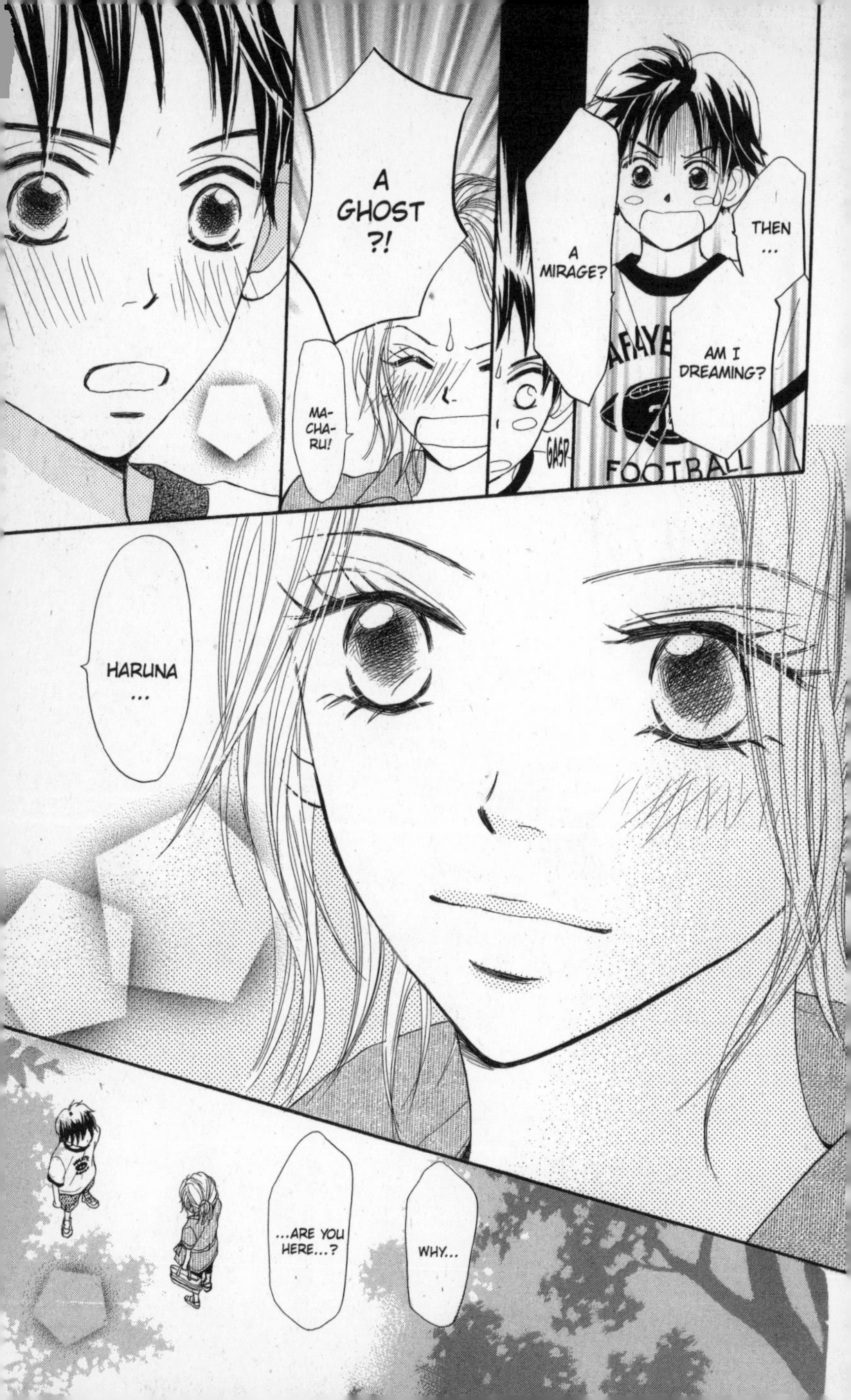
THEN ...
A MIRAGE?
AM I DREAMING?
AFAYE
FOOTBALL
GASP
A GHOST ?!
MA-CHA-RU!
HARUNA ...
WHY...
...ARE YOU HERE...?

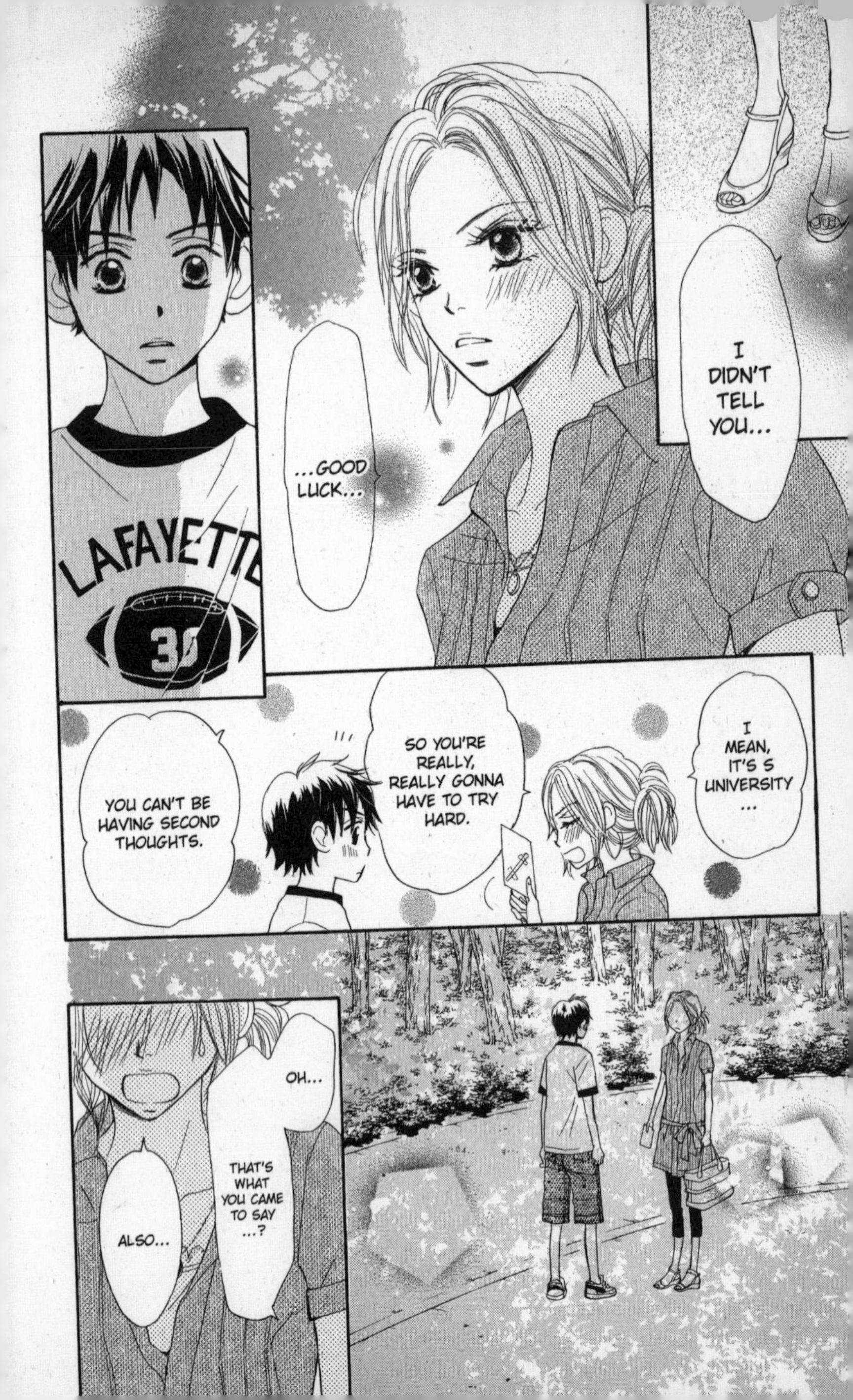
I DIDN'T TELL YOU...
...GOOD LUCK...
LAFAYETTE 30
I MEAN, IT'S S UNIVERSITY ...
SO YOU'RE REALLY, REALLY GONNA HAVE TO TRY HARD.
YOU CAN'T BE HAVING SECOND THOUGHTS.
OH...
THAT'S WHAT YOU CAME TO SAY ...?
ALSO...

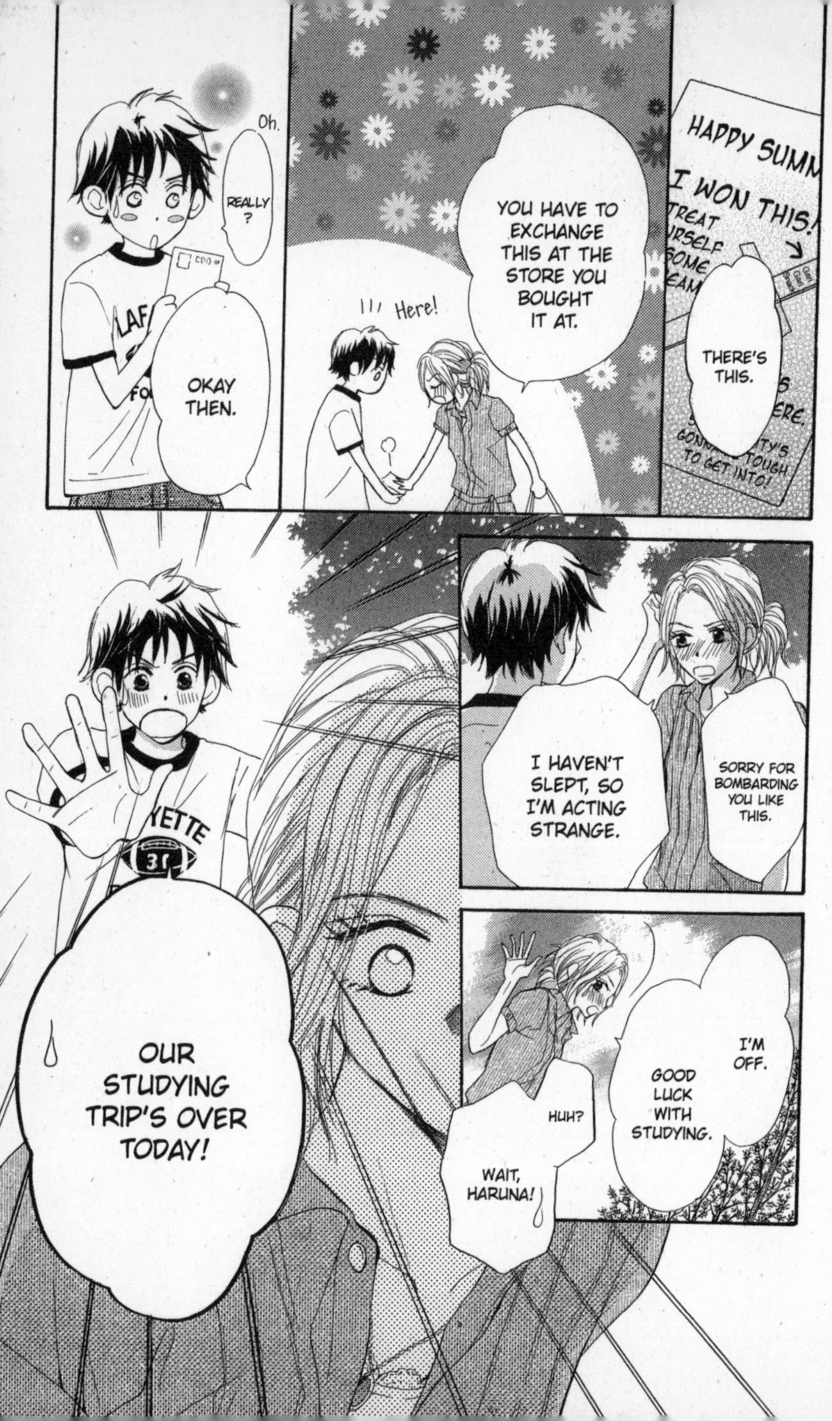
HAPPY SUMM
I WON THIS!
THERE'S THIS.
GONNA BE TOUGH TO GET INTO!
YOU HAVE TO EXCHANGE THIS AT THE STORE YOU BOUGHT IT AT.
Here!
Oh.
REALLY?
OKAY THEN.
SORRY FOR BOMBARDING YOU LIKE THIS.
I HAVEN'T SLEPT, SO I'M ACTING STRANGE.
I'M OFF.
GOOD LUCK WITH STUDYING.
HUH?
WAIT, HARUNA!
OUR STUDYING TRIP'S OVER TODAY!

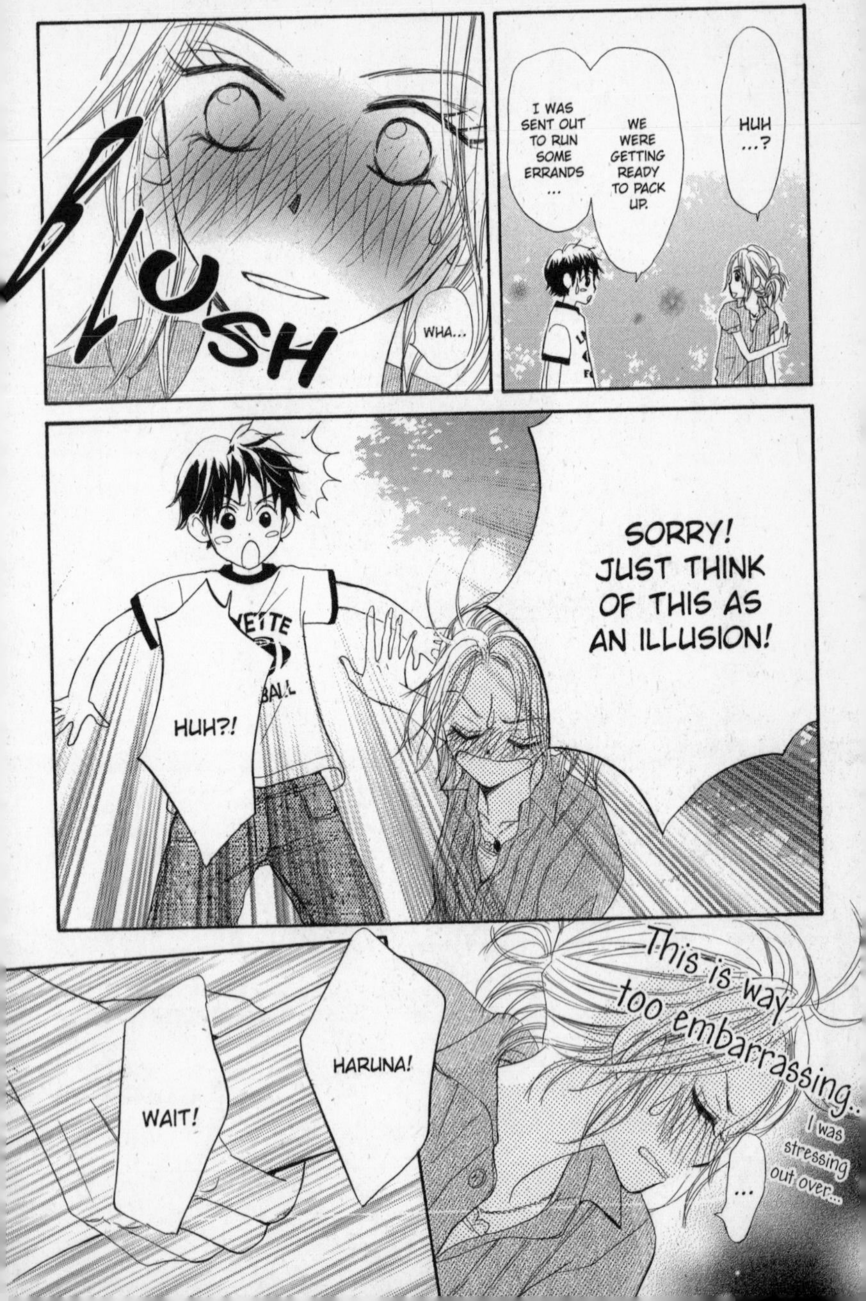
HUH ...?
WE WERE GETTING READY TO PACK UP.
I WAS SENT OUT TO RUN SOME ERRANDS ...
WHA...
BLUSH
SORRY! JUST THINK OF THIS AS AN ILLUSION!
HUH?!
This is way too embarrassing..
I was stressing out over...
...
HARUNA!
WAIT!

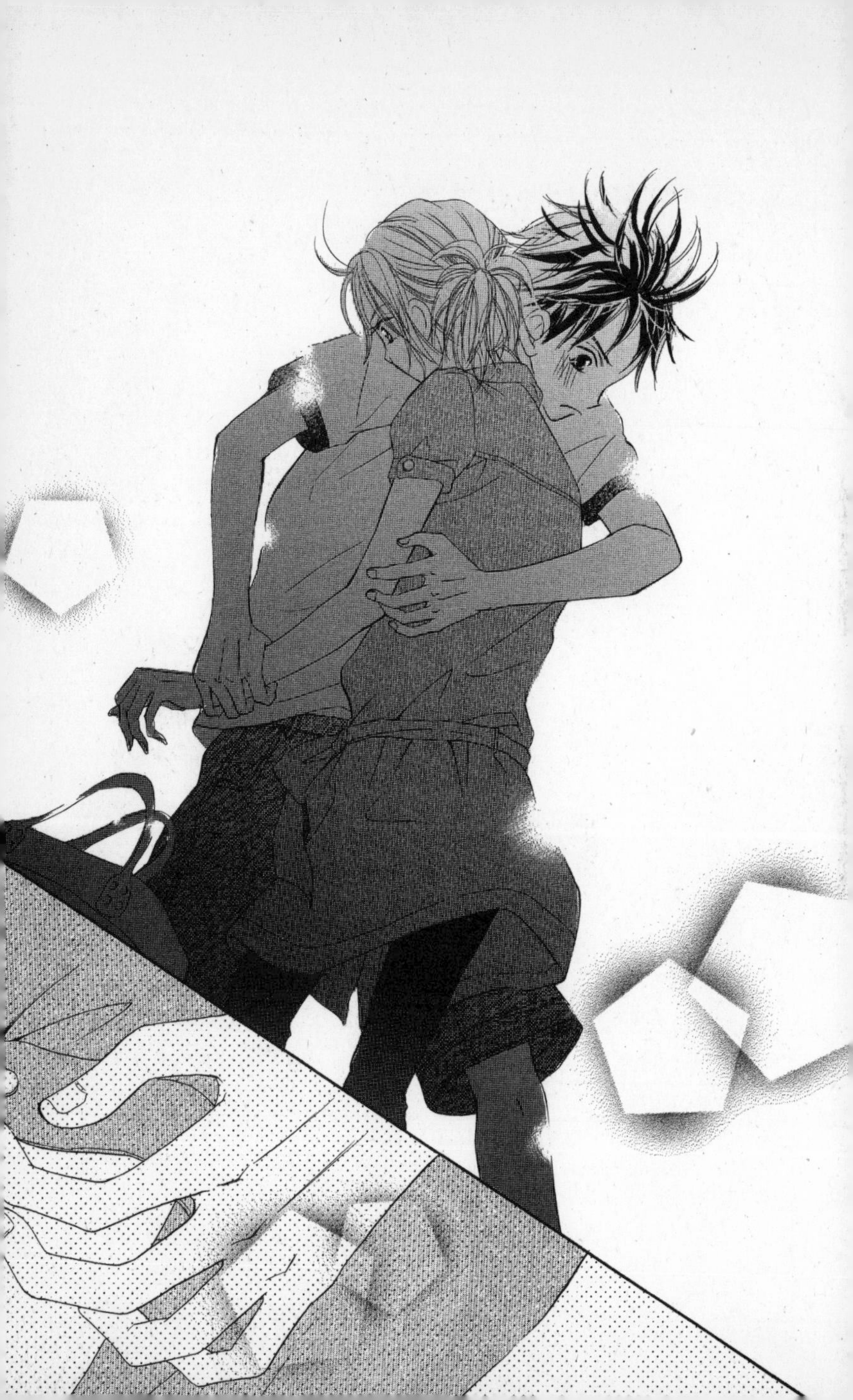

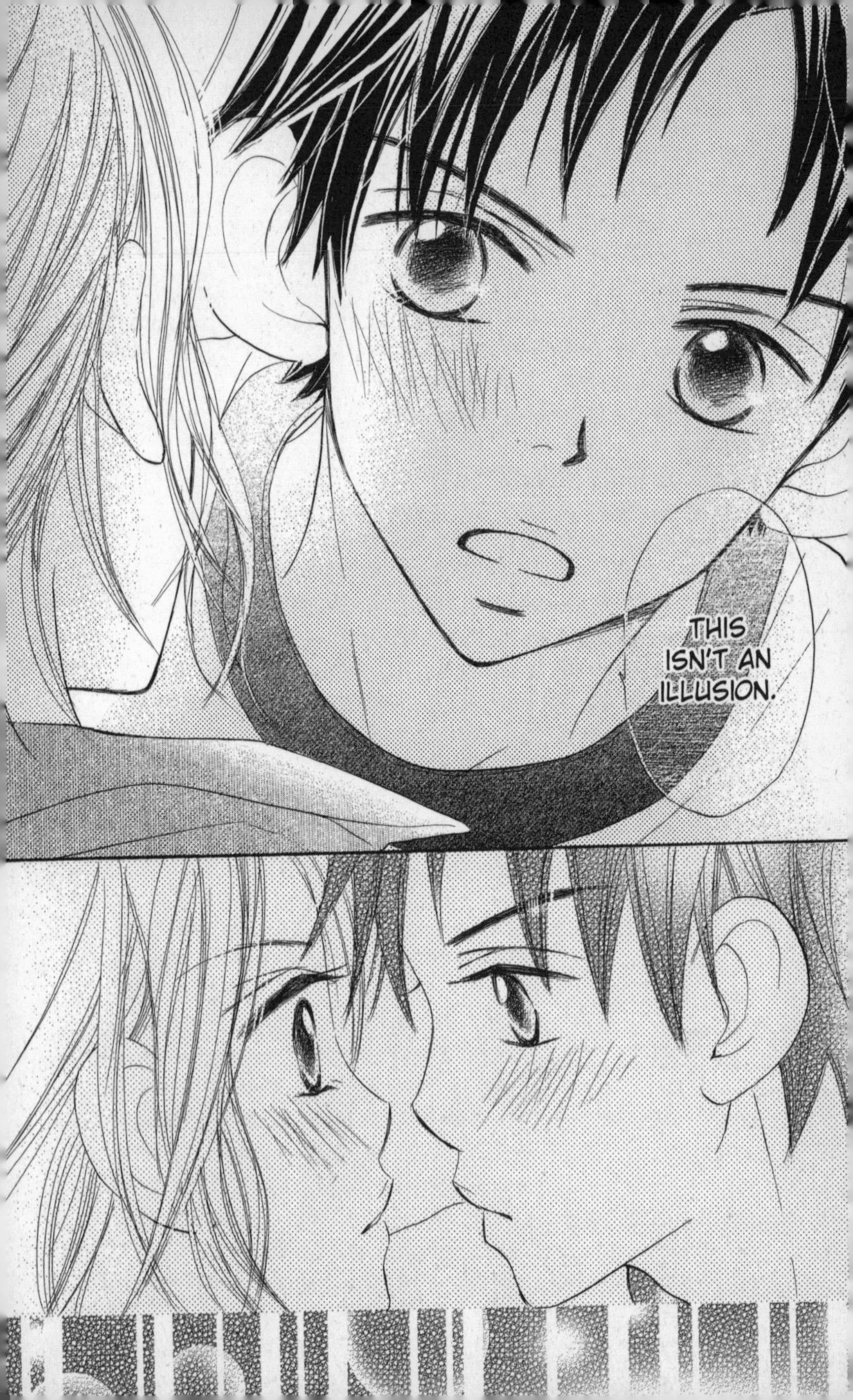
THIS ISN'T AN ILLUSION.

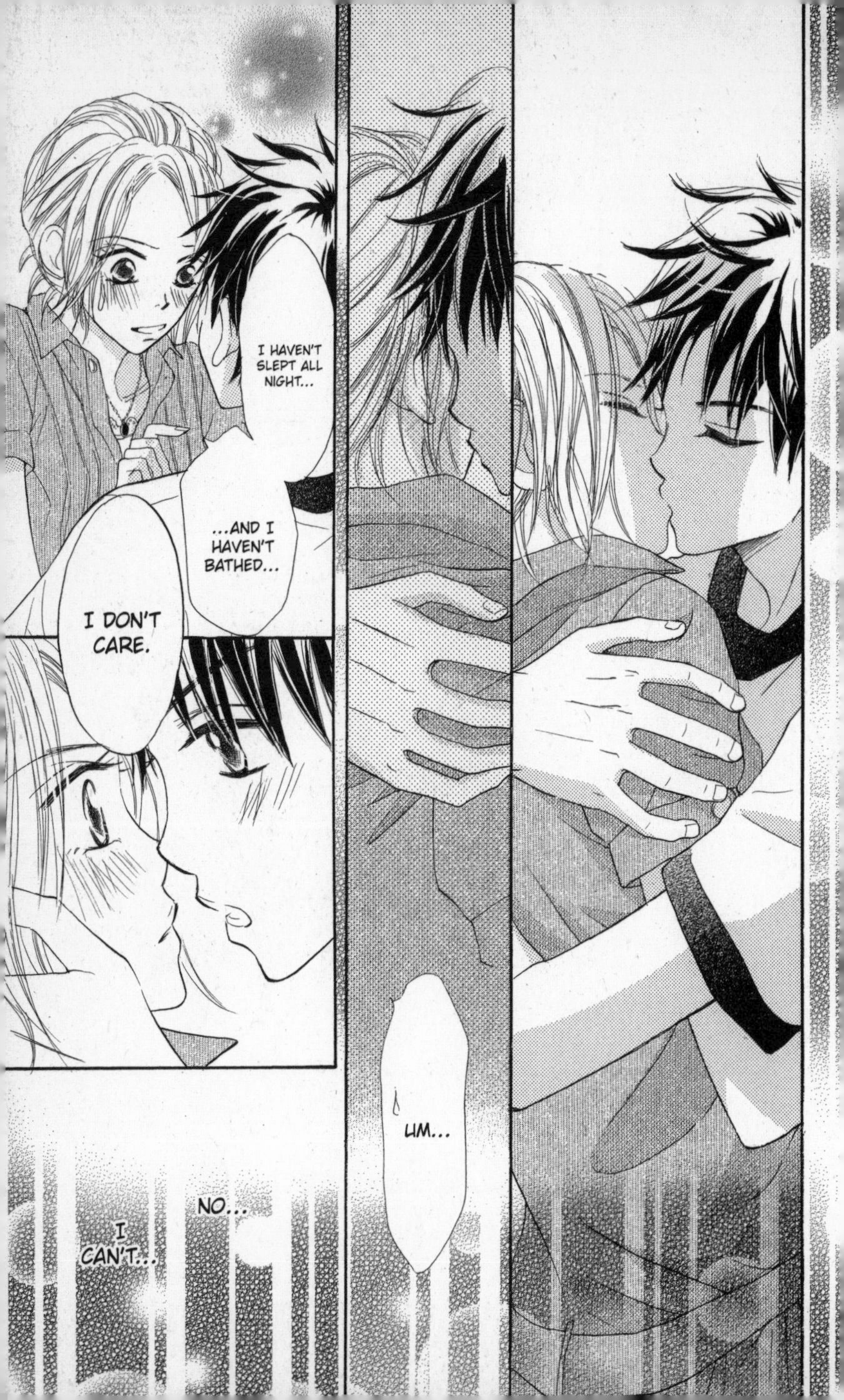
UM...
I HAVEN'T SLEPT ALL NIGHT...
...AND I HAVEN'T BATHED...
I DON'T CARE.
NO...
I CAN'T...

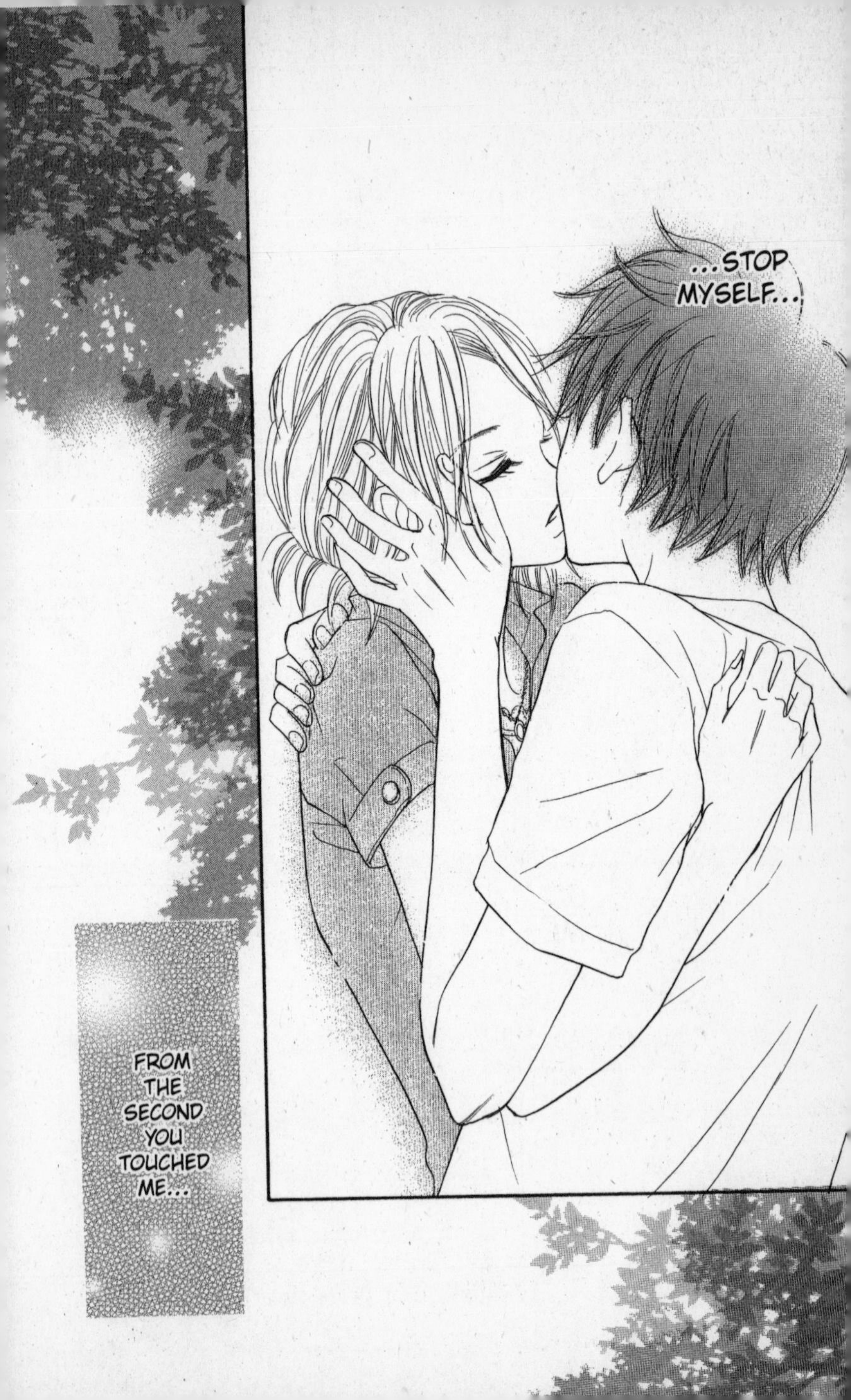
...STOP MYSELF...
FROM THE SECOND YOU TOUCHED ME...

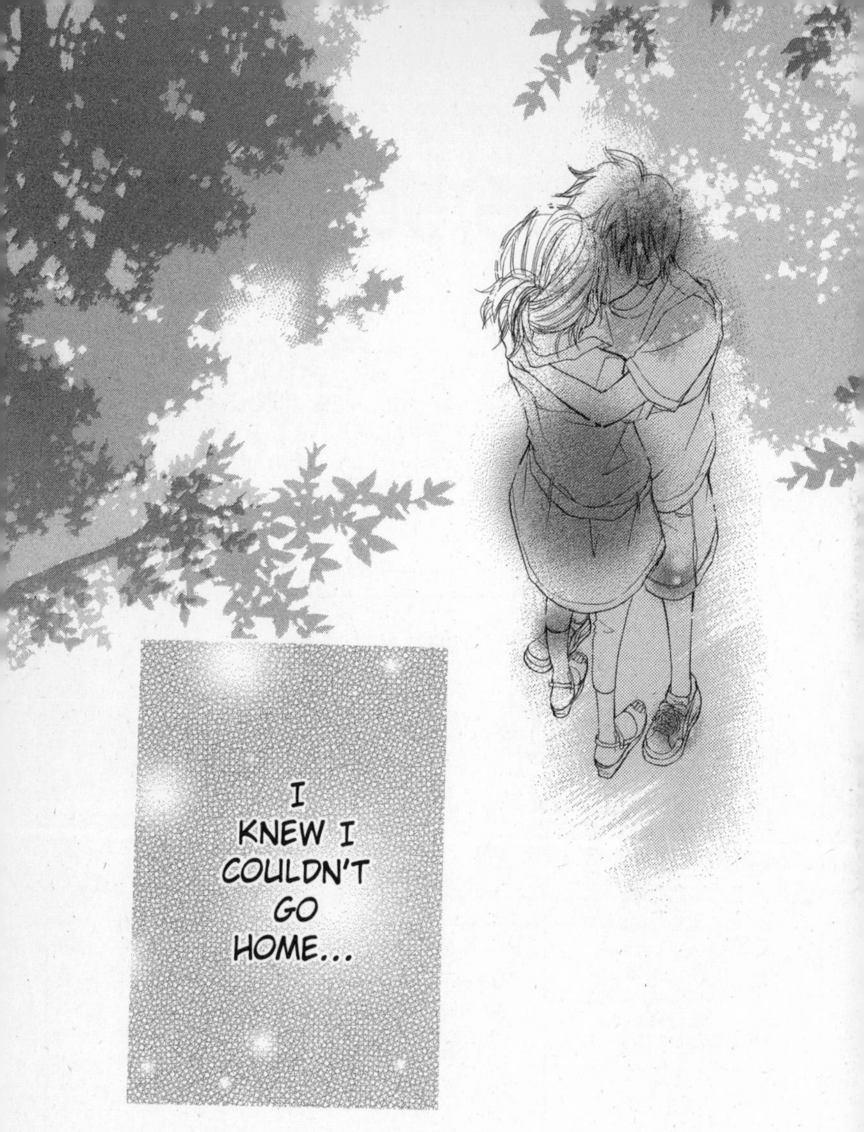
I KNEW I COULDN'T GO HOME...

MONKEY HIGH! ⑦ *THE END*

POSTSCRIPT

THANK YOU SO MUCH FOR READING! I'M SHOUKO AKIRA. WE'VE REALLY REACHED SEVEN VOLUMES... YOU'RE WITNESSING A MIRACLE. I'M GOING TO CONTINUE WITH SOME COMMENTS FOR EACH OF THE STORIES.

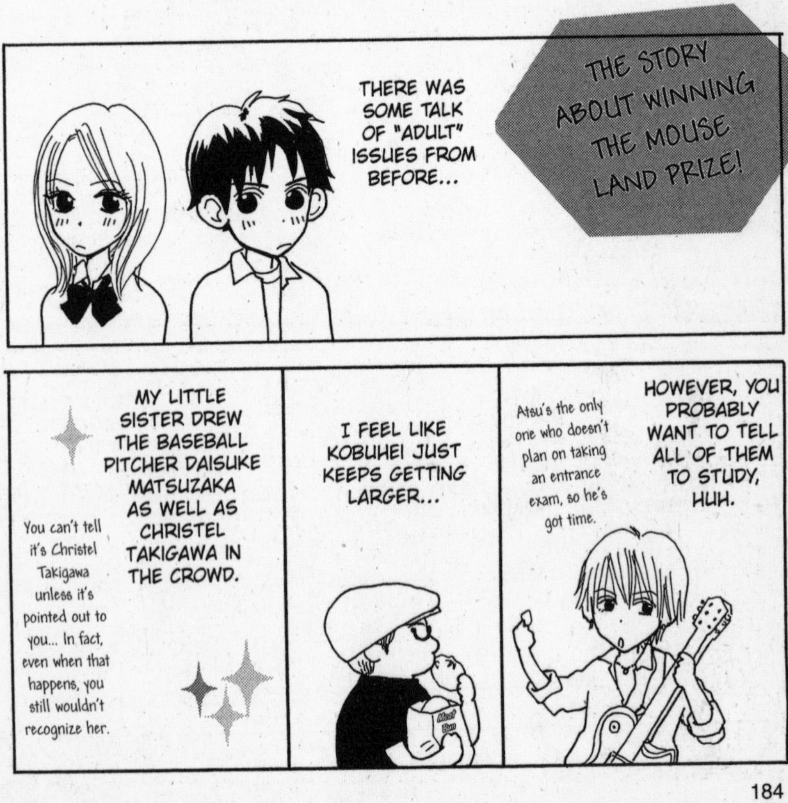
THE STORY ABOUT WINNING THE MOUSE LAND PRIZE!
THERE WAS SOME TALK OF "ADULT" ISSUES FROM BEFORE...
HOWEVER, YOU PROBABLY WANT TO TELL ALL OF THEM TO STUDY, HUH.
Atsu's the only one who doesn't plan on taking an entrance exam, so he's got time.
I FEEL LIKE KOBUHEI JUST KEEPS GETTING LARGER...
Meat Bun
MY LITTLE SISTER DREW THE BASEBALL PITCHER DAISUKE MATSUZAKA AS WELL AS CHRISTEL TAKIGAWA IN THE CROWD.
You can't tell it's Christel Takigawa unless it's pointed out to you... In fact, even when that happens, you still wouldn't recognize her.

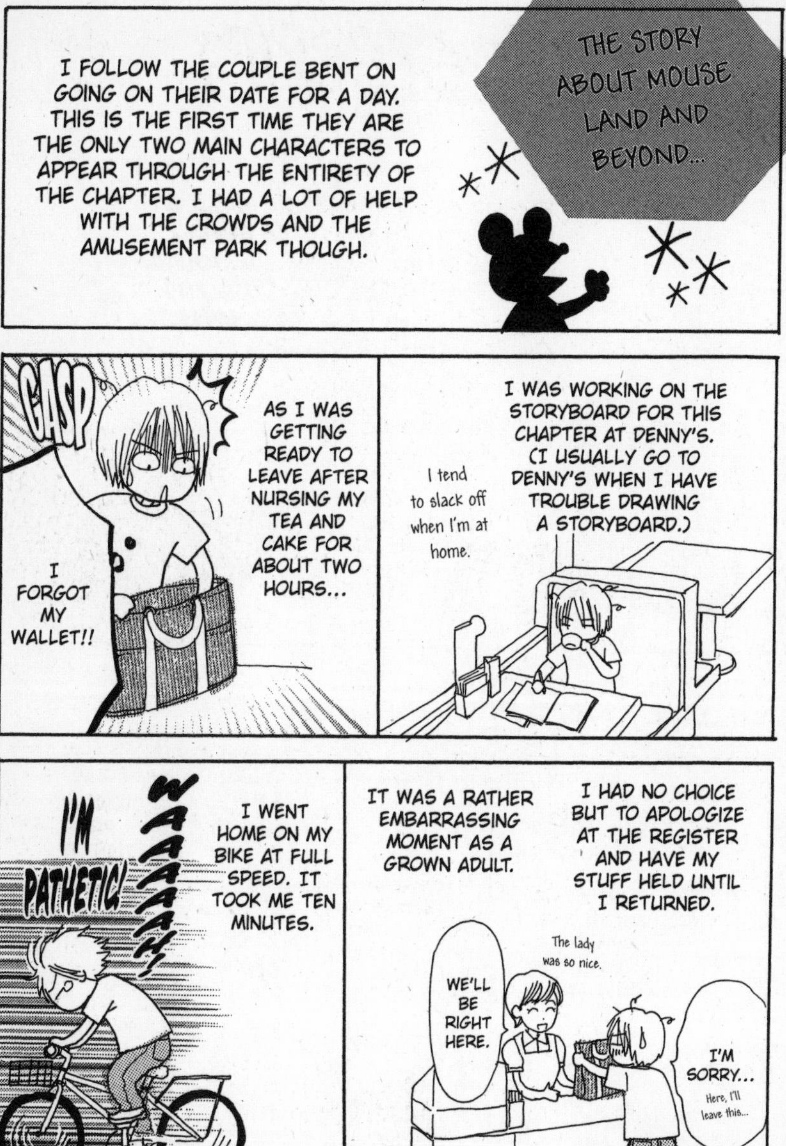
THE STORY ABOUT MOUSE LAND AND BEYOND...
I FOLLOW THE COUPLE BENT ON GOING ON THEIR DATE FOR A DAY. THIS IS THE FIRST TIME THEY ARE THE ONLY TWO MAIN CHARACTERS TO APPEAR THROUGH THE ENTIRETY OF THE CHAPTER. I HAD A LOT OF HELP WITH THE CROWDS AND THE AMUSEMENT PARK THOUGH.
I WAS WORKING ON THE STORYBOARD FOR THIS CHAPTER AT DENNY'S. (I USUALLY GO TO DENNY'S WHEN I HAVE TROUBLE DRAWING A STORYBOARD.)
I tend to slack off when I'm at home.
GASP
AS I WAS GETTING READY TO LEAVE AFTER NURSING MY TEA AND CAKE FOR ABOUT TWO HOURS...
I FORGOT MY WALLET!!
I HAD NO CHOICE BUT TO APOLOGIZE AT THE REGISTER AND HAVE MY STUFF HELD UNTIL I RETURNED.
IT WAS A RATHER EMBARRASSING MOMENT AS A GROWN ADULT.
The lady was so nice.
I'M SORRY...
Here, I'll leave this...
WE'LL BE RIGHT HERE.
WAAAAAAH!
I WENT HOME ON MY BIKE AT FULL SPEED. IT TOOK ME TEN MINUTES.
I'M PATHETIC!

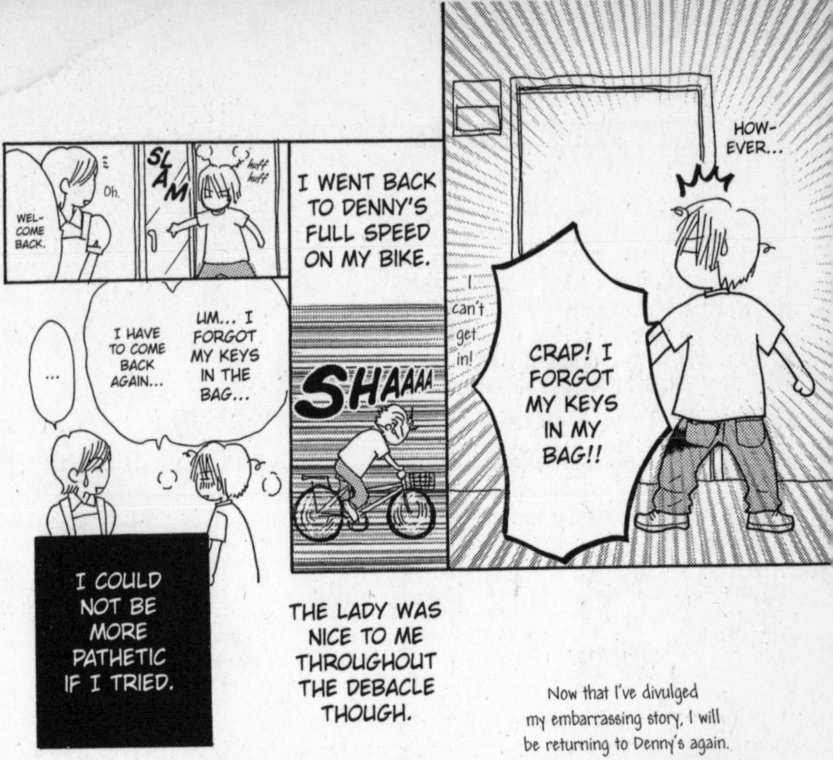
HOW-EVER...
I can't get in!
CRAP! I FORGOT MY KEYS IN MY BAG!!
I WENT BACK TO DENNY'S FULL SPEED ON MY BIKE.
SHAAAA
SLAM
huff huff
Oh.
WEL-COME BACK.
UM... I FORGOT MY KEYS IN THE BAG...
I HAVE TO COME BACK AGAIN...
...
I COULD NOT BE MORE PATHETIC IF I TRIED.

THE LADY WAS NICE TO ME THROUGHOUT THE DEBACLE THOUGH.

Now that I've divulged my embarrassing story, I will be returning to Denny's again.

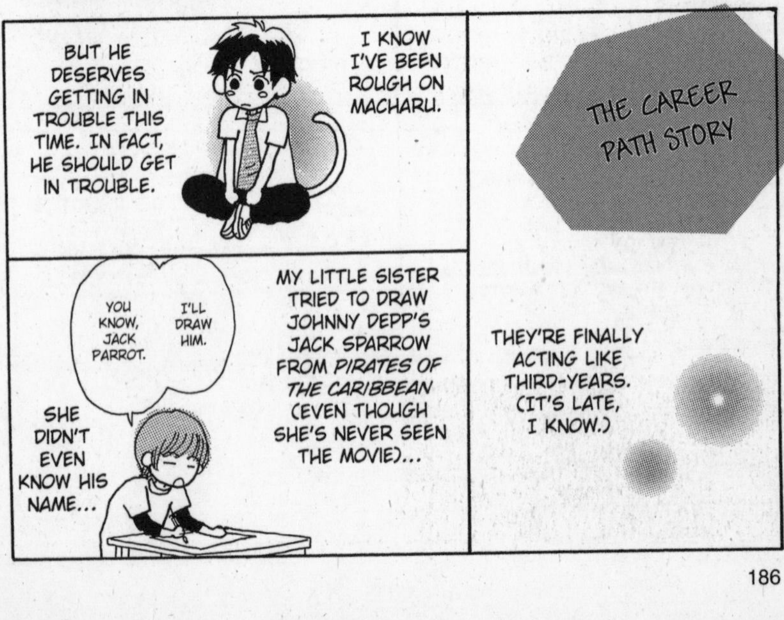
THE CAREER PATH STORY
THEY'RE FINALLY ACTING LIKE THIRD-YEARS. (IT'S LATE, I KNOW.)
I KNOW I'VE BEEN ROUGH ON MACHARU.
BUT HE DESERVES GETTING IN TROUBLE THIS TIME. IN FACT, HE SHOULD GET IN TROUBLE.
MY LITTLE SISTER TRIED TO DRAW JOHNNY DEPP'S JACK SPARROW FROM *PIRATES OF THE CARIBBEAN* (EVEN THOUGH SHE'S NEVER SEEN THE MOVIE)...
I'LL DRAW HIM.
YOU KNOW, JACK PARROT.
SHE DIDN'T EVEN KNOW HIS NAME...

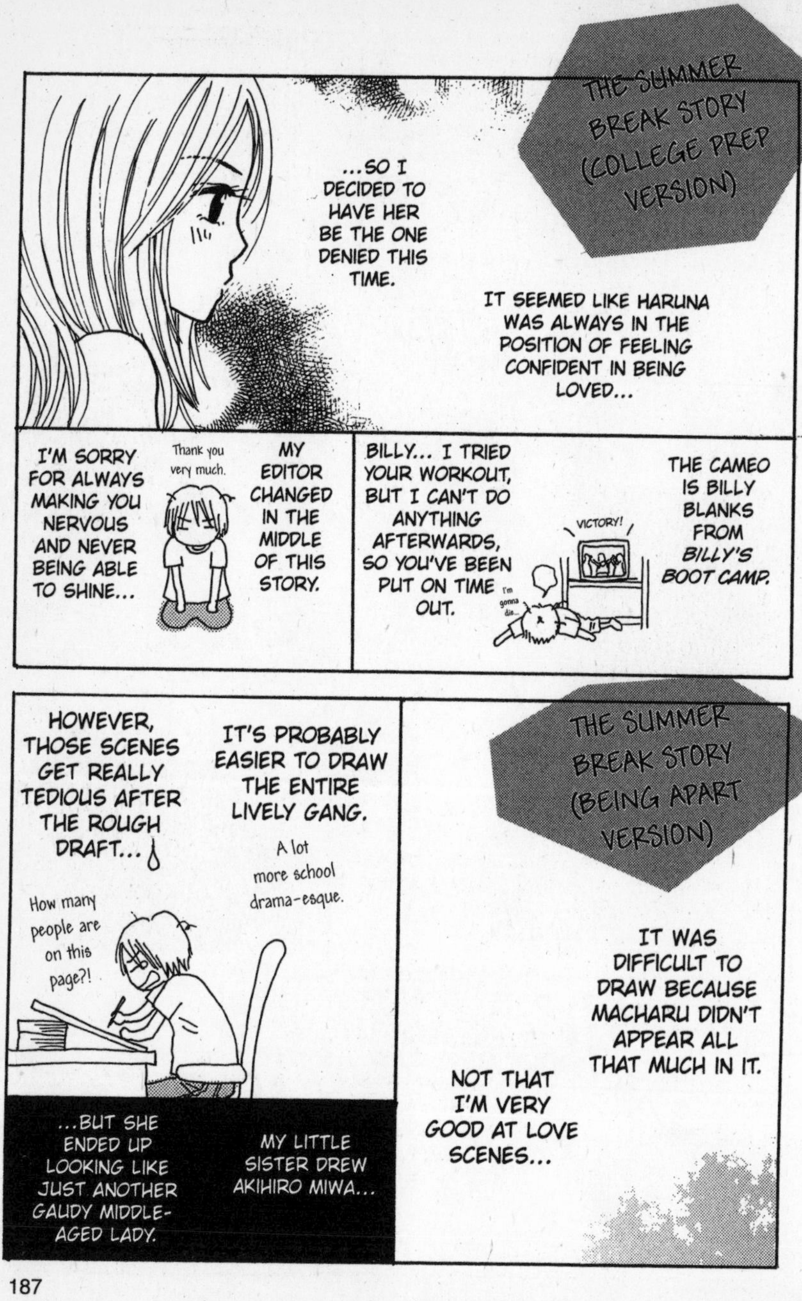
THE SUMMER BREAK STORY (COLLEGE PREP VERSION)
IT SEEMED LIKE HARUNA WAS ALWAYS IN THE POSITION OF FEELING CONFIDENT IN BEING LOVED...
...SO I DECIDED TO HAVE HER BE THE ONE DENIED THIS TIME.
THE CAMEO IS BILLY BLANKS FROM *BILLY'S BOOT CAMP.*
BILLY... I TRIED YOUR WORKOUT, BUT I CAN'T DO ANYTHING AFTERWARDS, SO YOU'VE BEEN PUT ON TIME OUT.
VICTORY!
I'm gonna die...
MY EDITOR CHANGED IN THE MIDDLE OF THIS STORY.
Thank you very much.
I'M SORRY FOR ALWAYS MAKING YOU NERVOUS AND NEVER BEING ABLE TO SHINE...
THE SUMMER BREAK STORY (BEING APART VERSION)
IT WAS DIFFICULT TO DRAW BECAUSE MACHARU DIDN'T APPEAR ALL THAT MUCH IN IT.
NOT THAT I'M VERY GOOD AT LOVE SCENES...
IT'S PROBABLY EASIER TO DRAW THE ENTIRE LIVELY GANG.
A lot more school drama-esque.
HOWEVER, THOSE SCENES GET REALLY TEDIOUS AFTER THE ROUGH DRAFT...
How many people are on this page?!
MY LITTLE SISTER DREW AKIHIRO MIWA...
...BUT SHE ENDED UP LOOKING LIKE JUST ANOTHER GAUDY MIDDLE-AGED LADY.

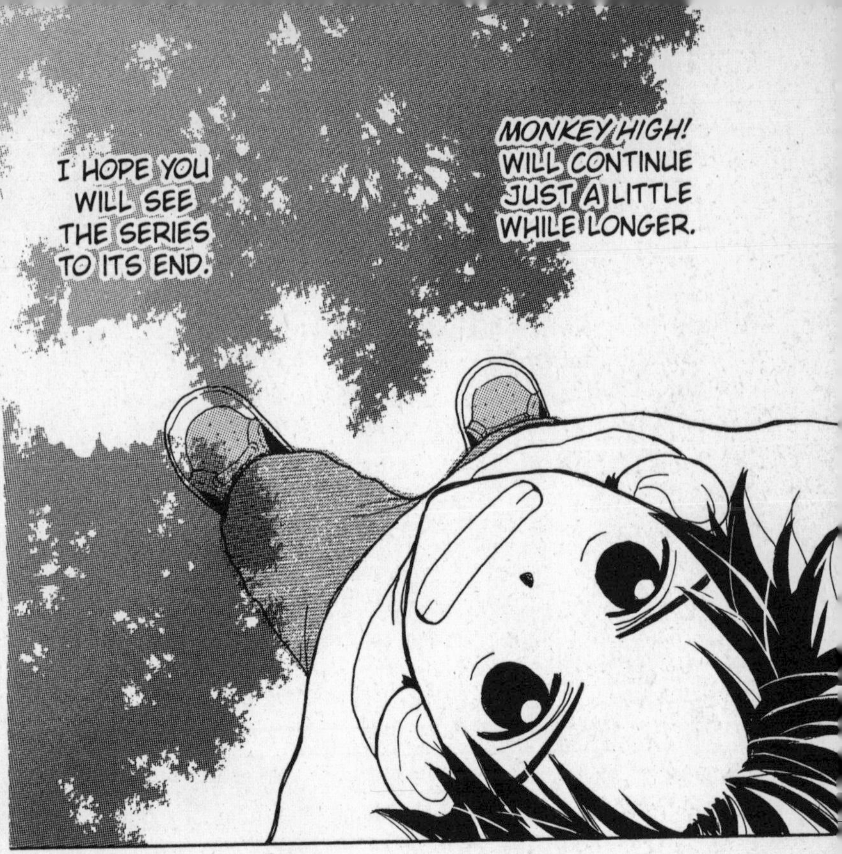
MONKEY HIGH! WILL CONTINUE JUST A LITTLE WHILE LONGER.
I HOPE YOU WILL SEE THE SERIES TO ITS END.

I WOULD LIKE TO THANK EVERYONE WHO ALWAYS HELPS ME: MY EDITOR, PEOPLE IN THE EDITORIAL DEPARTMENT, THE DESIGNER, MY FAMILY, FRIENDS AND ALL MY READERS. MY DEEPEST THANKS TO EVERYONE INVOLVED. I ASK FOR YOUR CONTINUED SUPPORT.

October 2007
Shouko Akira

Slightly confused by all the monkeying around? Here are some notes to help you out!

Page 4: **Masaru**
Even though everyone refers to him by his nickname, Macharu's real name is "Masaru," which means "superior" in Japanese. Interestingly enough, *saru* by itself means "monkey."

Page 21, panel 6: **Budokan**
A large arena in central Tokyo that functions as a venue for music concerts in addition to martial arts tournaments. For some musicians, being able to play at Budokan is a grand achievement.

Page 151, panel 4: **Nagano Prefecture**
Nagano Prefecture is located in the central region of the island Honshu in Japan.

Page 168, panel 6: **Yutaka Mizutani**
Japanese actor and singer who was born in 1952. (Yuka seems to like older and distinguished men, as her answer regarding her type isn't a typical one.)

Page 184, panel 5: **Daisuke Matsuzaka**
Baseball pitcher for the Boston Red Sox. He previously played for the Seibu Lions in Japan.

Page 184, panel 5: **Christel Takigawa**
A Japanese TV announcer and newscaster.

Page 187, panel 6: **Akihiro Miwa**
A famous singer, actor and writer who is also a transvestite. His signature look includes dyeing his shoulder-length hair bright yellow.

I've been shocked with every volume that's published. Thank you so much for your support. I forgot to add a tail to my self-portrait on the author bio page of volume 6. Please feel free to add one yourself.

—Shouko Akira

Volume 7!!

Lucky seven!!

Shouko Akira was born on September 10th and grew up in Kyoto. She currently lives in Tokyo and loves soccer, cycling, and Yoshimoto Shin Kigeki (a comedy stage show based out of Osaka). Most of her works revolve around school life and love, including *Times Two*, a collection of five romantic short stories.

MONKEY HIGH!
VOL. 7
The Shojo Beat Manga Edition

**STORY AND ART BY
SHOUKO AKIRA**

**Translation & Adaptation/Mai Ihara
Touch-up Art & Lettering/John Hunt
Design/Hidemi Dunn
Editor/Amy Yu**

**VP, Production/Alvin Lu
VP, Publishing Licensing/Rika Inouye
VP, Sales & Product Marketing/Gonzalo Ferreyra
VP, Creative/Linda Espinosa
Publisher/Hyoe Narita**

SARUYAMA! 7 by Shouko AKIRA © 2007 Shouko AKIRA
All rights reserved.
Original Japanese edition published in 2007 by Shogakukan Inc., Tokyo.

The stories, characters and incidents mentioned in this publication
are entirely fictional.

Printed in Canada

Published by VIZ Media, LLC
P.O. Box 77010
San Francisco, CA 94107

Shojo Beat Manga Edition
10 9 8 7 6 5 4 3 2 1
First printing, September 2009

www.viz.com

store.viz.com

PARENTAL ADVISORY
MONKEY HIGH! is rated T+ for Older Teen
and is recommended for ages 16 and up.
This volume contains sexual themes.
ratings.viz.com

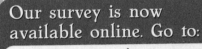